Russia's Peasants in Revolution ar

How did peasants experience and help guide Russia's war, revolution, and civil war? Why in the end did most agree to live as part of the Bolshevik regime? Taking the First World War to the end of the Civil War as a unified era of revolution, this book shows how peasant society and peasants' conceptions of themselves as citizens in the nation evolved in a period of total war, mass revolutionary politics, and civil breakdown. Aaron Retish reveals that the fateful decision by individuals to join the Revolution or to accommodate their lifestyle within it gave the Bolsheviks the resources and philosophical foundation on which to build the Soviet experiment and reshape international politics. He argues that peasants wanted more than land from the Revolution; they wanted to be active citizens. This is an important contribution to our understanding of the nature of the Russian Revolution and peasant–state relations.

AARON B. RETISH is Assistant Professor in the Department of History, Wayne State University.

Russia's Peasants in Revolution and Civil War

Citizenship, Identity, and the Creation of the Soviet State, 1914–1922

Aaron B. Retish

Wayne State University, Detroit

CAMBRIDGE
UNIVERSITY PRESS

CAMBRIDGE UNIVERSITY PRESS
Cambridge, New York, Melbourne, Madrid, Cape Town,
Singapore, São Paulo, Delhi, Tokyo, Mexico City

Cambridge University Press
The Edinburgh Building, Cambridge CB2 8RU, UK

Published in the United States of America by Cambridge University Press, New York

www.cambridge.org
Information on this title: www.cambridge.org/9781107404724

First published 2008
First paperback edition 2011

A catalogue record for this publication is available from the British Library

Library of Congress Cataloguing in Publication Data

Retish, Aaron B.
   Russia's peasants in revolution and civil war: citizenship, identity, and
the creation of the Soviet state, 1914–1922 / Aaron B. Retish.
      p.   cm.
   Includes bibliographical references and index.
   ISBN 978-0-521-89689-4 (hardback)
   1. Peasantry–Soviet Union–History.   2. Peasantry–Russia–History.
3. Soviet Union–History–Revolution, 1917–1921.
4. Russia–History–20th century.   I. Title.

   HD1536.S65R48 2008
   947.084´1–dc22
2008015646

ISBN 978-0-521-89689-4 Hardback
ISBN 978-1-107-40472-4 Paperback

Contents

Tables and illustrations

Tables

Illustrations

Note on terms and usage

Dates through January 1918 are given in Russia's Julian calendar, which ran thirteen days behind the Gregorian calendar. Russia adopted the Gregorian calendar in February 1918 and dates from that point forward reflect the change. I use the Library of Congress system of transliteration for Russian, Udmurt, and Mari except for names commonly known in English (for example, Trotsky instead of Trotskii). I have eliminated the soft sign at the end of place names (Kazan instead of Kazan') to make the text flow better. For style and readability, I have tried to keep foreign terms to a minimum and anglicise most plurals. This is a provincial history and I often refer to the province (*guberniia*), the districts (*uezdy*) of the province, and the rural administrative townships (*volosti*) within the districts. As *volost*s appear so often and an accurate English translation is clunky, I use the Russian term throughout the text without the soft sign (*volost*, instead of *volost'*). In the revolutionary era, Russia's peasants travelled in versts (approximately 1.07 kilometres), measured grain in puds (approximately 36 pounds or 16.4 kilograms) and funts (approximately .90 pounds or 0.41 kilograms) and marked off land in *desiatina*s (approximately 2.7 acres).

I use the following abbreviations when I refer to Russian archival materials: f. for collection (*fond*), op. for inventory (*opis'*), d. for file (*delo*), l. and ll. for folio and folios (*list* and *listy*), and ob. for verso (*oborot*).

Glossary

artel	cooperative organization of peasants
Cheka	Extraordinary Commission for the Struggle against Counter-Revolution and Sabotage
derevnia	village
fel'dsher	paramedic
gubispolkom	provincial executive committee
ispolkom	executive committee of soviet or committee
kolkhoz	collective farm
kombed(y)	committee(s) of the poor peasantry
Komuch	Committee of Members of the Constituent Assembly. Anti-Bolshevik regime in the Lower Volga in 1918
kustar'	peasant handicraft
kumyshka	alcoholic home-brewed ritual drink associated with Udmurts and Maris
Narkomnats	People's Commissariat of Nationalities
Narkomprod	People's Commissariat of Food Supply
Narkompros	People's Commissariat of Enlightenment
Narkomzem	People's Commissariat of Agriculture
NKVD	People's Commissariat of Internal Affairs
obshchina	land commune
otkhodnichestvo	network of peasant out-migration to the factories or urban areas
otkhodnik	peasant migrant worker
prigovor(y)	resolution(s) passed by village, communal or *volost* assembly
Prikomuch	The Urals Region Committee of Members of the Constituent Assembly. Anti-Bolshevik regime centred in Viatka in 1918
razverstka	compulsory levy of grain and goods

selo	village, usually a larger village that houses the main *volost* religious building
skhod	village, commune, or *volost* assembly
soldatka	soldier's wife
SR	member of the Socialist Revolutionary Party
starosta	village elder
starshina	*volost* elder
zavod	factory or factory town
zemstvo	semi-autonomous local governmental body

Map of Viatka province in 1914

Acknowledgements

It is my pleasure to acknowledge the institutions and people that helped make this book a reality. Fulbright-Hays, the International Research and Exchanges Board, the American Council of Teachers of Russian and United States Information Agency, and the United States Department of Education Title VI programme provided generous support for research in Russia and the Udmurt Republic. A Kennan Institute fellowship allowed me to scour the Library of Congress. Research at the Hoover Institution at Stanford University, as well as travel to several conferences, was funded by Ohio State University. A Social Science Research Council fellowship allowed unfettered time to write. Wayne State University funded a final research trip to Russia and managed to give me time off from teaching to write. I am grateful to all these institutions.

My time in Russia would not have been nearly as productive or enjoyable had it not been for the people in the archives and libraries. The Kirov academic community welcomed me with open arms and seemed sincerely interested in what this American had to say about their region's peasants. Elena Nikolaevna Chudinovskikh, Viktor Sergeevich Zharavin, and Natalia Vladimirovna Repina of the State Archive of Socio-Political History of Kirov Region (GASPI KO) are models of archival knowledge and fortitude. They tracked down many documents in lightning speed and are responsible for procuring the photographs in this volume. Galina Atem'evna Zemtsova and the archivists of the State Archive of Kirov Region (GAKO) went out of their way to accommodate me and share what is a gem of an archive. Valerii Egor'evich Musikhin drew from his deep knowledge of the archives and Viatka's peasantry to steer me on course at the beginning of research in Kirov. The tireless librarians in the Kraevedcheskii otdel of the Gertsen Library patiently helped me locate innumerable sources and still had time to invite me for tea. Larry Holmes (the 'other American' in Kirov) confirmed that I wasn't crazy to love a land where the sun sets at lunchtime. In Izhevsk, the archivists at the State Archive of the Udmurt Republic (TsGA UR) made their first American feel welcome. Galina Arkad'evna Nikitina discussed the complexities of Udmurt village life and introduced me to the wonderful ethnographic materials at the Scientific Subject Archive of the Udmurt Institute of History, Language and Literature of the Russian Academy of Sciences, Urals Branch (NOA UIIIaL URO RAN). I would also like to thank the archivists at the Russian State Historical Archive (RGIA) and the librarians at the Russian National Library in St Petersburg. In Moscow, the hard work and good cheer of the archivists at the Russian State Archive of the Economy (RGAE), the State Archive of the Russian Federation (GA RF), the Russian State Archive of Socio-Political History (RGASPI), the Russian Military Archive (RGVA), and the librarians at the Lenin and Historical Libraries made my time there a pleasure.

David Hoffmann guided this project from its beginning. He read chapters in all of their various stages, talked through ideas, and provided invaluable suggestions. He remains an ideal mentor and I thank him for his years of sage advice and unflappable support. Eve Levin and Nicholas Breyfogle read this work as a dissertation, have helped me mature as a historian, and continue to be sources of inspiration. The strong community of Russian and East Europeanists who I first met at Ohio State, including Sean Martin, Bill Risch, Matt Romaniello, Tricia Starks, and our honorary member Paul Hibbeln, have talked through almost every idea in this book, always with a humorous spin. My graduate training began under the late Allan Wildman and I hope that I have continued his legacy in this work.

Many scholars have helped me with their comments and insights. Michael Hickey read the manuscript more times than I care to admit and made me think about this work in several new ways. I was overjoyed to meet Sarah Badcock early on in the project for her work on 1917 gave me confidence that I was on the right track. Discussions with Sarah and Liudmila Novikova have shaped my understanding of the provincial perspective of the Russian Revolution. Fellow participants in the Study Group on the Russian Revolution commented on three sections of the work and I thank them for their feedback and general camaraderie. Several other scholars gave suggestions in informal conversations and at conferences, including Robert Argenbright, Mark Baker, Brian Bonhomme, Katherine David-Fox, Michael David-Fox, Kevin Deegan-Krause, Sheila Fitzpatrick, Corinne Gaudin, Robert Geraci, Tony Heywood, Steven Hoch, Peter Holquist, Stefan Karsch, Boris Kolonitskii, Yanni Kotsonis, David McDonald, Michael Melançon,

David Moon, Daniel Orlovsky, Gareth Popkins, Alex Rabinowitch, Chris Read, Bill Rosenberg, Franziska Schedewie, Jonathan Smele, Charles Steinwedel, Rex Wade, Paul Werth, Christine Worobec, and Greg Wu.

My colleagues in the Wayne State Department of History have welcomed me into an intellectually vibrant group. I would especially like to thank Marc Kruman who championed the theme of citizenship. Mel Small took the time to provide valuable comments on an earlier draft of the entire manuscript. He now knows more about Viatka's peasants than any other historian of US diplomacy and I have a better book in exchange. Janine Lanza, Kidada Williams, Carla Vecchiola, and James Buccellato gave invaluable suggestions on several chapters as well. I completed the manuscript as a fellow at the Wayne State Humanities Center. The director, Walter Edwards, and the other fellows created an inviting and energetic environment perfect for my work.

Some of the material in Chapter Two appeared in *Revolutionary Russia* and I thank the journal for permitting me to reproduce it here. I would also like to thank the anonymous reviewers who pushed me to think about several fundamental issues. Finally, I am grateful to Michael Watson of Cambridge University Press who adroitly shepherded the manuscript through to publication with good cheer.

Most of all, my family has given me love, friendship, encouragement, and energy; without them this work would have been impossible. Meeting my future wife Sarah Parmelee was the best thing that happened in Russian language class. Our daughter Eleanor reminds me that peasants and revolution should occasionally wait for slides and swings. The happiness that they have brought me cannot be put into words. I am also grateful to my brothers, Josh and Marc, and their families who ground me in the present. My father, Paul Retish, and mother, Esther Retish, have always encouraged my intellectual pursuits and have supported me whenever I began to lose hope. It is, then, to my parents that I dedicate this book.

Introduction: Peasants and revolutionary power

There is nothing in Russian history darker than the fate of Viatka and her land. – Nikolai Ivanovich Kostomarov, nineteenth-century historian.[1]

In successive waves, world war, revolution, and civil war swept away and remade the Russian countryside in eight calamitous years from 1914 to 1922. The First World War and Civil War conscripted over fifteen million young male peasants first into the tsarist, and then the Red and anti-Bolshevik armies, before placing the hardened survivors back in the village. Revolution destroyed the centuries-old peasant–landlord relationship, redistributed land, democratized the countryside, and allowed villages to install new governing bodies. War and social turmoil also brought massive famine and government requisitioning of grain and possessions, killing millions of peasants and destroying their means of existence. The Bolshevik victory, a defining event of the twentieth century, was ultimately determined by the support of peasants, the vast majority of Russia's population.

Russia's Peasants in Revolution and Civil War is a study of how peasants experienced and helped guide the course of Russia's war and revolution, and why in the end most agreed to live as part of the Bolshevik regime. This fateful decision by individuals to join the Soviet experiment or to accommodate their lifestyle within it gave the Bolsheviks the resources and philosophical foundation on which to build the Soviet experiment and reshape international politics. Taking the First World War to the end of the Civil War as a unified era of revolution, this book shows how peasant society and peasants' conceptions of themselves as citizens in the nation evolved in a period of total war, mass revolutionary politics, and the violence and devastation of civil breakdown.[2]

---

[1] Quoted in B. V. Gnedovskii and E. D. Dobrovol'skaia, *Dorogami zemli Viatskoi* (Moscow, 1971), 5.

[2] Peter Holquist astutely terms this period a continuum of crisis. *Making War, Forging Revolution: Russia's Continuum of Crisis, 1914–1921* (Cambridge, MA, 2002), 1–8.

Wartime mobilization and the destruction of the tsarist system created an ideal environment for many of the rural populations to break free from traditional roles. For peasants like Khadyi Diuniashev, a landless Tatar from southern Viatka province, war disrupted life and revolution gave it meaning. Diuniashev's youth was spent going to school and then working in the factories. His life would probably have followed the path of millions of other peasants – labouring as a seasonal worker and bringing back money and urban culture to his village each spring. Instead, like close to half of all other male peasants in Russia, Diuniashev was called to colours to fight in the First World War. Demobilized in 1917, he returned home politically radicalized and got caught up in the revolution. He found his future in the Soviet state, joining a food brigade in August 1918, then serving as the military commissar for his *volost* until the Soviet state, eager to co-opt national minorities into its system, appointed him to head the district administration. Four years after joining the Imperial Army, the formerly destitute peasant was a new member of the Bolshevik Party and one of the most powerful people in the province.[3] While his life changed much more than most, the kind of experiences and politicalization of his life happened to much of rural Russia.

To understand how Russia's turmoil shaped peasant support for the Soviet state, I analyse the interaction between peasants and political and cultural elites as the modern revolutionary state developed in the countryside. I do so through a study of peasant responses to tsarist, Provisional Government, Soviet and anti-Soviet schemes of mass mobilization and social intervention and the violence that often accompanied these projects. I highlight the complex diversity of peasant populations' reactions to the establishment of local administrations, as well as their participation in nation-building events. In examining peasants' interaction with the various states, I show that the population adopted, rejected, and helped to shape government power, just as it shaped them.

This book challenges the basic assumption that peasants dreamt of autonomy and held only limited political visions in war and revolution. Observers of the countryside in the early twentieth century, and most commentators since, believed that peasants dreamt of closing themselves off from the outside world. Peasants, in their eyes, held two political goals – to redistribute the land and resources as they saw fit and to achieve a mythical freedom (*volia*). Peasants' deep sense of collectivism

---

[3] Gosudarstvennyi Arkhiv Sotsial'no-Politicheskoi Istorii Kirovskoi Oblasti (hereafter GASPI KO), f. 1, op. 1, d. 211, ll. 19–19ob.

and communal solidarity, according to this view, shaped defensive responses to Russia's modernizing economy and interfering state officials and administration.[4] This picture has largely held intact despite social historians' rich analysis of the relationship between social groups and revolutionary power in the revolution, and recent studies of the village that have revealed acrimony and fissures within the village, the complexity of rural social networks, and the political morality of peasants' relationships with the outside world.[5] Such assumptions have deep implications for the critical issues of how peasants viewed and understood their political relationship with the state and nation, as well as what they wanted out of revolution and the revolutionary state.

Despite the thousands of works written on the Russian Revolution, there are remarkably few western studies on the peasants in revolution and none that examine the evolution of rural politics through the whole of the revolutionary era.[6] This work seeks to fill this great lacuna in the scholarship. If, as Orlando Figes writes of the Civil War, the key to understanding the social changes in the countryside and Bolshevik attempts to draw the peasants into the Soviet regime lies in a broad range of socio-economic, cultural, and institutional relations, then an analysis of the revolutionary environment already in place is crucial.[7]

---

[4] Orlando Figes, *Peasant Russia, Civil War: The Volga Countryside in Revolution (1917–1921)* (Oxford, 1989); Figes, *A People's Tragedy: A History of the Russian Revolution* (New York, 1996).

[5] For discussion on the impact of social history, see Ronald Grigor Suny, 'Toward a Social History of the October Revolution', *The American Historical Review* 88 (1983): 31–52; a recent addition is Christopher Read, *From Tsar to Soviets: The Russian People and their Revolution, 1917–21* (Oxford, 1996). On village life, see Esther Kingston-Mann and Timothy Mixter, eds, *Peasant Economy, Culture, and Politics of European Russia, 1800–1921* (Princeton, 1991); David Moon, *The Russian Peasantry, 1600–1930: The World the Peasants Made* (London, 1999).

[6] On provincial Russia in general during the revolutionary era, see, for example, Donald Raleigh, *Experiencing Russia's Civil War: Politics, Society, and Revolutionary Culture in Saratov, 1917–1922* (Princeton, 2002); Michael Hickey, 'Local Government and State Authority in the Provinces: Smolensk, February–June, 1917', *Slavic Review* 55 (1996): 863–81; Sarah Badcock, *Politics and the People in Revolutionary Russia: A Provincial History* (Cambridge, 2007); Peter Holquist, *Making War*; and Igor' V. Narskii, *Zhizn' v katastrofe. Budni naseleniia Urala v 1917–1922 gg.* (Moscow, 2001). Only Holquist studies the revolutionary era as a whole.

[7] Orlando Figes, *Peasant Russia*. For similar analyses, see V. V. Kabanov, *Krest'ianskoe khoziaistvo v usloviiakh 'voennogo kommunizma'* (Moscow, 1988); V. P. Danilov, *Sovetskaia dokolkhoznaia derevnia: sotsial'naia struktura, sotsial'nye otnosheniia* (Moscow, 1979); Graeme Gill, *Peasants and Government in the Russian Revolution* (New York, 1979). The term revolutionary ecology comes from Katerina Clark, *Petersburg: Crucible of Cultural Revolution* (Cambridge, MA, 1995), 1–28.

Ties that bind: citizenship, national identity, and revolution

Tremendous changes in the countryside in the pre-war era allowed peasants to begin to dream beyond their village. The First World War interrupted a dynamic transformation of peasant life and the villages in which they lived. As in other countries, a complex combination of economic modernization, political reform and revolution, and the growth of agencies of change such as schools, administrative organs, transportation networks, and universal conscription in the armed forces unsettled traditions of rural society and laid the foundation for many peasants to identify with the greater culture. These changes threatened the traditional, agriculturally based society where custom dominated and the commune had hegemony over its members.

Traditional forms of power had emanated from a variety of sources in the village. Elderly male leaders of the commune, village and *volost* officials such as policemen, scribes, and tax collectors, and economically strong families dominated village politics and sought to uphold the status quo in their favour. Within the household, elders, married folk, and those able to work, traditionally held more sway over family matters than the young, elderly, feeble, or widowed. Power also came from popular coercion to uphold traditions.[8] Culturally embedded misogyny dictated gender relations. Women maintained and ensured the physical needs of the household but because females were not considered as able labourers as men, peasant heads of households saw them in the long term as a weight on the economic viability of the family unit. Nevertheless, as Christine Worobec has shown, women carved out a position for themselves within this patriarchal system.[9] The economic standing of the peasant household within the village was fluid and based on a generational cycle of the household's number of labourers, but economic hostilities between wealthier and poorer peasants existed within the village.[10]

By 1914, economic change and contact with urban culture put traditional village culture on the defensive and altered everyday life in the

---

[8] Stephen P. Frank, 'Popular Justice, Community, and Culture among the Russian Peasantry, 1870–1900', in Ben Eklof and Stephen Frank, eds. *The World of the Russian Peasant: Post-Emancipation Culture and Society* (Boston, 1990), 133–53.

[9] Christine Worobec, *Peasant Russia: Family and Community in the Post-Emancipation Period* (DeKalb, 1991), 177–8.

[10] A. V. Chayanov, *The Theory of Peasant Economy*, ed. Daniel Throner et al. (Madison, 1986); Teodor Shanin, *Russia as a 'Developing Society'. The Roots of Otherness: Russia's Turn of Century*, vol. I (New Haven, 1985).

Plate 1. Peasants at harvest, Glazov district, early twentieth century. Courtesy GASPI KO

villages. Peasant families enjoyed new products such as factory-made clothing, metal roofs, and printed literature, showing, as Jeffrey Burds argues, the development of a conspicuous consumer culture in the countryside.[11] Contact with urban life also provided immaterial opportunities for the exchange of ideas, ways of life, and political organizing between peasant migrants and urban dwellers. The mostly young peasant migrants took these notions back to the village, which increased tensions between younger and older generations and threatened the power of the commune. These links to the urban culture and economy and generational tensions would continue during war and revolution. Peasant factory workers returned to the village with news, ideas, and networks with political groups, serving as mediators of the larger political changes and winning especially young fellow villagers to revolutionary parties such as the Bolsheviks.

Arenas of elite and popular intercourse necessary for nation building existed before 1914, even if Russia did not enjoy the civil society and public sphere free from state intervention of western European countries. The countryside had already begun to blend into the national economy and culture at the beginning of the twentieth century by participating

---

[11] Jeffrey Burds, *Peasant Dreams and Market Politics: Labor Migration and the Russian Village, 1861–1905* (Pittsburgh, 1998), ch. 6.

in the legal system, industrialization and urban migration, the growth of cash crops and the market-driven handicraft (*kustar'*) trade, greater schooling, and reading the commercial press.[12] Although peasant communities engaged these modernizing institutions, they resisted their transformative power and often 'peasantized' them. As Ben Eklof shows, primary schools were ineffective, rural literacy hovered around fifty per cent, and parents pulled children out of schools after they had learned just enough to help them deal with the outside print-based world.[13] However, by 1914, the effects of the interaction between town and country had profoundly altered the village community. Literacy was much higher for youths and allowed peasants to read the popular press and recognize national symbols – points that would be vital during war and revolution.

Traditional gender relations were slowly breaking down by the eve of the First World War as growing literacy rates and urban migratory labour gave young men and women new ideas about less misogynistic gender relations and provided them with opportunities to rise up the social ladder or escape village life entirely.[14] Peasants also found ties to the imagined community in several other arenas of contact such as religious pilgrimages, military conscription, theatre, and artwork. Simultaneously, peasants asserted political rights within the late-Imperial regime, even if they were not grounded in law. Peasants turned to the rural administration, courtroom, and the zemstvo to solve internal village quarrels and improve their social condition.[15] From the 1905 Revolution they also gained experience forging alliances with non-peasants, organizing political groups, and airing their grievances on both local and political issues to the highest authorities.[16] Taken as a whole, these modernizing changes put the village on the threshold of a transformation of political imagination.

Mass politics from war and revolution, patriotic sentiment, total warfare, and state mobilization pushed peasants remaining in the village

---

[12] S. A. Smith remarks that these economic and political transformations built upon a long-held 'protonational identity' to create at least the foundation for national sentiment, 'Citizenship and the Russian Nation during World War I: A Comment', *Slavic Review* 59 (2000): 316–29.

[13] Ben Eklof, *Russian Peasant Schools: Officialdom, Village Culture, and Popular Pedagogy, 1864–1914* (Berkeley, 1986).

[14] Barbara Alpern Engel, *Between the Fields and the City: Women, Work, and Family in Russia, 1861–1914* (Cambridge, 1994).

[15] See Corinne Gaudin, *Ruling Peasants: Village and State in Imperial Russia* (DeKalb, 2007); Jane Burbank, *Russian Peasants Go to Court: Legal Culture in the Countryside, 1905–1917* (Bloomington, 2004).

[16] Scott Seregny, *Russian Teachers and Peasant Revolution: The Politics of Education in 1905* (Bloomington, 1989); Andrew Verner, 'Discursive Strategies in the 1905 Revolution: Peasant Petitions from Vladimir Province', *Russian Review* 54 (1995): 65–90.

Plate 2. Peasant handicraft production, early twentieth century.
Courtesy GASPI KO

to embrace the national polity.[17] As in other warring powers, the First
World War gave birth to a broader participatory regime in Russia that in
turn reinvented what made up the Russian nation. Nation building and

[17] For an argument contra, see David Moon, 'Late Imperial Peasants', in Ian D. Thatcher,
ed., *Late Imperial Russia: Problems and Prospects. Essays in Honour of R. B. McKean*
(Manchester, 2005), 120–45. On nationalism as modernization, see Eugen Weber,
Peasants into Frenchmen: The Modernization of Rural France, 1870–1914 (Stanford, 1976);
Eric Hobsbawm, *Nations and Nationalism since 1780: Programme, Myth, Reality*
(Cambridge, 1993).

revolution in 1917 were not only top-down projects to create invented traditions by political and cultural elites. As Florencia Mallon argues for Mexico and Peru, nationalism is a 'broad vision for organizing society, a project for collective identity based on the premise of citizenship'. There is much room for disagreement and competing discourses within this vision. This view of nationalism applies equally to revolutionary Russia.[18] For Russia's peasants, revolution meant political participation, equality, new political languages, and new economic relationships, and they at first embraced their rights and responsibilities as citizens in the national polity.

Members of educated society were not so sure about giving 'backward' peasants the keys to their revolution so soon and instead preached duty and the need for patient cultural advancement. Russia's cultural elite in the early-twentieth century described the peasants as a homogenous, isolated, and culturally backward people. Fearing social breakdown from a period of rapid industrial modernization, commentators created a rural 'other' that expressed their own societal and cultural dreams and anxieties. They saw the idyllic, autarkic village increasingly corrupted by the dangers of a modern world – endemic crime, disease, and poverty.

While the balance between rights and duties revealed one of the tears in citizenship, the boundaries and very definition of membership in the polity constantly shifted and were contested throughout the revolutionary era.[19] The Soviet state adopted both discourses, drawing the peasantry into the national polity and asserting the need for state direction in creating Soviet citizens. The Bolsheviks were quick to resort to violence and coercion to foster class warfare and political power, but their ability to understand, connect to, and incorporate the various rural populations was central to their ultimate success in establishing power in the countryside. The Soviet state's willingness both to serve as a point of

---

[18] Florencia E. Mallon, *Peasant and Nation: The Making of Postcolonial Mexico and Peru* (Berkeley, 1995), 4; Benedict Anderson, *Imagined Communities: Reflections on the Origins and Spread of Nationalism* (New York, 1991). On the give and take of nationalism, see James Lehning, *Peasant and French: Cultural Contact in Rural France during the Nineteenth Century* (New York, 1995); Keely Stauter-Halsted, *The Nation in the Village: The Genesis of Peasant National Identity in Austrian Poland, 1848–1914* (Ithaca, 2001).

[19] T. H. Marshall's liberal view of increasing rights to all members of society equally has shaped current scholarly approaches to the subject. *Citizenship and Social Class, and Other Essays* (Cambridge, 1950). On a pessimistic view of the possibility of citizenship bestowing emancipatory rights in Russia, see Yanni Kotsonis, '"Face-to-Face": The State, the Individual, and the Citizen in Russian Taxation, 1863–1917', *Slavic Review* 63 (2004): 221–46; for a more optimistic view, see Eric Lohr, 'The Ideal Citizen and Real Subject in Late Imperial Russia', *Kritika* 7 (2006): 173–94.

mediation and to expand the social rights of citizenship helped it to survive the Civil War. Russia, and indeed the world, came into the modern age through the active participation in and accommodation of national politics by those living in the fields.[20]

As war and revolution gave new rights and opportunities for peasants to participate as members in the polity, wartime mobilization began a period that witnessed a more interventionist state. The revolutionary state officials mobilized, intervened, and tried to transform society to fit their rational ideals, the essence of a modern state.[21] The village became a laboratory for these state agents to test their methods and ideologies. Political and cultural elites' imagination of the peasantry as backward in this way shaped state policies during this era. Even though mass mobilization and modern politics created the worrying dilemma that educated society and state officials had to rely on active participation by the still-backward peasant to survive, war and revolution also presented them with the opportunity to transform and incorporate the 'helpless' rural other into the political system without tsarist autocratic interference.[22]

Peasants engaged, adopted, and resisted interventionist and transformative projects. For example, peasants in 1917 who sought educational opportunities eagerly proclaimed their ignorance and hope that education would make them 'enlightened citizens'. Simultaneously, peasants resisted elites' political tutelage and voted for their own candidates over the educated society's parties. Peasants later adopted the Soviet state's language of class to present themselves as poor peasants to gain access to grain and political organizations, while resisting the state's military conscription policies. At several points, individuals reinvented themselves and had to express publicly who they were and fit this persona into given categories. A complex web of political and social networks constructed public social identities during Russia's revolutionary age. How people placed themselves in a social category, and how other people and political bodies constructed and placed them in this category, not only created the popular experience of political change but also moulded the state and elite political discourse.[23]

---

[20] On popular political culture's influence on the state, see George Steinmetz, ed., *State/Culture: State-Formation After the Cultural Turn* (Ithaca, 1999).

[21] See David L. Hoffmann, *Stalinist Values: The Cultural Norms of Soviet Modernity, 1917–1941* (Ithaca, 2003), 7–10.

[22] Yanni Kotsonis, *Making Peasants Backward: Agricultural Cooperatives and the Agrarian Question in Russia, 1861–1914* (New York, 1999). On the state's influence on popular political identity, see Peter B. Evans, Dietrich Rueschemeyer, and Theda Skocpol, eds, *Bringing the State Back In* (New York, 1985).

[23] Sheila Fitzpatrick, *Tear off the Masks! Identity and Imposture in Twentieth-Century Russia* (Princeton, 2005), 9; David L. Hoffmann, *Peasant Metropolis: Social Identities in*

Like all studies of revolution, this book is also a discourse on power: how state power affected village politics, how peasant elites dominated their societies, how peasants understood their subaltern or subordinate position in society, how peasants influenced state power, how the power relationships altered Russian society and its polity, and how Russia's turmoil tore the power system asunder. It thereby examines the interconnections of power and identity between peasant and non-peasant society during a time of great social and political upheaval. The wartime Imperial state, the short-lived democratic Provisional Government, and the Soviet and anti-Soviet states all relied on coercion to maintain power over the peasantry, but they also tried to build support for their respective regimes through official persuasion and popular complicity: the hegemonic process.[24] The relationship between peasants and political power was more complicated than one with two distinct groups and a clear aggressor and victim. The peasantry influenced the state and its politics, breaking down the barriers between the dominated and the dominator. Moreover, rural populations did not always act as a cohesive unit. Different peasant populations moved in and out of the local state administration and villagers experienced war and revolution differently. The way in which power affected state and peasant identity and how peasants in turn shaped and affected power is the overarching theme of this work. Below it laid interwoven discursive ribbons of citizenship, ritual, and the myth of popular political participation.

The era's emancipatory politics cannot be understood outside the everyday struggle to survive in a society violently ripping apart.[25] Russian society was already out of joint before the First World War and the crescendo of destruction beginning in war, and culminating with the ruin from the Civil War, undercut the possibility of stable political relationships between social groups.[26] State sponsored violence, often directed at its own population, hastened and extended social breakdown. If years of death numbed both state actors and the population to the horrors of famine, endemic disease, and murder, then it also sharpened their sense that politics needed to transform society so this

---

Moscow, 1929–1941 (Ithaca, 1994). Rex A. Wade, *The Russian Revolution, 1917*, 2nd edn (Cambridge, 2005) shows the complexity of social identities in revolution.

[24] For a theoretical discursus on the hegemonic process and its failures, see Antonio Gramsci, *Selections from the Prison Notebooks*, eds and tr. Quintin Hoare and Geoffrey Nowell Smith (New York, 1992); Ranajit Guha, *Dominance without Hegemony: History and Power in Colonial India* (Cambridge, MA, 1997), 100–51.

[25] Raleigh, *Experiencing Russia's Civil War*; Narskii, *Zhizn' v katastrofe.*

[26] Leopold Haimson, 'Civil War and the Problem of Social Identities in Early Twentieth-Century Russia', in Diane P. Koenker et al., eds., *Party, State, and Society in the Russian Civil War: Explorations in Social History* (Bloomington, 1989), 24–47.

devastation would not happen again. Violence redefined both the lived experience and popular perceptions of revolutionary emancipation.

The revolutionary period therefore needs to be placed within the larger pan-European shift towards liberating popular politics and, as Peter Holquist has argued, the more immediate violent political turmoil of modern warfare.[27] Indeed, my work extends and challenges the new wave of scholarship on the Russian Revolution that explores the development of state practices across the revolutionary divide. These works, influenced by post-structuralism and the opening of Russia's archives, represent a sea change in the historiography of twentieth-century Russian history away from limited cold war arguments obsessing over the legitimacy of the October 1917 Bolshevik seizure of power and towards a more expansionist survey of Russia's history. My book agrees with their conclusions on the Revolution yet challenges their focus on institutional practice. In so doing, I show how peasants reacted to and helped to create the changing political world. Observing the Russian Revolution through the lens of rural society brings local politics and the formation of individual identities into focus.

This work also aims to unveil the complexity of peasant identity through a close study of the northeastern province of Viatka.[28] An understanding of the complex interaction of peasants' geographical locale, ethnic identity, social status, age, and gender is integral in fully understanding peasant participation in Russia's transformations. The Soviet government's ability to connect to and incorporate the various rural populations was central to its ultimate success in establishing power in the countryside. Previous studies of the revolutionary countryside rest on conclusions drawn from the Black Earth region of central Russia. This focus has led to a misleading portrait of a homogenous Russian peasantry who had been recently emancipated as private serfs and hungered for land.

Viatka province is an ideal location to re-examine peasant experiences and participation in the revolutionary era. Like their counterparts in northern Russia and western Siberia, most of Viatka's peasants did not know a landlord economy and did not suffer from acute land hunger.

---

[27] Holquist, *Making War*; see also Joshua A. Sanborn, *Drafting the Russian Nation: Military Conscription, Total War, and Mass Politics, 1905–1925* (DeKalb, 2003); Yanni Kotsonis and David L. Hoffmann, eds, *Russian Modernity: Politics, Knowledge, Practices* (New York, 2000).

[28] The Soviet government disassembled Viatka in 1929 and conglomerated it with the Gorky region. In December 1934, following the assassination of Viatka's native son Sergei Kirov, the government recreated the region and renamed it Kirov. Today, Kirov is one of the only regions in Russia that has not reverted to its pre-revolutionary name.

The region's peasant–state relationship highlights the multiplicity of the popular interaction with the state. A study of Viatka calls into question the long-held paradigm based on studies of the Black Earth region – that peasants tried to close themselves off from the outside world. Many peasants of Viatka sought out the state and actively worked to be part of the larger polity. Through a study of the significant, yet largely over-looked, peasant population of the Viatka countryside, this project paints a more complicated picture of Russia's peasantry and peasant–state relations, and creates a fundamentally new understanding of the Russian Revolution and the foundations of the Soviet Union.

Redefining the centre: Viatka province as metaphor

Viatka province lay amidst the tall pine trees and meandering rivers beyond the Volga, hundreds of miles from Moscow. Nestled in the north-east corner of European Russia (north of Kazan, on the foothills of the Ural Mountains), the province occupied a vast physical space. Viatka was one of the largest provinces in European Russia (roughly the same size as all of the Black Earth region) with the second largest rural population of all the Russian Empire's provinces.[29] Viatka resided on the border between central Russia and the northern and Siberian peripheries. Tatars, linguistically Finno-Ugric Udmurts and Maris, and smaller Slavic tribes inhabited the region in the tenth century and developed large settlements and a vibrant trade. Novgorod, a commercial partner of the Hanseatic League, established economic ties with the region and incorporated it into its empire in the fourteenth century. Following the decline of Novgorod, Muscovy integrated the territory into its kingdom in the next century. The first Russians to colonize Viatka came in the twelfth century, but they began systematic colonization only in the sixteenth century, establishing monasteries and economic networks, and by the eighteenth century constituted a majority of the region's population.[30] The Russian Orthodox Church began mass conversions of the local indigenous populations in the late-eighteenth century and most Udmurts and Maris converted to Orthodoxy.[31]

---

[29] S. N. Kosarev, *Zemel'noe ustroistvo v Viatskoi gubernii* (Viatka, 1917), 1; *Rossiia 1913 god: Statistiko-dokumental'nyi spravochnik* (St Petersburg, 1995), 18–22. At 89,160 square miles, Viatka was the approximate size of present-day Romania, with a surprisingly large population of 3,369,000, equal to that of Sweden in 1917 or Ireland in 2003.

[30] A. V. Emmausskii, *Istoriia Viatskogo kraia v XII-seredine XIX veka* (Kirov, 1996).

[31] Paul Werth, *At the Margins of Orthodoxy: Mission, Governance, and Confessional Politics in Russia's Volga–Kama Region, 1827–1905* (Ithaca, 2002).

At the beginning of the twentieth century, scholars and literary figures painted an image of Viatka as a remote wasteland, caught in the cross-roads of East and West, North and South. Viatka's liminal state created a space for writers to endow it with their own dreams, criticisms, and images.[32] Viatka's population, economy, and society were 'backward' and its distance from civilization punctuated by its function as a land of political exiles. For Viatka's most famous exile, the nineteenth-century philosopher and revolutionary Aleksandr Herzen, Viatka represented both the eastern wildness of Siberia, and the western despotism of Russian officials.[33] While literati constructed Viatka's environment as unspoiled by mankind, they still painted Viatka as a whole in dark hues.[34] The negative imagery is not unique to Viatka province. Other areas of Russia were certainly called the *glush'* (backwater), but Viatka embodied the extremes of this image of the remote countryside. Scholars have maintained this negative picture of Viatka under the tsarist regime. As one author writes, 'the vast Viatka region gradually became one of the most backwater and "God forsaken" of the Russian provinces'.[35] If this portrait of Viatka as a remote wasteland, hardly touched by modern governance or national unity is accurate then its peasants should have been cut off from the larger national changes. This was not the case. As a borderland and cross-cultural point, an analysis of war and revolution in Viatka illuminates the multiplicity of locals' experiences. Some of the differences stem from local conditions, but others highlight themes glossed over by those studying the centre.

A study of Viatka province thereby allows us to re-examine scholars' homogenizing perceptions of peasants in war and revolution. Viatka's ecology, land tenure system, and social structure differed from the Black Earth region but resembled other under-studied regions of Russia, such as the north, Urals, and western Siberia. Ninety per cent of the province's peasants were emancipated as state peasants in 1866. They had never had to labour for a squire and fulfilled their obligations with cash or in-kind goods (*obrok*). By the beginning of the twentieth century

---

[32] For discussion on other constructed liminal spaces in Russia, see Mark Bassin, *Imperial Visions: Nationalist Imagination and Geographical Expansion in the Russian Far East, 1840–1865* (Cambridge, 1999); Yuri Slezkine, *Arctic Mirrors: Russia and the Small Peoples of the North* (Ithaca, 1994); and Robert P. Geraci, *Window on the East: National and Imperial Identities in Late Tsarist Russia* (Ithaca, 2001). These works have intellectual connections to Edward Said's concept of orientalism. See Edward Said, *Orientalism* (New York, 1979).

[33] Aleksandr Gertsen, *Byloe i dumy* (Moscow, 1962), 210–20.

[34] See A. A. Titov, ed., *Nikolai Vasil'evich Chaikovskii: Religioznyia i obshchestvennyia iskaniia* (Paris, 1929).

[35] V. P. Danilov, *Rural Russia under the New Regime*, tr. Orlando Figes (Bloomington, 1988), 49.

these former state peasants had their 'forty acres and a mule', or an average of fifteen *desiatina*s of land (40.5 acres) and at least one horse per household. Most of the remaining peasants (6.1 per cent of the population) had lived as crown peasants, owned by members of the tsar's family before their 1863 emancipation. While crown peasants held on average less land than former state peasants, eight *desiatina*s (21.6 acres) of land, they had also never experienced the direct oversight of a squire. Viatka enjoyed the highest percentage of privately owned land in all of European Russia.[36] Economic standards varied greatly by *volost* and even village, but Viatka's peasants as a composite still did not suffer from land hunger like their fellow peasants who tilled the black earth. The majority of peasants in the Black Earth region had been the property of gentry before their emancipation in 1861. Although free, they still resented the landlord who kept the most, and often the best, land. In 1917, after the tsarist regime collapsed, peasants of the Black Earth channelled their anger against the estates. Viatka's peasants, like the millions of other former state peasants who did not have a single individual on whom to focus their aggression, waited for land reform laws, rather than autonomously seizing land, as happened in the Black Earth region.

While peasants of the Black Earth lived off some of the richest soil in the world, most of Viatka's peasants suffered from poor soil and a harsh climate, making it difficult to survive off the crops in the field.[37] Peasants in the northern regions could not sow the fields until the mid-May thaw and it was not unheard of to have frost in July. The soil was a frustrating mixture of soil and clay in the north but grew closer to the fluffy loam of the Black Earth in the south, allowing the latter to serve as the province's breadbasket. Thanks to the south's fertility, Viatka was one of the only non-Black Earth provinces to produce a grain surplus, however slight, on the eve of the First World War. It enjoyed an 8.2 per cent surplus of crops, especially oats, potatoes, flax, and hemp.[38] The concentration of surplus agricultural products prompted the state to establish a pattern

---

[36] In 1905, there were only 115 noble estates concentrated in the southern districts, half of which had 100 *desiatina*s of land or less. By comparison, there were over two thousand nobles with land in Tambov province, of whom approximately 1,300 owned over 100 *desiatina*s of land. *Statistika zemlevladeniia 1905 g. Svod dannykh po 50-ti guberniiam Evropeiskoi Rossii* (St Petersburg, 1907), 50–1 and 74–5.

[37] *Statisticheskii spravochnik po Viatskoi gubernii, 1917* (Viatka, 1917); A. Novikov, *Ekonomicheskiia nuzhdy Viatskago kraia (po dannym zemskoi statistiki)* (Viatka, 1896).

[38] A. N. Chelintsev, *Russkoe sel'skoe khoziaistvo pered revoliutsiei*, 2nd edn (Moscow, 1928), 37, 78, 87–8, 113–14, 116, 219, 223, 228–9. Based on calculations of average crops between 1907 and 1910, Viatka produced an average annual surplus of 9,547,000 puds of grain for these years. By comparison, Riazan produced an annual surplus of 11,130,000 puds, Saratov 41,166,000, the Don region 108,101,000. Arkhangel'sk had a shortfall of 3,829,000 puds, and Vladimir's shortfall was 9,570,000.

Plate 3. Viatka ploughman struggling with the land, early twentieth century. Courtesy GASPI KO

early in the First World War in which it targeted the southern regions when it needed to procure grain.

Viatka's peasants, especially in the less fertile central and northern regions, did not hunger for control of finite arable land like their brethren in the Black Earth. This is not to say that land was unimportant. Peasants in 1917, and especially after the Soviet Land Decree, rejoiced at the opportunity to take land they saw as rightfully theirs. The economics of ecology, however, had pushed many peasant households to rely on the dense state- and factory-owned forests that surrounded the villages and non-land based markets to supplement their crops. Most scholars argue that the Bolshevik regime gained initial peasant support from legalizing seizures and redistribution of their landlord's land and property and crucial acquiescence to Soviet rule in the Civil War because peasants feared the landlord system's return with the anti-Soviet forces. This was simply not the case in Viatka where the Black Earth manorial system did not exist. Peasant populations instead sought out Bolshevik authority to help solve intra-village disputes and increase their social standing. Peasants looked beyond the field in their political dreams and relationships with the polity. The region's peasant–state relationship thereby highlights the multiplicity of the popular interaction with the state.

Viatka's ethnic diversity shows the resonance of ethnic difference on state practice and peasant experience. State programmes through the revolution marked ethnic distinction. Tensions from Imperial rule and Russification were most charged on Russia's western borderlands and Central Asia and these areas witnessed the most pronounced national movements during the revolution, but they also resonated in European Russia.[39] Udmurts (the largest national minority in the province), Maris, and Tatars made up twenty-three per cent of the province's total population, and represented a majority of the rural population in the province's southern and eastern districts.[40]

Members of late-Imperial educated society were fascinated with studying and categorizing non-Russians. Ethnographers placed non-Russian peoples into an evolutionary hierarchy of culture, based on their assumptions of organic nationality.[41] Herzen, for instance, dabbling in ethnographic surveys during his Viatka exile, created an evolutionary ladder of cultural and physical progress with Russians on the top rung, Tatars below them, and Maris and Udmurts lagging behind as primitive savages. Established ethnographers D. K. Zelenin and N. N. Blinov also described Udmurts and Maris as physically, linguistically, culturally, and spiritually undeveloped.[42] Ethnographic description of Udmurt paganism and savagery continued in the notorious Multan Case in the 1890s, in which a group of seven Udmurts in southern Viatka were falsely convicted of human sacrifice.[43] The public uproar over the possibility that Udmurts were engaging in human sacrifice highlighted the

[39] Richard Pipes, *Formation of the Soviet Union: Communism and Nationalism, 1917–1923* (Cambridge, MA, 1964).

[40] For a general description of Viatka's non-Russian population, see M. Ostrovskaia, *Iz istorii Viatskikh inorodtsev* (Kazan, 1912). In the early-twentieth century Udmurts were known as Votiaks and Maris as Cheremisy. These terms now have pejorative connotations. For simplicity and cultural sensitivity, I use the terms Udmurts and Maris throughout the book.

[41] Nathaniel Knight, 'Ethnicity, Nationality and the Masses: *Narodnost'* and Modernity in Imperial Russia', in Kotsonis and Hoffmann, eds, *Russian Modernity*, 41–61; Charles Steinwedel, 'To Make a Difference: the Category of Ethnicity in Late Imperial Russian Politics, 1861–1917', in Kotsonis and Hoffmann, eds, *Russian Modernity*, 67–86.

[42] Aleksandr Gertsen, *Sobranie sochinenii v tridtsati tomakh*, t. 1 (Moscow, 1954), 371; D. K. Zelenin, *Kama i Viatka: Putevoditel' i etnograficheskoe opisanie prikamskago kraia*, (Viatka, 1904), 74–5, 168. E. I. Kiriukhina, 'Iz istorii natsional'nogo stroitel'stva v Viatskom krae', in A. V. Emmauskii, ed., *Voprosy istorii Kirovskoi oblasti* (Kirov, 1974), 6. See also Geraci's discussion of the ethnographer I. N. Smirnov, *Window on the East*, 202–7.

[43] Geraci, *Window on the East*, ch. 6; G. V. Korolenko, ed., *Delo multanskikh votiakov, obviniavshikhsia v prinesenii chelovecheskoi zhertvy iazycheskim bogam* (Moscow, 1896); L. S. Shatenshtein, *Multanskoe delo 1892–1896 gg.* (Izhevsk, 1960).

popular view that non-Russians needed cultural advancement and more stringent Christian teachings.

While officials and educated society marked distinctions based on national categories, everyday ethnic interaction in the countryside was more complex. Peasants of Viatka felt a greater bond as a social group than they felt divided by ethnic difference.[44] Peasants of different nationalities interacted on a daily basis. Markets and fairs were multi-ethnic meeting points where Russian, Udmurt, and Mari peasants traded goods with one another. In the district centre of Elabuga, for example, Russian peasants exchanged their cucumbers for Udmurts' forest materials.[45] These multi-ethnic gathering points were also places to get news of political events and during the revolutionary era became sites of contestation over economic relationships between peasants and state and the urban population, as well as between ethnic groups.[46] Russians lived in and around almost all the villages inhabited by non-Russians and these quarters grew closer as Russians resettled to southern and eastern Viatka during the great Siberian migration.[47] Although ethnographers believed that Maris 'feared and disdained Russians' and were 'barely subjected to Russification', by the end of the nineteenth century, these two groups shared agricultural techniques, instruments, and crops.[48] Russian and non-Russian peasants were also members of the same commune. In fact, in the second half of the nineteenth century, 30% of all communes in Sarapul district and 75% of all communes in Glazov district had a multi-ethnic composition.[49]

---

[44] Ethnicity, a relational term for a group of people who consider themselves and are considered by others as distinctive, best describes the self-understanding of non-Russian peasants at the beginning of the twentieth century and provides a better terminology than national identity. Thomas Hylland Eriksen, *Ethnicity and Nationalism: Anthropological Perspectives* (Boulder, 1993), 4, 10–12; Geoff Eley and Ronald Grigor Suny, 'Introduction: From the Moment of Social History to the Work of Cultural Representation', in Geoff Eley and Ronald Grigor Suny, eds, *Becoming National: A Reader* (New York, 1996), 21–2.

[45] *Trudy komisii po issledovaniiu kustarnoi promyshlennosti v Rossii.*, vyp. XI (St Petersburg, 1884), 15; N. P. Ligenko, 'Bazary, iarmarki, torzhki–aktivnaia sfera mezhetnicheskikh kontaktov. XIX-nachalo XX veka', in K. M. Klimov, ed., *Slavianskii i finno-ugorskii mir vchera, segodniia. Sbornik statei* (Izhevsk, 1996), 91, 97; G. E. Vereshchagin, *Votiaki sosnovskogo kraia* (St Petersburg, 1886), 17–18.

[46] Ligenko, 'Bazary', 103–4.

[47] Vereshchagin, *Votiaki Sosnovskogo kraia*, 1.

[48] Zelenin, *Kama i Viatka*, 168; G. A. Sepeev, 'Mariisko-Russkie etnokul'turnye vzaimosviazi v XIX veke (po materialam Urzhumskogo i Iaranskogo uezda)', in A. G. Balyberdin et al., eds, *Viatskaia zemlia v proshlom i nastoiashchem (K 500-letiiu vkhozhdeniia v sostav Rossiiskogo gosudarstva). Tezisy dokladov i soobshchenii k nauchnoi konferentsii Kirov, 23–25 maia 1989 goda* (Kirov, 1989), 278–80.

[49] G. A. Nikitina, *Sel'skaia obshchina buskel' v poreformennyi period (1861–1900 gg.)* (Izhevsk, 1993), 25; M. M. Martynova, 'Agrarnye otnosheniia v Udmurtii vo vtoroi

Ethnic groups still defined themselves in relation to other ethnicities. Popular stereotypes of local nationalities underscored the differences and pointed to tension brewing beneath the surface.[50] Udmurt expressions, such as 'when you talk with a Russian let your mouth and ears be on guard', and 'when you talk with a Russian have a knife in your pocket', show suspicion of Russians.[51] Similarly, Udmurt ideas of Tatars as dishonest in commercial relations, and as thieves, are seen in the expressions, 'a Tatar was born to cheat and to haggle', and 'a Tatar upon his birth steals a horse'. However, they did see the fellow Finno-Ugric Maris as their kin, saying, 'Udmurts and Maris grow from the same root'.[52]

Most of the villages of Viatka had become tied to the national economy and culture on the eve of war. Over ninety per cent of Viatka's peasant households relied on non-land-based peasant handicraft production and out-migrant labour (*otkhod*) markets to supplement their income. In 1897, sixty-three per cent of households, and an even greater amount in central Viatka, engaged in handicraft production, more than any other province in European Russia.[53] The vibrant and diverse peasant handicraft trade produced lace weavings, furniture, harmonicas, carriages, clay dolls, samovars, fishing tackle, matchboxes, and boots.[54] Peasants sold their wares to middlemen and at local fairs, further integrating them into the market economy. Migratory labour (*otkhodnichestvo*) also linked the household to the industrial economy and urban culture. Like peasants throughout Russia, Viatka's rural dwellers, especially youths, established patterns of out-migration near and far. Peasants supplied the armament and metalworks factories in Izhevsk, Votkinsk, and Glazov.[55] In Viatka

---

polovine XIX veka', in M. M. Martynova, M. I. Gnedin and N. P. Ligenko, eds, *Agrarnye otnosheniia v Udmurtii vo vtoroi polovine XIX-nachale XX vv.: Sbornik statei* (Izhevsk, 1981), 5.

[50] Such underlying hostility and stereotyping among neighbouring peasant national and ethnic groups paralleled those in Transylvania. Katherine Verdery, *Transylvanian Villagers: Three Centuries of Political, Economic, and Ethnic Change* (Berkeley, 1983).

[51] K. P. Gerd, 'Poslovitsy i pogovorki votiakov', in K. P. Gerd and V. P. Malimova, eds, *Votiaki. Sbornik po voprosam byta, ekonomiki, i kul'tury votiakov* (Moscow, 1926), 59. The sayings in Udmurt are, 'Dzuchen veras'kykyd ymyd pel'yd sak med-lo', and 'Dzuchen veras'kykyd – kisiiad purted med-lo'.

[52] 'Biger – orekchasykyny no vuz karny kyldem', 'Biger – vordskykyz-ik mumizles' valze lushkam', and 'Poren udmurten – odig vyjiys' potem pispu'. Gerd, in 'Poslovitsy', eds, 60.

[53] A. A. Rybnikov, *Kustarnaia promyshlennost' i sbyt kustarnykh izdelii*, (Moscow, 1913), 16–17.

[54] *Materialy po issledovaniiu promyslov Viatskoi gubernii, Viatskii uezd osnovnyia tablitsy (podvornoe izsledovanie 1909 goda)*, (Viatka, 1912), II, 70, 76; V. E. Musikhin, 'Krest'ianstvo kak osnova Viatskoi samobytnosti', V. F. Ponomarev et al., *Entsiklopediia zemli Viatskoi*, t. 10, *Remesla* (Kirov, 2000), 15.

[55] Izhevsk continues to be a major producer of armaments in Russia, now producing the Kalashnikov machine gun, designed by its native son, Mikhail Kalashnikov.

city and in smaller local factories peasants produced leather products, woven baskets, wooden furniture, and barrels. They also journeyed to factories in Kazan and Moscow, the mines of Perm, and the barges on the Volga. Many more peasants carried out temporary work in villages and cities closer to home.[56]

The transportation network and urbanization created a closer network with the national political and economic world. The railroad came to Viatka in 1898 and opened up opportunities to migrate eastward or travel easily to the provincial towns. At the beginning of the twentieth century the city of Viatka had a bustling economy and a population of 25,000 inhabitants (about the same size as the cities of Vladivostok, Vladimir, and Vologda) and growing. As the province's capital, peasants travelled to the city to lodge complaints with the government, made pilgrimages to the Trifonov monastery, and used the city's market to sell and buy goods.[57] The industrial towns of Izhevsk and Votkinsk, in southeast Viatka, provided further links to urban culture. Finally, peasants held a majority of seats on the zemstvo board of Viatka, as in other provinces without a strong cohort of landowners, and they donated exceptional amounts of money to support programmes like education, which they deemed valuable to living within the larger world.[58]

Structure

To show the evolution of peasant political experience and to give the reader a sense of how the catastrophes built upon each other, I follow a chronological account of the eight years of war and revolution. Chapter One begins the story of the revolution in the village with the call to arms on 18 July 1914. Wartime quickly militarized the village and made it into a front in the war. While mobilization for total war brought Russian peasants into the national struggle, it reinforced that the political and cultural elites defined Udmurts, Maris, and Tatars as marginal groups occupying a liminal space within the national struggle but outside the nation. Wartime footing and the changing population and economy also exacerbated social cleavages and altered gender dynamics in the village.

---

[56] Gosudarstvennyi Arkhiv Kirovskoi Oblasti (hereafter GAKO), f. R-1062, op. 1, d. 338, ll. 1, 17ob.

[57] *Naselenie Rossii za 100 let (1897–1997). Population of Russia: 1897–1997. Statisticheskii sbornik. Statistical Handbook* (Moscow, 1998), 58–9.

[58] Dorothy Atkinson, 'The Zemstvo and the Peasantry', in Terence Emmons and Wayne S. Vucinich, eds, *The Zemstvo in Russia: An Experiment in Local Self-Government* (Cambridge, 1982), 119–21; Carsten Pape, 'The "Peasant Zemstva": Popular Education in Vjatka Gubernija, 1867–1905', *Jahrbücher für Geschichte Osteuropas* 27 (1979): 498–519.

Mobilization, cataclysmic destruction, and peasants' new understanding of their place in the nation accelerated the popular desire for political changes. Chapters Two and Three explore peasant participation in the 1917 Revolution. If the war brought peasants into the nation, the February Revolution that overthrew the Tsar and established the democratic Provisional Government made them full citizens. Chapter Two, 'Peasant Citizens', shows the peaceful transition to a new government in the countryside and the ephemeral unity of peasants and rural educated society. Peasants were at first content to follow the new political elites' tutelage in parades, oaths, and other rituals meant to teach a citizenship heavy on duty to the nation and the wartime struggle. By summer, peasants bristled under elite constructions of them as politically backward. Chapter Three, 'Peasant and Nation in Revolution', explores how peasants clashed with rural elites and demanded an equal voice as full citizens in an increasingly fractured and polarized world. It documents the economic breakdown and growing tensions over grain between peasant and state agents that in turn broke apart the democratic experiment of the Provisional Government.

The fourth chapter, 'Bringing the State Back In', re-examines the crucial issue of land following the Bolshevik Decree on Land in October 1917 that sanctioned peasant seizures of land. The chapter refutes the picture of the peasantry obtaining freedom from outside interference to divide land as they saw fit, finding instead that peasants involved the nascent Soviet state to help resolve village conflicts. Peasants understood that land rights extended social citizenship rights under the Soviets. In fact, land became a trope for villagers to express community cleavages, and the chapter details the generational, social, and gendered fractures in the village through land court cases.

Chapters Five through Eight examine how peasants coped with the violent changes of the Civil War from 1918 to 1922. Chapter Five, 'Civil War and the Village', explores the confluence of grain politics and military conflicts in Viatka's countryside. In the summer of 1918, the Bolshevik state experimented with a levy system and forced grain requisitions in southern Viatka that it applied to the rest of Soviet Russia. The chaos from the requisitions and other Bolshevik excesses led to a fascinating triangular civil conflict in the countryside among Bolsheviks, anti-Bolshevik rebels, and peasants. Chapter Six, 'The Resurrection of Soviet Power in the Countryside', begins a two-chapter study of how the Soviet state and Communist Party planted themselves inside the village. In the immediate aftermath of anti-Soviet revolts, the state built rural institutions and established alliances with peasant populations. Chapter Seven, 'Big Tent Bolshevism', shows that peasant language and identity became more Soviet following state and Party cultural enlightenment and propaganda campaigns. The final chapter, 'The Citizens' Hunger', underscores the devastation of the Civil War and resulting famine on rural society that led to millions of deaths, popular revolts, and the largest migration of people from their home to date. The chapter argues that the Soviet state's willingness to sponsor relief efforts created a lasting relationship built on reciprocal ideas of social citizenship. The story of peasants in revolution is one of violence and terror as much as it is of freedom, emancipation, and negotiation. In the end, peasants helped to create a participatory political system committed to the improvement of peasants' lives. In 1922, Russia's modern revolutionary state held as many possibilities to include its populace in an emancipatory system as it did to steer the country down a murderous path.[59]

---

[59] Like Raleigh, I chart the end of the Civil War to 1922. See *Experiencing Russia's Civil War.*

1 The masses mobilized: militarization, conscription, and the First World War in the village

[T]he Russian Government addressed the people with an appeal to forget internal divisions and to unite in the fight against the terrible enemy, and Russia rose to this call. With an enthusiasm never before seen in history, those from the wealthiest estates to those of the poorest huts joined the ranks of the army, regardless of differing religions, nationalities, and social place. Everyone saw themselves as citizens, children of one common beloved motherland. They went, leaving behind wives, children, elderly parents, brothers and sisters. But as they were departing, they left us with one desire, one command: 'look after our families. Do not let them be forgotten in our absence while we defend your freedom, your beliefs, your nation, and your property. For the love and care of sacred mother Russia, do not let there be any sense of need in our homes'.[1]

For those in the countryside, the revolution truly began when the call to war on 18 July 1914 reached the village. From that moment, through the next eight years, peasants experienced a connected string of social and political upheaval that would only end with the gradual conclusion of civil war and slow recovery from famine. Wartime mobilization forced peasants to participate in mass politics and national rituals that would consume the nation in 1917 and pave the way for peasant participation in the early Soviet state.

Peasants had more immediate concerns in the middle of July than the growing threat of war. The winter wheat had ripened and the villagers needed to harvest it quickly.[2] Peasants nevertheless looked beyond their fields when they learned of the call to arms. Russia's peasants brought in their yield in the autumn, and gave out the village's wealth to the

---

[1] *Otchet o deiatel'nosti Slobodskogo otdela obshchestva pomoshchi sem'iam zapasnykh i ratnikov opolcheniia, prizvannykh v mobilizatsii 1914–1915 gg.* (Slobodskoi, 1916), 3.

[2] War interrupted the height of the winter rye harvest in Viatka's southern districts and peasants' preparations for the harvest in the north. M. Sadakov, 'Udmurtiia v gody pervoi mirovoi imperialisticheskoi voiny', *Zapiski Udmurtskogo NII* vyp. 16 (1954), 57.

national cause, sacrificing grain from their harvest, money from their savings, and, most importantly, able-bodied men from their households.

Economic modernization and political reforms of the late-nineteenth and early-twentieth centuries pushed Russia's peasants to confront representatives and images of the state and nation, and the war suddenly enveloped them completely in the national project. Wartime footing transformed existing points of cultural contact and gave birth to many new ones. It also revolutionized rural society itself. War created new economic realities including state-controlled markets, labour shortages, and inflation, and augmented the movement of populations by removing a sizeable amount of the male population and replacing them with foreign prisoners of war and refugees. The changing population and economic conditions also exacerbated social cleavages and altered gender dynamics in the village. Wartime mobilization and the conflict's cataclysmic destruction transformed peasant political discourse and how peasants understood their place in the nation. These changes accelerated the popular desire for political changes. A year of economic hardships and huge losses on the front made peasants question the war effort and the governmental structure as a whole.

The tsarist state and its agents in the countryside depended on mobilization of the population and its continued commitment to the war effort.[3] As the report that begins this chapter illustrates, officials and educated society used peasants' local concerns for the welfare of their men conscripted into the army, as well as abstract notions of political participation, patriotic duty, and nationalism to spur peasants to act. Zemstvo activists and reform-minded state personnel guided visions of national unification and tried to promote their modernizing visions among the peasantry. The result was the mobilization – indeed the militarization – of the village's resources through an intensification of state and zemstvo presence in the countryside. The village quickly became a front in the war against foreign enemies as well as peasant 'backwardness'. The impact of war created the political foundation for

---

[3] I see three overlapping actors during the pre-revolutionary war: the peasantry, state officials, and educated society (including zemstvo activists, professionals, and the intelligentsia). Some zemstvo activists were part of the peasant *soslovie* (estate) and some peasants acted as state officials, for example. As Peter Holquist notes, wartime mobilization in Russia and other combatants created 'a "parastatal complex", a dense network of professional and civic organizations that became closely intertwined with the state'. Throughout the text I try to specify when the categories overlap, but often state and educated society are too intertwined to extract one from the other: *Making War*, 21; Holquist derives the parastatal complex from Michael Geyer, 'The Militarization of Europe, 1914–1945', in John R. Gillis, ed., *The Militarization of the Western World* (New Brunswick, 1989), 65–102.

the course of the upcoming revolution in the countryside: an expansive state demanding popular mobilization, and peasants seeking greater participation in governance, becoming increasingly aware of their inclusion in the national state project.

Patriotism, conflict, and conscription

Villagers and urban dwellers across Russia participated in pro-war rallies and valediction rituals in the first months of the war. The village of Suna in Nolinsk district (*uezd*) was one of those that turned out to see its men off to war. The church bells rang to mark the occasion and mothers, children, and well-wishers attended a special service to pray for victory, the tsar, and the military. A huge crowd followed the conscripted men from the church carrying icons and gonfalons. Amidst their tears, the villagers cursed 'the monster Wilhelm'. The village ladies' circle adorned the reservists with gifts and the villagers yelled 'farewell countrymen' as their men rode off to war.[4] The beginning of war created a patriotic atmosphere, making Russia's subjects feel united and responsible to the government and country.[5] The solemnity of the occasion in Suna, however, underscored that the peasants understood these men might not return home alive.

Contemporary officials and newspapers defined peasant reaction to the war as patriotic, but based on blind unquestioning allegiance to the tsar. In the first days of the war, Viatka's Ministry of Internal Affairs remarked to its affiliate in the capital on the peasantry's 'strong sense of patriotism and outstanding empathy, mercy, and love' towards soldiers' families and the war effort in general. District administrators echoed their superior. As one noted, 'the simple Russian people (*narod*) instinctively feel that war is being waged in the name of the highest interests of the Russian people and they recognize the need to sacrifice fully until certain and final victory'.[6] Conservative pundits saw the peasantry as unconsciously patriotic and driven by religious fatalism. The monarchist newspaper *Severnoe slovo* commented that in the village 'there is not a single murmur about anything. Our villagers are fully submitted to fate and as one say "heaven created its will". They instinctively wait for Russia's decisive victory'.[7] Government officials and

---

[4] *Viatskaia rech'*, 10 January 1915, 3–4.
[5] On patriotism, see Rogers Brubaker, 'In the Nation of the Nation: Reflections on Nationalism and Patriotism', *Citizenship Studies* 8 (2004): 121. On the burst of patriotic culture and its failure to unite Russia, see Hubertus F. Jahn, *Patriotic Culture in Russia during World War I* (Ithaca, 1995).
[6] GAKO, f. 574, op. 2, d. 961, l. 83.   [7] *Severnoe slovo*, 4 January 1915, 3.

conservative writers were guided by their own conceptions of patriotism. Their nationalistic language, which equated material sacrifice by a simple, folkloric people with instinctive patriotic sentiment, imagined an ideal but outdated, naively monarchist, and tradition-bound peasantry.

The peasants of Viatka were neither fatalistic nor blindly patriotic in their initial support of the war and the Tsar. Peasants did feel inchoate patriotic ties to Russia's national struggle and often expressed this in religious services and prayers for the Tsar, markers of primordial national unification. But they had complex and conflicted reactions to the war effort stemming from the enormity of the task and an under-standing of mobilization's consequences for the village, as well as from pre-existing suspicions between peasants and tsarist authorities. At the outset of war peasants felt conflicting emotions – obligation to support the country's war effort, and dread of its effects on the village.[8]

In the autumn of 1914, peasants actively engaged in the war effort. Villagers took an interest in the war's proceedings and sought out the latest news of military operations. The Viatka government and zemstvo, after realizing peasant fascination with the war, fostered this interest and patriotic culture. At least while the war was going well, they published regular updates on its progress, a map, and biographies of Russia's military leaders, and disseminated them to all 22,500 of Viatka's villages. In turn, peasants displayed a knowledge of the complexities of the war – news from the front, government policies towards the countryside, and who were the leading political figures.[9] Most of all, peasants in general meetings (skhods) supported the cause with charitable donations to zemstvo hospitals and the Red Cross. Peasants also donated money and goods at public charity events. For example, during a fair on 27 October to mark the processional of an icon in Sernur village, Urzhum district, peasants bought flags to mark 'unity with our government'. In Glazov district, peasants purchased crosses during the intelligentsia-organized Red Cross Day. Several villages throughout the province also staged performances, with profits going to the war effort.[10] Newspapers

---

[8] My argument in part parallels that of Joshua Sanborn in 'The Mobilization of 1914 and the Question of the Russian Nation: A Re-examination', *Slavic Review* 59 (2000): 267–89.

[9] RGIA, f. 1284, op. 194, d. 13, l. 4ob; *Viatskaia rech'*, 6 December 1914, 3. For peasant interest in the war's movement, see Scott Seregny, 'Zemstvos, Peasants, and Citizenship: The Russian Adult Education Movement and World War I', *Slavic Review* 59 (2000): 294, 304; and response by S. A. Smith, 'Citizenship and the Russian Nation', 316–29.

[10] *Viatskaia rech'*, 12 November 1914, 3; 19 November 1914, 3; 6 February 1915, 3. See also, 29 October 1914, 4; 17 January 1916, 3.

Plate 4. Reading a letter from the front, 1915. Courtesy GASPI KO

publicized these events and helped to create a patriotic atmosphere in the countryside.

While a majority of the peasants supported the war effort, a number of peasants resisted the call to arms. Popular ambivalence, suspicion, and even hostility towards the war effort revealed that not all peasants shared in the patriotic enthusiasm, and that peasants overall felt ambivalent towards state mobilization efforts. Peasants petitioned the military to excuse themselves or family members from conscription by claiming illness or physical disability and complained that mobilization took them

away from summer fieldwork.[11] Some peasant families used the 1912
legal provision allowing the only son or sole able-bodied male worker of
a household to be freed from conscription and pleaded with the state to
disoblige a family member from the army by claiming that he was their
last working hand.[12] For example, in October 1914, in Bobinskaia *volost*,
Viatka district, Kozma Myshkin, an elderly peasant, petitioned the district military leader to return his eldest son Iakov from military service.
The petitioner already had two sons in the military and both he and his
wife were old, leaving the household without an able-bodied labourer.
Kozma asked that only Iakov be returned since he had a family with a
young child.[13] Peasants like Kozma Myshkin willingly sacrificed what
they considered a just amount for the nation. Since there was such a slim
margin between starvation and existence for most peasants, they were
unwilling to endanger their subsistence by letting go of too many
workers so they could not gather sufficient crops.

   Peasants also actively resisted the call to war by participating in
popular demonstrations. Draft riots erupted throughout Russia,
including Viatka.[14] Alongside these riots, and often indistinguishable in
the official records, thousands of peasants protested the war's immediate
effects on the food and alcohol markets. On 22 July 1914 over six
thousand local peasant conscripts to the army rose up in the city of
Kotel'nich following the closure of all spirit concessionaries. Soldiers
confronted their military officers and the district police, simultaneously
demanding vodka and protesting rising grain and tobacco prices. Failing
to force the officers to give them alcohol, they broke into a liquor store,
got drunk, and ran through town engaging in 'hooliganism', including
breaking into the store of a Tatar. The police fired into the crowd and
finally suppressed the riot after ten people died and another twelve were
wounded.[15] A similar instance occurred in Glazov district the night
before, when conscripts terrorized officials in a multi-village hunt for
alcohol that spanned the whole of Gordinskaia *volost*. In the village of

[11] GAKO, f. 589, op. 1, d. 352, ll. 29–31; O. S. Porshneva, *Krest'iane, rabochie i soldaty
   Rossii nakanune i v gody pervoi mirovoi voiny* (Moscow, 2004), 464–5.
[12] For more on exemptions based on ethnicity and family status, see Sanborn, *Drafting the
   Russian Nation*, 22; Emily E. Pyle, 'Village Social Relations and the Reception of Soldiers'
   Family and Policies in Russia, 1912–1921' (PhD diss., University of Chicago, 1997).
[13] GAKO, f. 589, op. 1, d. 352, l. 45. I have kept the adjectival endings of *volosts*, but
   have shortened the district names.
[14] Sanborn, 'The Mobilization of 1914', 274–8.
[15] GAKO, f. 714, op. 1, d. 1493, ll. 3, 10–13ob; A. B. Berkevich reports that thirteen
   people were wounded and another thirteen killed in uprisings in Viatka during July,
   'Krest'ianstvo i vseobshchaia mobilizatsiia v iiule 1914 g.', *Istoricheskie zapiski* 23
   (1947): 41.

Korabli they broke a window of the spirits store, shrugged off the guards, and drank several pints of wine. The group then set off to Ser'gino village (*selo*) where the soldiers threatened to destroy the local spirits store if they were not given wine. In Sergeevo village, the presence of the police, *volost starshina*, and several guards convinced the soldiers to pay for the spirits. The drunken spree turned ugly when the conscripts continued to the village of Korsovai and were once again given wine. Local villagers, reportedly influenced by the conscripts, assaulted a group of three policemen, almost killing one of them.[16]

Both incidents involved peasant conscripts' belief that they had the right to free alcohol. The riots were overtly driven by their desire to get drunk during male bonding rituals on the eve of an uncertain future at the front. While singling out a Tatar store, conscripts revealed ethnic tensions and their particular suspicions of Tatars. Their willingness to flout the law, destroy state property, and violently disobey the authorities points to animosity towards local authorities and officers of the tsarist order.

In fact, secret military correspondence revealed popular disquiet towards the war. The newly-formed war censor reported on 7 December 1914 that less than two per cent of perused correspondence from local soldiers expressed patriotic enthusiasm. Seventy per cent of correspondents felt a need to fulfil their duty, but dissatisfaction with their material situation, such as inadequate state provisions for their families, and complaints about their officers, prevented them from being 'happy and patriotic'.[17] The gendarmerie also arrested several peasant conscripts for refusing to serve and insulting the Tsar.[18]

Peasant apprehension of the war must be put into the larger context of peasant–state relations in late-Imperial Russia. Local and provincial officials, sensitive to violations in established rituals of the peasant–state discursive relationship even during peacetime, were more wary of perceived threats of disorder, rebellion, and resistance during wartime. At a time when the existence of the state itself was under threat, state officials expected peasants to support the regime and its policies publicly.[19] The war's opening revealed the hegemonic process quite clearly. Cultural and political elites redefined peasant action as patriotic, supporting the

---

[16] GAKO, f. 714, op. 1, d. 1493, ll. 27–8ob.

[17] GAKO, f. 714, op. 1, d. 1453, ll. 282, 340; Iu. P. Khranilov, 'Chto im delo do chuzhikh pisem, kogda briukho syto': voennaia tsenzura Viatskoi gubernii v bor'be za pobedu nad germantsami', *Voenno-istoricheskii zhurnal* 2 (1997): 22–9.

[18] GAKO, f. 714, op. 1, d. 1497. For cases in 1916, see d. 1679 and 1696.

[19] James C. Scott, *Domination and the Arts of Resistance: Hidden Transcripts* (New Haven, 1990), ch. 1; Ranajit Guha, *Elementary Aspects of Peasant Insurgency in Colonial India* (Delhi, 1983).

establishment. At the same time, the state read deeper meanings into even verbal asides at the beginning of war and inserted its own fears of popular upheaval into peasant statements of discontent. For their part, peasants' conflicted feelings towards government mobilization efforts foreshadowed their turn away from the tsarist war campaign and its mobilization programmes.

Some intellectuals, military officials, and historians have put forward the idea that the peasants' failure to identify themselves with the Russian nation was one of the main causes of Russia's defeat in the war. After the war, General Iurii Danilov famously described Russia's fatal predicament that peasants identified themselves with their region, 'as a Viatskii, Tul'skii, or Permskii', rather than with the nation, as a Russian. They did not see the national fight against Germans as their own.[20] Villagers, in this view, after a burst of enthusiasm, felt no obligation to sustain a prolonged sacrifice of goods and men. Peasant apprehension about the war and the government certainly manifested itself early in the military campaign. However, rather than the peasants' parochialism destroying the national military campaign, the wartime environment created ideal conditions for peasants to go beyond their regional affiliations and develop and express nationalist identities, including dreams of full political participation in the creation of the Russian nation. Total mobilization pushed Russian peasants to think of themselves as integral parts of the wartime effort. State and zemstvo officials' views of the peasantry as a malleable resource still foreshadowed future conflicts over the place of peasants in the Russian nation.

The art of mobilization

Total mobilization in Viatka for the First World War was part of the nexus of long-term, pan-European developments expanding the boundaries of governmentality. State and military practices during the war extended the government domain into the home and even the soul. Wartime conditions created the atmosphere for state and military officials, social scientists, and social activists to implement far-reaching

[20] Iu. N. Danilov attributed the absence of popular nationalism to Russia's multi-national population, vast space, and inadequate communications. These conditions caused the people to act in an infantile manner and so they could not be steadfast against the German threat. *Rossiia v mirovoi voine, 1914–1915 gg.* (Berlin, 1924), 111–12; N. N. Golovine refuted Danilov's dismissal of popular patriotism, but shared the sentiment of Viatka's state officials and journalistic editors that Russians felt a primitive, primordial patriotism. *The Russian Army in the World War* (New Haven, 1931). Richard Pipes has repeated Danilov's findings in, *The Russian Revolution* (New York, 1990), 203.

programmes upon the population that they had conceived in the decades preceding the war. These programmes transcended nineteenth-century military activities and attempted to exploit the full amount of the country's resources by mobilizing its people (both in being and in labour), livestock, economy, and inventory to a degree not seen before.[21] Officials' ideas about the cultural level and political reliability of the country's population moulded wartime mobilization. State-sponsored programmes in the Viatka countryside reveal a close connection between positive, 'low conscription' programmes that attempted to shape and incorporate populations and negative, suspicion-based programmes that sought to control and possibly exclude populations.[22]

Despite the public exclamations of popular monarchism, in internal conversations state officials expressed fear of the effects of mobilization and braced themselves for popular resistance to war.[23] On 14 July, on the eve of the call-up of reserves, St Petersburg ordered Viatka's governor to maintain order at all costs while securing militarily strategic positions and implementing measures to counter espionage and flight. Russian district police suspected both a group of Udmurts 'not speaking Russian' in conversations among themselves, and Chinese merchants doing business in the province, of being spies.[24] Local officials were equally concerned with preventing another 1905 Revolution in the countryside, when the power vacuum left by mobilization of military personnel and the Russo-Japanese war's hardships allowed massive and violent popular protest against the tsarist order. They increased police presence throughout the province and closed liquor stores ahead of schedule in areas that rose up in the previous war.[25] Fuelled by the growing polarization between the autocracy and educated society before 1914, high officials also initially feared that zemstvo workers and educated society would not support a tsarist regime whose politics they vocally opposed.

Extinguishing these fears, rural-educated society eagerly organized and worked diligently to advance Russia's cause. Accenting the recent convergence of the social sciences and the modern state, specialists such as ethnographers and statisticians offered their expertise to help categorize and study the population's efficacy as a state resource. Although contemporaries believed professionals skirted military conscription,

[21] Geyer, 'The Militarization of Europe'; Holquist, *Making War*.
[22] On the politics of low conscription, see Sanborn, *Drafting the Russian Nation*, ch. 1.
[23] See Scott, *Domination and the Arts of Resistance* on public and hidden transcripts in the hegemonic process.
[24] GAKO, f. 582, op. 154, d. 55, ll. 98, 101.
[25] GAKO, f. 582, op. 154, d. 55, ll. 1–1ob, 157, 162–5; d. 122, l. 2.

several teachers, doctors, and paramedics (*fel'dshers*) answered the army's call to colours.[26] By the end of the war, mobilization of the male rural intelligentsia caused severe shortages of male teachers and medical personnel in the countryside.

The zemstvo played a central role in the war effort in the countryside. In the pre-war era, its activists had created a solid link between villagers and non-peasant society and its policies became foundations on which to mobilize village resources. As part of the wave of patriotism at the outbreak of war, zemstvo leaders agreed to form an All-Russian Union of Zemstvos, building upon existing public organizations and using their technical expertise to mobilize the nation's home front.[27] On top of its extensive existent duties, the zemstvo eventually ran the food campaign, organized hospitals, helped care for refugees, established public aid foundations to collect monetary donations and make clothing, and gathered data on the population and economy.[28] Clearly those elements of society that felt the autocracy unduly limited their right to full participation in state governance jumped at the opportunity of mass public mobilization.

It helped that zemstvo activists' aims at the beginning of the war in part paralleled those of the tsarist state. Both groups shared the immediate aim of Russian victory in the war and both believed institutional popular mobilization of resources was the key to that goal. Despite initial disagreements between zemstvo technocrat activists, who wanted to use their aid in the war to push the tsarist government towards greater social

---

[26] The famous ethnographers D. K. Zelenin and N. N. Blinov were active members of the Viatka Province Statistical Committee and oversaw the collection of data on population fluctuations and harvest sizes. GAKO, f. 574, op. 2, d. 984, ll. 13–14ob. On ethnographers and social scientists in the service of the modern state, see James C. Scott, *Seeing Like the State: How Certain Schemes to Improve the Human Condition Have Failed* (New Haven, 1998). For Russia, see Robert Geraci, *Window on the East*; Francine Hirsch, *Empire of Nations: Ethnographic Knowledge and the Making of the Soviet Union* (Ithaca, 2005).

[27] Gosudarstvennyi Arkhiv Rossiiskoi Federatsii (hereafter GA RF), f. 102, op. 1915, d. 167, ll. 3–3ob; Rossiiskii Gosudarstvennyi Istoricheskii Arkhiv (hereafter RGIA), f. 1284, op. 194, d. 13, ll. 1–2ob. The Minister of Internal Affairs even reported that while the eager zemstvo agents brought technical expertise to the war effort, local city administrators were neither talented nor energetic. On zemstvo and agricultural specialists' attempts to break down the insularity of the village, see Kotsonis, *Making Peasants Backward*.

[28] William Gleason, 'The All-Russian Union of Zemstvos and World War I', in Emmons and Vucinich, eds, *The Zemstvo in Russia*, 365–82; Tikhon J. Polner, *Russian Local Government During the War and the Union of Zemstvos* (New Haven, 1930), 52–88; Kimitaka Matsuzato, 'The Role of Zemstva in the Creation and Collapse of Tsarism's War Efforts During World War One', *Jarbücher für Geschichte Osteuropas* 46 (1998): 322; S. A. Kukoviakin, *Zemskaia meditsina Viatskoi i drugikh severnykh gubernii evropeiskoi Rossii* (Kirov, 1998), 157–91.

and political reforms, and the more conservative zemstvo leadership who favoured unity with the state, zemstvo war management policies appeared to the peasants to be unified.[29]

Zemstvo activists militarized existent peasant-oriented programmes by tailoring and extending them to help in the war effort. They put their faith in state power (*gosudarstvennost'*) to achieve their aims of economic and social modernization and the war provided them the opportunity to integrate themselves into state programmes.[30] But zemstvo activists had their own view of the war and mobilization that diverged from official politics. Alongside mobilization for war they also hoped to foster their own conceptions of the nation and civic identity among the peasantry, as well as cultivate a rational, modernist culture in the village.[31] Because zemstvo activists saw themselves as part of a national war effort, they consciously drew the peasantry into their vision of the nation. Peasants as a whole welcomed the programmes that benefited the village economy, just as they had before the war, but did not share educated society's dream of the peasants' subordinate role in the nation. An examination of some of the most telling and often overlooked programmes reveals the close, multi-layered connections between peasants and cultural and political elites during the war.[32]

The guarantee of the future supply of foodstuffs for the army, discussed in greater detail below, was as important a task as the conscription of men and livestock. Zemstvo and state officials' plans to increase the food supply through improvement and modernization of peasant agriculture had great urgency during the war. Military mobilization took many of the young peasants who were more apt to heed experts' lessons than older, more traditional peasants. Zemstvo officials honed their pre-war focus on 'disseminating agricultural knowledge among the adult population' and stepped up efforts to support use of fertilizer, new agricultural tools, and preventative measures against common village catastrophes.[33] For

---

[29] On the divisions within the zemstvo during the war, see Alessandro Stanziani, 'The First World War and the Disintegration of Economic Spaces in Russia', in Judith Pallot, ed., *Transforming Peasants: Society, State and the Peasantry, 1861–1920* (Houndmills, 1998), 174–81.

[30] Alessandro Stanziani, 'Spécialistes, Bureucrates et Paysans les Approvisionnements Agricoles Pendant la Première Guerre Mondiale 1914–1917', *Cahiers du Monde Russe* XXXVI (January–June 1995): 71–94, Holquist, *Making War*, 12–46.

[31] Seregny, 'Zemstvos, Peasants, and Citizenship', 292–3. My argument diverges with Matsuzato and Stanziani who see zemstvo activists acting as a barrier between the peasantry and the national. I see the opposite – that zemstvo activists built discursive arenas for discussions and contrasting ideas of the nation.

[32] Polner provides a comprehensive description of zemstvo policies during the First World War, *Russian Local Government*.

[33] *Obzor Viatskoi gubernii za 1915 god* (Viatka, 1916), 6.

example, zemstvo officials published booklets explaining to peasants the dangers of anthrax, a bacterium that killed hundreds of heads of livestock each year. Zemstvo and state officials also implemented land improvement projects in 1915, such as draining swamps and improving meadows. When the state funded the land projects, many peasant communities embraced the improvements because they increased the quantity and quality of land without threatening their sustenance.[34]

If the war created the ideal conditions for zemstvo activist and specialists' drive to build a cultured, rational, modern state, the exigencies of war limited zemstvo dreams. Zemstvo fire prevention policies notably illuminate the problems of material shortages. Viatka's villages suffered from some of the worst rates of fire in all of European Russia, enduring over four thousand incidents of fire per year since the 1870s. Fire could quickly engulf a whole village, so the zemstvo implemented fire insurance, village planning, and volunteer firefighter brigades, supported with peasant finances. Viatka's zemstvo, though, was unique in its level of sponsorship of fire-resistant structures.[35] In 1916, personnel from the zemstvo and land settlement commission tried to build on ambitious plans to fund the construction of fire-resistant roofs and buildings throughout the province. Unfortunately, the war took much of the technical personnel and materials that the plan demanded. Officials in the governor's office fought the zemstvo's bid to devote scarce resources to a seemingly superfluous project, revealing a re-emerging chasm between zemstvo and state goals. Although the initial programme called for 260,000 bricks, the local brick factory could only produce less than half that amount. By November 1917, only twelve of the planned buildings were complete.[36]

Suspect ethnicity in the village

A discussion on ethnicity and the tenuous place of non-Russians in the mass participatory nation lay beneath zemstvo and state programmes. Ethnicity most acutely shaped state mobilization and local wartime

---

[34] RGIA, f. 426, op. 3, d. 824, ll. 1, 14, 24. On communes' acceptance of agricultural improvement, see Esther Kingston-Mann et al. eds, 'Peasant Communes and Economic Innovation: A Preliminary Inquiry', in *Peasant Economy, Culture, and Politics of European Russia*, 23–51.

[35] Cathy A. Frierson, *All Russia is Burning! A Cultural History of Fire and Arson in Late Imperial Russia* (Seattle, 2002), 74, 93–4, 225.

[36] RGIA, f. 397, op. 1, d. 291, ll. 2ob, 44–6. *Pravila obiazatel'nogo vzaimnogo zemskogo strakhovaniia ot ognia stroenii v Viatskoi gubernii* (Viatka, 1915).

experience for rural dwellers in Russia's peripheries. On the western borderland Jews suffered from state deportation and popular violence; in Central Asia, Kazakhs fought the state's 1916 reversal of their exemption from military conscription.[37] Ethnicity's effect on mobilization in the rest of Russia's villages, including Viatka's, was more subtle but equally important for shaping popular wartime experience and future membership in the Russian nation. State and zemstvo administers' views of non-Russian ethnic groups shaped everyday wartime policies, and, in turn, non-Russians' place in the wartime effort. They saw the region's linguistically Finno-Ugric Udmurts and Maris as economically and culturally immature, and tried to lift them while mobilizing their resources. Udmurt and Mari national backwardness channelled officials' fears that the people's shortfalls would threaten the war effort. Zemstvo and state officials also fretted over the political loyalty of local Tatars. Wartime politics reinforced the fact that the political and cultural elites defined Udmurts, Maris, and Tatars as marginal groups occupying a liminal space both within the national struggle and outside the nation, and made them feel tied to their distinct national identities just as they were becoming part of Russia.[38]

Viatka's zemstvo activists paid special attention to the beekeeping industry to maintain sweeteners and wax for popular, military, and church consumption. They encouraged disabled soldiers to learn beekeeping as a way to continue to be productive and benefit their country. The state placed such significance on beekeeping during the war that it allocated scarce wood, metal, and labour to the construction of a building for *kustar'* manufacturing of beehives in Malmyzh and stationed an apiarist there to instruct on the courses.[39] The zemstvo's wartime beekeeping policy extended a pre-war plan to train Udmurts and Maris in beekeeping, an occupation historically associated in Viatka with its Finno-Ugric peoples. At the turn of the century, zemstvo programmes headed by A. P. Batuev and I. E. Shavrov, the latter known as 'the apostle of rational beekeeping', began to transform traditional non-Russian beekeeping into a more 'rational' production.[40] The zemstvo established courses and training programmes in beekeeping and called for peasants throughout southern Viatka to switch from keeping

---

[37] Peter Gatrell, *Russia's First World War: A Social and Economic History* (London, 2005), 176–83.
[38] S. A. Smith argues a related point that the war exposed 'the incapacity of the rossiiskii state to serve as a framework for articulating multinational aspirations', 'Citizenship and the Russian Nation', 322.
[39] RGIA, f. 395, op. 2, d. 3406, ll. 10–10ob, 26–31.
[40] *Viatskoe pchelovodstvo*, January 1914, 1–2.

beehives in customized tree stumps, to storing them in miniature, orderly houses storing frame beehives.[41]

Zemstvo officials thought that construction of beehives was the easiest of the *kustar'* industries and established short courses on beekeeping to increase production and as an instrument to teach the principles of cooperation. The zemstvo attempted to push peasants engaged in *kustar'* into artel cooperatives, arguing that an artel could combine resources in order to buy enough materials and instruments to serve up to ten thousand beehives a year and also mechanize the preparation of honey. The zemstvo saw artels as the way to collectivize and modernize beekeeping while instilling cooperative ideals among the Udmurt and Mari peasants.[42] Peasants eagerly enrolled in beekeeping courses and followed instructions on switching methods of housing bees.

State officials also tried to mobilize Udmurt and Mari national agents for the war effort, beginning a relationship between cultural elites and the state that would grow after the Bolsheviks took power.[43] Before the war, the Russian state pursued the small group of Udmurt and Mari nationalists, shutting down fledgling publications and nationalist meetings. Once the war began, the Russian censors did an about-face and allowed national cultural elites (such as teachers and priests) to publish newspapers in their own language. In 1915, for example, the first Udmurt and Mari language newspapers, *Voinays ivor* and *Voina uver* (War News), began circulation. They published news from the front as well as advice on agriculture and hygiene, paralleling zemstvo activist and educated society's aims of raising peasant, especially non-Russian, culture while mobilizing them for Russia's war aims.[44] The war thereby provided the environment for national cultural projects to blossom after the February Revolution in 1917.

---

[41] *Krest'ianskaia sel'sko-khoziaistvenno-tekhnicheskaia gazeta*, 12 July 1914, 5–6; 10 January 1915, 12–13; N. A. Badov, *Sostoianie pchelovodstva v Viatskoi gubernii (po dannym ankety 1910 goda)* (Viatka, 1912), 76–8.

[42] RGIA, f. 395, op. 2, d. 3406, ll. 5, 8. In *Making Peasants Backward*, Kotsonis reaches similar conclusions with the pre-war cooperative movement.

[43] I define national agents as urban and rural teachers, clergymen, zemstvo agents, and other members of educated society who championed their ethnic or national identity. On the tsarist state's turn from oppression to mobilization of ethnicity, see Mark von Hagen, 'The Great War and the Mobilization of Ethnicity in the Russian Empire', in Barnett R. Rubin and Jack Snyder, eds, *Post-Soviet Political Order: Conflict and State Building* (New York, 1998), 34–57; Sanborn, *Drafting the Russian Nation*, 75.

[44] L. S. Khristoliubova, 'Prosvetitel'naia i etnokonsolidiruiushchaia rol' pervykh udmurtskikh gazet i kul'turno-prosvetitel'nykh obshchestv v pervoi chetverti XX v', in S. Lallukka and T. Molotovaia, eds, *Etnicheskaia mobilizatsiia vo vnutrennei periferii: Volgo-Kamskii region nachala XX v* (Izhevsk, 2000), 44; Seppo Lallukka, *From Fugitive Peasants to Diaspora: The Eastern Mari in Tsarist and Federal Russia* (Helsinki, 2003), 158.

Through the official promotion of rational beehives and national language literature the state gently differentiated the rural population by ethnicity. The Tsar's prohibition of the sale of most alcohol during the initial mobilization brought to the fore elite suspicion of non-Russians and heightened ethnic conflict. Peasants quickly responded to the prohibition of alcohol by developing stills and an imaginative array of home brews – beer, wines, and especially distilled spirits like *samogon* (moonshine).[45] For public officials and commentators in Russia's provinces, the persistence of the 'green serpent' manifested other culturally constructed ills of peasant culture, such as sloth-like laziness and drunkenness that potentially endangered the country's victory in the war and peasants' cultural advancement. In Viatka, the official and public struggle against alcohol displayed significant ethnic dimensions as well, since public officials, educated society, and the popular media equated *samogon* with *kumyshka*, a prohibited fermented alcoholic ritual drink most often associated with Udmurts and Maris.

In the late-Imperial era, state and church officials saw *kumyshka* as a sign of Udmurts' persistent paganism, cultural and economic insularity, and unhealthy lifestyle, while Udmurts defended *kumyshka* as an aspect of their cultural heritage. These tensions of empire show the non-Russians' straining to maintain a coherent system of spiritual and cultural beliefs in a homogenizing system, pushing a uniform nationality. The prohibition of alcohol, combined with larger economic, social, and political pressures, transformed *kumyshka* into a larger discussion of the place of Udmurts in the Russian nation and the state of peasant culture as a whole.

Kumyshka took hold of the popular imagination as Russians feared contamination of its detrimental effects on all society during the war. Official discourse on *kumyshka* portrayed it as an ethnic weakness that threatened Russia's war effort. Reporting to the capital on the situation in Viatka during the first month of the war, the Governor's office devoted half its account to the problem of containing *kumyshka*. The report touched on several central cultural constructions of Udmurts as both romantic primitives and backward peoples. Regional ethnographers in the late-nineteenth century had characterized Udmurts as meek, unenlightened pagans who lagged behind other local nationalities in culture, physical stamina, and sense of hygiene. The Governor's office account drew upon these depictions of Udmurts, calling them 'very

---

[45] David Christian, 'Prohibition in Russia, 1914–1925', *Australian Slavonic and East European Studies* 9 (1995): 89–118; Patricia Herlihy, *Alcoholic Empire: Vodka and Politics in Late Imperial Russia* (New York, 2002).

timid and sober'. Drinking *kumyshka*, however, destroyed their calm, childlike nature and reverted them to a violent, untamed people. 'Upon imbibing in *kumyshka*', the Governor's office wrote, Udmurts 'turned into wild people' (*obrashchaiutsia v dikikh liudei*) and 'savages'.[46] The government therefore sponsored pamphlets in Udmurt that confronted drunkenness and *kumyshka* in particular.[47]

Zemstvo newspapers during the war also underlined the pernicious affect of *kumyshka*, although they emphasized the harmful qualities of alcohol, rather than national character. Zemstvo writers used the temperance movement's motifs shunning alcohol for hampering productivity, health, and spirituality.[48] A typical article stated that Udmurts 'were unable to give up' the drink, wasting 'grain, wood, and time' and leading to 'many drunken arguments and fights'.[49] The Finno-Ugric peoples' supposedly benighted condition threatened Russia's wartime success and engendered more invasive policies.

However much officials fretted over the political and economic unreliability and cultural backwardness of Russian, Udmurt, and Mari peasants, they were most concerned with the possible contamination and political leanings of Tatars. The Imperial state had built a strong relationship with Muslims of the empire by promoting confessional tolerance and forging alliances with Muslim religious elites.[50] Official fear and suspicion of Islam's potential religious and political threat to the Russian empire persisted, though, especially in the Volga–Kama region. Around the turn of the century, state officials became obsessed that a pan-Islamic alliance existed among all Muslim populations of the world.[51] During the Russo-Japanese war, Russia's government worried about the loyalty of its 'Asian' peoples.[52] Scholars identified the Volga–Kama region as the centre of pan-Islamic and pan-Turkic movements in Russia and recommended that the government concentrate its efforts there on stopping the spread of these movements. The

[46] RGIA, f. 1284, op. 194, d. 13.
[47] *O p'ianstve* (Viatka, 1915); *Kumyshkaez an no iue, en no pos'te* (Viatka, 1916).
[48] Herlihy, *Alcoholic Empire*, ch. 6–8.
[49] *Krest'ianskaia sel'sko-khoziaistvennaia gazeta*, 20 September 1914, 10–11.
[50] Robert D. Crews, *For Prophet and Tsar: Islam and Empire in Russia and Central Asia* (Cambridge, MA, 2006). Not all Tatars were Muslim, and not all Muslims in the region were Tatars, but state officials homogenized the diverse group in its correspondence.
[51] Wayne Dowler, *Classroom and Empire: The Politics of Schooling Russia's Eastern Nationalities, 1860–1917* (Montreal, 2001), 216; Abeed Khalid, *The Politics of Muslim Cultural Reform: Jadidism in Central Asia* (Berkeley, 1998), 194.
[52] Robert Geraci, 'Russian Orientalism at an Impasse: Tsarist Education Policy and the 1910 Conference on Islam', in Daniel R. Brower and Edward J. Lazzerini, eds., *Russia's Orient: Imperial Borderlands and Peoples, 1700–1917*, (Bloomington, 1997), 141.

Viatka police focussed on Elabuga, Glazov, and Malmyzh districts, where most of the province's Tatars lived. Police followed Muslim political activists and attempted to quash pan-Islamic groups.[53] Influenced by the conflict in the Balkans, the police in 1913 believed that Muslim Tatars would unite with other countries with large Muslim populations, especially Turkey and China. As one police officer noted, Muslims 'do not hide their sympathy with the Chinese', and in the event of war with China, they would side with the enemy.[54] An agent of the secret police recorded a Malmyzh bourgeois Tatar stating to many Tatar peasants in Kokshinskaia *volost*, Malmyzh district,

Thank God that Turks again have gathered strength and were victorious over Slavs. All Muslims of course need to unite and help Turkey. No one should be afraid of the Russian tsar, since if we will support Turkey and unite with her, as well as with Afghan and Chinese Muslims, then we will be more than enough to win our freedom and regain the past khanate.[55]

This same fear that pan-Islamic Tatars and mullahs would convert unconscious Tatar Muslim peasants to anti-Russian movements was transferred to the First World War as Russia fought Turkey to the southeast.[56] Total warfare affecting all aspects of society and total mobilization of the population meant that state, educated elite, and military concerns regarding population groups' political allegiance became more important than they had in previous conflicts. Viatka police supposed that Tatars' natural sympathy was with Turkey and fellow Muslims. As Adeeb Khalid has shown for Central Asia, a small but influential group of urban cultural elites participated in the pan-Islamic and Jadidist phenomena at this time.[57] Although these movements existed in Viatka's countryside with the support of some mullahs, mosques, and educators, the state's fear of popular pan-Islamic and pan-Turkic movements was greatly exaggerated.[58] Speakers and teachers exposed Tatar Muslim peasants to these ideas, but there is no evidence that many of them accepted these elites' notions of Islam's role in a modernizing world. As Robert Geraci has argued, Russia's concern with a Tatar Muslim international conspiracy reflects a revised orientalist

---

[53] GAKO, f. 714, op. 1, d. 1364, ll. 24, 26–26ob, 28.
[54] GAKO, f. 714, op. 1, d. 1364, ll. 7–7ob; f. 582, op. 154, d. 122, l. 9.
[55] GAKO, f. 714, op. 1, d. 1364, ll. 36, 41.
[56] Tsentral'nyi Gosudarstvennyi Arkhiv Udmurtskoi Respubliki (hereafter TsGA UR), f. 96, op. 1, d. 195, l. 102.
[57] Khalid, *The Politics of Muslim Cultural Reform*, 216–44.
[58] A. A. Mashkovtsev, 'Viatskie musul'mane i gosudarstvo v ikh vzaimootnosheniiakh v 90-e gg. XIX v.-1917 g.', in V. I. Bakulin, ed., *Iz istorii Viatskogo kraia kontsa XIX-pervoi poloviny XX veka: Sbornik nauchnykh statei* (Kirov, 1998), 12–13.

stereotype.[59] Such images of Tatars as savage and conspiratorial transferred to state politics during the war. Russian police 'knew' that there
was an anti-Russian, pan-Turkic conspiracy in Viatka's southern cities
and villages and spent enormous resources trying to confirm their
beliefs. Police surveillance even expanded to non-religious Tatars.
An officer reported in 1915 that in Sarapul district, Zaliamotdin Fakh-
rutdinov had pro-Turkish propaganda in his fruit store, displaying
women laying a wreath on the head of a Turkish officer. In fact, the
'propaganda' was an advertisement from Kazan for a fruit company in
Krasnovodsk.[60]

Police records documented a significant Tatar Muslim political network preaching anti-tsarist rhetoric in the region, but it had little effect
on Tatar peasants' sense of belonging to the war effort.[61] For example,
in November 1915 the police arrested the Novyi Smail village mullah in
Sardykbazhskaia *volost*, Malmyzh district, for uttering that we 'need to
be happy about the German victories because all law and order will
collapse and we will choose a king from among ourselves'. Land captain
reports still systematically refuted upper-level state suspicions of Tatar
Muslims, stating that local Tatars felt no special political sympathy with
Turkey, even though Tatars and Turks shared the same religion. They
concluded that Tatars did not feel animosity towards Russia.[62] Tatar
peasants, and Muslims in general, in the region joined the army, sacrificed grain and livestock, and expressed patriotic sentiment at the same
level as their rural Russian counterparts.[63]

Official suspicion of certain non-Russian populations in Viatka
reflected Russia's long-term move to a modern nationalizing state, using
surveillance and scientific analysis to study and categorize its national
populations into reliable and unreliable parts.[64] As with the army's
isolating policies towards Jewish minorities living in the frontline zones,
the government fixated on Tatar Muslims as inherently dangerous. The

---

[59] Geraci, in Brower, 'Russian Orientalism', 152.
[60] GAKO, f. 582, op. 190, d. 6, ll. 511, 513–20. The Imperial government expressed
similar fears of Jewish treason during the war.
[61] GAKO, f. 714, op. 1, d. 1552, l. 1.   [62] TsGA UR, f. 96, op. 1, d. 195, ll. 103–8.
[63] Crews, *For Prophet and Tsar*, 360–2.
[64] Peter Holquist, 'To Count, to Extract, and to Exterminate: Population Statistics and
Population Politics in Late Imperial and Soviet Russia', in Ronald Grigor Suny and
Terry Martin, eds., *A State of Nations: Empire and Nation-Making in the Age of Lenin and
Stalin* (Oxford, 2001), 115–23. I take the term 'nationalizing state' from Eric Lohr and
Rogers Brubaker. Like Brubaker, I understand the nationalizing state as the project of
building a nation–state in which the state constructs what defines a national minority.
Rogers Brubaker, *Nationalism Reframed: Nationhood and the National Question in the
New Europe* (Cambridge, 1996), 55–69. Eric Lohr, *Nationalizing the Russian Empire:
The Campaign Against Enemy Aliens During World War I* (Cambridge, MA, 2003), 8.

Russian secret police worried about possible espionage and treason and continued its surveillance of religious Muslim leaders from the pre-war era.

State fear of Tatar nationalism and pan-Islam was a discussion about empire – how a state that defined itself through its Russian ethnicity and Orthodox Christian religion could rule over, and sometimes with, those of competing religions and national projects. It thereby highlights official insecurity about the place of non-Orthodox Christians in a modernizing nation. While the war necessitated mobilizing the population and making state subjects into citizens, the police and military resisted full inclusion of Tatars into the Russian nation and its war effort.

Official suspicion of the political reliability of Tatar Muslims did not lead to exclusion from Russia's national war effort. Tatars occupied a liminal space between the military's attempts during the war to incorporate more ethnicities into conscription policies and its exclusion of some population groups as inherently unacceptable people (such as Jews, Germans, and Austrians). Distance from the front, history of an alliance between Muslims and the state, and the absence of viable evidence of treason, allowed Viatka's Tatar population not to be subject to official ostracism.

Educated society, through the zemstvo, engaged in a process of self-mobilization to extract and control the nation's resources. They helped to mobilize villagers while imposing their ethnic stereotypes, social dreams, and political fears upon the population. The village, then, became a site of social intercourse and mass mobilization. Educated society and the state were not alone in promoting mobilization. Villagers, in part inspired by national sentiment, mobilized autonomously to help win the war. In this way, the war simultaneously introduced modern statist intervention and mass participation to the countryside.

The war comes home

Newspaper articles, mobilization of family members, and officials urging peasants to sell grain made villagers aware of a demanding but distant war. This feeling could last only a short time, as the far-off war quickly arrived in the village. Prisoners of war, deported suspect peoples, and refugees from the Russian empire brought the war to the village. An examination and comparison of how these populations changed the village economy and how peasants interacted differently with the three populations reveals how the war began to reshape peasants' relationship with the outside world.

Within the first month of combat, Viatka's larger villages began to receive their first German and Austro-Hungarian prisoners of war.[65] Through the course of the war, Russia would process a little over two million prisoners of war. Russia struggled to find adequate housing for such an unexpectedly large number of prisoners and shipped them to hastily constructed camps, vacant buildings, and private quarters in Viatka and several other provinces. The state also farmed out many prisoners to communities and individuals who policed them and, after autumn 1915, used their labour.[66] The Viatka government put most of its 8,000 prisoners of war to work in Viatka, Kotel'nich, Orlov, and Glazov districts – helping in the Viatka railway station, building the Viatka–Slobodskoi railroad line, repairing country roads, cleaning the streets, and working the land. Fourteen hundred prisoners of war worked for individual enterprises.[67] Although the state sent the vast majority of prisoners to work the land of the Black Earth region's large estates, they also worked for peasant farms.[68]

For peasants, most of whom had never seen a foreigner and had heard about the dastardly deeds of their wartime enemies, the sight of poorly clad soldiers speaking foreign languages was a shock. Peasants saw the prisoners of war as carriers of filth and the cause of remarkable inflation.[69] As a newspaper account from a village in Viatka district recounted, after a party of around sixty German prisoners was settled in the village, they quickly ate all the food causing the price of flour to rise. The Germans also filled available rooms, driving up rent for permanent inhabitants from two rubles to twenty rubles a month. The prisoners' poor health and diseases also strained medical resources.[70]

Living conditions for rank-and-file prisoners of war were terrible. Detainees were put under guard and forbidden to gather in groups, write

---

[65] *Viatskaia rech'*, 23 August 1914, 4.

[66] Alon Rachamimov, *POWs and the Great War: Captivity on the Eastern Front* (Oxford, 2002), 38, 87–97.

[67] *Pamiatnaia knizhka Viatskoi gubernii i kalendar' na 1915 g.* (Viatka, 1915), 109–11.

[68] A. M. Anfimov, *Rossiiskaia derevnia v gody pervoi mirovoi voiny (1914–fevral' 1917 g.)* (Moscow, 1962), 103–04. Rachamimov, *POWs and the Great War*, 107–15. Russia was not alone in forcing POWs and enemy aliens to labour in the fields. Great Britain also made up for their labour shortage in the countryside by using prisoners of war as substitute workers. By November 1918, Great Britain employed over 30,000 POWs in agriculture. The British government also tried to use enemy aliens in agriculture, but suffered logistical problems, feared espionage, and could not get enemy aliens to volunteer: P. E. Dewey, *British Agriculture in the First World War* (New York, 1989), 120–7, 136–8.

[69] Eric Lohr notes similar popular images of deported enemy aliens, 'Enemy Alien Politics Within the Russian Empire During World War I', (PhD diss., Harvard University, 1999), 78.

[70] *Viatskaia rech'*, 3 September 1914, 3.

letters in German, engage in recreational activities, or leave the village.[71] Most detainees had no winter clothing and little food and money. The Hague Convention allowed Russia to use rank-and-file POW labour with minimal wages, and the state-paid prisoners' wages were often three to four times less than local workers.[72] Prisoners appealed for donations to the American embassy in Petrograd, and to charity groups, but with little success.[73]

Shortly after the outbreak of war, the Russian army also began to systematically deport German and Austrian enemy aliens living in Russia to the provinces, as politically and ethnically suspect elements.[74] The government often lumped enemy aliens together with prisoners of war, sending them both to ill-equipped rural 'concentration camps' and villages. In November 1914, Belokholunitskii *zavod* already housed 458 detainees: 327 men, 70 women, and 61 children. Detainees' pathetic living conditions even brought international condemnation.[75] The local government put enemy aliens to work repairing roads, loading river cargo, and making army boots in factories and transferred them where it needed labourers. If the prisoner committed an infraction of the rules, the government shipped him to a remote village.[76] The tsarist administration had a legacy of calling on its provincial population to watch a limited number of enemies of the state in internal exile, but the state had banished almost all its convicts to urban areas. During the war, the administration relied on the peasants and district police to a much larger degree than ever before to keep guard and watch the thousands of deportees. Peasants' daily interaction with these foreigners showed them that they were part of a national war.

---

[71] *Pamiatnaia knizhka Viatskoi gubernii i kalendar' na 1915 g.* (Viatka, 1915), 109–11.

[72] Rachamimov, *POWs and the Great War*, 72–4; Anfimov, *Rossiiskaia derevnia*, 103–4.

[73] GAKO, f. 582, op. 154, d. 115a, ll. 476–476ob. This account seems typical. Rachamimov describes the prevalence of theft and poor living conditions for POWs throughout Russia. *POWs and the Great War*, 44–60, 87–125. Military officers as a rule enjoyed more favourable living conditions as POWs, including not being shipped to the villages.

[74] Lohr, *Nationalizing the Russian Empire*, esp. ch. 5; Lohr transfers the term 'enemy alien' from the British usage. Interestingly, the government did not send Turkish citizens or prisoners of war to Viatka, presumably out of continued fear that Tatars and Turks would feel a natural alliance. GAKO, f. R-876, op. 1, d. 9, ll. 334–5.

[75] GAKO, f. 582, op. 154, d. 115a, l. 777; d. 122, l. 10. The United States' secretary to the ambassador of Russia used the term concentration camp (camp de concentration) in correspondence with the vice-governor of Viatka and requested that the Russians treat the prisoners better and allow the American embassy to provide assistance. GAKO, f. 582, op. 154, d. 115a, ll. 571–2.

[76] *Reports of Delegates of the Embassy of the United States of America in St Petersburg on the Situation of the German Prisoners of War and Civil Persons in Russia* (Zurich, 1917), 57–61.

Peasants saw German and Austrian detainees as physical incarnations of the enemy. While there were instances of warm, personal emotions towards the detainees (including a handful of marriages between peasants and prisoners), most often peasants' personal contact with the prisoners was filled with strife.[77] In December 1914, a German enemy alien detained in Kumenskaia *volost*, Viatka district, renting a place from a local peasant woman, wrote in a letter that he had to do everything himself, including make his own bed, fetch hot water, and prepare kerosene and the samovar. When he stepped out, his landlady and her daughter 'cleaned out his apartment and took the samovar'.[78]

Peasants also violently attacked the detainees. In April 1915, two German prisoners of war were strolling the streets of Belokholunitskii *zavod*, when they met up with four local peasants. The peasants beat the Germans with a rope.[79] In Iaransk an Austrian soldier was 'grossly mistreated' and an officer passing by 'was most rudely insulted and smacked in the face'.[80] Peasant attacks on foreign prisoners were common, especially in Belokholunitskii *zavod* and the village of Sinegor'e, where there was a concentration of prisoners. According to a report of an American investigator, there were twenty attacks in one month in Sinegor'e, including a peasant who kicked a female prisoner in the stomach.[81] In Spasopreobrazhenskaia *volost*, Kotel'nich district, peasants violently beat three prisoners of war. When the police began an investigation, six local peasants attacked and beat the policeman, yelling we 'must beat up the policeman because he defends prisoners of war'.[82] Against this backdrop, a general fear spread among prisoners across the province in 1915 of an outbreak of wholesale violence against them.[83]

Such attacks went beyond traditional peasant suspicion of outsiders. The extent and voracity of peasant violence against these state-defined foreign enemies shows peasant understanding that they were part of the nation's war. Popular violence against perceived foreign enemies surfaced in all countries of combat during the Great War. Peasants

---

[77] Rachamimov, *POWs and the Great War*, 109–10. *Viatskaia rech'* reported that peasants in the village of Kozantsevo, Pilinskaia *volost*, Urzhum district, met 320 Austrian POWs with bread and warm clothes, but the prisoners 'distrustfully' refused the bread: 6 February 1915, 3.
[78] GAKO, f. 714, op. 1, d. 1588, ll. 24–24ob.
[79] GAKO, 1276, op. 1, d. 8, ll. 44–44ob; f. 714, op. 1, d. 1569a, ll. 82bob, 83. One of the German victims, George Karolov Riprikh, fell into depression, complaining that it was better to end his life, and killed himself.
[80] United States National Archives, State Department Records, 763.2114/1913.
[81] *Reports of Delegates*, 57.
[82] GAKO, f. 582, op. 190, d. 6, ll. 332, 334.   [83] *Reports of Delegates*, 57–8.

understood the state's categorization of prisoners of war and enemy aliens as representatives of the nation's opponents and identified themselves in opposition to them.

When the war turned for the worse and the Russian army began its protracted retreat, refugees from the war zones began to flood the country's interior, swelling to at least 3.3 million refugees by the end of 1915 and over 6 million by 1917.[84] In Viatka, the provincial zemstvo organized the effort to transport and house the refugees. Beginning in the summer of 1915, those fleeing the front arrived en masse in the province. Because Viatka was a central railroad juncture, many refugees simply passed through en route to their final stop in Siberia. Viatka still received up to 100,000 of the first million refugees from the north-west front. The zemstvo put some refugees to work in factories and the Viatka railroad station alongside prisoners of war.[85] The zemstvo distributed the bulk of the newcomers to villages throughout the province. Each district received ten thousand refugees.[86] In Nolinsk district, the government divided the initial wave of refugees, dispatching three refugees for every ten homes.[87] The government provided initial clothing and food and donated twenty-five kopeks per day to every refugee (fifteen kopeks for youths), but asked its peasantry to care for this massive influx of (largely) women and children who had to flee their homes with little property and sustenance.[88] Many peasant communities welcomed refugees into their village, supplemented state aid with grain, flour, and money, gave them free housing, and some peasants even gave up their homes in order not to divide refugee families.

Peasants' aid does not mean that they welcomed refugees without reservation. Peasants contributed to the degree that it would not overly inconvenience them. For example, peasants of Filippovskaia *volost* provided shelter but refused to give clothes and provisions. In Vozhgal'skaia *volost*, peasants sheltered 250 refugees, but declined any more because they did not have enough room in their huts.[89] Refugees lived in the villages as guests and outsiders. Communes did not include them as equal members of the village and the state prohibited their legal

[84] Peter Gatrell, *A Whole Empire Walking: Refugees in Russia During World War I* (Bloomington, 1999), 3.
[85] *Viatskoe gubernskoe zemskoe sobranie 56-i chrezvychainoi sessii, 15 sentiabria 1915 g.* (Viatka, 1915), 128; *Krest'ianskaia sel'sko-khoziaistvenno-tekhnicheskaia gazeta,* 31 October 1915, 14.
[86] *Viatskoe gubernskoe zemskoe sobranie,* 96–134.
[87] *Krest'ianskaia sel'sko-khoziaistvenno-tekhnicheskaia gazeta,* 31 October 1915, 14.
[88] *Krest'ianskaia sel'sko-khoziaistvenno-tekhnicheskaia gazeta,* 12 September 1915, 5; 30 September 1915, 16–17.
[89] *Krest'ianskaia sel'sko-khoziaistvenno-tekhnicheskaia gazeta,* 12 September 1915, 5.

inclusion in local society.[90] Refugees were not even reported as local inhabitants in the 1916–17 census. Nevertheless, peasants made a clear distinction among the new denizens, between enemy foreign prisoners and national refugees. Peasants accepted refugees because they understood the inherent link between different social groups within an imagined community. The connection was not always positive. If prisoners of war and enemy aliens represented the filth of the country's adversaries, refugees were a daily reminder that Russia was losing the war. Whereas prisoners of war signified Russia's initial victories over their enemies, evacuees and refugees signalled that the tide of the war had turned. Peasants saw the refugees' poverty and read stories of their despair in the media.[91]

The war initiated massive population movements that would last through 1922. Prisoners of war, exiles, refugees, mobilized and demobilized soldiers, and families trying to find a better life in the east created a new population group of people wandering for years in the desert of war and revolution. These migratory people put further strains on the rural economy, brought outside political ideas to the village, and created greater geographic diversity and social cleavages among the peasant populations. Paradoxically, the war's traumatic effects on the village quickly transformed peasant conceptions of their role in the war and the Russian nation. By helping displaced people, policing detained enemies, and living with material shortages and popular conscription, peasants, at least while they felt able, accepted the consequence of war as their own burden. The tsar faded into the background as peasants replaced him with the Russian nation as the reason to continue their efforts on the home front.

Feminization of the wartime village

State policies during the war dramatically affected more concrete aspects of peasant society as well. As young peasant men left the village, women began to play a larger role in public life. They became a significant part of the labour force and, as they began to assume the role of head of the household, women participated in village and *volost* meetings with more frequency, as well as fighting for their rights to property inheritance and state aid as family members of soldiers. The war therefore rapidly destabilized traditional generational and gender dynamics, already unsettled before the war by the outflow of young males and females for

---

[90] Gatrell, *A Whole Empire Walking*, 66.   [91] Gatrell, *A Whole Empire Walking*, 73–83.

seasonal urban labour and the inflow of urban ideals and consumer culture.[92]

The war began a decade-long negative demographic shift in Viatka. Between 1913 and 1915 alone births fell 9%, deaths increased 19%, and marriages dropped 34%.[93] Mass mobilization robbed the Viatka countryside of adult males. Between 1914 and 1918, 24% of all males and 49% of able-bodied working-age men went into the army, creating a massive shortage of workers.[94] By summer 1917, over 40% of peasant households in Viatka were without a male worker. The Viatka countryside was one of the hardest hit of all European Russia, with only Moscow and Kaluga provinces enduring a greater percentage of households left without a male worker.[95] The rate of local demographic decline appears to have been based on proximity to transportation. For example, Liumskaia and Elovskaia *volosts*, Glazov district, suffered large population declines and were both situated on the Cheptsa River, and, most importantly, on the railroad. They were also relatively near the city of Glazov, which housed factories producing war supplies. State labour conscription or higher wages may have moved peasants from these areas and into the factories. While the decline in the male population varied among *volosts*, it hit Russian and non-Russian peasants equally.

Women with a family member in the army had to assume roles in the peasant economy normally left for males. Women were forced to work in occupations traditionally reserved for men, such as ploughing and mowing with a scythe.[96] The depletion of the rural workforce drove up wages for male workers so most peasant communes were unable to supplement their depleted workforce with labourers.[97] Since most of Viatka did not suffer from surplus labour (unlike the overpopulated Black Earth region), there was an acute labour shortage during the war. Prisoners of war and refugees sometimes took agricultural work, but more often it was left to women. Women had to shoulder a wartime double burden of their traditional roles of overseeing household chores

---

[92] Barbara Alpern Engel, *Between the Fields and City*; Jeffrey Burds, *Peasant Dreams and Market Politics*.

[93] *Obzor Viatskoi gubernii za 1913 god* (Viatka, 1914), 42; *Obzor Viatskoi gubernii za 1915* (Viatka, 1914), 61.

[94] *Rossiia v mirovoi voine. 1914–1918 goda (v tsifrakh)* (Moscow, 1924), 21.

[95] Anfimov, *Rossiiskaia derevnia*, 189. Viatka's losses stood above the national average of 22.6% of all males and 47.4% of able-bodied male workers. Moscow province stood at 44% and Kaluga 44.9% of peasant households without a male worker.

[96] Rose L. Glickman, 'Peasant Women and their Work', in Beatrice Farnsworth and Lynne Viola, eds, *Russian Peasant Women*, (New York, 1992), 56.

[97] GAKO, f. 574, op. 2, d. 978, l. 45.

Plate 5. Milling rye in Viatka district during the war. Courtesy
GASPI KO

such as clothing the family, cooking, cleaning, fetching water, mowing
grass, turning hay, and seeing to livestock, and their new responsibilities
in the field and public life.[98]

The departure of males also brought women into a more visible
position in village politics. Traditionally, peasant women played a minor
role in official village institutions such as the *skhod* and public service. In
the late-nineteenth and early-twentieth centuries, outside factors had
begun to break down these restrictions. Growing male labour migration
to cities meant that some women took the place of their husbands in
the assembly in their absence.[99] A rise in educational opportunities and
literacy for women also made them more valuable to the community.
Some communities had also allowed widows to become the head of

---

[98] Peasant women already carried a tremendous responsibility for domestic and
agricultural chores before the war. *Krest'ianskaia sel'sko-khoziaistvenno-tekhnicheskaia
gazeta*, 21 June 1914, 7–8.
[99] Glickman, in Farnsworth and Viola, 'Peasant Women and their Work,' 56–8.

a household and participate fully in the communal assemblies.[100] Nevertheless, only a small minority of peasant women in Viatka participated fully in the pre-war assemblies.

Communal and *volost* resolutions (*prigovory*) highlight the significant shift in women's public participation. As male heads of households went into the armed forces, women gradually assumed their husbands' or fathers' roles and participated in public forums. A sample of resolutions reveals that in the spring of 1914 women comprised only 2% of signatories. This number increased only slightly after the first mobilization, to 2.5%. The number of female signatories steadily rose, in 1915, to 8.7%, and by 1916–17 to around 13% of total signatures.[101] However, women's participation varied among regions and even villages. In places where women had little or no history of voting in public life, such as Arkhangel'skaia *volost*, Nolinsk district, their role changed little. In areas where women had a tradition of participation in public forums, their role greatly increased during the war. The rise in women's participation is most clearly seen in resolutions of elections of peasants to public service in three communes of Bogorodskaia *volost*, also in Nolinsk district, where in the autumn of 1915, women constituted 3.6% of participants and a year later reached 21.8%.[102]

While the war gave some peasant women the opportunity to participate in public, it was rarely on an equal level with men. Moreover, women overall did not appear to aspire to social or political equality or even to encroach permanently on traditionally held male spaces. Individual women did not usually go against social norms to fight for public representation of their households. If a village allowed a woman to participate actively in the communal gatherings, then others would join her. A woman's name would often be repeated on resolutions, showing that she was a frequent participant at the meetings. Women also on occasion signed their name with the addendum 'wife of', as the conditional replacement of the more usual head of the household at the gathering. The war, then, accelerated the movement of women into male agricultural labour roles and the traditionally patriarchal public sphere of village politics.

---

[100] Moon, *The Russian Peasantry*, 235.
[101] These figures come from a random sample of fifty-three resolutions on a variety of topics throughout Viatka province. GAKO, f. 976, op. 4, d. 206, d. 209; f. 589, op. 1, d. 319, 324, 400, 401; f. 940, op. 1, d. 679, 693, 694, 709; f. 927, op. 1, d. 22, 31; f. 593, op. 1, d. 190, op. 2, d. 2; f. 941, op. 1, d. 207; TsGA UR, f. 96, op. 1, d. 2159.
[102] GAKO, f. R-1620, op. 2, d. 3, ll. 2–3ob, 8–11; f. 927, op. 1, d. 22, ll. 21, 22, 28–30. In one commune, women went from 0 to 12.3% of the total; in the second, they went from 8.67 to 11.2%; and in the third commune they jumped from 2.2 to 42% of the total participants.

Participants of village political gatherings changed during the war, but the composition of its leadership did not. Village and *volost* officials (such as the *starosta*, *starshina*, and scribe) traditionally ruled over social and political life as the official link between state and village and held significant power over the distribution of communal responsibilities and enforcement of the law. Village elites and male elders, especially from wealthier peasant families, continued to control these positions.[103] In Kliuchevskaia *volost*, Glazov district, peasant officials in 1916 remained prosperous, middle-age, male peasants. They all enjoyed large households and most owned more than one horse and a large amount of livestock; the average age of the officials was 53 years. In mixed Russian and Udmurt villages, power was based on gender, age, and prestige over ethnicity. In Kypkinsk commune, the village policeman and tax collector were both Udmurt and in Syginsk village, Syginsk commune, the village elder and the head of the *volost* court were Russians and the policeman Udmurt.[104] These power dynamics persisted throughout the war and revolution, even as revolutionary politics favoured young, poor, and non-Russian peasants more than in the tsarist era.

Soldiers' family members, and wives (*soldatki*) in particular, personified the war's effects in the village and, as such, became political objects as well as radicalized actors. *Soldatki* traditionally lived on the margins of village society and often at the mercy of their families and the charity begrudgingly provided by the commune. Villagers had labelled *soldatki* as pitiful victims, economic leaches, and women of low sexual morals.[105] In June 1912, the Duma transformed the position of *soldatki* by expressing the nation's obligation to support those who fulfil their duty and sacrifice for the nation by promising soldiers' wives and families a food stipend while their man was in the military or disabled while on duty. State officials acknowledged the reciprocal relationship between soldiers serving the nation and state duty to care for their families. As Emily Pyle notes, 'by September 1915, the government had spent almost a half billion rubles on support of soldiers' families', and 'a seventh of the entire government budget'.[106] The *soldatka* moved to the

---

[103] Moon, *The Russian Peasantry*; Steven L. Hoch, *Serfdom and Social Control in Russia: Petrovskoe, a Village in Tambov* (Chicago, 1986), 128–36.

[104] Compiled from a comparison of a list of officials in 1916 and the 1917 census. TsGA UR, f. 94, op. 1, d. 214, ll. 9–11; GAKO, f. 574, op. 4, d. 1674, 1691.

[105] Beatrice Farnsworth, 'The Soldatka: Folklore and Court Record', *Slavic Review* 49 (1990): 58; Barbara Alpern Engel, *Women in Russia, 1700–2000* (Cambridge, 2004), 61–2.

[106] Pyle, 'Village Social Relations', 159–60; Melissa Stockdale, 'United in Gratitude: Honoring Soldiers and Defining the Nation in Russia's Great War', *Kritika* 7 (2006): 461–5.

centre of village life as members of educated society and government joined together in forming societies for the aid of soldiers' families.[107] The societies' overwhelming list of responsibilities included helping to distribute monetary stipends, aiding orphans, organizing day nurseries, establishing a home for disabled veterans, providing clothes, books, and hot breakfasts to students, and raising money through charity concerts and galas.[108] The public joined the state to implement the nation's duty to support soldiers' families. As the report from the Slobodskoi Society for Aid to Families of Soldiers that began this chapter shows, public charity towards soldiers' families became a central expression of patriotism and support of the war effort.

Soldiers' families received monetary and food stipends from village and state, but aid societies' central aim was to make up for lost field labour, especially during the sowing and harvesting periods.[109] State aid to soldiers' families was therefore in practice much more than traditional charity or fulfilment of a state duty by caring for citizens who sacrificed for their country. The state saw the peasant household as an economic unit and used the promise of assistance to maintain agricultural production levels in order to sustain the economy and military, reinforcing the militarization of zemstvo programmes. To achieve this goal, committees and agronomists joined together to maximize modern, technocratic knowledge. At least in the province's southern grain belt, agronomists for the first year of the war distributed modern agricultural equipment to soldiers' families. In Urzhum they provided soldiers' families with threshing machines and a clover huller; in Malmyzh, families were to receive 500 quality ploughs from the Votkinsk factory.[110] Soldiers' wives supported such efforts. A consortium of 250 *soldatki* petitioned the Sarapul zemstvo, stating that they would manage all fieldwork if the zemstvo supplied them with ploughs.[111] To distribute aid most effectively, district committees in 1915 delegated the district agronomist and statistician to design a questionnaire to families receiving aid, asking such questions as what was the family's economic status,

---

[107] On the prominent role of *soldatki* in village economic life during the war, see Barbara Alpern Engel, 'Not by Bread Alone: Subsistence Riots in Russia during World War I', *Journal of Modern History* 69 (1997): 708; Mark Baker, 'Rampaging Soldatki, Cowering Police, Bazaar Riots and Moral Economy: The Social Impact of the Great War in Kharkiv Province', *Canadian–American Slavic Studies* 35 (2001): 137–55.

[108] *Otchet o deiatel'nosti*, 3.

[109] *Otchet o deiatel'nosti*, 12.

[110] GAKO, f. 1254, op. 2, d. 1537, ll. 21–2ob, 24–5, 30. The zemstvo introduced clover in Viatka for hay, soil rehabilitation, and pollen for bees only in the 1870s, but peasants quickly took to it. Zemstvo agronomists continued to promote it throughout the war.

[111] *Krest'ianskaia sel'sko-khoziaistvenno-tekhnicheskaia gazeta*, 31 December 1915, 17.

if the household received income from non-agricultural work, how much land the family tended, and the amount of livestock the family owned. After distributing 14,000 questionnaires, the Slobodskoi district committee calculated that families needed to hire 15,000 rubles worth of labourers; a sum well beyond its means.[112]

Since the scarcity of labour made private hiring of working hands too costly and inefficient, the state as early as spring 1915 decided to foist prisoner of war labourers into homes in Sarapul district as a form of assistance to soldiers' families. Soldiers' families billeted the prisoners during spring sowing and became, in essence, their Russian guards. Most families did not want them in their homes, both out of fear and the reasoning that the cost of feeding them outweighed any gratis labour. The Sarapul district government reported that despite peasant complaints, if the state was going to provide aid in labour to families of soldiers, then 'the use of POW labour would be inescapable'. The main problem, according to the government, was not peasant resistance to the plan, but the lack of agricultural equipment. The report suggested an alternative that presaged Soviet state agricultural initiatives – travelling POW brigades with ten ploughs and four seed drills that moved throughout the *volosts* during the sowing season.[113]

Once again debate over ethnicity and confession also guided the state's administration of aid. In the autumn of 1914, provincial military officials argued about whether to support Udmurt and Mari wives who had not been married in an Orthodox Church and therefore were living an 'illegitimate life', and Muslims who had more than one wife. The official response was mixed. The Religious Affairs Department of the Interior Section argued that since the 1912 law only supported Orthodox Christians, Old Believers, and sectarians, the state had no obligation to dispense aid to those married under non-Christian customs. However, provincial government agencies found no obstacles to dispensing aid to Muslim families.[114] Despite the original spirit of the law, state officials gave non-Christian women state support.

---

[112] GAKO, f. 1254, op. 2, d. 1537, ll. 8–9, 12–13, 62–9. The Glazov district committee distributed a similar questionnaire.

[113] GAKO, f. 1254, op. 2, d. 1537, ll. 78–78ob.

[114] RGIA, f. 1292, op. 7, d. 262, ll. 1–3, 5–6, 11–12, 15, 22, 26, 31, 33, 36. The matter was never settled. Other provinces in which non-Christians lived were just as confused as Viatka about aid to non-Christian families. The governments of Samara, Orenburg, Astrakhan, and Perm wrote to the military asking about money for Muslim families. The religious affairs letter should be seen as part of a long-term debate about the nature of Udmurt and Mari religious convictions. The Church categorized these non-Russians as Orthodox, pagan, holding a 'dual-belief' (*dvoeverie*), and those who had backslided to paganism or Islam (*musul'manstvo*). For more on the complexity of the

If the Duma marked off a significant, yet insufficient, amount for assistance to soldiers' families, the public, and especially peasants, tried to make up for the shortfall in donations. Most peasant donations at the beginning of the war went to support soldiers' families. The Ministry of Internal Affairs even noted that local Red Cross organizations and societies distributing aid to soldiers' families 'functioned solely on peasant donations'. While urban merchants contributed little to Viatka's local aid organizations, peasants sacrificed over double the amount of money requested by aid foundations in the first months of the war. Fellow villagers gave their labour to help gather the harvest of 1914 to households affected by conscription. Communes also issued resolutions pledging to help soldiers' families in all aspects of their fieldwork.[115]

Soldiers' families were far from simply helpless objects of political dreams; they fought for state and communal assistance and played a significant role within village political life. *Soldatki* in particular sent waves of petitions to all levels of government, seeking assistance, complaining of unfulfilled promises of support, and inadequate levels of compensation. Soldiers' wives led the fight for subsistence that they saw as rightly theirs as part of a state-created social group. The struggle for state and communal aid was a family affair as children, husbands, and parents also wrote numerous letters and petitions to all levels of government to win relief. Petitions usually emphasized the family's hopeless economic destitution in light of the loss of labour and their need for state charity.[116] All peasants, and especially women, commonly used self-subalternizing language in written petitions to get what they wanted. The individual and mass demonstrations of the soldiers' wives show that they saw assistance as their right, owed to them by the state and nation. Soldiers on the front also came to their wives' aid, writing requests to their *volost starshina* and offering advice on strategy to their spouses. In December 1914, in an intercepted letter, a reserve in Iaroslavl counselled his wife to 'demand a subsidy from the *volost* administration and if you do not receive it, write me and we will carry out measures'. He echoed a belief that would grow over the next two years, that the administration was corrupt and filled with the nation's enemies: 'The authorities who distribute the allowances are thieves and line their

---

term *dvoeverie*, see Eve Levin, '*Dvoeverie* and Popular Religion', in Stephen K. Batalden, ed., *Seeking God: The Recovering of Religious Identity in Orthodox Russia, Ukraine and Georgia* (DeKalb, 1993), 31–52.

[115] *Krest'ianskaia sel'sko-khoziaistvenno-tekhnicheskaia gazeta*, 29 August 1914, 3–4; 16 February 1915; RGIA, f. 1284, op. 194, d. 13, l. 3.

[116] Emily E. Pyle, 'Peasant Strategies for Obtaining State Aid: A Study of Petitions during World War I', *Russian History/Histoire Russe* 24 (1997): 41–64.

pockets. The Germans push the bureaucrats into the fire. In my opinion, all the authorities are Germans.'[117]

The generosity of communal aid to *soldatki* varied by region. *Soldatki*, especially in regions with a high level of male migrant labour, 'were less likely to receive free communal assistance than *soldatki* in predominantly agricultural regions'.[118] In villages with a history of migratory labour, peasants believed that workers' wives were well off from their spouses' extra wages. Not all *soldatki* suffered in desperate economic straits; many became the head of their household and managed the fieldwork and household economy with success. Less fortunate soldiers' wives had to move into their in-laws' or other family members' homes, fight for a relatively meagre state subsistence, and work their household's land with a reduced labour supply.

Strife filled these adapted households. Soldiers' wives who moved into their in-laws' home had to adjust to the new power relationship. As daughters-in-law, women were in an ambiguous relationship, below the head of the household, his wife, and her husband's siblings. The relationships could turn violent. In Slobodskoi district, the head of a household (*khoziain*) murdered his daughter-in-law, a *soldatka*. He had refused to help her work her fields while her husband was at war. Although she still managed to work her household's land, the *khoziain* still demanded money from her, which she refused. Upon returning home one day, they fought and he killed her.[119] Tension could also boil over when the husband died. Several *volost* and regional court cases involved inheritance disputes. As heads of households and future inheritors perished in the war, their relatives scrambled to claim their property. In Toropovskaia *volost*, Kotel'nich district, Pelagiia Osipova and her son moved in with her in-laws when her husband went to the front. When he died, Osipova moved to her brother's home but left her son. However, she insisted on inheriting her deceased husband's movable and immovable property, including his arable land and home. The *volost* and regional courts upheld her claim.[120]

If women coped with the war's effects by assuming male roles in the family and turning to village and outside institutions for support, they also took matters into their own hands by leaving their village. Women who had worked in the city often migrated permanently to an urban area. Women raised in a nearby village returned to their families. While overall migration beyond the province dropped significantly during the

---

[117] GAKO, f. 714, op. 1, d. 1453, ll. 340–340ob.
[118] Pyle, 'Village Social Relations', 183.   [119] GAKO, f. 582, op. 194, d. 6, ll. 1–1ob.
[120] GAKO, f. 584, op. 54, d. 275, unlisted. See also, d. 288, 290.

first years of the war, from 17,817 in 1913, to 6,079 in 1915, peasants still attempted to escape their village.[121] Soldiers' families took advantage of migratory networks and government policies that eased travel for soldiers' families to resettle in Siberia and the Far East. For example, in June 1916, Fekla Timshina, a *soldatka* of Shoran village, Urzhum district, petitioned the government for free rail passage for her and her infant son to join her father-in-law in the Amur. In accordance with the 1912 assistance legislation for soldiers' families, and after a review of her desperate economic situation, the government granted her request. Likewise, the *soldatka* N. I. Shiriaeva successfully petitioned for free rail passage to Krasnoiarsk for her family.[122]

War reshaped the social composition of the village and made women central actors in the militarized village. Newspapers described, with only slight exaggeration, villages comprised of only women and the elderly. Females composed the majority of the village population and expanded the boundaries of gendered activities, but did not overturn the patriarchal village structure. Instead they worked within it, or used the current wartime policies to leave or better their lot. *Soldatki* and their families became objects of communal and state charity, and patriotic rallying points to remind citizens of war's harmful effects and the need to sacrifice. Peasant women became modern political actors during the war by demanding entitlements that they felt the state owed them as relatives of soldiers. Women were also integral to the success of the mobilization effort and provided labour in the fields and farms and oversight of detainees and refugees.

The village at war

It is easy to understand why peasants tired of a war that many entered with conflicting feelings. Wartime drained the village of its most basic items. Conscription and the astounding number of casualties stole one and, often, multiple male members from households, disrupting peasant traditions and the family cycle; the opportunity of extra-village paid labour virtually vanished; manufactured goods as well as prime necessities disappeared. The conscription of horses and cows began a decline in working livestock, making ploughing and carting difficult. Factories converted to weapons production and the state funnelled metal and steel to the army. If a farm implement broke it was nearly impossible to repair or replace.

---

[121] *Obzor Viatskoi gubernii za 1915 g.*, 61–2.
[122] RGIA, f. 391, op. 6, d. 391, ll. 5–6ob; d. 710, ll. 1–6. The rest of the *delo* contains peasant petitions for the right for passage to Siberia and the Far East.

Peasant communities transformed traditions and customs and integrated outside aid to stabilize their economy and maintain their households. The commune, under attack by governmental reform, continued to impose social control. In July 1915, Gachinsk commune in Kotel'nich district petitioned to evict Egor Sechiukhin to Siberia as a serial thief and pernicious member of the community, as a way to protect village property. In December 1916, Pechmashsk commune in Iaransk district evicted 54-year-old Grigorii Sofronov for stealing his neighbour's pig and sheep from a nearby village.[123] The commune simultaneously reasserted itself by extending welfare programmes. Villagers had to provide for the scores of new orphans in the village, defined by Russia's peasants as the loss of one parent. Most often, the household provided for the orphaned child after dividing up the father's property. When the household could not provide for the orphan, the commune placed the child in trust with other relatives and sold the house and other possessions to help defray the costs of feeding another mouth.[124] The zemstvo, Ministry of Agriculture, and charitable organizations ostensibly provided support for orphan relief programmes, but the peasant communes actually carried out the aid.[125] Peasant households also mitigated the war's deteriorative effects on the household economy by broadening the tradition of adoption. In order to sustain a household, a typical peasant inheritance strategy was to adopt a current or future son-in-law. The new son would then have the right to inherit the household's land and property but he would be obliged to provide and care for his new family.[126] Although approximately twenty per cent of households before the war did not have an heir, the decimation of the male peasant population from the war forced many more peasant families to consider adoption.[127] Peasants extended traditions to save their household by adopting nephews and peasants from other nearby villages as well.[128]

War threatened the integrity of the village but the virtual end of the Stolypin agrarian reforms also stabilized the commune. By the outbreak of war, 50,254 peasants in Viatka had submitted requests to the state to

---

[123] GAKO, f. 584, op. 54, d. 105, 106.
[124] GAKO, f. 584, op. 54, d. 107, 108, 109, 110, 155; f. 941, op. 1, d. 223–42 involve village communities throughout the province selling orphans' property and putting them in trust with relatives.
[125] Polner, *Russian Local Government*, 141–5.
[126] Worobec, *Peasant Russia*, 57–62; Rodney Bohac, 'Peasant Inheritance Strategies in Russia', *Journal of Interdisciplinary History* 26 (1985): 26, 36–9.
[127] Worobec, *Peasant Russia*, 57. GAKO, f. 976, op. 4, d. 231, ll. 4–8ob, 17–18, 20; f. 927, op. 1, d. 26, ll. 3–3ob.
[128] GAKO, f. 927, op. 1, d. 37, ll. 4–4ob, 7; d. 26, ll. 3–3ob.

leave the commune.[129] The number of applications declined with the loss of the able-bodied men who sought to establish their own farm. Between September 1914 and May 1915, 1,106 peasants applied to establish individual farms, but from 1915 through to January 1917, only 663 more applications were submitted. Similarly, between 1906 and 1915, 23,526 peasants established individual farms, but from 1915 until 1917, they only established an additional 707 farms.[130] The trend was reflected in Bobinskaia *volost*, Viatka district, where, between June 1910 (when the reforms came into full effect) and May 1914, 187 households submitted applications to establish private farmsteads, and from May 1914 to 1917 no more applications were submitted and the land captain and *volost skhod* even rejected one of the previous applications brought before it.[131]

The initial destabilizing effect of the Stolypin Reforms on the village economy and community ran counter to the state's goal of full mobilization of resources. State funds to encourage private farms dried up and the land settlement commission changed its focus to maximizing crop yield and increasing land put under the plough. It promoted land improvement and internal colonization in the sparsely populated northern districts of Orlov and Slobodskoi.[132]

Growing peasant resistance to separators and individual farmers during the war also helped persuade the Ministry of Agriculture in February 1916 to suspend the reform movement and limit land organization to cases in process. Communes and separators clashed over resources. In Bel'skaia *volost*, Glazov district, villagers of Goglevskaia harboured hostility about the amount of land that a recent separator consolidated and attempted to force him back into the commune by felling his trees and refusing to provide him with winter rye seed to sow. The separator turned to the land captain for help; he went from door to door to convince the villagers to help the separator, but most of the villagers categorically refused.[133] Peasants' explicit insubordination to

---

[129] S. M. Dubrovskii, *Stolypinskaia zemel'naia reforma: Iz istorii sel'skogo khoziaistva i krest'ianstva Rossii v nachale XX veka* (Moscow, 1963), 579.

[130] Dubrovskii, *Stolypinskaia zemel'naia reforma*, 576–9.

[131] GAKO, f. 589, op. 1, d. 347, ll. 2–5; d. 394, ll. 4–5, 7–9.

[132] GAKO, f. 1254, op. 2, d. 1522; f. 1254, op. 2, d. 2156, ll. 47ob–48; Judith Pallot, *Land Reform in Russia 1906–1917: Peasant Responses to Stolypin's Project of Rural Transformation* (Oxford, 1999), 8, n. 14.

[133] GAKO, f. 582, op. 190, d. 6, ll. 21–2. In 1915, in Malmyzh district, peasants also seized the land for an entrance road to a separator's farmstead. A. M. Anfimov, ed., *Krest'ianskoe dvizhenie v Rossii v gody pervoi mirovoi voiny iiul' 1914 g.–fevral' 1917 g.: Sbornik dokumentov* (Moscow, 1965), 488. See also GAKO, f. 714, op. 1, d. 1543, ll. 49–50b for a case in Sarapul district in which peasants felled trees owned by a separator.

a governmental power shows many peasants' continued vehemence against separators from the commune. Peasant–separator conflicts over land boundaries and access to resources were endemic since the implementation of the reforms seven years earlier, but the war exacerbated tensions between the two parties.[134] Some peasants in communes felt that separators, most of whom had larger families than the norm, were not as badly hurt by male conscription into the army as they had been. Added strain on grain and livestock made peasants even more guarded about disputed arable land, meadows, and forests. Moreover, separators did not have assured support from local government officials. As seen in the above example, the land captain tried to help the separator, but could not, and did not attempt to force the commune to acquiesce to the separator. The state attempted to extract the maximum resources out of the population, and this meant that separator interest was often sacrificed to the national good.

Psychological and material constraints on the peasant economy and modern mass mobilization converged and escalated tensions between peasants and the tsarist government, and peasants wearied of the tsarist order.[135] Total war necessitated that the military conscript and control the food supply and have the ability to exploit peasants' labour and money as needed. The peasants acquiesced to a limit of a moral economic relationship with the state.

Peasant–state relations revolved around peasants supplying grain and livestock to the army and urban areas. The government joined forces with the zemstvo and allowed it to coordinate local purchase of grain.[136] In the first months of the war peasants sold and donated their grain and livestock to the war effort. In Viatka, the government established

---

[134] For pre-war commune–separator conflict in Viatka, see RGIA, f. 1291, op. 121, d. 63, ll. 40, 54, 78.

[135] Scholars debate whether the war helped or hurt the peasant economy. Soviet scholars argued that state mobilization of young men and requisitioning of livestock and grain caused the rural economy to deteriorate and increased the gap between rich and poor peasants. Other scholars have argued that peasants profited from the war since they had surplus labour and livestock and the loss of livestock actually helped the rural economy because peasants had to sacrifice too much grain to feed their animals. Alexis N. Antsiferov, Alexander O. Bilimovich et al., *Russian Agriculture during the War* (New York, 1968), 116–41.

[136] Peter Fraunholtz, 'State Intervention and Local Control in Russia, 1917–1921: Grain Procurement Politics in Penza Province', (PhD diss., Boston College, 1998), 44–9. As Fraunholtz points out, the relationship between state and zemstvo and centre and local was filled with tension and disrupted the efficacy of food supply programmes. K. I. Zaitsev, N. V. Dolinsky, and S. S. Demosthenov, *Food Supply in Russia During the World War* (New Haven, 1930); N. D. Kondrat'ev, *Rynok khlebov i ego regulirovanie vo vremia voiny i revoliutsii* (Moscow, 1991).

points in larger villages for peasants to bring their grain for sale. In Vodozerskaia *volost*, Iaransk district, in 1915, the state offered from eighty-five kopeks to one ruble per pud of oats and an additional five kopeks per pud for every verst peasants had to travel to deliver the food in a timely manner.[137] Many villages agreed to the price and sold thousands of puds of oats from their storage. Some villages even sold or donated nearly all their stored oats. Newspapers ran stories of villages conducting mass collections and donating hundreds of puds of grain, flour, flax, linen, potatoes, cabbage, carrots, beets, and other goods for the war effort.[138]

Food supply policies did not work and, as the war dragged on, they became increasingly convoluted. The military took most available goods, leaving little left over for the market. Prices of grain, kerosene, salt, tobacco, soap, matches, sugar, and other basic necessities skyrocketed. By the end of 1914, the price of rye increased by forty per cent in Sarapul district; between 1914 and 1917, sugar prices multiplied twenty-seven times.[139] This inflation, along with the absence of goods to purchase and the prohibition of alcohol may have helped the village economy in the short-term by leaving it awash in money. But the shortages of primary goods by 1915 created the first of a recurring 'scissors' crisis, in which grain prices decline in relation to escalating prices on manufactured goods, and so peasants did not have a concrete reason to sell their grain. The zemstvo and state did not offer prices either to match speculator and open market prices on grain and primary goods, or even inflationary pressures. At the beginning of the 1916 grain campaign, zemstvo officials in Nolinsk offered only one ruble, seven kopeks for the highest quality rye.[140] Yet peasants in the province calculated that it cost two rubles and twelve kopeks just to produce a pud of grain. Much of Viatka also suffered from poor weather that threatened the harvest, suggesting that even the above calculation was an under-estimation.[141]

Instead of giving the state their grain, Udmurt peasants distilled it into *kumyshka* to sell on the black market. In 1913, the Viatka Finance Ministry reported only nineteen cases of the sale of *kumyshka*. In 1914, that number escalated to 184 and in 1915 it reached 638 cases.[142] Certainly, peddling in *kumyshka* was more profitable than selling grain at

---

[137] GAKO, f. 976, op. 4, d. 206, l. 76.
[138] See, for example, *Viatskaia rech'*, 1 January 1915, 4.
[139] Sadakov, 'Udmurtiia v gody pervoi mirovoi imperialisticheskoi voiny', 56.
[140] GAKO, f. 940, op. 1, d. 706, l. 40.
[141] GAKO, f. 593, op. 1, d. 190, l. 46; Lars Lih, *Bread and Authority in Russia, 1914–1921* (Berkeley, 1990), 27.
[142] GAKO, f. R-876, op. 2, d. 78, ll. 44–5.

fixed prices, especially with the growing disparity between prices of agricultural and manufactured goods. In February 1917, the newspaper *Kama* reported that for a pud of flour that Udmurts could sell to the state for two rubles, they could make fifteen bottles of *kumyshka* that sold for three rubles each. After labour and materials, producers made thirty-nine rubles profit.[143]

Udmurts overtly protested against state attempts to close down their production. In January 1915, policemen arrived in the Udmurt village of Kyrlud, Poninskaia *volost*, Glazov district, to search for *kumyshka* paraphernalia. Their search of huts and storehouses turned up nothing, but a group of approximately seventy Udmurts armed with sticks met them on the street and surrounded the commander and an officer. Someone from a nearby hut shot and wounded the officer, and another peasant struck the village policeman in the head with a shaft. The police fired randomly and fled the village. District police later returned and confiscated the suspected material without incident and brought twelve peasants before a military court who, according to reports, continued to express bitterness towards police for conducting the searches. The court sentenced eleven of the peasants to terms ranging from fifteen years of hard labour to two months in prison.[144] These trials happened simultaneous to the popular press admonishing Udmurts for selling *kumyshka* rather than sacrificing grain to the military. These articles became a way to reproach peasants for not sacrificing enough grain, while displacing criticism on to a marginal group.

Although peasants sold their grain and dipped into their stock in the first year of the war, in 1916, the food crisis, continued uncertainty about their future, and the government's new compulsory requisitioning policy made many peasants balk at sacrificing more grain. Viatka, like the rest of Russia, began a levy system in which the central government determined the amount of grain that a province needed to deliver and the provincial and local governments allocated levies to each *volost*. In December 1916, the land captain, *volost* elder and scribe, and ten guards came to Aleksandrovskii village, Smetaninskaia *volost*, Iaransk district, to requisition oats. The villagers refused to deliver the oats, arguing that they had to supply their livestock and horses, so they did not have any surplus to give. The land captain tried to force his way into household grain storehouses (*ambars*). In the three households the land captain entered, he only found elderly women who claimed not to know where the keys to the storehouses were located. The villagers then openly resisted the land captain, who had to retreat for lack of forces. The Viatka governor later

---

[143] *Kama*, 15 February 1917, 4.   [144] *Viatskaia rech'*, 25 November 1915, 3.

ordered an armed detachment to the village.[145] The villagers defended their resistance in a petition later that month. They argued that they were willing to supply oats for the army and 'respond to the needs of the fatherland' (*otkliknut'sia k nuzhdam otechestva*), but they were living in a perilous state. The government would only pay one ruble, fifty kopeks per pud of oats, while they could get two rubles, thirty kopeks at the bazaar.[146] Even in the last months of the tsarist regime, peasants acknowledged their duty to the nation and their willingness to come to its aid. But the state's seemingly incompetent grain policy, which paid uncompetitive prices, failed to supply primary goods, and finally relied on the threat of force, undercut the population's patriotic sentiment.

Peasant resistance to state grain policies should also not be construed as peasant insularity. Peasants throughout the war stayed interested in national events and the situation at the front. They demanded news and literature about the war, continued to donate goods for soldiers and their families, and evoked the nation and patriotism in their petitions and resistance. Peasants refused to give grain because they felt they did not have much to spare. Moreover, peasants exasperated with state policies felt that they had sufficiently contributed to the war effort. For example, in refusing to give up oats, a peasant community wrote, 'We are carrying out forced carting of firewood for the Izhevsk factories and deliver other obligations of demanded fodder, but there are not enough oats. The crops were bad due to the exhausted land and we could not bring in the harvest because there were not enough able-bodied male workers. This is why livestock and the population are starving.'[147]

From the end of 1916 to the collapse of the tsarist regime in February 1917, clashes between peasants and government brigades, like the one above, occurred in a number of locales.[148] Women, and especially *soldatki*, were often at the forefront of such resistance, defending their household. As Barbara Alpern Engel has shown in her analysis of peasant protests, women took the lead in resistance when they perceived that the private sphere, a space that peasant women traditionally controlled, was under attack.[149] When grain requisitioning threatened the food supply, women resisted the state.

[145] Anfimov, *Krest'ianskoe dvizhenie*, 295–9; Lih, *Bread and Authority*, 49–50.
[146] Anfimov, *Krest'ianskoe dvizhenie*, 300–1.
[147] Sadakov, 'Udmurtiia v gody pervoi mirovoi imperialisticheskoi voiny', 63.
[148] Anfimov, *Krest'ianskoe dvizhenie*, 511–12. In December 1916, two hundred peasants in Viatka district resisted state requisitioning of grain. In January–February 1917, several *volost*s resisted grain requisitioning.
[149] Barbara Alpern Engel, 'Women, Men, and the Language of Peasant Resistance, 1870–1907', in Stephen P. Frank and Mark D. Steinberg, eds, *Cultures in Flux: Lower-Class Values, Practices, and Resistance in Late Imperial Russia*, (Princeton, 1994), 34–53;

The provincial government also conscripted the peasant women, children, and elders for labour. Before the war, Udmurt peasants supplied most of the wood fuel for the essential armaments factories of Izhevsk and Votkinsk, in eastern Viatka. By early 1915, to supplement the depleted male Udmurt workforce, land captains called *volost* assemblies throughout southern Viatka and mobilized the Russian and non-Russian peasant populations to gather wood for fuel for the factories. Peasants travelled up to 180 versts (119 miles) to deliver the fuel. This continued for a year, but by 1916 the poor wages and terrible working conditions, including having to sleep in the forests during the winter, made many peasants decide simply to leave work. Other peasants refused to leave their villages.[150]

Finally, rumours circulating around the countryside underscored growing peasant fears and dreams about the war and social tensions that erupted in 1917. Most rumours reflected growing concerns about the fate of their menfolk in the deteriorating war and placed blame on a treasonous political and military elite. For example, in January 1916, peasants of Viatka district heard of a brigade of forty soldiers freezing in the city of Viatka. In March a rumour in the same district spread that on the frontlines commanders of German heritage in the Russian army beat soldiers with birch rods. News that draftees ate meat during Lent further enraged these peasants and they called on the local police to prohibit the sale of meat during this fast.[151] In Sarapul district, rumours in the second year of war focussed on the high number of casualties. Rumours that ran through the nation also manifested themselves in the Viatka countryside. One of the most popular rumours was that after the war the Tsar would take gentry land and give it to the peasants.[152] Others reported German infiltration from the highest government officials to the factories, as expressed in the soldier's letter to his wife, discussed above. Several peasants reiterated the rumour that the tsarist family was in league with the Germans. One version in 1915 had it that the Tsar made an underground passage from his palace to Germany and that he

Lynne Viola, '*Bab'i Bunty* and Peasant Women's Protest During Collectivization', in Farnsworth and Viola, eds, *Russian Peasant Women*, 189–205.

[150] Sadakov, 'Udmurtiia v gody pervoi mirovoi imperialisticheskoi voiny', 59–61; Anfimov, *Rossiiskaia derevnia*, 194; GAKO, f. 574, op. 2, d. 978, l. 44.

[151] GAKO, f. 582, op. 158, d. 14, ll. 22, 29–29ob. On popular rumours during the war, see Figes, *A People's Tragedy*, 284–5. On peasant rumours as the prose of peasant culture in opposition to political elites: see Guha, *Elementary Aspects*, 251–77. David Moon documents the long history of the centrality of rumour in peasant knowledge and political action: *Russian Peasants and Tsarist Legislation on the Eve of Reform: Interaction between Peasants and Officialdom* (Basingstoke, 1992).

[152] Porshneva, *Krest'iane, rabochie i soldaty*, 107.

had already fled to Germany by automobile. The following year a peasant in Urzhum blamed the treachery of the Tsar's mother, Mariia Fedorovna, who supposedly informed on Russia's condition to Germany by telephone.[153] A letter written in September 1915 to the leading Kadet Party (Constitutional Democrat) figure and Duma member, Pavel Miliukov, insisted that the Minister of the Court, Vladimir Frederiks, was a German and must be removed from office. The author also reiterated a rumour floating through Izhevsk that rifle production at the factory went so slowly because of German sabotage.[154]

Conclusion

The peasantry was the vital ingredient in Russia's total war. Wartime conscription and mobilization seized the traditional village, already under attack by market forces, and shook it forcefully until the nature of the village was completely rearranged. In the summer of 1914 peasant men and women lived in a symbiotic, misogynist relationship, in which men dominated over women in a changing but still traditional peasant society. Two years later, the newly militarized village was overwhelmingly composed of women, elders, and children, and, in many villages, foreign prisoners, enemy aliens, and refugees.

The war was a catalyst for peasant nationalism and revolution. While the Imperial government had opened up the civil ranks and allowed more public involvement in governance, it still resisted bringing peasants (and other estates) into the regime's rule as equal partners. The necessities of total war forced the state to integrate the population into the national cause, although without political rights. Military conscription, labour mobilization, and peasant participation in local war efforts made peasants feel part of the nation's war. Even though the tsarist government officially continued its old, restrictive ideology of the Tsar ruling over his subjects, popular participation in the war effort provided fertile soil for the upcoming public discussion in 1917 of the citizens' roles in the nation.

State mobilization and total war created an environment that bred mass political activism. Zemstvo officials, traditionally the centre's contentious allies in the countryside, rallied to help the nation and acted as the essential link between the state and its population. War brought

---

[153] RGIA, f. 1405, op. 521, d. 476, ll. 261ob–62, 342. I thank Boris Kolonitskii for providing me with these and several other citations of colourful rumours during the war.
[154] GARF, f. 102, op. 2, d. 1030, l. 1337.

popular peasant patriotism and even national sentiment to the forefront. Initially, it helped Russia's government utilize the country's resources. However, when food supplies dwindled, casualties mounted, and popular perceptions of the centre's corruption and alienation from the people grew, peasants felt connected to their nation and not to their tsar. The war laid the necessary foundations for a revolutionary regime based on popular participation in governance. At the same time, zemstvo activist and state officials' role as unequal leaders in social engineering projects, including policies categorizing population groups based on ethnicity, military service, and gender relations, also widened existent fissures in rural society and revealed the bases of future social and political upheaval.

2 Peasant citizens: freedom and revolution in the village

As church bells rang through the countryside to celebrate the end of autocratic rule in March 1917, villagers understood that a new political order was upon them. In the first months of the revolution, there was a true sense of unity and endless possibilities for Russia to overcome past differences and the dismal military campaign, and to build a new nation now that the obstructive autocratic regime was gone. Peasants, rural educated society, and state officials created and acted out their ideas of this nation through the construction of new administrative bodies, new symbolic ceremonies, and a new discourse surrounding these activities. If the first two years of war brought peasants into the Russian nation, the post-February order elevated them into full citizens of the polity. But what did citizenship mean? This question stood at the centre of a complex debate on state formation and political inclusion in the new Russian republic.

The wartime environment shaped this crucial political conversation. Mobilization for total war had merged the interests of the tsarist state, zemstvo, and rural educated society.[1] The February Revolution empowered zemstvo personnel and they glided into governmental positions vacated by the old order. At the same time, local members of educated society served as political interpreters, imparting state values to the peasants. The new political leaders then refashioned the war as a defence of the revolution and the resurrected Russian nation in which peasants needed to continue to sacrifice and remain mobilized to sustain an increasingly unpopular war. The critical military situation sharpened state and rural educated society's focus on citizen obligations over political rights. The war also transformed peasants. Wartime both destabilized the rural community and brought it into the national political order. After the February Revolution, provisions and wartime crises added additional strain on the new governmental order, and by the summer a sense of failure, exacerbating social tensions. The decaying military environment thereby charted the path for the revolution.

[1] Holquist, *Making War.*

The revolutionary state became a site of negotiation and contestation for social groups.[2] Modern military mobilization transformed into modern political mobilization and peasants quickly came into their own as powerful political actors. Peasants partially embraced the ways educated society and state representatives defined their role in the revolutionary state – the revolutionary discourse, administrative responsibilities, and even their apprenticeship as citizens – but they also challenged other more onerous obligations.[3] Holidays, revolutionary symbols, and elections allowed peasants, local members of educated society, political representatives, and state agents to discuss what revolution meant. The post-February order presented citizenship in its laws and governmental institutions as a guarantee of rights to political participation and freedom within the state, with concomitant duties and obligations for the good of the nation.[4] However, tensions of political inclusion tore at the stability of the order from its inception. These arguments intertwined with social fragmentation from economic and military crises and evolved into class conflict.

Many scholars argue that peasants saw the end of the tsarist regime as an opportunity to free themselves from an oppressive order. The old order disintegrated and 'peasants in all villages embarked on the same broad path, that of rejecting the authority of the formal administration and of establishing an authority of their own'.[5] While peasants attempted to reorder the political establishment to fit their views of a just relationship with the state, they did little to indicate that they wanted a break with the outside world. Villagers continued communication with higher-level authorities and took cues to establish village and especially *volost* governing bodies from the district and provincial governments. Peasants showed themselves to be complex political actors and they understood that the revolution altered their traditional identification of themselves as subordinates in the political community. In 1917, they

---

[2] William Rosenberg, 'Social Mediation and State Construction(s) in Revolutionary Russia', *Social History* 19 (1994): 171–2.

[3] I take the concept of apprenticeship as citizens from the large body of literature on political apprenticeship as a popular conversation of sociability, acculturation, and resistance in the French Revolution. For example, see Catherine Duprat, 'Lieux et temps de l'acculturation politique', *Annales historiques de la Révolution française* 66 (1994): 387–400; Suzanne Desan, 'What's After Political Culture? Recent French Revolutionary Historiography', *French Historical Studies* 23 (2000): 170–5.

[4] For Provisional Government edicts banning discrimination based on class, nationality, and gender, see Robert Browder and Alexander F. Kerensky, eds., *The Russian Provisional Government, 1917: Documents*, vol. I (Stanford, 1961), 157–77, 191–242.

[5] Gill, *Peasants and Government*, 29.

quickly realized that they had the opportunity and rights to become full members in the newly reinvented political community.

The very term citizen, *grazhdanin*, was an integral part of the revolution.[6] Peasants saw the term in newspapers, on posters, in government propaganda, and heard it on the streets. Government authorities and educated society further reinforced the idea by freely using the term in newspaper articles and addressing all their appeals to the 'citizens' of Russia. Clearly, though, educated Russian society's construction of a benighted peasantry moulded its views on peasant citizenship. Newspaper articles, pronouncements, ceremonies, and speeches expressed different terms of citizenship for the peasantry. Educated society and the Provisional Government pointed out time and again that coinciding with freedom was a duty (*dolg*) to the nation. Peasants must keep order, raise their cultural level through education and public organizations, refrain from alcohol, seek spiritual fulfilment through the church, respect private property, and especially continue the war effort. These duties mirrored the elites' fears of anarchy (in part from the legacy of the 1905 Revolution) and cultural understandings of the Russian peasantry. In a seeming contradiction between the new government's liberation of all the peoples from the legally hierarchical estates (*sosloviia*) system, local elites attempted to continue a paternalistic cultural and political hierarchy. While granting freedom to the people, educated Russia still imposed a constricting discourse that attempted to make the peasants into second-class citizens.

Citizenship also wove peasants into the political fabric. It presupposed active participation in political rituals and the commitment of one's self, one's soul, to the defence and growth of the polity. Resistance, non-compliance, apathy, or unwillingness to defend the state and revolution became a rejection of citizenship and membership in this polity. Citizenship was an effective form of state mobilization and intrusion into peasants' identity that raised the political stakes by prohibiting peasants from separating themselves from politics. The meaning of citizenship and its correct articulation thereby became a source of social tension.

Many peasants, for their part, quickly adopted the term 'citizen' and used it in petitions and letters to newspapers. Use does not always constitute understanding. Did peasants understand the term citizen to be an equal member of the state, or did they view citizenship differently than the elites? Orlando Figes argues that the peasantry did not construe citizenship as equal rights for all, since the peasants acted

---

[6] Orlando Figes and Boris Kolonitskii, *Interpreting the Russian Revolution: The Language and Symbols of 1917* (New Haven, 1999), 141.

against non-peasant groups in 1917. Instead, according to him, peasants had a limited definition of citizenship based on a traditional kinship that did not go beyond the village borders. The peasantry, in his view, could not understand the complex modern political terms and mutated them into peasant-talk.[7] Peasants in Viatka, however, understood how the elite discussed and defined the ideas of citizenship. The population accepted parts of it, such as the right to national political participation and the need for education, but rejected or ignored other elements of the elites' definition, such as the obligation to sacrifice unjust amounts of grain to the army and metropole. Multiple visions of the Russian nation therefore took shape in 1917.

Peasants eagerly fought to become full citizens and to play a major role in reconstructing the nation. They defended a complex peasant economy and local interests that only in part concerned acquiring long-sought-after land rights.[8] They also moved to be active political participants in the Russian nation's reinvention. Nascent popular Russian nationalism certainly existed before 1917 and the war brought the peasants into acting as part of the national cause and thinking of themselves as citizens of the Russian nation, even without universal political rights. The over-throw of the Tsar made elites and peasants transform and redefine the symbols of the Russian nation.

Freedom and order

Violence reigned in the first days of the February Revolution in Petro-grad. People tore down symbols of the old order and destroyed statues of the tsars. They raided police stations, freed prisoners, and brutally murdered police officers.[9] In striking contrast, peasants rejoiced at their freedom then calmly set out to construct a new political order in the countryside.[10] Even in the darkest days of the autumn crises, when

---

[7] Figes and Kolonitskii, 141–4.

[8] A. D. Maliavskii, *Krest'ianskoe dvizhenie v Rossii v 1917 g. mart-oktiabr'* (Moscow, 1981); Kabanov, *Krest'ianskoe khoziaistvo*.

[9] Figes, *A People's Tragedy*, 322.

[10] *Slovo i zhizn'*, 3 March 1917, 1; Report of head of Viatka provincial *ispolkom* on the events of February 1917 in the city of Viatka (31 October 1917), A. S. Bystrova et al., eds, *Ustanovlenie i uprochenie sovetskoi vlasti v Viatskoi gubernii: Sbornik dokumentov* (Kirov, 1957), 90–1. As in other provinces, tsarist officials, in this case Viatka's Governor N. A. Rudnev and the Vice Governor P. P. Kandirov, attempted to keep the events in Petrograd a secret. News of unrest was not published until 2 March. The city Duma, in step with local soldiers, pushed the governmental transition along, arresting gendarmes and police officers. On 6 March workers in Viatka established a soviet parallel to the Provisional Government. See the memoir of the Bolshevik A. P. Kuchkin, in *Za vlast' sovetov: Sbornik vospominanii starykh bol'shevikov–Uchastnikov Velikoi Oktiabr'skoi*

Russian society was gripped with a great fear as peasants in Russia's heartland attacked police and military detachments and burned manors, Viatka's peasants did not turn the world upside down.

News of the revolution in Petrograd travelled fast. Rumours of massive strikes spread to the city of Viatka as they were happening, on 25 February, and news reports two days later confirmed the rumours.[11] Like everywhere else in the Empire, Viatka learned the stunning news of the Tsar's abdication by telegraph. The announcement of the 2 March abdication arrived that night in Viatka and appeared in the local press the next day. The news spread quickly, albeit unevenly, across the countryside. Within two weeks of the historic announcement, by mid-March, virtually every village had heard of the end of the Romanov dynasty.

The abdication manifesto that soon followed the news and rumours of the overthrow of the Tsar became the first material symbol of the new era. The local clergyman or a zemstvo official, as one of the most literate residents of the village, was often the one to read the declaration and explain its significance. In what would begin a pattern in the conversation with the peasantry, the member of educated society inserted his own political dreams and fears into the explication of the document. For example, on 10 March in Pishchalintsy village, Orlov district, peasants held a 'crowded *volost* meeting in which the district agronomist read the manifesto of the abdication' of Tsar Nicholas and Grand Duke Mikhail's declination of the throne and the decree establishing the Provisional Government. The agronomist 'tried to explain to the meeting the significance of the revolution (*perevorot*) and that it was the duty of everyone to maintain tranquillity and to do all measures to help the Provisional Government in the elimination of the remaining legacy of the old order'.[12] Parroting the revolutionary state's first decrees, the agronomist stressed order over freedom.

Having heard formal word of the end of autocracy, villagers came together at general gatherings or crowded meetings (*obshchie sobraniia, obshchie skhody, obshchie mitingi*) at the nearest major village to discuss and celebrate the extraordinary situation. Peasants understood the significance of the news and so allowed villagers of both sexes and all ages

  sotsialisticheskoi revoliutsii i grazhdanskoi voiny v Viatskoi gubernii, V. D. Letiagin et al., eds. (Kirov, 1957), 9.
[11] Iu. N. Timkin, '1917 god: Ot revoliutsii po telegrafu k revoliutsii na shtykakh', in L. S. Tatarenkova et al., eds, *Entsiklopediia zemli Viatskoi*, t. 4. *Istoriia* (Kirov, 1995), 337; and Timkin, *Smutnoe vremia na Viatke. Obshchestvenno-politicheskoe razvitie Viatskoi gubernii vesnoi 1917–osen'iu 1918 gg.* (Kirov, 1998), 6.
[12] *Krest'ianskaia gazeta Viakskago gubernskago zemstva*, 11 April 1917, 10.

to attend the meetings. The *skhod* in Karakulino, Sarapul district, brought together over five hundred people, including women and residents from neighbouring Permiakov village, who came 'to hear the truth' about the revolution. Many attendees had never before been to a *skhod*. So many people appeared that the meeting hut overflowed and the *skhod* had to be held outside.[13] From the beginning, the peasantry of Viatka acted with cautious exuberance and embraced the new national republican rhetoric and ideals. On 4 March peasants in Orlov district heard the abdication manifesto and broke out in the 'Marseillaise' and other 'songs of freedom'.[14]

A peasant described the scene in his village of Elgan, in Glazov district: 'The first sign of the events in Petrograd came on 5 March from soldiers arriving on leave' who told locals of the tsar's abdication. The local intelligentsia rallied to action and organized a *volost* gathering two days later attended by four hundred people, half of whom were women and soldiers. Someone read the manifesto and the priest took the floor and spoke on the significance of the national events for the people (*narod*) and told them, 'fate is in your hands'. An orator followed and urged the villagers to keep order and be calm. The citizens answered with a huge 'ura' in honour of free Russia. Many people, it was reported, had tears in their eyes. The following week, the village celebrated with a special holiday of freedom and collection, with streets adorned with red flags flying overhead and speeches. Villagers collected over 110 rubles for families who had members killed 'fighting for freedom'. On 28 March the village held another assembly attended by over five hundred people and elected *volost* officers.[15]

Gatherings welcomed the Provisional Government, called on it to improve their material wellbeing, and to convene the Constituent Assembly as soon as possible. The *volost skhod* in Stulovskaia *volost*, Slobodskoi district, sent a resolution (*prigovor*) on 14 March to the Provisional Government in Petrograd, recognizing the new regime and asking about peasant rights in elections to a land gathering.[16] The *volost skhod* in Iangulovskaia *volost*, Malmyzh district, called on the Provisional

[13] *Kama*, 16 March 1917, 4.
[14] *Slovo i zhizn'*, 7 March 1917, 4. On a 7 March revolutionary general gathering of Okat'evo village, Kotel'nich district, see 14 March 1917, 4. It is surprising that villagers knew the 'Marseillaise' but they may have learned it as a revolutionary sign from 1905, or from urban connections. For parallel gatherings in Kazan and Nizhegorod provinces, see Sarah Badcock, *Politics and the People*, ch. 6.
[15] *Krest'ianskaia gazeta Viatskago gubernskago zemstva*, 21 April 1917, 15–16.
[16] GA RF, f. 1788, op. 2, d. 91, ll. 194–5ob. See also a telegram to the Petrograd Soviet from Buiskaia *volost*, Urzhum district, from 1 May 1917, Bystrova et al., eds, *Ustanovlenie*, 119.

Government leader Prince L'vov to convoke the Constituent Assembly and to better its population's desperate situation. The villagers emphasized their anxiety and fear for their livelihood and the future. As 'free and law-abiding citizens', a phrase repeated by peasants writing to the newspapers in 1917, they asked the Provisional Government to allow them access to public land.[17]

In many *volosts*, but certainly not all, peasants overthrew the land captain, *starshina*, and other foremen and established a new government, as happened in Semerikovskaia *volost*, Nolinsk district, when peasants elected a new *volost starshina*, arrested the former office holder and 'gave him a beating'.[18] Some peasants also overthrew unpopular religious leaders. The Isenbaevskaia *volost* public safety committee dismissed the Sosnova village mullah, Nazmitdin Tukaev, for leading a life of debauchery, not attending to the funeral needs of the poor, and cosying up to the police and gendarmes.[19] Villages established new governments of varying names and sizes to replace the *volost* and communal leaders. The change in power should not be overemphasized. Meetings were open to all villagers but elders and those who had traditionally held power still ruled. In many villages peasants reappointed the same men to represent them in the new committees.[20] But democratic politics undermined the older, and often wealthier, governing group by including new and traditionally marginal populations into *volost* and even village politics. From 1917 onwards, soldiers, returning workers, outsider political representatives, and women played a greater role in deciding how the village ran.

For all the excited commotion of the heady early days of revolution, the tight communication between peasants and district officials is striking. Most often the district government created the impetus to establish new administrative bodies in the *volost*. Even those *volosts* that autonomously selected a ruling body reshaped them just a few days later to match the formal instructions.[21] On 6 March in Orlov, the district

---

[17] *Malmyzhskaia zhizn'*, 29 April 1917, 3. Peasants of Osinov district, Perm province, also asked the government for land after proclaiming, 'We former peasants who are now equal citizens (*ravnopravnye grazhdane*) enthusiastically welcome the Provisional Government . . . and we new citizens will give the new government everything it asks of us for the general happiness of our dear motherland.' *Kama*, 10 March 1917, 4.

[18] GAKO, f. 582, op. 194, d. 8, l. 8ob.   [19] *Kama*, 7 May 1917, 4.

[20] For example, GAKO, f. 976, op. 4, d. 248, l. 22. The same was true in Saratov. Donald J. Raleigh, *Revolution on the Volga: 1917 in Saratov* (Ithaca, 1986), 174–6.

[21] Viatka district established a committee for public safety on 4 March, Glazov on 6 March, Kotel'nich on 9 March, Urzhum on 3 March, Orlov on 4 March, Nolinsk on 7 March. L. A. Obukhov, 'Vopros o vlasti na mestakh posle fevral'skoi revoliutsii (Po materialam Viatskoi gubernii)', in G. Krysova et al., eds, *Istoriia i kul'tura Volgo-Viatskogo kraia (K 90-letiiu Viatskoi uchenoi arkhivnoi komissii)* (Kirov, 1994), 224–6.

Plate 6. Soldiers on leave during the war, Viatka district. Courtesy
GASPI KO

zemstvo administration instructed the *volost*s to establish provisional
public committees (*vremennye obshchestvennye komitety*) that would mirror
the newly established government in the town. The committees were
given detailed instructions for sweeping powers, akin to the former *volost*
administration, to help the new government maintain order and continue the supply of food to the cities and army. The committees
appointed police and a people's militia, made certain that the people
continued to work, and instructed the population about important

matters.[22] In May, the Viatka provincial commissar, Pavel Pan'kov, reported to the Ministry of Internal Affairs that, 'power in the localities is organizing itself with fair success and at the present time almost every locality has a people's militia'. By June, most *volost*s had established permanent executive committees (*ispolkom*s) to govern.[23] The revolution in the town and country were linked together. The Provisional Government recognized changes in leadership in the village, and peasants solicited help in designing the new rural state. Most significantly, members of the rural intelligentsia found a position in the vast majority of *volost ispolkom*s and in several large villages.[24] While their representation declined during the summer, in the spring peasants welcomed these mediators with the outside world. Educated society also positioned itself for appointment by playing leading roles in meetings and accompanying public festivals. Provincial Provisional Government administrators, many who were themselves active in the zemstvo, also encouraged their counterparts in the countryside to play a leading role in rural government.

Peasants were concerned with under government and crime in the countryside, even more than the new state administrators. The establishment of rural administrative organs transpired peacefully, but tensions in the dialogue between peasant and state administrators over how best to keep order in the village reveal the fundamental divergence in ideas of citizenship and peasant political participation in the revolutionary state. On 23 March in Iaransk district, representatives from various *volost* administrations discussed the problem of establishing a viable government and rule of law with the district administration. The representatives expressed concern that the new government was not allocating sufficient personnel to maintain peace in the countryside. A peasant asked, 'whether [the newly elected] *volost* elder will be able to cope with maintaining order in all of the *volost*, as previously the *volost* official had help from village policemen, but now the elder will not have such aides'. The administrator dismissed his concerns.[25]

The district administration proposed instead to mobilize the local intelligentsia to teach the peasants how to be citizens. Teachers and

---

[22] GAKO, f. 1345, op. 1, d. 22, ll. 6–6ob. GA RF, f. 1788, op. 2, d. 64, ll. 13–14ob; *Izvestiia Kotel'nicheskago vremennago ispolnitel'nago komiteta*, 14 May 1917, 7.

[23] GA RF, f. 1788, op. 2, d. 91, l. 36ob; GAKO, f. 1345, op. 1, d. 21. Thirty-two were organized in Malmyzh district, fifteen in Glazov district, twenty-five in Nolinsk district, and in every *volost* of Slobodskoi district. The Right SR and member of the provincial Peasant Union organizational committee, Petr Salamatov, replaced Pan'kov as provincial commissar later that month.

[24] GAKO, f. 1345, op. 1, d. 21, ll. 47–51.   [25] GAKO, f. 976, op. 4, d. 248, ll. 22–3.

students would, 'explain to the semi-literate peasants the rights of citizenship'. The administration planned to have students in the local schools descend on the villages during Passion Week and engage the 'dark people' (the peasantry) in general discussions about current events.[26] Similarly, the Information Section of the Kotel'nich *ispolkom* held a course during Passion Week attended by eighty teachers, training them to go to the villages and prepare peasants for voting in the Constituent Assembly. The class was so successful the committee organized another the following month.[27] The local government hoped that education could end peasants' ignorance and make them into good, law-abiding citizens. The district administrators, mostly zemstvo agents, extended their reliance on education and short courses that they had promoted throughout the war to train peasants.

Within a month, then, villages and *volosts* had new governments. There was real excitement that the people had put the government on course to achieve historic victories over political tyranny and in war. However, future tensions between peasants and the rural intelligentsia can already be seen. These tensions stemmed from intellectuals' views of peasants as benighted and whose need of cultural and political education would potentially block Russia from advancing. They also came from competing visions of revolution and the role of the state. Peasants, rural intellectuals, and district administrators expressed these views as they celebrated and came to terms with the revolution.

Rituals of power, rituals of citizenship

Villagers celebrated the revolution with songs, holidays and festivals, speeches, meetings, and other events marking their new life and mediating the transition from tsarist despotism to democratic freedom. These ceremonies strived to invent new understandings of the Russian nation and customized old signs and symbols to bring coherence to the political changes and shape a new national discourse. They sought to unify groups and express the jubilant emotions of the people.[28] They also

---

[26] GAKO, f. 976, op. 4, d. 248, l. 22.
[27] *Izvestiia Kotel'nicheskago vremennago ispolnitel'nago komiteta*, 27 April 1917, 14–15.
[28] On popular celebrations in the Provisional Government era, see B. I. Kolonitskii, *Simvoly vlasti i bor'ba za vlast': K izucheniiu politicheskoi kul'tury Rossiiskoi revoliutsii 1917 goda* (St Petersburg, 2001), esp. 5–13; Figes and Kolonitskii, *Interpreting the Russian Revolution*; Richard Stites, *Revolutionary Dreams: Utopian Visions and Experimental Life in the Russian Revolution* (New York, 1989), ch. 3–4; James von Geldern, *Bolshevik Festivals, 1917–1920* (Berkeley, 1993), ch 1.

aimed to establish order, exercise power, and solidify claims of political legitimacy, all in the environment of war.

These rituals were integral to the popular experience of revolution and gave meaning to the new government and the political changes as a whole. The heyday of the rural festivities occurred in the spring and early summer, at the same time as the establishment of reorganized local bodies of authority. The celebrations, like the state administration, acted as sites of negotiation over the revolutionary value system and myth-ologies, political power, and the terms of citizenship. Rural educated society of various political stripes, as self-proclaimed representatives of the new order, conducted the rituals of power and used them to establish political legitimacy and build a tutorial relationship for the post-tsarist era. On the surface, the festivities were quite successful, with hundreds and sometimes thousands of locals participating, which was especially significant in May and June as peasants spent most of their days in the fields. Large public gatherings were crucial events for controlling the public discourse on the revolution, for it was there that the elites could act as the narrators of the new master fiction and appropriate 'the field of cultural production'.[29] Members of educated society tried to use cul-tural production to solidify their own standing in a political world based on popular sovereignty and to calm their worries of otherwise unfettered mass participation. A ceremony, as James Scott writes, is, 'the *self-portrait* of dominant elites as they would have themselves seen'.[30] Members of educated society attempted to portray the values of demo-cratic reform, popular sovereignty, duty to the nation, and obligation to provide for its well-being from the first village and *volost* meetings of the revolution. They had gained valuable experience overseeing mass mobilization during the war. Now that the autocracy that had blocked their dreams of cultural modernization was gone, they just needed to convince the benighted peasantry to follow them.

Educated society and state agents organized most celebrations to create a unified public identity under the Provisional Government, but they never gained full control of the rituals.[31] Peasants had lived in a world that legitimized their subordinate role in society through rituals that consecrated the tsar, but self-mobilization during wartime, followed by the February Revolution, upset this traditional role and by spring 1917 peasants saw themselves as more equitable participants in a larger,

[29] Pierre Bourdieu, *Outline of a Theory of Practice*, tr. Richard Nice (Cambridge, 1995), 184.
[30] Scott, *Domination and the Arts of Resistance*, 18.
[31] Michael C. Hickey, 'Discourses of Public Identity and Liberalism in the February Revolution: Smolensk, Spring 1917', *The Russian Review* 55 (1996): 624–5.

national struggle. They happily participated in the revolutionary rituals and at first accepted educated society's tutelage but they also took the revolutionary symbols and rechannelled them to project unity across the peasant social estate.

Reminiscent of the emancipation from serfdom and most significant imperial decrees, the new authorities linked the Tsar's abdication to religious credence.[32] Many peasants heard the official abdication at church on 12 March, the first Sunday after news reached the countryside. This happened in Nikuliata village, Iaransk district, where the peasants heard the liturgy and then were read the manifesto of the Tsar's abdication and the establishment of the Provisional Government. There was a short service and then the attendees welcomed the new regime.[33] Other ceremonies greeting the new era featured religious processions and sermons by the village priest. Peasants could not have missed the solemnity of the occasion and link between 'the spiritual authority of the Church', and their responsibilities under the new regime. Educated society, supported by state decrees, offered the peasantry a new notion of political freedom but used the same symbolic reference point in the church as the old tsarist regime and transferred the church's consecration of local tsarist authority and power to themselves. Marches resembled religious processions, and requiems and masses continued the stream of services for those called to colours or killed in the war over the past two years. Revolutionary ceremonial symbols looked both forward, to a modern democratic nation in which the new power came from the people, and backward, to the tsarist system and political legitimacy from divine sanction. In doing so, they established contradictory symbols of the pre-modern divine rule and the modern nation state.

These were emotional and spiritual days for both peasants and local intellectuals. The revolution could not have come at a more symbolically charged time of year, coinciding with the Great Lent and Easter, and with animist springtime celebrations. The population's religious hopes for Russia's miraculous resurrection and revolutionary political dreams intermixed in ceremonies and gatherings. People gave each other Easter kisses to celebrate the revolution and the holiday and proclaimed, 'Russia

---

[32] For the tsarist government's use of the moral significance of the Church in 1861, see Daniel Field, 'The Year of Jubilee', in Ben Eklof, John Bushnell and Larissa Zakharova eds, *Russia's Great Reforms, 1855–1881* (Bloomington, 1994), 40–57.

[33] *Krest'ianskaia gazeta Viatskago gubernskago zemstva*, 11 April 1917, 11. The phrase 'spiritual authority of the Church' comes from Jeffrey Brooks, *When Russia Learned to Read: Literacy and Popular Literature, 1861–1917* (Princeton, 1985), 244.

Plate 7. Relaxing during a holiday in Viatka, 1917. Courtesy *National Geographic* Image Collection

has arisen' alongside 'Christ has arisen'.[34] Citizenship, blended with images of Russian nationalism, also took on spiritual connotations. Local clergy helped to fuse citizenship and religion. On 3 March Bishop Nikandr of Viatka and Slobodskoi districts publicly blessed the revolution as a way for the country to have strength to finish the war. He urged the population to remain calm and believe in the goodness of God.[35] On 5 March, the village of Zagar'e eagerly gathered in the church and parish school. The rector described the shocking events in the capital that culminated in the hasty end of the Romanov regime and the audience 'in rapture welcomed the resurrection of its fellow people (*rodnogo naroda*)'.[36] Ishlyk village held a children's holiday in the zemstvo school on 30 April to celebrate the revolution. The classroom was decorated in green, with flags and placards reading, 'Glory to the sacred work' (*slava sviatomu trudu*),

[34] Kolonitskii, *Simvoly vlasti*, 56–79, esp. 76; Wade, *The Russian Revolution*, 89, 127. For more on the popularity of religious metaphoric language in 1917, see Mark D. Steinberg, *Voices of Revolution, 1917* (New Haven, 2001), 30–1.

[35] *Slovo i zhizn'*, 3 March 1917, 2; Badcock finds a similarly active church in Kazan and Nizhegorod provinces, *Politics and the People*.

[36] *Slovo i zhizn'*, 7 March 1917, 4; Villagers in Shorkan village, Sarapul district, held a service commemorating the revolution on 5 March and heard the Tsar's abdication. The following week a full religious procession followed the normal Sunday service. A clergyman then gave a speech on the fate of Russia. Villagers formed a provisional public safety committee that evening. *Kama*, 21 March 1917, 4.

'Freedom – the good fortune of Russia', and 'May the memory of those killed fighting for freedom live forever.' Before a service, the local priest, O. A. Zavarin, gave a sermon to children and parents about the new sacred life in a free Russia.[37] Father Zavarin was the most visible of the scores of parish priests who got caught up in the revolution and helped guide its celebrations. Many clergymen had supported revolutionary reforms and sympathized with demands for raising the economic and cultural standard of living.[38] Beneath the piety of both peasant parishioners and clergymen expressed in these rituals, however, laid the seemingly contradictory celebration of secular politics and popular sovereignty without reliance on a divinely imposed tsar. Peasants also used religious events to engage in politics. During the congregation at Easter, many peasants began the process of political organization. In summer festivals, peasants gathered information about national politics and organized voting coalitions for the zemstvo elections.[39]

Holidays by their nature are a time outside normal time – a period reserved for relaxation and revelry. The celebrations in 1917 were certainly joyous events marked by church bells ringing and villages bedecked with striking red ribbons and flags. Banners flew proclaiming, 'Long live the democratic republic' and 'land and freedom' (*zemlia i volia*).[40] Peasant tradition would not consider the holidays festive, however. Many were planned events with tight schedules that did not have room for games, dancing, drink, and food. Instead, the elite wanted the peasants to attend church, learn new songs, and then go to school. Holidays illuminate the conflicting images that peasants, local educated society, and officials held of citizenship and the hopes of the new regime. The holiday rituals around Viatka province in 1917 were formulaic. Celebrations of the Holiday of the Revolution, May Day, Easter, and the Holiday of Freedom invariably included speeches by the local priest

---

[37] *Kukarskaia zhizn'*, 7 May 1917, 2.
[38] Chris J. Chulos, *Converging Worlds: Religion and Community in Peasant Russia, 1861–1917* (DeKalb, 2003), 97–111.
[39] *Kukarskaia zhizn'*, 30 July 1917, 2. Such was the case when peasants in Il'inskaia *volost* celebrated the holiday of their patron saint, Il'ia, in late July. At the gathering, the local teacher gave a lecture to both male and female peasants on the national political atmosphere and the situation at the front.
[40] *Krest'ianskaia gazeta*, 18 April 1917, 11; 16 May 1917, 10–11; and 19 May 1917, 11. Some locales celebrated Workers' Day on 18 April, corresponding to 1 May New Style, and others on 1 May Old Style. Newspapers' descriptions of holidays were themselves attempts to control the meaning of holidays. The author in this SR paper emphasized the dramatic significance of the holiday by proclaiming that peasants celebrated for the first time in their lives. Obviously, this is not true. It is still possible to find an accurate picture of the holidays from the plethora of diverse sources and an understanding of the filters of the reporters and newspaper publishers.

and teacher explaining to the peasants how to act and the significance of the regime.

The local intelligentsia and the district government told the villagers in concrete terms how to celebrate and emphasized obligations to the country over freedom. The Orlov zemstvo administration's minutely detailed plans for the Smirnovskaia *volost* provisional public committee's celebration of the Holiday of the Revolution on 30 April was typical. Members of educated society were deeply involved in the elaborate celebration. All inhabitants of the *volost* were to participate according to government orders. A liturgy in Verkhoivskoe village would begin the day and all villagers would parade to the zemstvo school en route to a platform in front of the church where they would hear a memorial service (*moleben*) and a speech, then sing the 'Marseillaise'. They would then go in solemn procession to the school where the schoolmaster would give another speech. Following the oratory, the peasants were to sing revolutionary songs while proceeding to the neighbouring village of Vozhgaly, where they would hear a speech yet again, and then return to the Verkhoivskoe church square. At the square would be a requiem for the combatants and those who had fallen in the struggle for freedom. After the service would be another speech, followed by a return march to the school accompanied by revolutionary songs, and then a final speech. The village was to be decorated with flags, posters, and coloured ribbons. The *volost* government was ordered to distribute holiday programmes with the lyrics to revolutionary songs and a special edition newspaper. During the holiday, the government would try to collect donations for families of those killed at war. Before the holiday the teacher and local priest were supposed to teach the villagers the proper revolutionary songs, such as the 'Marseillaise', 'Bravely Comrades Keep Together', the 'Varshavianka', and the 'Funeral March'.[41] The dense script of the holiday in Smirnovskaia *volost*, and its near duplication throughout the province, shows how local state officials and educated society consciously imposed symbolism upon popular celebrations of the revolution. Their messages conveyed mass participation and political empowerment that were the promises of the February Revolution, alongside regimented tutelage.

Festivals of Russia's new freedom physically centred around the school, and ceremonies reinforced the metaphor of education through the prominent role of the teacher. Village instructors built upon courses and conversations begun at the beginning of the war and gave general speeches on the current moment and lectures on topics that they

[41] GAKO, f. 1345, op. 1, d. 22, l. 18.

believed should concern the peasantry. In Slobodskoi district, three thousand peasants celebrated the Holiday of the Revolution by attending a mass at the village square. They sang revolutionary songs and heard the local doctor speak about buying freedom bonds. The crowd proceeded to the school, where an arch had been built where on one side read, 'Learning is enlightenment, and ignorance is darkness', and on the other side was written, 'Welcome universal, free education'. The teacher gave a speech about the need for education before this backdrop.[42] The arch represented the agreement of educated society and peasants on educational reform. Educated society hoped that the revolution would finally bring enlightenment, both rationally and spiritually, to the people. Unimpeded by the tsarist autocracy, zemstvo officials and reformist administrators believed that they could fulfil their dreams of raising popular culture as they had dreamt at the start of the war. With education and cultural development, peasants could overcome their ignorance and become proper citizens.

Peasants used the emphasis on education to try to gain resources for their village schools to make their children literate and thus more capable of brokering relations with the larger society.[43] The Viatka zemstvo, spurred on by the peasantry, had consistently devoted more of its budget to primary schooling than any other province.[44] Peasant political declarations in 1905, and again in 1917, demanded that such schooling be free and universal. Peasants adopted elite rhetoric on educational enlightenment and cultural development to try to get the new government to repair or build a school in their village. For example, peasants in Petropavlovskaia *volost*, Iaransk district, had a meeting in which they unanimously supported the democratic republic of Russia and demanded the immediate opening of a school and reading hut in their area so their children would have 'the ability to enter a new life as enlightened citizens'.[45]

Provisional Government celebrations went well beyond general education and training of proper citizenship. They also foreshadowed Bolshevik holidays by mobilizing the masses for a targeted state aim. The government needed a way to motivate the population to fulfil the urgent necessities of the all-encompassing war – supplying food, materials, and human resources. For example, Liberty Bond Day rallied the people to support the government financially. The special edition newspaper, *Vo imia svobody Rossii* (In the name of the freedom of

---

[42] *Krest'ianskaia gazeta*, 6 June 1917, 11.
[43] Eklof, *Russian Peasant Schools*.   [44] Pape, 'The "Peasant Zemstva"', esp. 516–19.
[45] *Kukarskaia zhizn'*, 11 May 1917, 2.

Russia), called on comrades and citizens of Russia to 'do one's bit' to bond freedom.[46] It asked citizens to defend freedom by giving to those protecting the country (*rodina*). Repeating what the intelligentsia told the peasantry during the announcement of the Tsar's abdication, the newspaper asserted that freedom was not something to be taken for granted; it was everyone's duty.[47] As citizens, peasants had to pay for their freedom. Newspapers also attempted to convince the peasants to buy freedom bonds. For example, the top banner of the first issue of the *volost* newspaper, *Kukarskaia zhizn'*, announced: 'citizens, the fatherland (*rodina*) demands our effort in order to defeat the enemies. It needs grain, guns, arms, and shells, and for this it needs money.'[48] At meetings, officials and local elites spoke to the peasants about buying bonds and contributing foodstuffs to the government. The peasants listened and at holidays and meetings gave considerable donations for the war effort.

Peasants understood the transfer of governmental power as intrinsically linked to the military campaign. The tsarist regime had undermined the war effort, but the people's government would now direct the war properly. As at the beginning of war, many peasant communities in the early months of the revolution expressed renewed patriotic enthusiasm with symbolic donations of support for the redefined war.[49] In a general *skhod* on 9 March, peasants of Berezovskaia *volost*, Orlov district, elected a new local *volost* committee and sent the Provisional Government a telegram thanking it, 'for the great matter of giving Russia its freedom. Please receive this small contribution [of 74 rubles, 47 kopeks] as a gift for the soldiers in the trenches.'[50] Support for the war temporarily went beyond support just for the soldiers. Peasants of Shcherbininskaia *volost*, Viatka district, sent a 140 ruble donation for military needs along with a telegram to L'vov: 'We welcome the Provisional Government and are prepared to support all of its measures overseeing the homeland's (*rodnaia zemlia*) struggle with foreign enemies.'[51] Through the spring and early summer, peasant meetings sent donations to the Provisional Government. Villagers equated the Provisional

---

[46] *Vo imia svobody Rossii*, 25 June 1917, 1.

[47] *Vo imia svobody Rossii*, 25 June 1917, 2. On Liberty Bond Day celebrations in Petrograd, see von Geldern, *Bolshevik Festivals*, 19–20.

[48] *Kukarskaia zhizn'*, 30 April 1917, 1. The newspaper printed several similar messages to the people. For example, on 14 May 1917, a banner proclaimed, 'Today collect for freedom bonds. Citizens! (*Grazhdanki i grazhdane*) Sacrifice for a speedy victory over the enemy and for securing the achievements of freedom!'

[49] *Viatskaia rech'*, 31 May 1917, 4; 2 June 1917, 4; 7 June 1917, 4; 13 June 1917, 4; 17 June 1917, 4.

[50] *Viatskaia rech'*, 20 March 1917, 4.   [51] *Viatskaia rech'*, 11 April 1917, 3.

Government with the military effort and its early failure to end the hardships of war doomed its popular support.

Holidays were just one of several means that educated society used to try to create a new political language and tradition that did not include the tsars. Zemstvo agents and the rural intelligentsia taught the villagers how to speak in school, holidays, speeches, and newspapers. The zemstvo press put great effort into creating a new revolutionary language for the peasants and published brochures of revolutionary songs that contained such revolutionary songs as 'Dubinushka', the 'Marseillaise', and even the rarely heard 'Internationale', alongside popular folk songs like 'Ekh ty, dolia, moia dolia' and new songs that merged plebeian solidarity, assumed revolutionary dreams, and images of the Russian nation.[52] It also published a dictionary of common political and foreign terms for peasants to comprehend the political rhetoric of 1917. The pamphlet contained long explications of elections, democracy, specific political parties, and the land issue.[53]

Oath-taking became another symbolic ritual of power in which the state and educated society attempted to define and control peasant citizenship and loyalty. In mid-April, the provincial-level leaders passed an instruction down to the *volost ispolkom*s to have the local inhabitants take an oath (*prisiaga*) of loyalty to the Provisional Government. Like the revolutionary holidays, the church was intimately involved in the administration of the oaths. The district government directed the *volost ispolkom* to gather all the local inhabitants on the following Sunday or local holiday and have the parish priest or rector (*nastoiatel'*) of the local church give the oath. Everyone in the *volost*, both 'men and women' sixteen years and older were supposed to take the oath. The state now saw women as well as men as members of the political community.[54]

The state provided special instructions for 'citizens who are not Orthodox Christians'. They were instructed to take the oath before the head of the *volost* committee, rather than a clergyman, and did not have to make the sign of the cross when giving the oath. The fact that the state specified that non-Orthodox peasants were to take oaths before a member of the Provisional Government rather than one of their own clergymen, shows that the new political elite assumed the church as a

---

[52] *Pesni revoliutsii* (Slobodskoi, 1917); Kolonitskii, *Simvoly vlasti*, 16–18, 285–303; Badcock, *Politics and the People*, ch. 5.

[53] *Slovar'-spravochnik. Pri chtenii knig i gazet*, 2nd edn (Viatka, 1917).

[54] Oath-taking in the Viatka countryside, as in the French Revolution, represented a sacralization of citizenship and a bond of solemn loyalty between citizen and state. Lynn Hunt, *Politics, Culture, and Class in the French Revolution*, ed. V. E. Bonnell and Lynn Hunt (Berkeley, 1984), 27.

natural ally and viewed the loyalty of non-Orthodox clergy to the Russian state with suspicion. In this way, Provisional Government administrators continued tsarist military and state mistrust of Tatar Muslims. Pagans who would not take oaths due to religious beliefs were supposed to begin their oath with, 'By honour of a citizen I promise on my conscience to be loyal and perpetually dedicated to the Russian state as my Fatherland.' Muslims were to finish their oath as, 'Concluding my oath, with a kiss to the glorious Koran and sign below.'[55]

Like the public spectacles, the state's imposition of oaths was the immediate attempt to impose a new discourse of power, control, and order in the countryside. Peasants were certainly familiar with oath-taking, as swearing before a cross or an icon was common practice in village courts, and those who served in the army had taken an oath to serve upon conscription.[56] In the superstitious peasant world, an oath was an exceptionally serious undertaking. Russian peasants had a mixed reaction to the oaths. In Ishlyk village in Petropavlovskaia *volost*, Iaransk district, the villagers swore an oath to the Provisional Government. Father Zavarin, who would oversee the village's holiday four days later, explained the significance of the oath and urged the population to support the Provisional Government. The peasants immediately followed this up by acting out their own definition of citizenship under the new regime by organizing a local branch of the Peasant Union.[57]

The peasants of Ostrovnovskaia *volost*, Slobodskoi district, simply refused to take the oath based on their principles of citizenship. They stated that:

1. Free people do not need an oath and the people must not swear to the Provisional Government, but to the people.
2. All citizens of the *volost* know very well that they belong to the Russian state and thus do not need an oath to our fatherland, inasmuch as the composition of the government is provisional and may change.
3. All commands of the Provisional Government leading the people toward the strengthening of freedom will be precisely fulfilled by the population without an oath.[58]

Peasants of Ostrovnovskaia *volost* displayed a recondite understanding of political liberties and citizenship. They defended their rights as free

---

[55] GAKO, f. 1345, op. 1, d. 22, l. 25.
[56] Stephen Frank, *Crime, Cultural Conflict, and Justice in Rural Russia, 1856–1914* (Berkeley, 1999), 181–2.
[57] *Kukarskaia zhizn'*, 30 April 1917, 2.
[58] Resolution by the *volost ispolkom* on 26 April 1917, Bystrova et al., eds, *Ustanovlenie*, 116.

people while acknowledging their inherent duties as equal citizens to uphold the nation's interests.

Through building a new government administration and participating in national rituals, peasants, educated society, and regional state administrators reinvented what constituted the Russian nation. While all sides wanted popular participation in the new Russia, they had differing ideas of how the peasants should become citizens. However, peasants also understood their new rights and demanded freedom and equality guaranteed to them as citizens. Beneath the symbolic unity that the ceremonies of citizenship displayed in the early months of the revolution, the peasantry and elites held inherently different ideas about the role of the peasantry as citizens in the new Russian nation. Rather than unifying the countryside, rituals of power and the struggle to establish local administration helped create social-based politics.

Peasant politics and the nation

Peasants engaged Russia's political world through formal organizations and used them to promote their own social and political agendas. Political and public organizations, like celebratory rituals, flourished in the first months of revolution. Both gave meaning to the new political landscape and helped create political identities. In fact, many of the organizations were formed at holiday celebrations. Peasants built upon their experience in 1905 and in the war to create alliances with other social groups, learn the political discourse of the day, and became adroit political actors. Contemporaries, and many historians, have emphasized peasants' limited political aims of defending traditional interests, notably ownership of land, and their penchant for expressing political aims through violent action – seizing land, burning manors, and creating general mayhem.[59] While control of land was a central aim of peasants' political dreams, revolution meant far more than that one local issue, especially for those residing outside the Black Earth region. Indeed, in Viatka, where most peasants did not endure antagonism with the gentry, peasants expressed their revolutionary visions in popular interaction with elite politics and nation building.

Thousands of villagers joined groups with wide political objectives. The 1905 Revolution in this regard acted as a dress rehearsal for 1917.[60]

---

[59] See, for example, Figes, *A People's Tragedy*, 331.
[60] Roberta Manning convincingly shows that peasants in Smolensk province built on their political experiences in 1905. 'Bolshevik Without the Party: Sychevka in 1917', in Donald J. Raleigh, ed., *Provincial Landscapes: Local Dimensions of Soviet Power, 1917–1953* (Pittsburgh, 2001), 36–58.

Older peasants' memories of political activism and the legacy of structural organizations guided political developments in the spring of 1917.
As in 1905, peasants formed local associations and sent representatives
to provincial and national congresses where they discussed national
matters of importance to them. While peasant organizations did not
enjoy the political weight of urban-based soviets, they played a major
role in local and district-level politics.[61] The historical significance of
peasant organizations lies beyond their immediate political might,
though. Peasants actively participated in local organizations with the
understanding that they were part of a national political order. They
discussed, debated, and passed resolutions on a number of issues – the
war, deserters, foodstuff campaigns, land reforms, and the role of capitalism in international economics that went far beyond localist views.

Peasant discussions and participation in political organizations show
that they had a complex view of national events and attempted to
influence state policies. They also exercised power by countering and
negotiating state proclamations. As with local administrative reform
and rituals of citizenship, peasant acceptance of tutelage from above
in political organization was short-lived. Peasants preferred to engage in
politics to unite and promote the interests of the working people of
Russia. This was an imagined community – the peasant nation – that
linked this socio-economic group beyond individuals' village or *volost*.
Peasants' sense of social unity trumped party politics or adherence to a
party platform.

Village political activism in Viatka quickly coalesced around the
All-Russian Peasant Union (*Vserossiiskii Krest'ianskii Soiuz*), a loosely
structured organization with the aim of promoting peasant interests.
Formed in the summer of 1905 in Moscow by a group of liberal
socialists, the Peasant Union gained wide support in villages throughout
Russia, including Viatka. In its short lifetime, peasants formed village
and *volost* chapters, sent representatives to a congress in Moscow, and
used the organization to engage in radical political change by over-
throwing *volost* governments and demanding land and tax reform, universal education, and local control of government, only to be suppressed
by the government.[62] Peasant Union members had wide political goals

---

[61] V. M. Lavrov, '*Krest'ianskii parlament' Rossii (Vserossiiskie s''ezdy sovetov krest'ianskikh deputatov v 1917–1918 godakh)* (Moscow, 1996).

[62] A. A. Kurenyshev, *Vserossiiskii krest'ianskii soiuz 1905–1930 gg.: Mify i real'nost'* (Moscow, 2004), 20–34; Scott Seregny, 'A Different Type of Peasant Movement: The Peasant Unions in the Russian Revolution of 1905', *Slavic Review* 47 (1988): 51–67. See Oliver Radkey, *The Agrarian Foes of Bolshevism: Promise and Default of the Russian Socialist Revolutionaries, February to October 1917* (New York, 1958), 60, 244;

and, as Scott Seregny notes, their activity 'reveals the existence of an organized peasant movement seeking to effect agrarian reform, civil and political rights, local control, and access to education through political channels and in concert with other groups'.[63] In early March 1917, moderate socialists affiliated with the Popular Socialist Party revived the Peasant Union in Moscow and chapters quickly blossomed in Ukraine, southern Russia, Siberia, and other peripheral regions, rooting themselves much deeper than in 1905.[64] In Viatka, prominent moderate socialist intellectuals, fronted by the populist and leading Popular Socialist figure Nikolai Charushin, reorganized a provincial committee on 18 March and local chapters throughout the province followed.[65] By June, every *volost* but three in the whole province boasted a *volost*-level chapter. In Nolinsk district alone, up to twenty-seven thousand people joined the Peasant Union.[66]

District government and zemstvo administration advanced the Peasant Union to be the political representation of the peasantry as a social estate. With hints of corporatism, the Peasant Union was to advance peasant needs to the Provisional Government while preparing the population for the Constituent Assembly election.[67] The Peasant Union central leadership believed that they could build a supraparty organization in which 'a Socialist Revolutionary, a Social Democrat, a People's Socialist, and a person without party loyalty could enter'.[68] However, the Union platform reflected the organizers' political moderation. It demanded that members fully support the Provisional Government, execute all decrees including its unconditional war aims, do not seize land and forests without authorization, and 'wait peacefully for the Constituent Assembly to decide these matters'. It also called for members to contribute to foodstuffs committees and participate in the cultural–educational activities of the zemstvo and other organizations.[69]

A. A. Papyrina, *Revoliutsionnoe dvizhenie v Viatskoi gubernii v 1905–1907 gg.* (Kirov, 1975), 85–95.

[63] Seregny, 'Peasant Unions', 67.

[64] E. M. Shchagin, 'Revoliutsiia, vlast', politicheskie partii i sud'by vsekrest'ianskoi organizatsii v Rossii', in A. F. Kielev, ed., *Vlast' i obshchestvennye organizatsii v Rossii v pervoi treti XX stoletiia* (Moscow, 1993), 51.

[65] *Viatskaia rech'*, 19 March 1917, in Bystrova et al., eds, *Ustanovlenie*, 97.

[66] Report from A. I. Moshkin, a provisional member of the Viatka province *ispolkom*, 9 August 1917 in A. V. Shestakov, *Sovety krest'ianskikh deputatov i drugie krest'ianskie organizatsii*, tom 1, ch. 1 [Mart–Oktiabr' 1917 g.] (Moscow, 1929), 118; E. D. Popova, *Krest'ianskie komitety Viatskoi gubernii v 1917 godu* (Kirov, 1966), 5.

[67] Daniel Orlovsky, 'Corporatism or Democracy: The Russian Provisional Government of 1917', *The Soviet and Post-Soviet Review* 24 (1997): 15–25.

[68] Quotes in Shchagin, 'Revoliutsiia, vlast", 50.

[69] *Kak ustroit' krest'ianskii soiuz*, (Viatka, 1917), 6; GAKO, f. 1353, op. 1, d. 2, ll. 1, 9–68.

As in 1905, zemstvo workers, like cooperative instructors, played a leading role in organizing *volost* and village chapters.[70] A representative would appear at a meeting or revolutionary holiday and discuss the national situation and the promise of the Peasant Union. As when the rural intelligentsia read and explained the fall of the Tsar to peasants, these mediators between peasant society and the nation helped to bring villages into the national political scene. The Peasant Union reinforced the themes of the rituals of revolution and citizenship – active political participation, cultural and spiritual enlightenment, and economic support of the government and war. The organization of Peasant Union chapters, then, was tightly bound to other revolutionary rituals of citizenship orchestrated by educated society. In other cases, the *volost starshina*, who probably remembered the Union from twelve years earlier, received word from zemstvo, government, or Union representatives and organized the local chapter. In regions with a strong tradition of worker out-migration, a local returned and helped to organize chapters, as happened in Malmyzh district where a master worker in the Izhevsk factory returned to his *volost* to form chapters of the Peasant Union. The latter case was rare, as peasant workers were drawn towards soviets and more overt party politics.[71]

The Peasant Union movement swept through the countryside. *Volost skhod*s passed the same model resolution of support drawn up by the Peasant Union and established a local chapter.[72] Once the campaign gathered steam in mid-May the statement even changed from handwritten to machine-copied. Peasants gave their written support for the Union platform and welcomed the alliance with the zemstvo and educated society. The political goals of village communes, if not individual peasants, coincided with the corporatism of the Peasant Union leadership. Most peasants saw themselves as peasants first in the political struggle and eagerly joined the organization that promised to promote these interests beyond the village. The proclamation behind which they had put their vote supported the Union to improve the deteriorating situation for the working peasantry and to establish 'freedom, equality, and brotherhood'. Villagers added proclamations, consciously placing

---

[70] GAKO, f. 1345, op. 1, d. 22, ll. 32–3.
[71] GAKO, f. R-885, op. 1, d. 48, ll. 53–4. Some *zemliachestva* (fellow-villager associations) organizations from Moscow helped form Peasant Unions in Vladimir province. A. S. Smirnov, 'Zemliacheskie organizatsii rabochikh i soldat v 1917 g.', *Istoricheskie zapiski* 60 (1957), 95. On *zemliachestvo* in general, see Michael C. Hickey, 'Urban Zemliachestva and Rural Revolution: Petrograd and the Smolensk Countryside in 1917', *The Soviet and Post-Soviet Review* 23 (1996): 143–59.
[72] The *volost skhod* was the official way to organize a local chapter. *Kak ustroit'*, 3.

their Peasant Union chapter as part of a larger imagined community of all peasants throughout Russia. A common refrain in resolutions stated that only the unity of the peasantry could improve its condition.[73] Peasant Unions acted as the political arm of the commune or *volost,* reaching out to the provincial and even national political scene, a point made by the Savali village *skhod* when it resolved to 'join our commune with the peasant All Russian Union' because it promised to 'defend peasant interests before the government'.[74]

Since peasants formed Union chapters at the democratized *skhod,* women witnessed and voiced their approval for its formation. They were by no means equal participants. Like other *skhod*s during the war, women signed as surrogates of their male partners. Some labelled themselves as a *soldatka,* to mark their temporary social position. Active female membership in the Union, though, varied by village. While in many of Viatka's villages, no women were represented as members in the Peasant Union, in others up to twenty per cent of the participants were women.[75] Moreover, women were almost never elected to Union councils or as representatives to district congresses. Women, like others traditionally excluded from power in the village, participated more frequently in the newly democratized public meetings, but their limited participation mirrors gender roles in other peasant activities in the public sphere in 1917.[76] Few women went beyond roles that supported their own survival or the welfare of the home and family.

The probability of a village organizing a local chapter depended on geography and personality more than anything else. Villages near provincial cities, major roadways, or the railroad organized more quickly than those located away from the economic intersections. For example, the prominent village of Savali, located just north of the city of Malmyzh, where two major roads intersected and an agricultural school sat, organized a chapter on 3 April.[77] Most of the other villages in Malmyzh district did not form cells until the end of April and the beginning of May. Ethnicity did not play a strong role at first in political

---

[73] GAKO, f. 1353, op. 1, d. 2, ll. 2–2ob.

[74] Resolution of Savali village *skhod,* 3 April 1917. Bystrova et al., eds, *Ustanovlenie,* 101.

[75] GAKO, f. R-885, op. 1, d. 48, ll. 6ob–7; f. 1353, op. 1, d. 3, l. 24; f. 1353, op. 1, d. 2, ll. 1, 2–2ob, 6, 24–5, 26ob–7, 28ob–9, 40ob–1, 58ob–9. Out of a random sample of ten villages, the average percentage of women as the total number of participants was seven per cent.

[76] Figes, *Peasant Russia,* 33; Badcock, *Politics and the People,* ch. 7.

[77] GAKO, f. 1353, op. 1, d. 2, ll. 1–2ob. The same pattern occurred in Urzhum district where, for example, Buiskaia *volost,* located just north of the town of Urzhum and containing a factory, organized a local chapter on 4 April. *Krest'ianskaia gazeta,* 2 May 1917, 13.

participation in the Peasant Union, as Russian and non-Russian villages organized chapters with equal frequency.[78]

The dominance of a cohesive Union under the platform that its leadership envisioned lasted only a short time in the countryside. The Union competed with other organized political parties in a countryside radicalized by war and foodstuffs crises and a society fracturing along class lines against 'bourgeois' elements. Villages appropriated the Union organization, but felt no allegiance to its platform. Soviets soon challenged its authority in the countryside as well. In mid-May, the SR-dominated Viatka soviet began to reach out to the peasants. Delegates travelled all the way to Malmyzh district where they discussed the current situation with the same *volost skhods* that a month earlier had welcomed Peasant Union representatives.[79] This time the peasants issued identical *prigovory* supporting the soviet position. In the resolution language the soviets played off popular nationalism and class interests. In flowery prose, the *skhods* reframed their support for the war defending freedom against the Germans and 'the despot Kaiser' as 'free citizens of the Russian state (*gosudarstvo*)', along with 'all true citizens of Russia' who are 'moved by patriotic feeling and love for our people's army'. They now only conditionally supported the new Provisional Government coalition, as long as 'representatives of the people's democratic masses' were represented; they sent greetings to the Petrograd and Viatka soviets, called for the quick convening of the Constituent Assembly, and all land to toiling people.[80] The most powerful workers soviet in the province emerged in Izhevsk and dominated the politics of the city. Representatives of the Izhevsk soviet spread out in the surrounding areas and along in-migrant worker paths. The Kronstadt soviet sent agitators to their native districts, including Iaransk and Viatka, to agitate for the end of war, the immediate seizure of land, and support for the Bolsheviks, with only limited success.[81]

---

[78] GAKO, f. 1353, op. 1, d. 2, ll. 2, 4, 6–7. The predominantly Udmurt village of Tyloval-Pel'ga, Velipel'ginskaia *volost*, Malmyzh district, and the mixed Udmurt–Russian village of Izopel'ga of the same *volost*, both organized local chapters at the end of April. The largely Tatar *volost* of Starotrykinskaia, the mixed Tatar–Russian *volost*, Viatskaia-Polianskaia, and the mixed Russian–Mari Serdykbazhskaia *volost* also formed chapters of the Peasant Union.

[79] Badcock has found that soviets in Kazan and Nizhegorod provinces also sent representatives to enlighten the peasants, even though the Peasant Union there did not represent a major political challenger. 'Talking to the People and Shaping Revolution: The Drive for Enlightenment in Revolutionary Russia', *The Russian Review* 65 (2006): 617–36.

[80] GAKO, f. 1345, op. 1, d. 204, ll. 63–6ob, 77–77ob, 80–1, 83–4ob, 86–86ob. Quote on l. 63; GA RF, f. 1791, op. 2, d. 178b, l. 34.

[81] Smirnov, 'Zemliacheskie organizatsii', 99, 102–3. The provincial Provisional Government even drove out a native Viatka resident turned Kronstadt agitator, Pavel Khokhliakov,

The peasants balanced multiple political visions – a more conservative Peasant Union in line with the Provisional Government platform and state, and its dream to be non-class based, and the class-based soviet. The Peasant Union had an early advantage as older peasants remembered it as the political mobilizer in 1905. Villagers' political dreams broadened quickly in 1917 and the revolution itself was more democratic and better suited for soviets. Peasants had the option to ally with the apparently moderate Peasant Union and the worker-based, more radical soviets. Peasants decided to ally with both. Peasants did not see a problem in being a member of a Peasant Union under a national or provincial peasant soviet, a point the peasants from Savali, and several other communities, stated in proclamations in the spring.

The debate over Union or soviet power, though, was not contested on the village or *volost* level. The fight for the peasant voice erupted at district and provincial peasant congresses in May and early June. Peasant representatives from almost every *volost* gathered alongside worker delegates from urban soviets, rural intellectuals, and members of urban educated society at the district centre to discuss national politics and organize for upcoming elections. Congress protocols varied widely among the districts. The Congress of the Urzhum Peasantry and the Peasant Congress in Glazov issued wide-ranging, radical programmes on 7 May. The Glazov congress supported an expropriation of land owned by landlords and Stolypin separators, and transfer of these lands and state, monastery, church, and crown land to a general fund. It failed to mention waiting for the Constituent Assembly. The congress also demanded an eight-hour day and a forty-two-hour working week, a progressive income tax and exemption for the poor, far-reaching personal freedoms, and the right of education for both sexes to age sixteen in the native language. It also condemned the war as a capitalist tool.[82] Peasant representatives at the First Peasant Congress of Malmyzh District were more fractured over the war and fiercely debated war aims. A minority no longer saw Germans as the enemy and praised Kaiser Wilhelm's intelligence and kindness towards his people. Instead they viewed the war as a struggle against capitalism. The majority argued

from the province; E. I. Kiriukina, *Ocherki istorii Kirovskoi organizatsii KPSS.* (Kirov, 1965), 404, 426–7.

[82] *Krest'ianskaia gazeta*, 19 May 1917, 8; 23 May 1917, 10; *Izvestiia Kotel'nicheskago vremennago ispolnitel'nago komiteta*, 14 May 1917, 10–11. The Slobodskoi District Congress of Peasant Deputies issued similar proclamations – that workers and peasants must be united in the struggle for truth and freedom, and that the government must initiate an eight-hour working day, defend female and child labourers, and implement insurance for workers. E. S. Sadyrina, *Oktiabr' v Viatksoi gubernii* (Kirov, 1957), 56–7.

against a separate peace and held the Provisional Government's position, 'to carry on the war mercilessly and with increased energy', and to turn the war into 'a people's war for law, justice, independence, and freedom'.[83] Glazov, Malmyzh, and Sarapul, the three districts closest to the Izhevsk soviet, transformed all their Union organizations into soviets of peasant deputies.[84] At what was otherwise an amicable meeting at the Viatka district peasant congress, urban leaders of the Peasant Union fought with soviet liaisons over renaming and reorganizing the congress. While the Peasant Union name remained, delegates resolved to establish parallel organizations, overlapping soviet and Peasant Union power.[85]

By the First Provincial Peasant Congress, held in the city of Viatka from 6 to 10 June, the Peasant Union's meteoric rise was over. The Peasant Union had organized the congress and the organizational committee acknowledged the Union's role by electing its leader, Charushin, as honorary chair. Almost half of the *volost* Peasant Union chapters and rural soviets sent representatives, many of whom were peasants. Most speakers, however, came from the intelligentsia and SR leadership, a point of contention in the halls. Although the overlapping group of moderate SRs and Popular Socialists had prominence in the provincial-level Provisional Government and soviet, the final congress resolutions followed the leftist district congresses. They also replicated the fracture between the Peasant Union and soviets that the SRs pushed through at the national All-Russian Congress of Peasant Deputies held in Petrograd in May. The First Provincial Peasant Congress claimed loyalty to the Petrograd Soviet and passed moderate socialist resolutions, including support of the Provisional Government, as long as it worked in unison with the soviet. It rejected the government's war aims and stood behind Revolutionary Defencism. While stating that the final decision on land must be provided by the Constituent Assembly, it still resolved that the land question must be decided in the interests of those who worked the land and that 'all citizens of the Russian state have the right to land so long as they work it under their own labour'. Most alarmingly to the Peasant Union leadership, the congress repeated the national Congress of Peasant Deputies' attacks on the Peasant Union's local organization as 'unable to satisfy the basic demands of the present moment' for its universal, non-class based membership. The congress

---

[83] GAKO, f. 1353, op. 1, d. 1, ll. 1–5; quote on l. 2.
[84] Shestakov, *Sovety krest'ianskikh deputatov*, 118; Bystrova et al., eds, *Ustanovlenie*, 128–30.
[85] *Krest'ianskaia gazeta*, 9 June 1917, 11–12; Shestakov, *Sovety krest'ianskikh deputatov*, 116–17.

condemned the Peasant Union since, 'It is in essence an individual party in which half-conscious peasants join, rather than all the masses of the working peasantry. Moreover, the most conscious members are leaving to socialist parties.'[86]

For a short time, the Peasant Union channelled political power alongside the Provisional Government and the soviet. Sarah Badcock has shown in Kazan and Nizhegorod provinces province that the term dual power does not adequately convey the diffusion of power in the provinces in 1917.[87] The same held true in Viatka. The Peasant Union in Viatka decentralized power across the countryside, where its base lived. Members sat on social mediation, provision, and land committees as equals with representatives of the provincial-level soviet, *ispolkom*, and commissar. Peasant Union members also briefly controlled the Malmyzh *ispolkom* in the summer.[88] As a decentralized mediator of power, the Peasant Union challenged the authority of soviet and Provisional Government power. In Petrograd and Viatka, the Congress of Peasant Deputies and the SRs wrested power from the Peasant Union, but the organization collapsed for larger reasons.

The Peasant Union leadership's dreams of a centrist supraclass organization failed because peasants were not satisfied with the Union leadership's visions of state power limited to social mediation.[89] By the late spring, peasants sought a more active government with radical political solutions. They also felt more kinship to other toilers than they did to rural intellectuals. The Peasant Union's decentralized structure gave peasants the room to keep the organizational apparatus, but safely reject its platform. This happened in Iaransk district and other locales that retained their appellation, but charted more aggressive policies. Many *volost* Peasant Union chapters followed the provincial peasant congress recommendation and relabelled themselves soviets. Nevertheless, they continued relations with the district- and provincial-level Peasant Union. In *volost*s the Peasant Union and soviets served as public organizations linking the local to the provincial and national political scene. In a short time, peasants showed their ability to organize and make strategic alliances with non-peasants. They parlayed their experience under the tutelage of rural educated society and the Peasant Union into class-based peasant soviets and congresses, which would dominate the political world of the countryside in 1917.

[86] GASPI KO, f. 45, op. 1, d. 118, ll. 6–32. Quotes on ll. 22 and 29. The Peasant Union experienced a similar trajectory in Saratov. Raleigh, *Revolution on the Volga*, 180–1.
[87] Badcock, *Politics and the People*.   [88] Bystrova et al., eds, *Ustanovlenie*, 105–7.
[89] Hickey sees the demise of liberal *obshchestvennost'* dreams in Smolensk, 'Discourses of Public Identity', 615–37; Rosenberg, 'Social Mediation', 169–88.

Peasants in Viatka proclaimed loyalty and melded their identity to peasant public organizations, not political parties. In part this was because the peasant-oriented SR Party did not actively campaign through the Viatka countryside as it did in several other central provinces.[90] The lack of party alliance did not inhibit Viatka's peasants from joining the national process and displaying amazing power for political change. As in 1905, however, the ruling body was unwilling to accept peasants as equal members of the polity, leading the population to accept more radical political organizations in the years to come.

Beyond opening up emancipatory politics for the peasant estate, the Revolution also highlighted ethnic and national differences. Udmurt and Mari peasants came into the Revolution with a strong sense of ethnic identity with a distinct language, culture, and customs, but had not envisioned the ideological demand for a nation-based state. Their national agents (urban and rural teachers, clergymen, zemstvo agents, and other members of educated society who championed their ethnic or national identity), though, could now embrace their national identity without fear of political reprisal.[91] Freedom of the press and the popular obsession with political organization and congresses allowed national agents to create arenas to coalesce and mobilize their ethnic group, telescoping the development of national identity. These agents built upon a history of popular resistance to Russification and national cultural work enhanced by the relaxation of censorship during the war.

National agents organized a series of regional and provincial congresses to promote national awareness and cultural autonomy. In mid-May, representatives of non-Russians of the Volga region met in Kazan, which included an Udmurt (Votiak) section. The following month, Mari leaders came together for their First All-Russian Congress of Mari. In July, national minorities held a provincial congress and Muslims formed a Muslim soviet. In September, Maris held their first provincial congress. Educational autonomy dominated all the congresses. National agents accepted elite notions of non-Russians' backwardness but used them as a means to gain resources for education. They argued that the tsarist regime's policy of Russification had culturally oppressed their nationality by only teaching their children Russian. Mari, Udmurt, and Tatar youths must be educated by teachers of their own nationality in

[90] Sarah Badcock, '"We're for the Muzhiks' Party!" Peasant Support for the Socialist Revolutionary Party During 1917', *Europe–Asia Studies* 53 (2001):133–49.
[91] Wade, *The Russian Revolution*, 147–8.

their mother tongue, representatives argued.[92] The Mari provincial congress resolved to establish schools to teach Mari culture, history, ethnography, and geography in the mother tongue and to prepare teachers from the Mari population. It also resolved to open libraries and reading huts with books and newspapers in Mari.[93]

Nationality politics, though, accented non-Russian peasants' distinction from the larger nation. While Udmurt, Mari, and to a lesser extent Tatar peasants lived alongside Russian peasants, traded with them, and shared many of the same political dreams of political emancipation, they held different cultural traditions. Demands for a differential citizenship, greater cultural autonomy with equal political rights, had resonance among non-Russian peasants who had compromised cultural traditions and fought against the Imperial regime. Such nationality politics that fostered ethnic identity, though, also undermined the democratic experiment in the countryside and the national project by solidifying non-Russians' place on the margins of the nation. As will be seen in the next chapter, the growing political and provisions crises in the summer and autumn further marginalized non-Russians, especially Udmurts and Tatars, whom educated society targeted as corruptive and pernicious populations in democratic Russia.

Conclusion

What is most striking about the end of the tsarist regime in the Viatka countryside is how peaceful was the transition to a new government and how focussed were the peasants on establishing a new political system. In the first months of the democratic regime, peasants listened to rural intellectuals on how to practice citizenship and willingly bound themselves to the state. They briefly accepted elite language, symbols, and cultural constructions that put peasants in a position of apprenticeship. While peasants were at first content to follow the political elites' rituals of power and instructions for political tutelage, by summer they had gained sufficient experience to express their visions on the regional and even national political world and their political ideals increasingly differed from their elite leaders.

---

[92] O. I. Vasil'eva, *Udmurtskaia intelligentsiia. Formirovanie i deiatel'nost'. 1917–1941 gg.* (Izhevsk, 1999), 15–16; N. P. Pavlov, *Samoopredelenie, avtonomiia: Idei, realii* (Izhevsk, 2000), 20–9.

[93] *Kukarskaia zhizn'*, 30 July 1917, 2; 21 September 1917, 2; *Krest'ianskaia gazeta*, 28 July 1917, 12–13; *Postanovleniia i resheniia s"ezda mari (cheremis') Viatskoi gubernii* (Viatka, 1917).

The Provisional Government created democratic institutions and fostered social practices to develop popular citizenship but failed to develop long-lasting support for the regime. Members of educated society who had taken power attempted to create peasant citizens based on their long-held notions of how peasants were supposed to act. Their restricted views, along with their ideology rooted in the enlightenment tradition with all its trappings of cultural evolution, created a disconnect between peasant and state. While both sides wanted popular participation in the new Russia, they had different ideas of how the peasants should become citizens. Rather than unifying society, the elite political symbols and relationship of spring 1917 widened social fissures and helped to breed social and class identity. By the summer, where we now turn, tensions from the political relationship exacerbated the crises of provisions, land, the war, and growing social instability in the countryside. Peasants threw off their political tutelage, state officials reverted to coercion to force the population to act as they wanted, and the democratic experiment quickly collapsed.

3   Peasant and nation in revolution

The February Revolution promised that all citizens could participate in political change and transform economics to build a more just and equitable society. Peasants' fight for peace, land, and bread was therefore tied to their participation in national politics. Peasants believed that they had a right to land and natural resources, not only as people who believed that the land had always been theirs, but also as equal members of the political community. They welcomed state intervention to resolve these issues. When state agents turned to coercive policies to get grain from peasants, however, peasant citizens resisted this revocation of the terms of citizenship and rejected the Provisional Government experiment as a whole.

By the summer of 1917, the honeymoon between peasants and the political leaders was over. Peasants bristled under elite constructions of them as politically backward and unable to form political action. Peasants increasingly clashed with rural elites and demanded an equal voice as full citizens in the political world. Through the drawn out preparation for national electors, and culminating in the Constituent Assembly elections, most peasants became disillusioned with elite politics and wanted instead their own representatives who championed peasant causes within an evermore fractious nation. The political elite's failure to accept popular peasant participation in the Russian nation's reinvention must be placed alongside the Provisional Government's other major shortcomings – the war, land reform, and food – in an assessment of why it could never achieve the popular support necessary for survival.

Peasant dreams and the politics of land and grain

For many peasants the revolution grounded their economic claims for access to natural resources in the political world. Peasant communities in the Black Earth region notoriously seized land and burned the manors of their landlords. In stark contrast to the vaunted tales from the Black Earth region, Viatka did not experience a wave of unauthorized peasant land seizures. A national congress of provincial commissars even noted that Viatka was one of the calmest provinces in the spring of 1917.[1] The economic structure of much of Viatka, as well as the northern European Russian and Siberian regions, partly explains this. All lacked an entrenched landlord tenure system and peasants did not suffer from land hunger to the extent of those in the Black Earth region. Peasants of Viatka therefore did not have one figure on whom to focus their attention. When placed in the context of the larger political world, the Viatka peasants acted in much the same way as other peasants of Russia, who hoped to gain greater access to the resources that were so important to the rural economy. Some peasant communes and individuals engaged in unauthorized acts to claim or utilize natural resources and did so increasingly as the sense of economic crisis grew. Most often, though, peasants pursued a concurrent legal, interactive campaign with the government to win access to much-needed resources. The peasantry built upon existing discourses of justice and moral responsibility to justify both actions.

Villages and communes acted as one to take advantage of the overthrow of the tsarist order and claim land and forests that they had coveted. Seizures of merchant and landlord estate land in the southern districts received the most press and space in the official documents as it was what educated society feared the most, but such heated clashes were rare. The main focus of peasant aggression was over public (*kazennaia*) forests and lands that surrounded many villages in the central and northern districts. Chesnovko village, Iaransk district, was surrounded by public forest and residents could not expand their already small plots. Locals were forced to resettle in search of arable land. Villagers demanded the right to clear enough forest to ease their land hunger, graze their cattle for free, and collect three *sazhen*'s (twenty-one feet) of dead wood and fallen trees per house (*na pechku*). The peasants grounded their demands in political rights as free citizens (*svobodnye grazhdane i grazhdanki*) and in moral economics as a measure to stave off starvation. Peasants also took extra legal measures and began to hoard wood from forests as winter neared. The incidents of illegal felling in public forests became epidemic and the provincial commissar requested troops from Moscow to be sent to guard them.[2]

Ironically, when peasants finally had the possibility of obtaining more land, most households continued to suffer from a shortage of working

[1] *Kukarskaia zhizn'*, 18 May 1917, 2; GA RF, f. 1788, op. 2, d. 64, l. 12.
[2] Bystrova et al., eds, *Ustanovlenie*, 142–4, 179–80.

hands and struggled to work their existing land allotments. Voluntary demobilization and the military's release of soldiers over the age of forty to work in the fields provided some relief, but certainly not enough. Viatka's agricultural economy was already in decline.

Land also held great importance for the public and government leaders. Peasant land seizures underscored public fears that the countryside was descending into a state of rampant crime and anarchy. The agricultural ministry also fretted over an adequate food supply to the army and cities and so was intent on maintaining land productivity. Agriculture ministers delayed a major land reform that could upset production until the Constituent Assembly and their chant for patience was echoed in Viatka by the provincial newspapers, Peasant Union, and soviets. This promise of a future state-approved land redistribution became intertwined with peasant notions of the Constituent Assembly and they too stated in petitions and resolutions that the land question must be resolved by the Constituent Assembly. In the meantime, the government adopted minor land policies to increase productivity, such as allowing peasants to use unsown fields and the tsar's former land. The inability to devise a system to encourage producers to give up their grain undermined these efforts.

In April, the Provisional Government established a network of land committees with the limited goal of preparing for land reform by inventorying land, as well as resolving land disputes and ensuring reliable agricultural productivity.[3] The provincial and district committees, both controlled by zemstvo leadership, began to meet in mid-summer.[4] *Volost* land committees established themselves only in the late autumn.[5] Until then, the *volost ispolkom*, commune, or the barely working court system resolved local land issues. District land committees were the most active bodies in dealing with land.

District committees went beyond their jurisdiction to seek economic relief for peasants. In late August, the Elabuga district land committee took the radical step of calling for all unpopulated land to be distributed, settled, and put under the plough by winter. It also attempted to limit the exploitation of tenant peasants by tackling stifling rent payments.

---

[3] *Elabuzhskaia malen'kaia narodnaia gazeta*, 28 May 1917, 3. Dorothy Atkinson, *The End of the Russian Land Commune, 1905–1930* (Stanford, 1983), 123.

[4] GASPI KO, f. 45, op. 1, d. 143, l. 48. The Viatka district land committee first met on 5 June and the Iaransk district land committee on 17 June. Ten of the eleven district land committees were formed in June and July and by September all districts had land committees. Popova, *Krest'ianskie komitety Viatskoi gubernii v 1917 godu*, 20.

[5] GAKO, f. 1362, op. 1, d. 2, ll. 1–44. In Urzhum district, they were formed as late as October and November.

Plots of rented land had to be categorized by their quality and annual rent assessed accordingly; good land could not be charged over eight rubles, average land not over five, and poor land not over three rubles per *desiatina*. Rent for glades was limited to five rubles and if the existing rent was higher, the leaser had to return the extra money.[6] The zealousness of the district land committees stemmed in part from the ambiguous and overlapping administration, but also because members were committed to relieving the economic burden on peasants.

Peasant interaction with land committees shows villagers' willingness to use legal means to gain access to land and resources and to continue legal traditions established under the tsarist regime. In Viatka district, peasants filed complaints to the land committee even before it was formed when their struggles for land were denied by their *volost* administration.[7] Villagers also sent petitions to all levels of government, evoking the state's moral responsibility to its people and grounding claims on a peasant sense of justice.

If peasants believed that they had a right to land and resources, the state and urban dwellers posited that they had a right to its output. The food supply crisis destabilized the economy and radicalized both state action and peasant politics. The Provisional Government inherited a food supply system in freefall, unable to entice peasants to give up grain reliably or to distribute grain when peasants did deliver. By the end of 1916, the tsarist regime had even flirted with forced requisitions. The Provisional Government put its faith in the state to solve this fundamental problem. On 25 March, the Commission on Food Supply claimed ownership of all the nation's grain. The law instructed newly established *volost*-level provisions committees to determine the amount of grain that each peasant household needed, to allow the household to keep an additional ten per cent in case of unforeseen events, and to claim the remaining grain for state needs. The Provisional Government maintained the fixed price system established in September 1916 to compensate producers.[8] The grain monopoly continued the militarization of the village and extended the state's ability to intervene in individuals' economic lives.

The state's grain policy created a means to obtain grain from peasants, but gave little incentive beyond altruism and revolutionary zeal for the population to sacrifice its crops.[9] Most importantly, the government refused to establish a parallel monopoly on the non-agricultural basic goods that peasants desired, such as manufactured goods, salt, fuel, and

[6] GA RF, f. 1791, op. 6, d. 78, l. 12.   [7] GASPI KO, f. 45, op. 1, d. 143, l. 53.
[8] Lih, *Bread and Authority*, 57–80.   [9] Holquist, *Making War*, 96–8.

matches. The state-determined grain prices, raised slightly from 1916, still did not match the inflation on these items, when they were even available. To make matters worse, the government also rescinded its reimbursement to peasants for carting grain from the village to the supply stations, a decision that especially affected peasants in Viatka's vast countryside who had to travel on average 69 versts (46 miles) and, in extreme situations, 150 versts (99.5 miles) to deliver their grain.[10] The grain monopoly could not compete with the more profitable, and more convenient, black market.

Collections of grain and money were held during celebrations of the revolution, linking the new freedom to sacrifices of grain and the village donations widely publicized in the socialist and the moderate liberal press. Newspaper banners played on national unity, reading, 'Comrade peasants! Harvest grain for your starving brothers!'[11] Nevertheless, these actions failed to produce sufficient grain for the cities and army. Initial dreams that rural producers would distribute grain for revolutionary Russia were quickly dashed as few communities donated or even sold their grain.

Peasants let zemstvo administrators and moderate members of educated society take the lead in the political sphere in the early days of the revolution, but rejected their terms in the economic relationship. Peasants were unwilling to threaten their lives for the public good when the state refused to provide for them. The Provisional Government had not established a moral relationship with the population in which the peasantry would agree to an amount of exploitation in exchange for the guarantee of subsistence welfare. This hesitancy was seen as the Congress of Peasant Deputies in June welcomed the grain monopoly for 'freeing the peasantry from the power of sackmen', but demanded that the government provide equitable prices on manufactured goods. It also called for more state intervention: 'The government must immediately and decisively enter into the economic life of the country to plan and assist in the output of the most demanded provisions.'[12] By the autumn peasant communities regularly complained of the state's urban bias and demanded reciprocity. The Uninskaia *volost* assembly, Glazov district, wrote to the provincial commissar that it 'protests the establishment of fixed prices on agricultural products and demands the introduction of those very prices on fabricated goods of city industries needed in village

[10] I. Sigov, *Arakcheevskii sotsializm: Doklad o khlebnoi monopolii, zaslushannyi Vol'no-Ekonomicheskim Obshchestvom 25 maia 1917 goda* (Petrograd, 1917), 10.
[11] *Elabuzhskaia malen'kaia narodnaia gazeta*, 27 May 1917, 2–3.
[12] GASPI KO, f. 45, op. 1, d. 18, l. 14; *Postanovleniia gubernskago krest'ianskago s"ezda v Viatke 6–10 iiunia 1917 goda* (Viatka, 1917), 5.

Plate 8. Peasant market, 1917. Courtesy *National Geographic* Image Collection

life'.[13] Peasants listened to and engaged with outside agitators on political rights and land, but refused a dialogue over grain. In May, the district food provisions committee sent soldiers to the countryside to help peasants in the field but the peasants refused their help. The Viatka soviet and army garrisons dispatched agitators to appeal to the peasants to give up grain for the military, with little success.[14] In Sernur, a peasant stood up at a *skhod* and proclaimed, 'the army has enough grain, it doesn't need anymore'.[15]

Peasants complained that they did not have grain to give. Official inventories of grain were never completed so their claims are hard to prove, but many peasants' stock was depleted after giving up consecutive years of grain with insufficient labour. The harvest in much of Viatka was also below normal in 1917. Peasants in the province's breadbasket districts of Elabuga and Iaransk suffered from a bad harvest after they lost almost all of the spring wheat from cold and wind.[16] On top of that, the harsh winter killed most peasants' bees in Iaransk district, depriving

---

[13] GA RF, f. 1791, op. 6, d. 78, l. 87; f. 1791, op. 6, d. 463a, l. 112.

[14] *Krest'ianskaia gazeta*, 16 May 1917, 13; *Elabuzhskaia malen'kaia narodnaia gazeta*, 5 May 1917, 4; *Kukarskaia zhizn*, 21 May 1917, 2; *Vlast' naroda*, Moscow, 6 May 1917, 3. See also GAKO, f. R-1322, op. 1a, d. 30.

[15] *Krest'ianskaia gazeta*, 26 May 1917, 9.

[16] *Elabuzhskaia malen'kaia narodnaia gazeta*, 3 May 1917, 1–2; *Kukarskaia zhizn'*, 30 July 1917, 2.

them of a cash crop that was not controlled by the grain monopoly.[17] In May, I. Sigov reported to the Free Economic Society in Petrograd that the peasantry of Viatka, like the whole of Russia's peasants, stored their grain rather than deliver it, and that 'since the 25 March law, the new food provision organs have not procured one funt of grain'.[18] Even if peasants had grain, they resisted giving it over to support the grain monopoly.

Tensions over provisions surfaced in Viatka's grain surplus districts upon the announcement of the grain monopoly. A rumour spread throughout Urzhum district that peasants would have to give up all their crops.[19] Other rumours had it that the army did not even need food, or that in Siberia the grain monopoly did not exist. On 18 May, outside the village of Gol'iany in Sarapul district, an unknown person appeared on horseback yelling mother-curses at the Provisional Government. He shouted that 'the Provisional Government keeps all of you starving. There is already no sugar, tobacco, merchandise, or wheat flour (*krupchatka*). They are already beginning to take grain and flour and all of this is the Provisional Government's fault.' The police tried to arrest this 'harmful person' on charges of causing alarm, but could not detain him. The unknown man put his horse at a gallop, aiming directly towards the head of the police, while shouting even more mother-curses. The police shot at the man but he got away. They later enlisted the aid of three armed soldiers, but they still could not detain the unknown rebel.[20]

Peasants resisted the state's attempts to inventory grain. They often did so passively, refusing to register it or reporting incorrect quantities of grain.[21] A common tactic among local villagers throughout Viatka district was to take rye surreptitiously from the communal storehouses and distribute it among themselves. In October, the district provisions committee responded by conducting an inventory of grain, but it could not get the *volost* provisions administration to act.[22] Upon hearing that the administration planned to seize the grain in *volost* grain stores, the peasants of four communes in Medianskaia *volost*, Viatka district, gathered in their respective *skhod*s and resolved to take all the grain from their communal grain storage and redistribute it among the villagers. One commune actually went as one to the store and took the keys from soldiers guarding the building.[23]

[17] *Kukarskaia zhizn'*, 21 May 1917, 2.
[18] Sigov, *Arakcheevskii sotsializm*, 10, 12–13. Quote on p. 13.
[19] *Krest'ianskaia gazeta*, 26 May 1917, 9.   [20] GAKO, f. 582, op. 194, d. 5, ll. 39–39ob.
[21] GA RF, f. 1791, op. 6, d. 79, l. 3.   [22] GAKO, f. 1345, op. 1, d. 27, l. 24.
[23] GAKO, f. R-1322, op. 1a, d. 31; GA RF, f. 1791, op. 6, d. 78, l. 17.

State appeals to popular civic duty also failed to persuade peasants to give up their grain. By the late summer, provisions committees used force alongside persuasion. Peasants countered with more overt and violent resistance. District provisions committees dispatched military regiments to compel peasants to allow an inventory of their stock and prepare grain for market. In Sarapul district, punitive brigades systematically went through five *volost*s to force peasants who had resisted milling their grain to do so.[24]

In late September, hundreds of villagers throughout Staro-Ven'inskaia *volost* rose up against 160 soldiers dispatched by the district provisions administration to force peasants to thresh their grain. At a charged, rambunctious *volost skhod* of 150 peasants called by the soldiers, villagers refused to cooperate and four 'agitators' were arrested. Afterwards the brigade tried to requisition a threshing machine but the *volost starshina* alerted all the peasants who were at the *skhod*. The soldiers shot in the air and the crowd of peasants dispersed. That night, though, a call to action went out throughout the *volost* and the next morning close to 600 people arrived at the village. Seeing the chairmen of the *volost* electoral and provisions committees, the crowd yelled, 'Here are the ones who gave up our grain. Arrest them!' The peasants took the keys from the sentry of the jail, freed those arrested the previous day, and imprisoned their captives. The sentry returned with two other soldiers and the peasants, now armed, attacked them. The sentry shot into the crowd, killing two and wounding four. The rest of the soldiers heard the commotion and ran to the jail. The shedding of blood chilled the peasants. In the traditional, almost ritualized manner of peasant armed resistance, they apologized, said that they would never again oppose the state, and threshed their grain.[25] They put on the mask of obedient peasants for only a short while, however, for the next year they would again oppose requisitions.

Most of the protests were centreed in the grain-surplus southern regions, where food provisions officials focussed their efforts. Peasants resolutely resisted giving up food without adequate compensation. The state responded with force, provoking more adamant peasant resistance. Udmurts in Buranovskaia *volost*, Sarapul district, refused to give up their livestock and, as the official report noted, 'persuasion was unsuccessful', so a military detachment was sent.[26] In Staro-Ven'inskaia *volost*, Sarapul

---

[24] Kiriukhina, ed., *Ocherki istorii*, 439–41.
[25] Report of the head of the Sarapul district militia. Bystrova et al., eds, *Ustanovlenie*, 205–7.
[26] Bystrova et al., eds, *Ustanovlenie*, 161. This phenomenon was not unique to Viatka. Tatars in Kazan clashed with military detachments as early as March 1917. N. N. Kabytova, *Vlast' i obshchestvo v Rossiiskoi provintsii: 1917 god v Povol'zhe* (Samara, 1999), 50–1.

district, an army regiment compelled locals to thresh their grain. Those who refused were arrested, but the peasants armed themselves and attacked the convoy. A soldier fired into the crowd, killing two and wounding three.[27] Four hundred peasants in Konganurskaia *volost*, Urzhum district, attacked and arrested members of the provisions administration. The district soviet had to ask the Kazan military headquarters to send troops to quell the protest. Simultaneously, peasants in seven *volost*s of Iaransk aggressively protested the grain monopoly.[28] Tatars in Malmyzh district battled soldiers and a Muslim member of the district *ispolkom* was sent by the district provisions committee to oversee an inventory of grain and search for *kumyshka*.[29] Ominously, in mid-October, residents of Ikskii Ust beat up the chairman of the Elabuga district provisions committee and the 150 soldiers in the area refused to arrest the instigators.[30]

Peasants as a whole resisted forced grain requisitions, but non-Russians clashed more often and more violently against the state's intrusions. Geography and economics only partially explain this. Non-Russians made up nearly half of the rural population in Viatka's southern districts but the tense historical relationship between Udmurts, Maris, and Tatars and Russian officials also drove their resistance in 1917. In the late-tsarist era, each group had resisted and accommodated religious conversion and official attempts to assimilate them into the Russian culture. State intervention in 1917 was a continuation of this struggle.

The tense atmosphere over grain supplies and popular fears of lawlessness exacerbated ethnic tensions and provided the discursive parameters for their expression. The revolution allowed free expressions of ethnic identity, but free press and social tensions fostered ethnic tensions. The urban public and state assumed that peasants hoarded grain and tried to bypass the monopoly for their own profit. The Udmurt and Mari ritual drink *kumyshka* continued to be a favourite target of the press and a sign that non-Russians had not yet reached the cultural level to be integrated fully into the Russian nation. In Kadet, zemstvo, and SR newspapers *kumyshka* (as a stand-in for Udmurts) became an enemy of freedom and the revolution. As the newspaper *Slovo i zhizn'* reported on March 1917, local 'Udmurts interpreted freedom (*svoboda*) for their own benefit and began a massive brewing of *kumyshka*. Extreme and strict measures must be taken to stop this

---

[27] GA RF, f. 1791, op. 6, d. 462, l. 32; d. 79, l. 53.
[28] GA RF, f. 1791, op. 6, d. 78, l. 86; Kiriukhina, ed., *Ocherki istorii*, 438–9.
[29] GA RF, f. 1791, op. 6, d. 463a, l. 88.   [30] GA RF, f. 1791, op. 6, d. 462, l. 43.

clandestine act.'[31] The zemstvo newspaper *Krest'ianskaia gazeta* also described Udmurts as misinterpreting political freedom, writing that 'The brewing of *kumyshka* is an invention of Udmurts and they are smitten by their skill. The Udmurt says, "while there is freedom we need to make [*kumyshka*] because there may one day be new laws published and then we will willy-nilly have to give up *kumyshka*."' However, the newspaper editorialized that 'The Udmurt loves money a lot and so will obtain it through the easiest method – brewing *kumyshka*. Brewing *kumyshka* does not take much labour and is easy, but it is also lucrative.'[32] Such portrayals of Udmurt cultural failings, such as selfishness, greed, and miscomprehension of the political arena, reflected both educated Russia's unease with peasants actively participating in Russia's politics, as well as popular cultural portrayals of benighted peasants as a whole. Discussions of *kumyshka* went beyond social or class tensions. 'The Udmurt', the article in *Krest'ianskaia gazeta* concluded, 'is still not completely enlightened and not completely developed. They see no harm in brewing *kumyshka* and no one teaches them about the harm in doing so.'[33]

Reflecting growing social divisions between intellectuals and peasants and fears of anarchy, newspapers created a sense that all peasants were making *kumyshka*. The local newspaper *Kukarskaia zhizn'*, in August 1917, reported that 'now almost all the villagers of Viatka are making this "boiled mind-dulling drink" (*otvaritel'nyi odurmanivaiushchii napitok*) and the local intelligentsia do not have the strength to stop it'.[34] An article in July reported that 'the skill of Udmurts to distil *kumyshka* was adopted perfectly by our peasantry of Troitsksaia and Norlianskaia *volost*s. The method of distilling is very easy and the instruments, if you will, are found in every home.'[35] The newspaper reiterated two months later that *kumyshka* had invaded Russian regions of Viatka province: 'In Nolinsk district, all the population is Russian. Up to the prohibition of the sale of strong drinks no one made [home brews] and no one was skilled in making beer and *kumyshka*. They learned from the non-Russians (*inorodtsy*) living in neighbouring districts.'[36] The press displayed a growing impotence to stop Udmurt-to-Russian peasant

---

[31] *Slovo i zhizn'*, 21 March 1917, 4.   [32] *Krest'ianskaia gazeta*, 26 May 1917, 13.
[33] *Krest'ianskaia gazeta*, 26 May 1917, 13.
[34] *Kukarskaia zhizn'*, 27 August 1917, 2. On related fears by educated society of urban hooliganism and rural crime in the late Imperial era, see Joan Neuberger, *Hooliganism: Crime, Culture, and Power in St Petersburg, 1900–1914* (Berkeley, 1993); Frank, *Crime, Cultural Conflict*.
[35] *Krest'ianskaia gazeta*, 14 July 1917, 20.
[36] *Krest'ianskaia gazeta*, 5 September 1917, 13.

contagion through 1917. As part of public fears that crime, mass desertion, and chaos in national politics was destroying Russia, by the autumn of 1917 newspaper articles expressed a sense of rampant *ku-myshka*. In the 'Anarchy Reigns' section of *Krest'ianskaia gazeta*, the newspaper reported peasants who had resolved not to punish those caught making *kumyshka* and to free the policeman from even searching for the illegal substance.[37]

The state's discursive tone shifted from positive patriotic ebullience in the spring to negative nationalist threats in the autumn. The Urzhum district commissar posted placards that framed the food crisis as the threat to the revolution. It equated General Kornilov's failed counter-revolution with the danger of famine. But, the poster declared, 'if you, citizens, are conscious of the danger facing the country (*rodina*), you will aid it. Immediately bring grain to collection points.' The poster rebutted 'lies, and dangerous and dark rumours' denying the existence of a grain monopoly and it created a dialectic between the positive image of 'citizens' and the negative image of 'people' (*liudi*). As in other state and elite discourse in 1917, the poster argued that a peasant became a citizen through good behaviour that benefited the state. The poster warned citizens that there are people who spread lies and engage in speculation. They are the 'enemies of freedom who line their pockets from your grain'. These people have 'their own interests' and not the state's in mind. A citizen, the poster posited, does not believe these rumours, reports them to the authorities, and sacrifices grain.[38]

Fractures in the village

Peasants identified themselves as a single collective to the outside world, concealing growing disagreements within the community. The strengthening of the commune from the beginning of the war helped to create a sense of a unified collective. Fractures, already dividing the village along generational, gendered, and economic lines grew under the revolution's pressures. Younger and traditionally marginalized populations played a greater role in village politics, threatening powerful elders. Returning workers continued to challenge elders' authority, as they had before the war. Village communities also revered peasant soldiers, whom the press and government hailed as heroes of the revolutionary nation and who had experience with the larger political arena. Villagers elected soldiers to leadership positions traditionally held by a select group of elder peasants and gave them their ear when they spoke. Returning

---

[37] *Krest'ianskaia gazeta*, 7 November 1917, 9.   [38] GA RF, f. 1791, op. 6, d. 237, l. 14.

soldiers' influence should not be overstated, though. Elders still held the majority of leadership positions.

Villagers heightened their acts against separators from the commune that had taken shape during the first years of war. From 1906 to the outbreak of war, tensions and sparring had followed the separation and consolidation of private farms (*khutora*) and semi-consolidated private farms (*otruba*), but the communes had been powerless to stop the government-supported movement. Commune members were emboldened by the new order and acted against the separators. Villagers ploughed separators' land, trampled grass and crops (*potrava*), dismantled boundary markers, and denied them access to forests. When news of the revolution reached Petropavlovskaia *volost*, Sarapul district, peasants began to return separators' land to the commune under the threat of force. The commune had a history of disputes with up to three hundred individual farmers (who had established *otruba*). The commune believed that the separators had the better land and had cut off access to the meadows needed for grazing livestock. Peasants in the commune had been subject to fines and had even had their cattle confiscated as punishment for trespassing over the separators' land. Under duress, most of the separators agreed to return to the commune.[39] Following the general trend of the peasant movement, attacks on separators followed the agricultural cycle, increasing in the spring, declining in late summer and resuming their climb in August and September. Commune members in Nemcheniata village, Kotel'nich district, obstructed the separators Golovostev and Manin from gathering their harvest. The militiaman was called to protect the separators from physical danger, but the peasants fought off the militia and beat Manin to death. A detachment of soldiers finally restored order.[40]

Peasant action against the separators reflected social norms of justice. The separators had violated communal norms of land use and responsibility. Separating from the commune, according to Judith Pallot, 'was a statement of disengagement from a nexus of mutual obligations and expectations upon which the Russian peasant community's survival had

---

[39] GA RF, f. 1791, op. 2, d.178b, ll. 11, 14, 16, 18. In May, separators in Glazov district complained that peasants, influenced by soldiers returning from the front, seized their land. In June, a separator in Orlov district complained that fellow villagers were not allowing him to fell trees even though they had agreed to this in 1915. Other villages in Orlov tried to tempt separators back with promises of more land than the separators once had in the commune. In June, villagers in Sarapul district ploughed separators' lands and destroyed their boundary markers. Bystrova et al., eds, *Ustanovlenie*, 105–7, 114, 132, 139, 154.

[40] GA RF, f. 1791, op. 6, d. 463a, l. 52; f. 1791, op. 6, d. 78, l. 84; f. 1791, op. 6, d. 237, ll. 6–7.

been historically founded'.[41] Villagers therefore attempted to right the wrongs through symbolic and concrete actions. They destroyed boundary markers demarcating separator land from the commune's and prevented ploughing and sowing of the land, thereby erasing the physical injustice and bringing all land back into the fold. Villagers prevented separators from reaping the benefits of their ill claims by disrupting their harvest. Finally, when separators would not comply, villagers relied on force, using violence and moral sanction to exact justice. Peasant action in 1917 against separators was the crescendo of a decade-long struggle among the peasant community over the separation process. Villagers used the same methods, on a larger and more overt level, to fight separators in 1917 that they had been using in the past ten years.

War and revolution's democratizing effect on the commune helped some women partially enter the public sphere. *Soldatki* most of all turned to the state and used their freedom to organize to improve their condition. *Soldatki* continued to press the provincial administration in letters and complaints for aid. In April, *soldatki* formed a provincial union, reflecting a sense of kinship and identity.[42] In the autumn, local *soldatki* congresses insisted that inflation ate away at their current subsidies and they needed a raise to purchase basic goods.[43] However, *soldatki* faced growing criticism for their government subsidies. *Soldatki* became targets for villagers' despair at their declining economic condition. As a peasant from Riazan province wrote in a letter to a local newspaper, 'They say that there is money in the village. There is, but who has it? Childless *soldatki* who receive state subsidies (*kazennoe posobie*) and hirelings and earn a good living without any expenses.'[44]

The presence of prisoners of war in the village also grew increasingly contentious throughout 1917 with peasant embitterment from the catastrophic war. If peasants had acted as guardians of the prisoners, they now used the breakdown of state power to take revenge on the loathed Germans and Austrians. The Swedish mission reported that the prisoners no longer enjoyed personal safety: 'Almost all peasants refuse to sell POWs provisions. While many locales do not have any, some do and don't sell them provisions out of malice. In these places people are starving with hunger.'[45] In early summer, in Polomskaia

---

[41] Pallot, *Land Reform in Russia*, 171.
[42] Kiriukhina, ed., *Ocherki istorii*, 396–7. *Soldatki* had the same demands in Nizhegorod, Kazan, and Tambov provinces. Sarah Badcock, *Politics and the People*, 145–80.
[43] Bystrova et al., eds, *Ustanovlenie*, 192–4.
[44] Quoted in Sigov, *Arakcheevskii sotsializm*, 15.
[45] GA RF, f. 1791. op. 2, d. 559, ll. 14–29; quotes on ll. 16–17.

volost, Orlov district, peasants even killed a prisoner. Neighbouring villagers defended their brethren and decried prisoner of war affluence and the 'brazen faced lies' spread in letters to Kerensky and the Swedish government. Peasants defined the prisoners as more than national enemies; they transformed them into class enemies who took advantage of poor, starving peasants. They stated that they lived in nicer homes and that their food 'is better than ours thanks to the money that they have'. Peasants noted that in their village one of the Germans, Rudolf Shpis, 'a rich man', even murdered a *soldatka*. Peasants complained of prisoners' 'arrogant, rude, and insolent behaviour' (*nadmennym, grubym i nakhal'nym povedeniem*) and concluded that, 'our population has had enough citizenly self-control and have not reacted to the extremely insulting conduct of the above German elements'.[46]

Peasants envisioned prisoner of war wealth, but the economic downward spiral hurt most prisoners' already desultory standard of living. The government could not provide funds for the prisoners and even demanded that they pay taxes on relief from the Swedish mission. Sensing the political disorder and economic collapse, prisoners of war disguised themselves as Russian soldiers and ran away en masse.[47]

It was against this backdrop of economic collapse, stress from failing wartime politics, growing intra-village tensions, polarizing social and class conflict, and political leaders' acceptance of the need to rely on coercion and force that the Provisional Government started the process to recast Russia's political system to be based on popular sovereignty. The contradictory push towards active participation in the recreation of the national polity, and the official violence and centrifugal forces pulling society apart, created a tragic paradox for the Provisional Government's electoral experiment.

The zemstvo elections as national trial

The Provisional Government implemented election laws upon its accession to power, establishing the largest democracy and the widest enfranchisement in the world. The state granted:

the right to participate to all Russian citizens of both sexes, i.e. men and women, regardless of belief and nationality. They need only to be twenty years old by the time of the compilation of the [electoral] lists and live in the stated *volost* or have

---

[46] GA RF, f. 1791, op. 2, d. 559, l. 78.   [47] GA RF, f. 1791, op. 2, d. 559, ll. 78, 95–6.

an established domicile or some kind of determined occupation, or belong there on service. [So] almost all citizens [have the right to vote].[48]

All peoples of Russia regardless of estate (*soslovie*), gender, or nationality enjoyed the legal right to participate in the recreation of the Russian nation. However, by making a special point to note gender, religion, and nationality, the Provisional Government showed itself to be aware of the historical and cultural tensions of political participation in Russia. The late-Imperial state allowed, and contended with, a growing civil society and public sphere. But both the state and the public sphere discriminated against women, non-Orthodox Christians, and non-Russians by denying them equal access or even a voice in the growing public movement.[49] If citizenship is a unifying national consciousness, though, then heterogeneous identities such as those based on gender, nationality, or religious belief also undercut the national project.[50] The Provisional Government's laws foreshadowed the problems that would plague the relationship between the state and its citizens.

Contradicting the euphoria of political freedom and the initial promises of a quick election to the Constituent Assembly, the Provisional Government established a prolonged initiation to prepare the population to vote for Russia's national future. In a process that would drag on from March through to December 1917, the state hesitantly moved towards national elections. Two interconnected issues exacerbated the delays: the administrative weakness that the Provisional Government inherited in the countryside, and local educated society's concern to control the political lives of the peasant population.

The success of popular electoral participation rested on the enumeration and registration of voters in a national census. The government schemed to merge the counting of the electorate with an inventory of grain – counting and controlling personal and perishable national resources. In this way the provisions crisis seeped into electoral politics. In the early summer, newly appointed administrative officials and census-takers roamed the countryside and counted people, livestock,

---

[48] GAKO, f. 589, op. 2, d. 19, l. 7ob. The state did exclude monks from voting; those declared by law to be insane or deaf and unable to speak; as well as those who had been convicted for a major criminal offence in the past three years.

[49] See Joseph Bradley, 'Subjects into Citizens: Societies, Civil Society, and Autocracy in Tsarist Russia', *American Historical Review* 107 (2002): 1094–1123. Several historians have shown how the public sphere was gendered. See Joan Landes, *Women and the Public Sphere in the Age of the French Revolution* (Ithaca, 1988).

[50] For further discussion on how citizenship as a unifying national consciousness undermines ethnic and local identities, see Greg Urban and Joel Sherzer, eds, *Nation–States and Indians in Latin America* (Austin, 1991).

and grain. Peasants, especially non-Russians in grain surplus regions, resisted the census in fear that it would result in a taking of their grain and to protest the grain monopoly. Ironically, peasants fought to be part of the political world, but resisted the economic relationship. The result was disenfranchisement of scores of peasants, especially non-Russians.

The census exacerbated historical tensions between the state and its non-Russian populations, revealing central problems in the creation of a unified citizenry of the Russian nation. Russian peasants did not resist the counting, but Udmurts, Maris, and Tatars refused to allow the government to categorize them. For example, the Urzhum district administration completed the census in Russian areas, but encountered resistance in almost all the non-Russian *volosts*. Government census-takers complained in July about their inability to carry out the census in Kosolapovskaia *volost*, a predominately Mari region. They requested a battalion of two hundred soldiers and officers to force the population to comply.[51] State officials feared non-Russian conspiracies to undermine official programmes. In Turekskaia *volost*, the census agents only partially completed their task. Officials blamed the 'Tatar part of the population, who under the influence of *kosolapovtsy* (people from Kosolapovskaia *volost*) are hostile toward the census.'[52]

Non-Russian peasants refused to give information about their population and possessions to the state. In the Tatar village of Paran'ga, a military regiment had to be called to fulfil the census. A crowd of peasants gathered to meet the detachment, demanded that the soldiers leave the village, and fired some shots. The soldiers returned fire, killing a Tatar peasant.[53] The census highlighted the tensions for populations living on the border of acceptance into the nation, and official suspicion. Tatars, Maris, Udmurts, and other nationalities did not have the sense of belonging that the Provisional Government attempted to convey. As the bureaucracy of the state reached into the non-Russian villages, peasants resisted its attempts at gaining knowledge in order to categorize and potentially separate them from the Russian population.

Despite the numerous problems, the census data did establish voting lists for the five major electoral campaigns in 1917: city dumas, the *volost*, district and provincial zemstvo, and the Constituent Assembly.

[51] GAKO, f. 1345, op. 1, d. 85, l. 4.
[52] *Krest'ianskaia gazeta*, 25 July 1917, 12–13; 8 August 1917, 11. The state also encountered resistance in Cheremiskaia, Turekskaia, and Sernurskaia *volosts*. Mari peasants also resisted the census in Kazan province. N. V. Gerasimova, 'Zemskaia reforma na territorii Chuvashii: vybory v volostnye i uezdnye zemstva (iiun'–dekabr' 1917g.)', *Vestnik Moskovskogo universiteta* series 8 (January–February 2003): 78–9.
[53] GA RF, f. 1791, op. 6, d. 78, l. 85; d. 460, l. 92.

The *volost* zemstvo and the Constituent Assembly elections were the most widely known and enjoyed the widest participation.[54] State officials and local intelligentsia saw the zemstvo elections as administrative preparation as well as practice for the peasants for the Constituent Assembly elections. Moreover, peasant organizations and the political activity that shaped the Constituent Assembly voting came into their own during the elections for the *volost* zemstvo.

The election process highlights one of the fundamental shortcomings and contradictions of the Provisional Government that ultimately led to its downfall. Viatka's local governmental and cultural elites, for the most part, saw the peasantry as irrational actors who needed patrimonial oversight. This constricting view precluded a synthesis between peasant and state under the Provisional Government. Popular participation in the government was also supposed to be a means to legitimize the new state. Indeed, the Bolsheviks accentuated this connection between participation and legitimacy by boycotting the Duma in order not to be tainted by the 'bourgeois regime'. In the provinces, the state hoped that rule by election would solidify mass support.

The zemstvo and Constituent Assembly elections, like elections in other democratic countries, were also symbolic rituals. In the same vein as mass festivals and oaths, elections were a means to emphasize the nation's sovereignty.[55] The population was supposed to renew its support for the governmental system through voting in the elections and to legitimize the myth of popular participation. It therefore tied together ideas of citizenship rights and responsibilities. The elections in the Viatka countryside, like the elections in revolutionary France, are important 'symbolic practices' as they 'offered immediate participation in the new nation through the performance of a civic duty, and they opened up previously restricted access to positions of political responsibility. Because they had such direct impact on the political structure, they attracted the attention of officials, and, as a result, they are one of the best documented revolutionary practices.'[56] As James Lehning shows for nineteenth-century France, elections were arenas of explicit power and its use in the dialogue between the peasantry and national cultural elites. The elections were therefore tied to ideas of citizenship rights and responsibilities.[57] Moreover, unlike festivals that relied on mass consensus and the appearance of the absence of resistance,

---

[54] See Timkin, *Smutnoe vremia*, 14.
[55] Hunt, *Politics, Culture, and Class*, 125.   [56] Hunt, *Politics, Culture, and Class*, 126.
[57] Lehning, *Peasant and French*, 179.

electoral results reveal differences among the population.[58] These differences were as varied as geography, gender, ethnicity, and status. The events surrounding the elections reveal that peasants and Russia's political leadership had inconsistent ideas of popular participation, the voting process, and the peasant–intelligentsia relationship.

In its first month, the Provisional Government had ordered the establishment of a popularly elected non-estate-based *volost* zemstvo with extensive power to replace the *volost* administration. The legislation fulfilled zemstvo officials' dreams, held since the system's birth, of extending the zemstvo to the *volost* level. Liberal reformers and moderate socialists touted the reform's 'liberation of the peasantry from its burdensome guardianship' of the tsarist state, but dreamt of supplanting benighted peasant *volost* officials with educated specialists who would govern the more powerful local state rationally.[59] Fear of peasant democracy over zemstvo rationalist dreams escalated in the summer months. The provincial administration also saw the zemstvo election as preparation for themselves and the peasants for the Constituent Assembly election. They were correct. Peasant organizations and political activity that later shaped the Constituent Assembly voting came into their own during the zemstvo election. The *volost* zemstvo election was finally held in Viatka province from 13 to 27 August, followed by elections to the district zemstvo from 29 August through to 10 September.

By August, when the state had completed its census, the democratic government was once again in crisis. The fallout from the July Days pushed the government leftward and the Provisional Government quickly lost credibility in a socially polarized country. Peasants sparred with the military and state officials over grain and there was a growing fear among landowners, educated society, and urbanites that the countryside was spiralling towards anarchy. On top of this, the harvest, itself laden with political symbolism and import in an economy in flux, was in full swing and preoccupied peasants. It was in this tense environment that the *volost* zemstvo election was held.

Reformers and local educated society lamented the failure of the *volost* zemstvo election (as have several historians). Structural problems, violence, corruption, suspicion, and peasant apathy marred the election in much of Russia. Swimming through the tangle of problems, the elections at least in Viatka show that peasants participated and urged on local governmental change. Peasants threw off the guardianship of educated

---

[58] Hunt, *Politics, Culture, and Class*, 126–7.
[59] Quoted in Jane Burbank, 'An Imperial Rights Regime: Law and Citizenship in the Russian Empire', *Kritika* 7 (2006): 427.

society and chose their own candidates to fill governmental posts. They disappointed government reformers and local educated society in both the process and the outcome of the election. The people did not look to the elites for aid and guidance in selecting their representatives, but rather those candidates from their own developed organizations. By the autumn, peasants' political acumen had ripened and they no longer showed the patience with educated society's political tutelage that they had in the first months of the revolution. Despite the growing social tensions, many peasants continued to participate actively in citizenship activities and nation-building events, including elections.

A litany of problems limited the efficacy of the zemstvo election as it had the census two months earlier. The wobbly rural administration could not handle the duties of a popular election. Several villages did not receive timely notification or were never told when the election would be held. Local governments did not distribute the lists of candidates as required by law. Electoral officials did not inform the peasants to which regional voting precinct within the *volost* they belonged. One commissioner received ballots for only one of the two days of voting, resulting in only 28 of a potential 786 voters being counted. Several others simply never counted the ballots.[60] In Viatka district, the zemstvo found the district administration guilty of determining the number of voters alone without consulting the zemstvo.[61] Corruption also marred the election. Also in Viatka district, people with 'especially bad reputations' supposedly hired a person of ill-repute and forced the illiterate to vote for him. This person was not even a candidate and, as a recently convicted criminal, was legally barred from standing for election. The local electoral commission knew all along of these misdealings and did nothing.[62]

Ethnic tensions once again threatened the viability of the national ritual. In Urzhum district, Maris spurned preparatory acts for the election by refusing to give information for zemstvo electoral lists.[63] In the mixed Russian–Mari *volost* of Ernurskaia, Iaransk district, a group of villagers stood outside the polling place making noise and rallying Mari peasants against the election. One of the instigators, Egor Kipdulkin, told the head of the regional electoral commission 'to trash' the election, and then hit him in the face. The head of the *volost* electoral commission claimed that Mari peasants were 'against all state power'. The local administration postponed the stormy *volost* zemstvo election and the

---

[60] *Krest'ianskaia gazeta*, 19 September 1917, 5.
[61] GAKO, f. 1345, op. 1, d. 105, l. 23. [62] *Krest'ianskaia gazeta*, 29 August 1917, 9.
[63] *Krest'ianskaia gazeta*, 8 August 1917, 11.

commissioner asked the district government to send a representative or the militia to restore order.[64] In the largely Udmurt *volost* of Nizhne-Ukanskaia, Glazov district, 111 peasants wrote a complaint that in the district zemstvo elections the secretary of the electoral commission wrote down a different list for illiterate peasants. In another instance in the same *volost*, a member of the commission conducted an open vote and then filled out the ballots himself.[65] Non-Russian peasants throughout Russia in fact resisted the zemstvo election, as they did the census. They feared greater government encroachment on ethnic independence.[66] Many non-Russian elites enjoyed the revolution's political freedoms and decentralization and fostered a cohesive ethnic identity, in contrast to the larger Russian political identity, and called for greater autonomy. Non-Russians' political actions focussed on garnering independence, not integrating themselves into the historically oppressive Russian governmental structure.

Peasants also resisted the election after hearing rumours from returning soldiers of pernicious state intentions to use the *volost* zemstvo to take their grain, a point that in fact had credibility. In Troitskaia and Pasegovskaia *volosts*, Viatka district, peasants responded to these rumours by refusing to give information to compile voter lists. They insisted that they did not need the new *volost* zemstvo and demanded the abolition of the district zemstvo as well. As a result, 11% of voters cast ballots in Pasegovskaia *volost* and only 7% of the potential voters participated in Troitskaia *volost*.[67]

Given these problems, highly publicized in the liberal and moderate socialist press, the zemstvo elections in Viatka were remarkably successful in turning out the vote. They failed as a national ritual, though, by broadening the distance between social groups. A close analysis of the elections in Kukarskaia *volost*, Iaransk district, illustrates these contradictions.[68] Five lists of candidates competed for votes – two of local intelligentsia, one clerical and two peasant, the Peasant Union and a local list. The electoral campaign was hard-fought and aggravated animosity between peasants and local intellectuals. The Peasant Union held mass rallies, while the editors of *Kukarskaia zhizn'* (who were also

---

[64] GAKO, f. 1351, op. 1, d. 17, l. 2.   [65] GAKO, f. 1345, op. 1, d. 91, ll. 38–41.

[66] For example, in the Don region, Cossacks resisted the zemstvo election for fear that it would weaken Cossack influence in the area. William G. Rosenberg, 'The zemstvo in 1917 and under Bolshevik Rule', in Emmons and Vucinich, eds, *The Zemstvo in Russia*, 397.

[67] *Krest'ianskaia gazeta*, 15 September 1917, 10–12.

[68] Kukarskaia *volost* is an ideal test case of the electoral campaign because of its diverse ethnic population, similar to much of southern Viatka.

candidates on one of the intelligentsia lists) lobbied for their list in a string of editorials. Peasants accused the intellectuals of electoral fraud in a petition to the district commissar. The complaint charged both intelligentsia lists of taking advantage of 'the most illiterate and ignorant people' from the villages by controlling the printing of ballots and distributing illegal ballots with the list number or candidate names on them. Young members of the intelligentsia and students from the *gimnasium* even handed out ballots on the street and from the porch of the school.[69]

The Peasant Union still won a lopsided victory, with 61% of the vote, trampling the intelligentsia lists that together received only 18%.[70] The results (see Table 3.1) show the solidarity of the peasants and the continued ability of the Peasant Union to mobilize its members. Kukarsk precinct (representing the large town and economic centre of south-west Viatka) was anomalous with a relatively low turnout of 44% and strong support for the intellectual parties (representing almost all of the parties' votes). Elections in the precinct presumably followed the law's prescript as free and secret and many voters supported their own urban party. In the remaining rural precincts, villagers probably voted as one for the Peasant Union at a village assembly, which would explain the 81% voter turnout. Peasants in village assemblies usually decided matters unanimously to give the impression that the whole community stood behind the assembly. While the extent of political organization in Kukarskaia was exceptional, other *volost*s throughout the province also saw contested elections and animosity between peasants and their self-appointed guardians. Voter turnout varied greatly among *volost*s based on the efficiency of *volost* officials, local political organization, the prevalence of rumours, locals' feelings towards the state, and ethnic makeup.[71]

Peasants of Kukarskaia *volost* gave the Peasant Union even greater support, with 75% of the vote, at the district zemstvo election. A reconstituted list of local intelligentsia received only 9%.[72] The peasants

---

[69] GAKO, f. 1351, op. 1, d. 24, ll. 14–18. Lists 16–18 are ballots showing evidence of fraud.

[70] Since the election determined 25 representatives for the *volost* zemstvo and almost 2,500 people voted, for every 100 votes, a list was able to send one candidate. The Peasant Union sent 15 representatives, the intelligentsia lists together sent 4.

[71] On Viatka district, see *Krest'ianskaia gazeta*, 15 September 1917, 12. The author of the report on the Viatka *volost* zemstvo elections posited that voting participation was related to where the *volost* administrators personally appeared to support the local electoral commissions.

[72] The list included one of the editors of *Kukarskaia zhizn'*, the wife of a doctor who had run in the *volost* zemstvo election, a technician, and a businessman.

Table 3.1 *Kukarskaia township zemstvo election result*

Voting precincts	Turnout (number of votes as a percentage of eligible voters)	Electoral Lists and Share of Total Vote					
		Intelligentsia List 1	Intelligentsia List 2	Clergy	Peasant Union	Local Village List	Total
Kukarsk	44	339 (14%)	95 (4%)	26 (1%)	19 (1%)	463 (19%)	942
Grekh.-Smolents	77	17 (1%)	1 (0%)	0 (0%)	556 (22%)	0 (0%)	574
Nemdinsk	78	2 (0%)	7 (0%)	0 (0%)	379 (15%)	0 (0%)	388
Shalakhovsk	89	1 (0%)	0 (0%)	0 (0%)	558 (23%)	0 (0%)	559
Overall	72	359	103	26	1512	463	2463
Share of Vote		15%	4%	1%	61%	19%	100%

Data from *Kukarskaia zhizn'*, 24 August, 1917, 2.

elected seven representatives to the district zemstvo. These peasant candidates held positions of respect in the village communities, including an elder (*starshina*), a head of committees, a worker, and a scribe. The Peasant Union candidates campaigned on their personal qualities. Union descriptions noted that one peasant was 'well known', another was 'quiet', and another a 'good peasant'. The representatives were not young; the average age was forty-five, the same age as village elders and heads of households.[73] There is no evidence that peasants sent excess men to the zemstvo.[74] Rather, peasants voted for good characteristics and those who were literate. This conflicts with new peasant leaders in the Black Earth region, who were young and often held marginal positions in the village.

The zemstvo election was the first opportunity for women to participate officially as equal citizens in the public sphere. Peasant women built on their expanded position from the war in village assemblies and economic life and parlayed it into voting for public officials, participating in the elections in numbers paralleling males. Such relatively large participation by women is in stark contrast to other parts of Russia, such as Petrograd province, where peasant women abstained from voting because it threatened traditional social practices.[75]

The election exacerbated tensions between peasant and educated society. The peasantry did not vote the way local educated society wanted and by selecting the peasant party over the intelligentsia, rejected the confines of the tutorial relationship. Before the election the editors had filled the newspaper with pleas to vote for the intelligentsia. As with the ceremonies described above, elites portrayed the election as a ritual of citizenship, both granting the peasantry an opportunity at freedom and participation in the state while still being tightly regimented. The editors of *Kukarskaia zhizn'* recounted an educational vignette in which an old peasant complained about the situation in the village because there was no tobacco. The newspaper editorialized that while conditions were tough in the village, 'freedom is not guilty, the people are guilty'. Old peasants and 'their fellow villagers are absolutely not interested in the fate of the nation (*rodina*) or social matters such as the zemstvo'. The newspaper warned that the elections are complicated and difficult to understand and cautioned the peasants not to vote for

---

[73] *Kukarskaia zhizn'*, 3 September 1917, 2.
[74] Burbank, 'An Imperial Rights Regime', 426.
[75] Rosenberg, 'The Zemstvo in 1917' in Emmons and Vucirich, eds, *The Zemstvo in Russia*, 398.

those who have given them tobacco. This was presumably a dig at the Peasant Union, which often distributed goods at local meetings.

Educated society blamed its loss on the ignorance of the peasantry and lashed out at the people. The newspaper editors printed the electoral results and below them wrote that it was clear from the numbers that 'the population of Kukarskaia *volost* considers itself to be more developed and conscious (*soznatel'nye*) than other places, but its activity in the elections showed the exact opposite. The village did not understand the significance of the elections to the zemstvo, and the conscious implementation of its duty of citizenship.'[76] According to the editors, by not voting for the intelligentsia, the peasants held a false consciousness and failed as citizens. The elites were the victims of the incongruities of their national viewpoint. They could not reconcile their image of the peasantry as a homogenous uneducated mass who needed the intelligentsia to mediate between village and nation, with the fact that peasants had a complex understanding of the democratic process and used it for their own good. The elite was in the process of losing control over the rituals of citizenship and the practices of nationalism.

Throughout the province peasants almost uniformly elected respected peasants. Nine-tenths of those elected to the district zemstvo in Kotel'nich and Viatka districts were peasants. Only five of the elected representatives were from the rural intelligentsia.[77] In Kadamskaia *volost*, Iaransk district, twenty-seven out of twenty-eight people elected were peasants. Notably, all of the representatives were literate. Similar trends of peasants electing educated peasants can be seen in both the *volost* and district zemstvo elections. Peasants understood the importance of literacy and education when representing their causes to the outside world.

For all its problems and pockets of resistance, almost half of registered voters cast a ballot in the zemstvo election.[78] An active and developed political culture and sense of citizenship had emerged in the countryside. Political allegiances coalesced around lists that engaged in a serious campaign to turn out the vote and win support. They advertised in the newspapers, published platforms, held organizational meetings, and

[76] *Kukarskaia zhizn'*, 24 August 1917, 2.
[77] GA RF, f. 1791, op. 6, d. 78, l. 46. Similar trends in which peasants beat intelligentsia candidates can be seen throughout Iaransk district. *Kukarskaia zhizn'*, 10 September 1917, 2. This corresponds with results in Simbirsk province. Gerasimova, 'Zemskaia reforma', 81.
[78] Documentary lapses in the archival records prevent an exact computation of the percentage of voters. I estimate it at forty-five per cent, based on evidence from two districts. *Krest'ianskaia gazeta*, 15 September 1917, 12.

tried to persuade voter groups. Political parties and soviets sent agitators to rally support.[79] By the autumn, many peasant communities had gained confidence and political experience. They could free themselves from the necessity of relying on rural educated society, a mediator to the nation, by electing those of their own social background who possessed the skills needed in fighting for peasant causes. It should then come as no surprise that peasants appropriated the zemstvo elections and made the zemstvo a peasant institution.

The elections for the zemstvo were more significant than the reconstituted bodies that began to meet at the end of September. *Volost* zemstvo officials sometimes replicated previous *volost* administrators and carried on their work as before. Overall, though, many *volost* zemstvos met sporadically over the next months, hearing petitions on land disputes and attempting to improve local material well-being.[80] Their work was undermined because constituted state power at the *volost* level became exceptionally confusing at this point. Land committees, food provisions, and *volost skhod*s all made declarations that asserted power over their constituents. *Volost* zemstvos over the winter either withered away or ceded power to the soviets.

The climax of the democratic experiment

The Bolshevik seizure of power in Petrograd happened against the background of a socially polarized world. By the autumn, peasants frequently spoke with disgust and bitterness towards public society and state officials. There was a general feeling that the state administration was collapsing under the pressures of food crises, social instability, and lack of popular confidence. Bolshevik rule did not affect the countryside until the winter transition to soviet power and the implementation of the popular Soviet Land Decree. This is not to say that the event went unnoticed by the more politically attuned *volost*s. Land committees of Bobinskaia and Kstininskaia, *volost*s abutting Viatka city with a vibrant *kustar'* economy tied to the city, condemned the Bolsheviks for usurping the right to transfer national democratic power from the Constituent Assembly. Neither committee defended the Provisional Government, but they did stand by the sovereignty of the state.[81] However, the democratic experiment of politics based on popular sovereignty and

---

[79] Gerasimova, 'Zemskaia reforma', 80–1.
[80] GAKO, f. 1351, op. 1, d. 15, ll. 10–18; f. 589, op. 2, d. 19, ll. 34–6ob.
[81] GAKO, f. 1345, op. 1 d. 27, ll. 100, 122–22ob.

mass participation continued despite events that transpired in Petrograd. The post-February order ended not in the last grains of the harvest in late October, but with the voting for the Constituent Assembly in the swirling snow of December.

The Constituent Assembly election marked the climax in the struggle over national politics in 1917. It seems odd that peasants would care about the Constituent Assembly elections, given the mixed success of the zemstvo elections, delays in calling the election, and popular mistrust of government provisions policies. Of any of the national political symbols in 1917, though, the Constituent Assembly had the most resonance with all inhabitants of the countryside throughout the nine-month marathon to its election.[82] For peasants, most political leaders, and government figures, the Constituent Assembly remained a pure, untainted symbol of the revolution's potential and the last chance to solve such seemingly insolvable problems as land reform. In the end, more than one million people came out to vote in Viatka, and over ninety per cent of them were peasants. If elections are symbolic, ritualistic events that reaffirm citizens' acceptance of the current order, the Constituent Assembly election, by November, was a contradictory symbol. Peasants engaged and participated in the elections, but did not support the post-February order or its representatives. The election also reveals the increasingly complex political field in the village as the peasantry became more experienced politically.

Peasants were hopeful of finally participating in the Constituent Assembly election. Peasants from all walks of life petitioned the provincial electoral commission to get their candidate lists on the ballot. Peasants young and old signed the application for a regional affiliate of the Peasant Union and 38 of the 115 peasant signatories were women.[83] While the above applicant succeeded in getting their candidates on the ballot, many peasant political groups failed. The commission rejected applications by a peasant community from Elovskaia *volost* in Glazov district, the Pachinsk Soviet of Peasant Deputies from Iaransk district, and a group of Mari peasants from Iaransk district attempting to make their teacher, Leonid Mendiiarov, a candidate in the election, all for applying past the 13 October deadline. Interestingly, all three rejected applications were dated before the deadline.[84]

---

[82] L. G. Protasov, *Vserossiiskoe uchreditel'noe sobranie: Istoriia rozhdeniia i gibeli* (Moscow, 1997), ch. 2; Oliver Radkey, *Russia Goes to the Polls: The Election to the All-Russian Constituent Assembly, 1917* (Ithaca, 1989).
[83] GAKO, f. 1349, op. 1, d. 29, ll. 3–4ob, 8.   [84] GAKO, f. 1349, op. 1, d. 41, 50, 59.

The commission favoured candidates from the moderate socialist parties. The Popular Socialist Party application was supported by 116 signatories, all but 2 of whom were members of educated society. The list contained two of the most famous figures of liberal Viatka – Nikolai A. Charushin and Nikolai V. Chaikovskii. The Popular Socialist Party clearly violated electoral regulations. Four of the candidates did not include their statements announcing intent to stand as candidates and the commission could not read other statements since they were in Mari, transcribed but not translated into Russian. The commission initially rejected the four candidates, but the following day mysteriously reversed its decision and allowed all the candidates to stand.[85] In a move to increase their odds of winning enough votes to send their representatives to the Constituent Assembly, the Popular Socialist Party formed a bloc with the National Union of Mari of Viatka Province and included a few Maris among their nineteen candidates. One was Mendiiarov, who the peasants three days earlier failed to get on their own ballot.[86]

Peasants had twelve lists from which to choose: the Bolsheviks, the provincial Muslim Union, the Popular Socialist Party and provincial Mari Union bloc, the Kadets, Mensheviks, a clerical party, a merchant's list, four local lists, and the Provincial Congress of Peasant Deputies and the Socialist Revolutionary Party (CPD/SR) bloc. The last alliance was forged only in late September at the Third Provincial Congress of the Soviet of Peasant Deputies.

The campaign for peasant votes and the electoral results reveal the strong social divisions in the autumn and winter of 1917. The CPD/SR bloc gained the most from the tensions. It had entrenched local organizations and experienced agitators. Villages had sent their representatives to the congresses since it had represented the Peasant Union in the spring. Now, as a more politically radical institution, it appealed to peasant solidarity and class antagonism. The Congress's political literature played off the peasants' antipathy towards the intelligentsia and political leadership's definition of the peasantry as 'dark and unconscious'. It urged peasants to disprove non-toilers' conceptions that peasants were willing to remain exploited, with the men in their field-work and the women in domestic chores. The CPD/SRs attacked the merchants' lists as rich industrialists, landowners, and lawyers, and dismissed the clergy list for its 'hope that the unconscious peasants will vote for them'.[87] In local meetings, the Congress of Peasant Deputies encouraged members to vote for its list because it would defend the

---

[85] GAKO, f. 1349, op. 1, d. 25, 26.   [86] GAKO, f. 1349, op. 1, d. 25, l. 33.
[87] *Narodnoe delo*, 8 November 1917, 1.

working peasant. Agitators for the Congress of Peasant Deputies travelled throughout the countryside and held meetings in every *volost* of Urzhum district.

Women were especially important in the 1917 elections as they remained in the vast majority in the village. Their participation in the zemstvo elections showed that their support was essential for a party's success. Of all of the lists, however, only the CPD/SR bloc campaigned for the peasant woman vote, and even it had a limited vision of women's emancipation and participation in revolutionary society. Its literature emphasized the danger of peasant women's ignorance and political isolation brought on, it argued, from exclusion from the *skhod*. This failing of political consciousness threatened the welfare of the state and class solidarity. It had already led to the failure of the zemstvo elections. Women supposedly said, 'the *baba* doesn't need a thing from the zemstvo, and so we do not need to vote'. Since the women did not vote, then people who 'were not for the working peasant' dominated the elections. The author warned that women's ignorance would also destroy the peasantry's fate in the Constituent Assembly elections, in which 'candidates of the rich' will out-vote the peasantry unless the women go to the polls. Women's participation in this public ritual was a necessary evil for the greater good. The CPD/SRs framed the ritual of the election, and the women's duty as citizens in terms of sacrifice for the greater good of the peasantry and for the good of their husbands:

If their husbands remain at the front for the nation, and the victory of the revolution and freedom, then their wives in the village are obliged to fight for land, by casting their votes for the candidates of the working people.[88]

It was therefore essential for all the peasantry to agitate and clarify to the women their duty to help the 'conscious inhabitants of the villages' and the CPD/SRs.

Agitators in 1917 were right to target women, for they made up a solid majority of the voters. Based on demographic data, the 'average' vote in Russia's Constituent Assembly election was a Russian peasant woman in her mid-thirties.[89] L. G. Protasov has also found that women were more likely to vote in the Constituent Assembly election than men.[90] Results from Slobodskoi district confirm his conclusions; 60.2% of registered women voted, over 54% of registered men. Women composed 52% of the population, but represented 55% of the vote. In Sochnevskaia *volost,*

---

[88] *Narodnoe delo*, 29 October 1917, 3.
[89] I determined the average age of the voter from Protasov's calculation for Moscow province, *Vserossiiskoe uchreditel'noe sobranie*, 201.
[90] Protasov, *Vserossiiskoe uchreditel'noe sobranie*, 202.

more than twice as many women registered to vote than men and they made up 68% of the final vote.[91] Women built on their experience in the zemstvo elections and used the electoral arena to enter the public sphere on equal legal grounds to men.

The electoral campaign also accented ethnic minorities' political marginalization and ethnic tensions in citizenship in general. Language barriers put many non-Russians at a disadvantage. For example, the *ispolkom* of the Soviet of Peasant Deputies sent a Muslim representative to the Tatar village (*selo*) of Karino, Slobodskoi district, to agitate. The representative went to the mullah, who announced to the people, 'This is one of ours who will speak in our way and explain everything in our language.' When the representative asked them if they knew about the parties for the Constituent Assembly, the peasants answered, 'We don't know anything. There were Russians here, but they talked something incomprehensible. We heard only that there is democracy, but what this is – we don't know.'[92] The Tatars in this village may not have been part of electoral politics in the autumn of 1917, but they were actively engaged with the larger politics of the Provisional Government. During the meeting they complained about the state's grain monopoly and inquired about the feasibility of establishing Tatar schools.

The Mari and Tatar national parties overcame communication hurdles and agitated to their rural constituents in the native language. Once again, the CPD/SR bloc was the only other party to place significance on targeting under-represented populations and distributed copies of its programme in both Russian and Mari. Udmurts did not enjoy special attention from any of the parties, despite being the largest ethnic minority in the province. The Udmurt national agents remained smaller and politically weaker than their respective Tatar and Mari groups and did not form their own national congress, the precursor to national party formation in the province. Non-Russians' resistance to the summer census also hindered their involvement in the elections since they were not registered on voter lists. For example, the voting precinct of Irnusk in Urzhum district, a heavily Tatar precinct, had only 17.5% of the total population registered to vote, 10% of women and 31.2% of men. Other heavily non-Russian regions had similar numbers. Popular protests against grain inventories led by non-Russians in the southern districts politically disenfranchised them. While they could fight to get on voter lists in the autumn, most did not.

[91] GAKO, f. 1349, op. 1, d. 14, ll. 384–92ob.
[92] *Krest'ianskaia gazeta*, 25 August 1917, 11–12.

The campaign lasted three weeks longer than expected. The vote was originally scheduled for 12 to 14 November but basic technical difficulties forced the commission to postpone the election. Like the rest of the Russian Empire, the Viatka provincial government lacked reliable resources and sufficient manpower. The commission realized that not only had Petrograd not sent enough paper for printing the twelve final lists of candidates, but the Viatka printing presses could only run off a portion of the required ballots.[93] The provincial commission and local administrators also fought over the size of voting districts. Using their experience from the zemstvo elections, the provincial electoral commissions tried to establish smaller voting districts. Most districts had corresponded to a major village within a *volost*, with *volost*s divided into three or more districts. The vast size of the province with its small, remote villages compelled peasants to travel more than ten versts (6.6 miles) to vote. Peasants in Elabuga district therefore demanded that the electoral commission increase the number of voting districts.[94] Nevertheless, some local election officials fought the provincial commission on this issue, arguing that while smaller districts 'would be more convenient for the population', the local administration simply did not have the personnel or money to man more districts. In Nolinsk district, officials unsuccessfully demanded that the number of voting districts be reduced from 177 to 25, so that every *volost* count as only one voting district.[95] Since the census went so poorly and the government lacked competent officials, the electoral commission struggled even to compile voter lists. In September it sent out urgent messages to the regions to finish their lists as soon as possible. Most localities did not compile definite numbers of voters until October or November, and even then the numbers were rough estimates. To make matters worse, the commission published the electoral lists only eighteen days before the elections, not giving voters enough time to know the candidates.[96] Only Elabuga district held its elections on time. The other ten districts conducted their elections from 2 to 5 December.

The technical problems that plagued the election's preparation continued on election day. Some peasants were not informed of the new election date. At least one village was never told that the election was taking place. The government's fear that they would not have enough

---

[93] GAKO, f. 1349, op. 1, d. 75, l. 38; GAKO, f. 1349, op. 1, d. 14, ll. 20–1; GA RF, f. 1810, op. 1, d. 178, l. 19. Several provinces struggled to find paper. Protasov, *Vserossiiskoe uchreditel'noe sobranie*, 92–3.
[94] GAKO, f. 1349, op. 1, d. 14, l. 50.   [95] GAKO, f. 1349, op. 1, d. 14, l. 78.
[96] S. P. Zubarev, *Za respubliku sovetov. Kommunisty Prikam'ia v bor'be protiv burzhuaznoi parlamentskoi respubliki (mart 1917–noiabr' 1918 g.)* (Izhevsk, 1970), 68–9.

personnel was justified. No election officials were present in Raevsk district, or Verkhoshizhemskaia *volost*, Orlov district during the voting. Soldiers on leave took it upon themselves to guarantee that the peasants could vote by going to the *volost* centre and demanding that the *volost* administration combine Raevsk district with the neighbouring district. The administration complied.[97]

Peasant celebrations during the elections, despite the government's debilitating technical problems, show the significance villagers placed on the Constituent Assembly vote. They had more time to spend on the Constituent Assembly elections in December than they had for the zemstvo elections during harvest time. They were finished in the fields and with the decline in factory production and overall turmoil, many out-migrants stayed at home. Villagers put on their best clothes and crossed themselves as they cast their vote.

Peasants voted by individual written ballots, not by communal voice vote. District administrators paid close attention to the validity of ballots. The Elabuga district electoral commissioners rejected open vote ballots not signed by the voter. Illiterate peasants were permitted to mark their ballot with an 'x' or other distinguishing mark.[98] The administration still threw out ballots erased or with extra marks, or if there were more ballots in the sealed envelope than that declared by the precinct.

Sixty-six per cent of registered voters in Viatka cast their ballot for the Constituent Assembly, slightly higher than the national average. More peasants voted in December than in the autumn zemstvo elections. Residents of Troitskaia and Pasegovskaia *volost*s, Viatka district, who had refused to vote for the zemstvo, were some of the most active voters for the Constituent Assembly in the district.

On the surface, the Constituent Assembly election results in Viatka look nearly identical to the national numbers. The SRs claimed a resounding victory, with 57% of the vote. Their bloc with the CPD received more votes than any other list in every district; indeed, the population was more likely to vote for it than the Bolsheviks by a ratio of three to one. The Bolsheviks still won a respectable second place, garnering 22.1%. The Muslim Union was a distant third, with 5.2% of the vote, and the Kadets fourth with 4.5% (see Table 3.2).

What appears to be a dominant Socialist Revolutionary Party victory is more complex when placed in the context of rural political organization since March 1917. Peasants supported organizations and political ideals

---

[97] GAKO, f. 1349, op. 1, d. 14, l. 251.
[98] GAKO, f. 1349, op. 1, d. 14, ll. 604–8ob. For some districts I was able to read the individual ballots.

Table 3.2 *Election results for the Constituent Assembly in Viatka province*

Districts	CPD/SR	Bolsheviks	Muslim Union	Kadets	Popular Socialist/ Mari Union	Kotel'nich Peasant Union	Mensheviks	Regional Parties[a]	Clerical Party	Union of Industry	Total Votes
Elabuga	66,425	3,823	19,015	3,900	2,566	147	4,901	700	293	552	102,322
Glazov	58,792	30,993	3,517	2,145	2,375	159	729	9,436	558	443	109,147
Iaransk	62,929	27,564	50	3,486	2,675	81	166	497	926	535	98,909
Kotel'nich	39,210	38,406	52	3,568	822	31,369	250	481	650	622	115,430
Malmyzh	75,590	11,004	19,609	2,114	1,664	158	140	440	798	353	111,870
Nolinsk	36,950	11,404	13	4,510	2,944	47	322	354	313	239	57,096
Orlov	42,197	33,884	27	3,101	1,819	139	346	419	468	456	82,856
Sarapul	57,753	34,115	8,705	11,988	1,224	167	7,857	2,073	1,978	393	126,253
Slobodskoi	50,499	16,476	1,585	1,825	1,460	108	713	551	1,154	911	75,282
Urzhum	87,661	15,693	2,892	4,577	14,767	53	1,088	443	569	291	128,034
Viatka city	1,682	2,474	100	4,082	1,635	10	2,000	68	675	962	13,688
Viatka District	32,837	11,116	20	2,810	3,670	102	655	553	1,014	571	53,348
Total	612,525	236,952	55,585	48,106	37,621	32,540	19,167	16,015	9,396	6,328	1,074,235
Share of Total Vote (Rounded to .5)	57%	22%	5%	4.5%	3.5%	3%	2%	1.5%	1%	0.5%	100

[a] Including the Glazov Regional Party, Iaransk Regional Party, and Petropavlovsk (Sarapul district) Regional Party. Data from GAKO, f. 1349, op. 1, d. 14, ll. 592–3ob.

rather than parties. The massive Peasant Union mobilization effort in the spring radicalized over the summer but initial participants continued their involvement in district and provincial politics. Villages sent representatives to congresses and remaining Peasant Union chapters, and peasant soviets folded themselves into peasant deputies in September. SR Party agitators only actively worked in the Glazov district countryside. Sarah Badcock has shown that peasants supported the SRs and allied groups as 'their' political party that championed peasant causes broadly conceived. They did not support a uniform party platform.[99] Viatka shows a similar pattern where peasants voted for the CPD/SR bloc as the extension of political action joining peasants in an imagined political community.

The Bolsheviks represented the main alternative political ideal to the post-February peasant political world. They enjoyed wide support among soldiers, as they did throughout Russia. They also won decisive victories along the main transportation arteries and even in smaller rural factories where there had not been signs of Bolshevik support in the summer, hinting at spreading Bolshevik influence carried by agitators and the news. The soldiers' garrison in Kotel'nich gave the Bolsheviks its support over the SR coalition, as did peasant-workers in rural factories in Glazov. National minority parties also fared well. The Muslim Union beat the Bolsheviks in Tatar regions of Elabuga and Malmyzh and pockets of Tatars strongly supported the Muslim Union in Glazov district. Maris backed the Mari Union, providing the majority of the votes for the Popular Socialist/Mari Union bloc.

Viatka province could send eleven representatives to the Constituent Assembly. The CPD/SR list sent six (four peasants, an engineer, and a doctor) and the Bolsheviks sent four. The Popular Socialist Party and Mari Union bloc that had won a mere 3.5 per cent of the vote combined their votes with the Mensheviks allowing enough votes to send the moderate socialist Nikolai Chaikovskii as a representative.[100] Present at the closure of the Constituent Assembly, Chaikovskii sent a frantic telegram to the Viatka provincial elections committee, seeking formal protest. The committee instead quietly noted that no more money was coming in and disbanded.

Conclusion

At a time when state and society should have been united through national rituals of active citizenship, they remained in opposition.

---

[99] Badcock, 'We're for the Muzhik's Party'.
[100] GAKO, f. 1349, op. 1, d. 14, ll. 764–5, 779–80.

Representatives of the political and cultural elite attempted to create national citizens in their own image. They used the electoral process as a method to integrate the peasantry into the national system as subaltern citizens – members of the nation subservient to their social superiors. At the same time, elites feared the potential political power bestowed upon the people through the elections. The population, though, had different understandings of what constituted a positive political citizen. Peasants as a whole actively attempted to participate in national rituals as equal members, as guaranteed by law.

But tensions within society also worked to undermine the national project. Equal legal citizenship for all necessitated that those tradition-ally excluded from the political world – notably women, non-Russians, non-Orthodox Christians, and the poor – would participate in elections in the same manner as those populations who had enjoyed a privileged position in the public sphere. While peasant women moved to play a major role in the national ritual, males resisted and tried to control their behaviour. While Russian peasants actively sought out the elections, many non-Russians tried to escape the new imposition of the state, fearing another attack on their culture and religion. Finally, the un-developed Russian administrative apparatus in the countryside could not carry out state elections successfully. The various peasant populations and the local elites pushed and pulled on the already fragile electoral system. The elections, the central symbol of the nation and an arena of state power, could not sustain the stress and simply crumbled. The Constituent Assembly election was the climax of the democratic experiment. Like the zemstvo elections, the process of voting and the symbolic representation of the Constituent Assembly mattered more than the end result.

As seen in the Peasant Union and consequent electoral campaigns, peasants demanded an equal voice in the political world, not just as followers of an 'enlightened' intelligentsia. Most peasants wanted their own representatives who championed such peasant causes as the implementation of democratic government, land reform, and a just grain policy. The failure of both top and local officials and members of edu-cated society who allied with the democratic experiment to accept popular peasant participation in the Russian nation's reinvention must be placed alongside the Provisional Government's other major short-comings – the war, land reform, and food – in an assessment of why it could never achieve the stable popular support it needed for survival.

Several complex social and political developments explain the failure of the Provisional Government experiment – the fracturing of Russian society and growing class conflict, underdeveloped rural administration,

and economic pressures exacerbated by a failing war effort undermined democratic development. Overarching these developments was
a philosophical problem. Peasants, on the one hand, and rural public
society and government administrators of various political stripes on the
other, had differing visions of citizenship and political participation.
Social and political polarization and the spiralling centrifugal force of
revolution, essential ingredients of civil war, were tearing apart Russia
in 1917. The Bolsheviks and their foes, despite great ideological
differences, would rely on mass mobilization and expanded notions of
citizenship to attempt to glue the nation back together.

4   Bringing the state back in: land disputes and Soviet power in the village

In late 1917, Russia's peasants obtained that for which they had hungered for hundreds of years and felt they had been denied in their emancipation from serfdom – full control of the land. It came when the Bolsheviks issued the Decree on Land as their second proclamation after seizing power in Petrograd in October 1917, following only the call for negotiating Russia out of the war. The short document, plagiarizing the SR programme on land, abolished private property and affirmed the right to land for all citizens of the Russian state who would work it with their own labour. The Bolsheviks hailed the Decree on Land as the will of the conscious peasantry. Lenin had spoken of allowing peasants to solve the land question on their own and the decree gave legal sanction to peasants' appropriation of the land, showing how desperately the new leadership needed peasant acquiescence to their rule.[1] The Constituent Assembly also affirmed the transfer of land in January 1918 with its own land reform, one of its only major pieces of legislation before being forcibly dispersed by the Bolsheviks. Both revolutionary bodies recognized peasant aspirations for land, solving the bedevilling problem of land reform in quick decrees, and used these dreams as tools to win support.

At a time when the new Soviet government was too weak to extend its arm formally into the countryside, land rights served as a crucial link binding peasants to the state. The Soviet revolutionary state's land reform thereby went well beyond a *post facto* acceptance of the peasant land takeovers of 1917. It extended peasants' social rights as citizens under the Soviet system to include a legal guarantee for all toiling

[1] V. I. Lenin, *Polnoe sobranie sochinenii*, 5th edn, vol. 35 (Moscow, 1959–1965), 27; *Sbornik dokumentov po zemel'nomu zakonodatel'stvu SSSR i RSFSR, 1917–1954* (Moscow, 1954), 11–12. On the intricacies of the Decree, see I. I. Mints, ed., *Leninskii dekret o zemle v deistvii: sbornik statei* (Moscow, 1979); D. S. Rozenblium, *Zemel'noe pravo RSFSR* (Moscow, 1925), 33–47; Atkinson, *The End of the Russian Land Commune*, ch. 10; John Channon, 'The Bolsheviks and the Peasantry: the Land Question During the First Eight Months of Soviet Rule', *The Slavonic and East European Review* 66 (1988): 594–600.

peoples to use the land. The Decree on Land, like Soviet power as a whole, marked a shift in the debates over citizenship during the revolution, away from political rights and towards social and economic benefits. The land reform, while seemingly recognizing autonomy for the peasants, in substance grounded the state in the village by acting as a mechanism of modern state intervention. This chapter will examine the transition to Soviet rule through the lens of the land question, a fundamental issue in rural politics for peasants and state agents.

Land brought peasants closer to the Soviet order. First, many village communities involved the state in land seizures and redistributions by asking for the authorities' permission and acceptance of land use. After dividing land at village or communal meetings, discontented individuals in the divided village turned to what they knew best to improve their lot and undermine communal control – the rural administration. The Soviet state did not have to impose its will upon the village in the early months of 1918 because most peasants did not want to cast away relationships and communication lines with the outside world. Especially for those who bristled under the control of communal elites and traditions, the implementation of the law codes helped to solidify social gains or right the wrongs wrought by their fellow villagers. It was this process of building a relationship using the trope of land that gave Soviet power an early advantage in the countryside. The mixture of a fortuitous mediator during a tumultuous political transition within the village and pragmatic state action helped to build a link between the Soviet state and village.

The new Soviet land sections established in the spring of 1918 extended in a radical direction previous state-sponsored social mediation practices. The highly contested land redistribution exacerbated deep cleavages and struggles splitting apart the village. The new Soviet state, through the land sections, became the mediator and beneficiary of village divisions as peasants engaged the state to help solve their problems. Soviet jurists, following Lenin's directives in the Decree on Land, and provincial and district allies of the Soviet state set the parameters of the conversations, favouring Bolshevik class conceptions of the village in laws and instructions on land use. Equally important, though, the Soviet administrators willingly sublimated ideological aims of class conflict for legal order or threats to the stability of the village as a whole. The government's willingness to act as a mediator among the peasantry helped to establish an early authority in the countryside and provide a solid foundation for the Bolsheviks and their allies to build a state.[2]

---

[2] The redistribution of land and resources in the countryside in 1917–18 has held a prominent position in both Soviet and western historiography. Most Soviet historians

Peasants built on a long tradition of using state organs to legitimize their actions and to help resolve intra-village disputes. As early as the seventeenth century, peasants had turned to the official court and petition processes when communal organs and customs could not solve their problems. This legal interaction between peasant and local state administration grew in the late-tsarist era with the establishment of the *volost* courts. In the early Soviet era then, rather than autonomously distribute the land, Viatka's peasants in unprecedented numbers used the government administration to help them through this momentous process, shaping the primitive local government just as it shaped them.

Moving towards 'Soviet' rule

In December 1917, just after peasants cast their ballots for the Constituent Assembly, local Bolsheviks orchestrated the overthrow of the Provisional Government in Viatka and its district towns in favour of soviet rule. On 7 December Bolsheviks and sympathetic SRs, in the guise of a Military Revolutionary Council (MRC) took control of the city of Viatka with support from the Red Guard and soldiers from the local garrison and Petrograd. In the next month, Bolshevik and sympathetic SR-controlled MRCs claimed power for the soviets and slowly asserted their control, or, as in Orlov district, seized power by force. The Bolsheviks came to power by popular demonstrations resembling the October Revolution mythology only in the factory cities of Izhevsk and Glazov.[3]

Soviet power was more popular than the discredited Provisional Government but 'the proletariat' did not rise up and install the Bolsheviks in power in 1917. The shaky Soviet government could hardly govern in the district towns and suffered from boycotts by government workers. The revolutionary committee in the town of Elabuga had to call on Red Guards from Sarapul in January 1918 to crush resistance from those loyal to the Provisional Government, while the Iaransk soviet barely put down its first uprising in the district in March.[4] Through

---

viewed the redistribution largely in class terms – as a struggle by the poor and middle peasant against the kulak, landlord, and former state power. Recent western scholarship has argued that the process of the reallocation of land was carried out by an autonomous peasantry with little influence from the new Soviet state. See P. N. Pershin, *Agrarnaia revoliutsiia v Rossii: Agrarnye preobrazovaniia Velikoi Oktiabr'skoi sotsialisticheskoi revoliutsii (1917–1918 gg.)*, vol. II (Moscow, 1966), 221–337; Figes, *Peasant Russia*.

[3] GA RF, f. 1810, op. 1, d. 178, l. 32a; For more on the Bolshevik takeover of power in Viatka's urban centres, see Timkin, *Smutnoe vremia*, 29–49.

[4] *Izvestiia Viatskogo gubernskogo ispolnitel'nogo komiteta*, 15 March 1918, 2; Bystrova et al., eds, *Ustanovlenie*, 330, 418–19.

August 1918, Soviet power, not Bolshevik power, ruled Viatka. Bolsheviks led the charge for all power to the soviets, but did not have the popularity or ability to rule any of these organs alone. The Bolshevik Party remained weak and poorly represented in the province and ruled in a coalition that threatened to swallow its rule. At the Second Provincial Congress of Soviets in April 1918, the Bolsheviks stood in a minority against a diverse corps of delegates. Leftist socialist SR-Maximalists and Mensheviks, moderate socialist Right SRs and Popular Socialists, as well as Anarchists, reminded the Bolsheviks that Russians' political loyalties may have shifted leftward but they were still fractured. A majority of district *ispolkom* representatives still belonged to the Left SRs and Bolsheviks could claim to control only three district soviets – Malmyzh, Slobodskoi, and Iaransk. On the provincial level, twenty Bolsheviks, eighteen Left SRs and Maximalists, one Anarchist, and ten non-Party representatives constituted the *ispolkom*.[5] In the villages, the move to a new Soviet order was even slower. The Constituent Assembly elections reminded peasants that they still engaged in national politics defined by the February Revolution. The Provisional Government administration lingered as neither central nor provincial government had the revolutionary authority or resources to force change.

Peasants did not usher in Soviet power with a triumphal 'October Revolution' but they welcomed its policies in the first months. Most peasants must have seen the Soviet government as an extension of the post-February order. Lenin's writings in 1917 and early Soviet decrees emphasized a decentralization of power that peasants had already felt in the autumn of 1917, and the Soviet's class-based language that championed the toiling peoples had been a part of village language since the summer. The villagers of Staryi Burets in Malmyzh and Lypskaia *volost* in Glazov, like scores of other rural citizens, continued to issue resolutions on national politics that they had learned about from newspapers or their representatives to soviet congresses. The declarations called for all power to the soviets and the immediate convocation of the Constituent Assembly, peace without annexations, and demands for land and progressive taxation that fit in well with the new Soviet regime. Peasants demanded freedom, equality, brotherhood, and full participation, much as they had under the Provisional Government. They saw Soviet rule with a Constituent Assembly as a means to provide these political dreams. A general gathering of citizens from Khristorozhdestvenskaia *volost*, Malmyzh district, therefore had no problem welcoming both the

---

[5] E. I. Riabukhin, *V bor'be s kontrrevoliutsiei (Pomoshch' trudiashchikhsia Viatskoi gubernii vostochnomu frontu v 1918–1919 gg.)* (Kirov, 1959), 32–3.

Constituent Assembly and the Soviet of People's Commissars and the Central Committee as 'the true spokesmen of the will of the toiling people'.[6] Provincial- and district-level Soviet governmental leaders still lamented the breakdown of authority in the countryside. As one Malmyzh official reported in 1918, 'Life in the district it seems was absolutely comatose.'[7] Apparently, he did not see the success in the gradual governmental transition to Soviet rule.

The October Revolution took a longer time to reverberate in the village than did the February Revolution. The bureaucratic style of the transfer of power starkly contrasted with the overwhelmingly inclusive, democratic, and spiritual feelings of March 1917. The few *volost* zemstvo administrations that were overthrown by peasants committed to Soviet power housed sizeable factories, had close political ties to the city, or politically active veterans. In Verkhodvorskaia *volost*, Orlov district, peasants formed a *volost* soviet on 16 December, immediately following the Bolshevik ascension to power in the district, and it governed with the existing administration until 14 January 1918, when the zemstvo was abolished and the *volost* elected a new *ispolkom*. Chepetskaia *volost*, Viatka district, was one of only a handful of *volost*s that actually formed MRCs or Red Guards to establish Soviet power. At a *volost* meeting on 31 December, among the usual calls for peace without annexations, control of factories for all toiling people, and land to all working peasants, energetic supporters of soviet rule moved to establish sole soviet power. Two weeks later, members of the soviet formed an MRC and replaced the militia with a Red Guard.[8] Such militarized instruments to secure soviet power were rare, though.

District congresses of deputies from each *volost* met in the first five weeks of 1918 and mediated the transition to full soviet rule in most locales. The congresses resolved to abolish the district and *volost* zemstvo in favour of soviets with an *ispolkom* and administrative sections. Resolutions took several months to implement and the zemstvo continued to govern under soviet auspices well into April 1918. On the district level, soviets replaced zemstvo committees by March, with the majority of *volost* zemstvo personnel remaining in their posts trying to work within the new state order.[9] The Slobodskoi Congress of Soviets

[6] Bystrova et al., eds, *Ustanovlenie*, 227, 316, 344. Quote from 344.
[7] S. A. Piontkovskii, ed., *Sovety v oktiabre: Sbornik dokumentov* (Moscow, 1928), 333.
[8] Bystrova et al., eds, *Ustanovlenie*, 302–4, 311, 313–14.
[9] TsGA UR, f. R-204, op. 6, d. 7, ll. 9, 13–14; GAKO, f. R-879, op. 1, d. 75, ll. 566–72; Iu. N. Timkin, 'Bolshevik i Viatskoe zemstvo v oktiabre 1917–marte 1918 gg.', in N. P. Gur'ianova and V. E. Musikhin, eds, *Viatskomu zemstvu – 130 let: Materialy nauchnoi konferentsii 8–9 Oktiabria 1997 goda* (Kirov, 1997), 113; On the tensions within

issued a resolution of praise for the zemstvo efforts to raise the well-being of the population before subsuming it into the economic section of the soviet. The Nolinsk district Soviet government even surveyed its *volost ispolkom*s on whether or not it should abolish the district zemstvo. From April to June, a variety of responses came back, reflecting local peasants' diverse standpoints on the zemstvo. Eight of the twenty responses repeated the district's language to abolish the zemstvo, but the others gently asked that the zemstvo be reorganized, moved under the jurisdiction of the soviet, or simply renamed since 'the district is in great need of its leadership in the economy'.[10]

On the *volost* level, most zemstvos elected just a few months earlier ruled alongside soviets, making up for the new order's lack of experienced administrators, before being subsumed by soviets. Most often, a *volost* meeting (*sobranie* or *skhod*) voted to reform the *volost* administration as a soviet, with nearly the same representation as before – either one representative per village, or one representative for every fifty households of a village. In Malmyzh and Glazov districts, the zemstvo remained in power alongside the soviet *ispolkom*s until April 1918. In Malmyzh, the district *ispolkom* made the *volost* zemstvos into a section of the local *ispolkom*s, along with sections on land, provisions, and social order. Village soviets were virtually non-existent during the first year of Soviet rule, and communal and village committee government remained almost unchanged, but most *volost*s slowly adapted their administration to meet Soviet reality.[11]

Simultaneously, the First Provincial Congress of Soviets of Peasant Deputies, echoed by the provincial land section, ordered the abolishment of old land committees and the immediate establishment of land sections under the auspices of the local soviets. Like the rural administration as a whole, land committees only gradually disbanded and began to function anew in mid-March 1918. The committees reformed with much the same personnel. The Novo-Multanskaia *volost* land committee, Malmyzh district, on 3 February 1918 heard applications

---

the zemstvo between professional obligations and political allegiance, and the demise of the zemstvo in early 1918, see Rosenberg, 'The Zemstvo in 1917' in Emmons and Vucinich, eds, *The Zemstvo in Russia* 403–16.

[10] Notes on resolutions of *volost* meetings of Nolinsk district; Resolution of the Second Slobodskoi District Congress of Soviets, 25 February 1918; Bystrova et al., eds, *Ustanovlenie*, 366–7, 397.

[11] *Vtoroi Viatskii gubernskii s''ezd sovetov krest'ianskikh, rabochikh i soldatskikh deputatov* (Viatka, 1918), 37, 57, 67, 74; Piontkovskii, *Sovety v oktiabre*, 334–5. In Kliuchevskaia *volost*, Glazov district, the *volost* zemstvo and the soviet ruled together in February 1918, but the soviet took power by March. Figes finds a similar transition from zemstvo to soviet rule in the Black Earth region, *Peasant Russia*, 61–9.

from peasants but decided to postpone deciding on them until the formation of a new land committee. A month later, a new land section of
fifteen representatives from local villages met and heard petitions from
peasants on the redistribution of land.[12] Zemstvo agents and peasants
who served on the zemstvo board still comprised the majority in *volost*
land committees in Urzhum district. In fact, in the district only the
Toktai-Beliakskaia *volost* land committee was composed solely of peasants. Many of the heads of the *volost* land committees also served as the
heads of the *volost* zemstvo administration in the transition period.[13]

Males dominated the elections to the *volost* land sections, although
generational tensions stirred beneath the quiet transitions on paper.
In March and April 1918 village leaders, called communal *skhod*s in
which they chose a representative to the *volost* land section. In contrast to
the more inclusive meetings in the transitional days of 1917, male heads
of households dominated these *skhod*s, even though the law called for
villages to elect representatives at open village meetings. Although women
dominated in sheer numbers in the countryside, voted two months earlier
in organized elections, and participated in public gatherings throughout
1917, peasants continued to elect males almost exclusively to represent
their interests.[14] Younger peasants and returning soldiers played a greater
role and challenged the older generation in some places, as happened at
a general gathering (*obshchee sobranie*) in Buranovskaia *volost* where they
'freed the elders (*stariki*)' from service on the land committee.[15]

Asserting rights to resources

Peasants did not wait idly for a change in government to assert their
land rights. They took advantage of the disintegration of authoritative
administrative power to pilfer or seize state land and forests. When they
did act, though, they did so cautiously or to offset the breakdown of the
economy and winter cold. Peasant appropriation of land, forests, and
agricultural resources reached its climax in the winter of 1917–18.
Winter was a time of scarcity, when peasants had a greater need for
access to historically restricted resources, such as public forests. Many
Soviet scholars emphasized the peasantry's violence and spontaneity in

---

[12] TsGA UR, f. R-204, op. 18, d. 1, ll. 2–9; in Nolinsk district, see GAKO, f. R-1620,
op. 2, d. 1, ll. 23–4ob.
[13] GAKO, f. 1362, op. 1, d. 2, ll. 9–26.
[14] TsGA UR, f. R-204, op. 59, d. 2, ll. 1–2, 5–6ob, 7–8, 16–17. These were general *skhod*s,
averaging almost ninety people. Viatka district also had an exclusively male composition
of *volost* land sections, GAKO, f. R-1062, op. 1, d. 4ots, ll. 10–18, 21, 60–1ob.
[15] TsGA UR, f. R-204, op. 15, d. 1, l. 2ob.

seizing resources in order to show long-standing primitive class tensions between peasants and nobles in the countryside. Peasants rarely destroyed grain and property. The few reported cases appear in southern Viatka, where most squires' estates were located.[16] Landlord estates, the target of peasant land takeovers in the Black Earth region, were virtually non-existent in Viatka and the rest of northern Russia.

Peasants turned their sights not on land but on coveted mills and forests. Four separate peasant communities in Malmyzh seized their local mill, drove away the owner or millwright, and redistributed the goods stored inside.[17] Peasants targeted mills because they kept much-needed food and wood and were long-coveted expensive instruments in agricultural production. Peasants ached most acutely for goods from the surrounding forests, especially in the winter when they needed wood to heat their homes. The growing fuel crisis and evaporation of guards and other deterrents engendered mass unauthorized felling of trees. In October, members of the Krupintsy village commune, having already stolen wood from the peasant Moshin's forest, declared that he had no right to it because the forest was so close to their village.[18] The Viatka land college complained in February 1918 of 'massive, rapacious felling of state, former crown, church, privately-held and even communal forests', causing 'huge damage to the forest economy and the interests of the whole state'.[19] The state administration's couching of forest pillaging in terms of national security demonstrates the significance of forestry to the national economy. In the centre, politicians and forest specialists argued for a centralized, rational management of the forests to protect the natural resource for the whole nation's well-being. The state relied on wood for basic necessities such as railroad supplies, fuel, paper, and building materials. It also needed wood to help heat the cities. Viatka province was one of largest exporters of wood to the other provinces in European Russia. In all of the state's various incarnations (the tsarist, Provisional Government, and Soviet), the defence of forests was therefore one of its highest priorities. State administrators passed decrees

---

[16] There were at least seven similar instances of peasants seizing estate property in Elabuga and Malmyzh districts. The only other reported case of a peasant attack on an estate happened in November 1917, in Morozovskaia *volost*, Kotel'nich district, when peasants burned buildings, grain, livestock, and agricultural implements of a local estate. Bystrova et al., eds, *Ustanovlenie*, 224–6.

[17] Report of the militia chief of Malmyzh district. I. P. Emel'ianov, ed., *Oktiabr'skaia sotsialisticheskaia revoliutsiia v Udmurtii: Sbornik dokumentov i materialov (1917–1918 gg.)* (Izhevsk, 1957), 205–6.

[18] GAKO, f. R-1287, op. 1, d. 3, l. 14; *Viatskaia rech'*, 15 October 1917, 3.

[19] GAKO, f. R-1287, op. 1, d. 8, l. 9; see also GAKO, f. R-1620, op. 2, d. 1, l. 58.

against illicit use of forest materials, placed guards around forests, and even sent armed forces to stop peasant felling of trees.[20]

Unending central- and provincial-level proclamations against felling highlight the central authority's inability to stop peasants who took advantage of the centrifugal force of decentralization in the winter months to ignore the decrees. As K. P. Metelev, the first Commissar of the Viatka Land Section (Zemotdel), stated, 'our published instructions on guarding forests are not having the desired results. It is very unfortunate, but it is a consistent fact that our directives vanish into thin air (*visnut' v vozdukhe*).'[21] Many village and *volost* authorities often did not attempt to enforce the anti-felling laws.

The Glazov district land section noted massive illegal felling by peasants of trees in state forests in February 1918, which denied forest materials for the city of Glazov. The land section called on the 'citizens' of the city to demand the *volost* land committee's certification every time they buy wood from a seller. It also demanded that the *volost* land committees send armed brigades to confiscate illegally felled trees. Official proclamations did no good, for the following month the Glazov district *ispolkom* complained daily of massive felling of trees by peasants as *volost* officials and village elders stood idly by. The *ispolkom* ordered the *volost* land sections, village elders, and village leaders (*desiatniks*) to take 'the most decisive measures' to stop felling and to request guards or other aid if needed.[22] Peasant felling of trees declined in spring only to pick up again in the winter of 1918. Forests remained a contested space for peasants and state because both viewed the vast wooded areas as a resource primarily for their own exploitation. Here was one area where peasants refused to abide by Soviet decrees. But it would be wrong to conclude that peasants completely opposed Soviet rule because, concurrently, peasants adopted Soviet land laws and used the state to help solve village problems.

Peasants continued to act with and without legal sanction to obtain their desired results. Neighbouring communes in Urzhum district fought to get the resources of three privately held estates in late 1917. In October 1917, Buiskii commune, Kriukovskaia *volost*, negotiated a deal with the landowner Bushkovyi and the *volost* land committee in which ownership of the mill would transfer to the land committee but members would work in the mill without pay for Bushkovyi. In December, though,

---

[20] Brian Bonhomme, *Forests, Peasants, and Revolutionaries: Forest Conservation and Organisation in Soviet Russia, 1917–1929* (Boulder, 2005), 83–94, 141–7.

[21] *Vtoroi Viatskii gubernskii s''ezd*, 28.

[22] Rossiiskii Gosudarstvennyi Arkhiv Ekonomiki (hereafter RGAE), f. 478, op. 6, d. 763, ll. 4–5, 22–22ob; GAKO, f. R-3238, op. 1, d. 2, l. 22; d. 5, ll. 1–1ob.

peasants seized Bushkovyi's enormous forest estate of almost 10,000 *desiatina*s and engaged in massive felling. The *volost* land committee put up guards but could not stop peasants from ransacking the forest. Locals coveted the neighbouring estate of V. S. Depreis, a noted conservative in local politics. On 7 December 1917, Depreis reported to the district government on rumours that the peasants were about to take all of his property. The following week, the peasants struck. They seized his pedigree livestock but decided to allow the district land committee to inventory and oversee the redistribution back to the villages. Simultaneously, seven villages in Terebilovskaia and Petrovskaia *volost*s fought the town of Urzhum in the faltering district land committee over the rightful use of a forest estate on the edge of town. The peasants stated that the commune had documents that the estate was owned in trust. After the regional land committee granted rights to both Urzhum city and the villages to collect firewood, the villages put up a guard to keep city dwellers away.[23]

Some villages employed the Decree on Land to help their cause in the winter months. For example, in January 1918, peasants of Bylerechensk commune, in Vodozerskaia *volost*, Iaransk district, wrote to the *volost* land committee, citing the language of the Decree, that the forest belongs to all the people of the Russian Republic, not to the state. They requested that the *volost* land committee stop individuals who aimed to seize and fell the forest.[24] The villagers stood together to fight for coveted land and forests. Logically, poorer peasants who could not afford wood were more likely to pilfer forests. Zemstvo statistics show, though, that land- and especially forest-hunger affected whole villages more often than individual peasants.[25] Soviet historians' picture of poor peasants leading the charge to seize land does not appear in the records. Once peasants gained control of these resources or decided to redistribute land in the new system, though, they turned on each other.

Reading the laws: initiating land redistributions

Blessed by the state, village communities across Russia in the spring of 1918 brought new land into communal assessment and redistributed existing allotments to match a population transformed by war and revolution. The process began with formal resolutions to divide

---

[23] GAKO, f. 1362, op. 1, d. 3, ll. 22ob, 31, 37–37ob.
[24] GAKO, f. R-1287, op. 1, d. 3, l. 11.
[25] *Trudy mestnykh komitetov o nuzhdakh sel'sko-khoziaistvennoi promyshlennosti*, t. X (St Petersburg, 1903), 325, 556.

communal (*obshchina*) land at village gatherings (*obshchie sobraniia*) in
the early spring as villagers began to think of sowing the fields. They had
to wait just a little longer in this extraordinary year to begin to tend their
new allotments because spring came late to Viatka (May 1918 is still the
coldest on record), leaving the fields too cold to seed.[26] Over the next
three years, almost two-thirds of Viatka's villages redistributed land,
many of them more than once. This was less than the nearly universal
distributions by the land-hungry communes in the Black Earth region,
but the wave of redistributions in both regions during this time was
equally staggering for its potential transformation of land tenure and as
a social act uniting peasants through the country.[27]

For all its social and political significance, the mass redistribution
movement in the early months of Soviet rule was not a 'Black Repartition' (*chernyi peredel*), a distribution of all of Russia's lands to the peasants without the interference of the hated landlord or state authorities.
The Black Repartition has been part of observers' construction of the
Russian peasantry's ideals, but it does not match the political and economic realities of the revolutionary countryside. As in 1917, after the fall
of the tsar, peasants did not seek isolation or reject government political
and social reform. In the Black Earth region peasants acted on their
own to take over estates, and peasant communes in that area may have
acted as 'autonomous agents' in the agrarian revolution, rejecting early
Soviet state attempts to organize the population and guide land reform.[28]
In Viatka, at least, the opposite occurred. The already emboldened peasant communes, encouraged by the monumental state decrees, divided
the land and often sought out the Soviet state to give their actions
legitimacy. Communes did not incorporate all the land, measured in part
by the new land laws.

The October Decree on Land guaranteed what peasants had demanded throughout 1917 – the right for all citizens to work the land with
their own labour – and subsequent laws in December 1917 establishing
land committees provided a general framework for implementing this
guarantee. The Decree on Land approved the 23 June First All-Russian
Congress of Soviets' resolution supporting the *volost* land committees'

---

[26] The average temperature for May 1918 was 3.8 degrees (C), while the historical
average temperature is 10 degrees (C). M. O. Frenkel, 'Klimat', in *Entsiklopediia zemli
Viatskoi*, ed., N. I. Perminova et al., t. 7, *Priroda* (Kirov, 1997), 144, 155.
[27] On land divisions in the Black Earth region, see Kabanov, *Krest'ianskoe khoziaistvo*,
60–1. According to a 1922 survey, almost every village in the Black Earth region (94%)
redistributed the land. In the Urals (Viatka and Perm provinces), 69% of villages
surveyed had redistributed land, while in the northern region, 63% redistributed land.
[28] Figes, *Peasant Russia*, 67.

oversight of peasant seizure and annexation of estate property. A more detailed 4 December 1917 decree on land committees provided a specific framework for *volost*, district, provincial, and central land committees and outlined the committees' tasks, responsibilities, and finances.[29] It was not until the publication of the Basic Law on the Socialization of Land (*Osnovnoi zakon o sotsializatsii zemli*) on 19 February 1918, however, that peasants and the land committees were given specific instructions on who actually had the right to use the land and forests, and how the controversial redistributions should be carried out. Published on the anniversary of the 1861 peasant emancipation from serfdom, the Basic Law was supposed to symbolize peasants' true emancipation. Whereas the 1861 emancipation bound the newly freed serfs to a life of redemption payments, the 1918 Basic Law spelled out the Soviet state's guarantee to redistribute land and agricultural goods for free (Basic Law, articles 2–7). Lenin personally oversaw the distribution across the countryside of the Decree on Land, which he viewed as critical to generate peasant support for the socialist state. The Soviet state advertised the Basic Law in the same way and by April 1918, the Viatka government had distributed 1,000 copies of the law throughout the province.[30]

Bolshevik land policy went well beyond propaganda and temporary compromise. The land decrees represented a larger shift in popular and educated society's extension of citizenship beyond political rights and into social and economic entitlements. In contrast to the Basic Law on Forests, issued into law on 30 May 1918, with its heavy focus on centralization of administrative oversight, the Basic Law on Land allowed localities much more control. Both, though, continued statist trends from the tsarist era whereby zemstvo agents, professionals, and the state emphasized from above the rationalization and modernization of agricultural production.

Provinces and districts promulgated their own instructions and resolutions that extended, and muddied, specifics of the Basic Law. To add to the confusion, many *volost*s and villages redistributed land as they made the transition to Soviet rule. Peasants were both jubilant and confused by the land decrees but still tried to adhere to the spirit of the decrees. Later, individual peasants would use the spaces and contradictions between the decrees to improve their lot.

---

[29] *Sbornik*, 13–14, 16–23.
[30] GAKO, f. R-1062, op. 1, d. 5, l. 157; *Vtoroi Viatskii gubernskii s"ezd*, 28–9; Atkinson, *The End of the Russian Land Commune*, 169.

The Basic Law contained 52 clauses clarifying how the local soviet was to oversee the distribution of land. According to article 12, land was to be redistributed to the working people in an equal manner and based on the historical land-tenure system and norms of the region. The land decree extended the social right to work the land for all citizens but the Basic Law established an economically tiered system of granting the entitlement. The laws gave preferable treatment to population groups within the category of 'toiling people'. Priority went to 'landless and small land owners of the local tillers of the land as well as local agricultural workers (*rabochie*)'. The second-tier group was 'those who arrived at the given locale after the publication of the law on the socialization of land who are part of the land tilling population'. This middle group would include artisans, workers, and other city dwellers who returned to their village to guarantee a source of food. The non-land-tilling population (*nezemledel'cheskoe naselenie*) who registered with the local land section could also receive land (Basic Law, article 22), assuming they worked it with their own labour.

Communes were not supposed simply to divide up all the land as they saw fit. Land that peasants did not own before 1917 (i.e., state, land bank, church, crown, and noble land) in theory went into a reserve land fund (*zapasnoi zemel'nyi fond*) that the *volost* land committee would oversee. The committee would keep part of the land for agricultural improvement and distribute the rest to landless and small land holders only after a survey of land and a census of the population to determine the number of consumers and workers, an impossible task given the dearth of surveyors and census-takers in the countryside in 1918.[31]

The Second Viatka Provincial Congress of Peasant, Worker, and Soldier Deputy Soviets in April 1918 expanded upon the central provisions of the Basic Law in a set of Provisional Instructions.[32] The Provisional Instructions organized the review of the redistribution process by local land sections. The instructions specified that the commune had to allot the amount of land by eater, regardless of gender

---

[31] *Sbornik*, 23–31; *Izvestiia soveta krest'ianskikh, soldatskikh i rabochikh deputatov Orlovskago uezda*, 7 March 1918, 3. The law also contained a variety of other clauses such as: insurance from fire, livestock moraine, death, and crop failure (articles 14–16); a state monopoly of grain (article 19); and legal migration (articles 27–34).

[32] *Vtoroi Viatskii gubernskii s''ezd*, 95–103; GAKO, f. R-1062, op. 1, d. 38, ll. 63–6ob. The congress showed the fractured politics at the provincial level in April 1918. The head of the provincial Bolshevik Party and soon-to-be chairman of the provincial executive committee (*gubispolkom*), Ivan Popov, opened the congress. A Left SR spoke in support of Soviet power followed by an SR-Maximalist who condemned the Bolsheviks for ruining the economy, terrorizing the countryside, and leading Russia to the brink of civil war.

(article 35), through a majority of votes of citizens eighteen years and older, also regardless of gender (article 36). These laws departed from tsarist law that called for two-thirds of the households to agree to a redistribution of the land and empowered younger peasants and women who traditionally had less of a say in communal decisions. The *volost*, district, and provincial land section committees all used the Provisional Instructions as the basis of their decisions during 1918. Regions also held congresses of *volost* land sections in March and April 1918 and passed further resolutions reinforcing and supplementing the provincial and national land laws. They also worked to resolve local land disputes.[33]

Communes followed the essence of the laws, but not always the details, when they redistributed land. Peasant members fully digested the language of citizenship and universally referred to all named individuals as 'citizens'. Their resolutions made a point to show that the ascribed followed the law. Many repeated the code's prohibition of buying and selling land and its order that landholders must use only their own labour to work the land. Explicit reference to legal codes continued peasants' discursive patterns in official communal documents. Some resolutions began by showing how they upheld the 1902 law for two-thirds of eligible voters to be present at a resolution; several others cited the Land Decree, provincial, and district land codes.[34] Villages sent their redistribution decrees to the *volost* land section for approval, as the Provisional Instructions demanded.

For all the excitement generated by the revolutionary land decrees, most communes enacted only a partial reallotment of land, incorporating some of the newly acquired land, cutting off strips from the wealthiest and depleted households, and transferring the land to the poor.[35] Resolutions often listed the personal movement of strips of land. In a general gathering of Verkh-Ushnur, Kurkumbal and Dundshtur villages, Konganurskaia *volost*, Urzhum district, the resolution specified that Nikolai Shcherbakov would take a strip of land from Vladimir Shcherbakov, and Stepan Solov'ev from Il'ia Solov'ev.[36] Rarely did communes fully level all the land. They did place a new emphasis on a

---

[33] RGAE, f. 478, op. 6, d. 760, l. 27; d. 761, l. 65; d. 101, ll. 2–7ob. Elabuga had a congress in February, Malmyzh in January, Iaransk in March, *Vtoroi Viatskii gubernskii s''ezd*, 52, 57, 85.

[34] A. A. Ivanov, ed., *Pervaia sovetskaia vesna v derevne: Krest'ianstvo Mariiskogo kraia i zemel'nyi vopros v 1918 godu: Dokumenty i materialy* (Ioshkar–Ola, 2002), 92, 141–2, 159–61, 165–6.

[35] *Materialy po zemel'noi reforme 1918 goda. Raspredelenie zemli v 1918 godu* (Moscow, 1919), 1–2; *Vtoroi Viatskii gubernskii s''ezd*, 43, 79.

[36] Ivanov, ed., *Pervaia sovetskaia vesna*, 139; see the same in Nolinsk district, GAKO, f. R-3224, op. 1, d. 5, ll. 1ob–3.

more egalitarian division, though. At a general meeting of citizens of Shantraner village, Urzhum district, peasants resolved to reallot land 'from those that have it to those that do not'.[37] As part of this egalitarian move, eighty to eighty-eight per cent of communes that redistributed land in Viatka, as in Russia as a whole, based their divisions primarily on the number of consumers (or eaters) in a household.[38] The consumer variable supported the Provisional Instructions and fitted the economic realities of the revolutionary village. Even though veterans were beginning to return, the village still felt an acute labour shortage from the scores of able-bodied peasants who died, were imprisoned, or disappeared at war. A division based solely on the number of workers would not have made sense when households could not say with certainty how many they still had. Many communes also accounted for the number of a household's workers to ensure that the unit could viably work the allotted land.

Overall, the increase in land per household was negligible. Russia's peasants already owned most of the arable land and the land committee held onto a portion of the newly acquired land in the reserve fund. Once the commune or land committee doled out parcels to newly divided households, landless or small landholders, and other residents with a tenuous position in the community, such as recent returnees from the city, average households did not gain much. Peasants as a whole in Viatka increased their land by only 3.2%, a far cry from the gains of the peasants of Samara province (127.7%) or Saratov (84.5%). The divisions succeeded in their mission of levelling land allotments, though. Between 1917 and 1919 communal redistributions cut off the extremes – the number of landless peasants dropped from 3.3 to 1.9% and households with over 13 *desiatina*s of land fell from 3.2 to 1.1% – while the middle bumped up. Households with 2.1 to 4 *desiatina*s of land jumped from 24.6 to 36% of the whole.[39] Comrade Kotov, a speaker at the Fourth Extraordinary Party Conference in March 1919, complained that traditionally strong elements in the village controlled the redistribution process and when peasants won new land it was too small to farm, especially with modern technology. He concluded

[37] Ivanov, ed., *Pervaia sovetskaia vesna*, 95.
[38] *Vtoroi Viatskii gubernskii s''ezd*, 41, 51, 54, 79; 'Sovremennoe zemlepol'zovanie po dannym spetsial'noi ankety TsSU 1922 g.', *Vestnik statistiki*, no. 1–3 (1923): 141–2; Atkinson, *The End of the Russian Land Commune*, 177.
[39] V. P. Danilov, 'Pereraspredelenie zemel'nogo fonda Rossii v rezul'tate Velikoi Oktiabr'skoi revoliutsii', in I. I. Mints, ed., *Leninskii dekret o zemle v deistvii*, 284–7; B. Knipovich, 'Napravelenie i itogi agrarnoi politiki 1917–1920 gg.', in P. Mesiatsev, ed., *O zemle: Sbornik statei o proshlom i budushchem zemel'no khoziaistvennogo stroitel'stva*, vyp. 1 (Moscow, 1921), 26; Ivanov, ed., *Pervaia sovetskaia vesna*, 374.

simply that, 'The socialization of the land gave nothing to the village.'[40] Kotov's conclusions may have been exaggerated but reflect Bolshevik agents' frustration that the land redistribution process did not do more for the economic viability of the village and the expropriation of what the Party saw as kulak property. The Soviet myth of class warfare in the village oversimplified the complex social dynamics in the countryside. Poor peasants did not simply struggle with kulaks over the spoils of the new land.

Peasants meditated on the divisions, waited for administrative guidelines and approval, fought over the spoils, and often re-divided assets a number of times. It is therefore important to see the villages' redistribution of land and resources as more than a single event transpiring in a raucous *skhod*.[41] The Soviet state played a crucial role in all of this by establishing new laws and administrative organs that guided the redistribution process and acted as a mediator among the peasantry, helping to solve village quarrels. After the villages and communes divided the land in their possession, new conflicts erupted. The Iaransk district land section reported in December 1918 that the 'levelling of land of course was not able to satisfy the toiling peasantry completely. Peasants in general do not want the land on a temporary basis, but forever (*navsegda*). Moreover small landholders and the landless do not get land from the reserve land fund equally.'[42] In 1922, forty-three per cent of surveyed peasants in the region remained unsatisfied with the land divisions.[43] The redistribution of land and resources brought to the surface long-standing and complex conflicts based on social standing within the village, kinship ties, and inter-village relations. In order to resolve these conflicts, many peasants actively sought government help. Peasants willingly used the new Bolshevik state apparatus for their own good, both to gain approval in the redistribution process and to resolve internal disputes. The land section was an arena in which peasants could challenge the village's power dynamics by using established laws.

Mediating conflict: village disputes and the Soviet state

Once villages redistributed land, thousands of disgruntled peasants and whole communes turned to the Soviet administration to resolve village disputes and to better their situation during this critical time. The

---

[40] *Chetvertaia chrezvychainaia Viatskaia gubernskaia konferentsiia RKP(b) 1919* (Viatka, 1919), 13.
[41] Figes finds the same patten in the Black Earth region, but he argues that the traditional peasant commune redistributed the land without the state's aid. *Peasant Russia*, 102–3.
[42] Ivanov, ed., *Pervaia sovetskaia vesna*, 317.   [43] 'Sovremennoe', 146–7.

Kotel'nich district land section stated in August 1918 that, 'during the period of land redistribution, fifty to a hundred citizens, if not more, appeared every week' to appeal to the state for help.[44] On top of those who asked for help in person, citizens submitted 1,239 written petitions on land to the district land section between February (when the district land section was established) and August 1918. The other districts of Viatka reported similar mass appeals to the Soviet administration to resolve local land conflicts.[45] Such a large wave of peasant petitions to the state was unprecedented in modern Russian history. The 1861–63 struggle between newly freed serfs and nobles over land charters (*ustavnye gramoty*) comes closest in sheer numbers of administrative filings, but more peasants involved the state in 1918 than in 1861–63, in part because post-emancipation peace mediators dealt with the whole community as one. A better comparison is to cases submitted to the late-Imperial era *volost* courts, but the courts had a different scope of cases and were established explicitly as an agency of intra-village social conflict mediation.[46]

Peasants regularly appealed all the way to the national level to have their case heard by a Moscow central committee. In agreement with the Basic Law (article 9) and Provisional Instructions (articles 31, 33, 48), peasants appealed first to the *volost* land section (*volzemotdel*), then worked up the chain of command to the district land section (*uzemotdel*), and the provincial land section (*gubzemotdel*) before turning to the Kremlin.[47] The whole process took months, and in some cases years, with uncertain results. Land sections beyond the *volost* level mixed agronomists, peasant officials, and city politicians, showing that peasants willingly engaged non-peasants in the land distribution proceedings. The majority of the district land committee officials in summer 1918 were SRs and Left SRs from the professions and representatives from the *volost*. The provincial-level land section was composed entirely of non-peasants and headed at first by Metelev', an SR-Maximalist who oversaw a committee of three Bolsheviks and three SRs. Other members of the provincial section included a statistician, eight agronomists, two forestry officials, a land surveyor, the head of the land division, and four 'knowledgeable people' (*sveduiushchie litsa*). While Metelev' and many

[44] GAKO, f. R-876, op. 1, d. 92, l. 372ob.
[45] GAKO, f. R-1062, op. 1, d. 74; GAKO, f. R-876, op, 1. d. 92, l. 372ob; and RGAE, f. 478, op. 6, d. 765, 766.
[46] Allan K. Wildman, 'The Defining Moment: Land Charters as the Foundation of the Post-Emancipation Agrarian Settlement in Russia, 1861–63', *The Carl Beck Papers in Russian and East European Studies* 1205 (1996).
[47] GAKO, f. R-1062, op. 1, d. 41, l. 16.

other SRs left the government, the tone of the land section resolutions did not change.[48]

Peasants turned to the Soviet administrative body without hesitation, often circumventing their local land section. In April 1918, the Glazov district *ispolkom* complained to the *volost* land sections that 'lately citizens are appearing at the district land section with various applications about allotment of land, allowing land redistributions, and other land matters, without [the necessary] applications from their *volost* land section'. The peasant petitions drive did not cease, for the following month the *ispolkom* ordered the *volost* land sections to announce that peasants must submit complaints to the *volost* land sections, rather than to the district-level administration.[49]

Lenin supported the egalitarian division of land in part because he believed that poor peasants would resist kulak-driven communal decisions. He was right to a degree. The guise of unanimity in the 1918 redistribution resolutions faded away almost immediately, revealing an even more fractured village. Divisions ran in multiple directions – one line cast communal solidarity against many people who lived in an uncertain status in the village, like tenant farmers, Stolypin separators, destitute families, alcoholics, lazy or sick individuals, beggars, refugees, clergymen, and migrant workers. The village was not only divided between insiders of the traditional community and outsiders, or the poor against the rich. Other lines divided the community and households when the young challenged their elders in the meetings and at home; widows and daughters-in-law demanded land; and poor and rich asked for more land or resources. With these and other cleavages, land became a trope for villagers to express their problems.

The levelling process provoked more prosperous peasants and those who felt wrongly identified as wealthy to seek redress. Those on the losing end of the levelling process included households with a large labour force and land allotments that lost land when their communities divided the land by consumer.[50] Petitioning peasants, categorized by the Bolsheviks as anti-Soviet kulaks, adopted Soviet language and used Soviet land law to better their situation. In 1919, Dmitrii Guzhavin, a peasant of Sovetsk district, took on his village over its appropriation of

---

[48] RGAE, f. 478, op. 6, d. 761, l. 9; *Vtoroi Viatskii gubernskii s"ezd*, 27; GA RF, f. R-393, op. 3, d. 104, l. 1.

[49] RGAE, f. 478, op. 6, d. 763, ll. 18, 28. In May 1919, The People's Commissariat on Land (Narkomzem) similarly complained that petitions and complaints on land matters must go to the *volost* land section first. GAKO, f. R-1062, op. 1, d. 38, ll. 76–76ob.

[50] The same was true in the Black Earth region. Figes, *Peasant Russia*, 108.

his fruit garden. In his petition Guzhavin did not deny that he had served a prison sentence as a counter-revolutionary earlier that year. While he was in jail, fellow villagers worked his fruit garden with the understanding that it would be returned to him when he was freed. When this did not happen Guzhavin filed grievances up to the national level. The district land committee found that he was not entitled to property because his father was an absentee landlord who did not work his own land and rented out his two houses. Guzhavin defended himself thus: 'Although I am a son of a wealthy peasant I must not be tied to his deeds.' He did not inherit or use his father's property and he worked the land with his own labour. His fellow villagers disagreed. They wrote in a resolution that his father worked the land but it was Dmitrii and his family who lived in the town and rented out the land. The central land committee agreed with the village.[51]

Strong conflicts emerged between the commune and peasants who had an uncertain status within the village. Landless and tenant farmers, refugees, clergy, returning soldiers, migrant workers (*otkhodniki*), and widows were often excluded by their communities during the redistribution process. In Kotel'nich district, a landless peasant who worked on his brother's allotment used the new Soviet law to acquire land. The commune, based on peasant common law, had refused to grant the peasant any land, since he did not own a plot in the village. The peasant appealed to the various land sections. The provincial land section finally granted him land, in agreement with the Provisional Instructions (article 36), which stated that those who live in the locality and work the land have the right to the land.[52] The law did not always help marginalized peasants, as a peasant who lived in Viatka city learned. He tried to gain land by claiming that he lived in a nearby village and worked the land. The provincial land section rejected his petition after it found out that he lived in a village for only a short period during the summer.[53]

Even peasants who thought that they were integrated into their village were sidelined during the land distribution. In Urzhum district, S. P. Bastrakov complained to the district soviet that he had lived in his village for nineteen years and worked communal land but the commune was now trying to take his land since he was not officially a member of the commune. Bastrakov had adopted a household in this village and had lived off its land as part of a customary communal social security system.

[51] RGAE, f. 478, op. 6, d. 138, ll. 41–3ob.
[52] RGAE, f. 478, op. 6, d. 761, ll. 84–84ob.
[53] RGAE, f. 478, op. 6, d. 761. ll. 68–68ob.

He was never viewed as a legitimate part of the commune, though, and his neighbours believed that he did not have a claim to their land.[54]

Parish clergy also found themselves left out of their community's land redistribution. While the clergyman had an esteemed role as a key link between village and nation in the first half of 1917, his position had become precarious by 1918. The Bolsheviks nationalized all land belonging to the church and monasteries and put it in reserve land funds. In February 1918, the Soviet government also enacted 'the Decree on the Separation of Church and State' which, among other things, forbade religious teaching in schools, made civil marriages the sole acknowledged ceremony, and put the survival of the village church largely in the hands of the local soviet.[55] The new restrictions on the clergys' daily functions threatened the viability of the already poor rural priests. As peasants redistributed land, priests had to depend on their parish's goodwill to allot them land. Most communities abutting church or monastery property allowed church workers and monks to continue to work their plots of land and brought the remaining property into the village for redivision by the land sections.[56]

Even though most communes allowed clergymen to continue to use their allotments, there were cases in which priests complained to the land section to better their situation. The priests played on the phrases and discursive strategies of socialism and citizenship to win their case. Pavel Miliutin, a clergyman in Buiskii *zavod*, Urzhum district, argued his case all the way to the provincial land section. Miliutin rested his argument on the foundation of all the major decrees on land – he presented himself as a land toiler who had worked twelve *desiatina*s of church land with 'his own labour' up to the present year. Miliutin thereby tried to meet the Basic Law's two major requirements of guaranteed land – to have worked the land with one's own labour up to 1917. Local peasants had given him a plot of two *desiatina*s already sown with oats, but it was eight versts away and he could not survive with such inaccessible land. The land section rejected his petition, since the Provisional Instructions stated that even though a clergyman works the land with his own labour, as a current employee of the church he was not entitled to land unless local citizens allotted a parcel to him.[57]

Another clergyman, Mikhail Maslov, however, fought to retain his land. As per the Basic Law, church land was inserted into the reserve

---

[54] Ivanov, ed., *Pervaia sovetskaia vesna*, 72, 174. The result of the case is unknown.
[55] Glennys Young, *Power and the Sacred in Revolutionary Russia: Religious Activists in the Village* (University Park, PA, 1997), 56–60.
[56] GAKO, f. R-3224, op. 1, d. 1, l. 3; Ivanov, ed., *Pervaia sovetskaia vesna*, 287–8.
[57] GAKO, f. R-1062, op. 1, d. 74, ll. 344–6, 350ob.

land fund that the Kliuchevskaia *volost ispolkom* began to distribute in May 1918. Already in April, Maslov appealed to the *volost ispolkom*:

I ask the Kliuchevsk *ispolkom* to provisionally rent me church land and hay fields for one year as a citizen without land and needing the use of land to support myself. Moreover, I will use the land . . . for rational vegetable gardening, horticulture, and beekeeping with the aim of showing the people of the village . . . I promise to work the rented land with my own labour.[58]

The clergyman evoked the rights of citizenship under the Soviet regime for all landless toilers to receive a land allotment as long as he works it with his own labour. He also pandered to the rural intelligentsia and the Soviet state's vocal goal of raising the standard of peasant agriculture through scientific example. In a subsequent petition in May, Maslov pleaded with the *ispolkom* to let him keep his land, emphasizing the collective good that would come out of his instruction of good farming practices to the people. He also promised to continue to distribute his goods so peasants could see the benefits of modern farming: 'This spring I gave out gratis to the people of Kliuchevskaia *volost* maple from the tree nursery and strawberries from the garden.' The *ispolkom* did not let him rent the land, something that the Basic Law forbade. It did, however, go against the Provisional Instructions and allotted him half a *desiatina*, enough land in its opinion to survive.[59]

Maslov's plea for land was tied up in a larger local struggle to receive church land from the reserve land fund. In the spring, the Kliuchevskaia *volost* land section decided to redistribute the reserve land fund's inventory and the Glazov district land section followed with further instructions to distribute all church land, 'regardless of whether or not clergymen work it with their own labour'. The district land section excluded plots of special cultural importance, such as church squares, cemeteries, land on which buildings were located, fences, gardens, and areas with beehives.[60] Peasants petitioned the land section to give them church land. Like the priest Maslov, villagers constructed themselves as good, landless citizens. Varmiia Merypova wrote, 'I ask the Kliuchevsk *ispolkom* to give me one and a half *desiatina*s of land from the church of Parzei village for me to toil with my own hands as a landless female citizen who has no occupational work.'[61] Peasants fitted themselves into

[58] TsGA UR, f. R-204, op. 6, d. 3, l. 48.
[59] TsGA UR, f. R-204, op. 6, d. 3, l. 45; GAKO, f. R-3224, op. 1, d. 1, ll. 9ob, 15ob, for similar cases where the soviet allotted one priest land, and returned a horse and harness to another priest because they were toilers.
[60] TsGA UR, f. R-204, op. 6, d. 3, l. 26.   [61] TsGA UR, f. R-204, op. 6, d. 3, l. 43.

the state's primary category to receive land from the reserve land fund. In May, the Kliuchevsk government distributed church land to several households. The receiving party had to sign a note in which they promised to abide by certain restrictions:

I, the below signed citizen of Kliuchevskaia *volost* . . . village, given the current note by the Kliuchevskaia *volost* land section to all those receiving land from the reserve land fund for rental use for one year, will work and harvest it during this time . . . I will guard and not fell trees growing on the allotments provided to me for temporary use. I sign . . .[62]

If clergy represented a small population who fitted awkwardly into the Soviet legal system, returning soldiers were one of the largest, and most important, populations for the Soviet system. Soldiers, who returned home in a steady stream in 1917, played a prominent role in politicizing the village. The Soviet state quickly recognized the importance of soldiers as political allies in the village and helped make a smooth transition for them into the new political world. However, soldiers did not always benefit from their standing. While they were at war, their villages frequently excluded them from the land redistribution process, even though the Provisional Instructions explicitly stated that communities must allot a soldier land if the government had not informed the family of his death (article 36). Villagers treated soldiers as they did other peasants who were away during the scramble for land. Uncertain whether the men would return, villagers did not want to risk forgoing valuable land. For example, a wounded Muslim soldier at war since 1914 complained to the provincial land section that he did not receive his land allotment because he was in the hospital when the village issued their redistribution resolution. His fellow villagers had confessed to him that they did not allot him land because he did not work it himself because he was away in the army.[63] In Kotel'nich district, the Mal'tsev brothers complained to the Central Committee in March 1918 that their *volost* soviet mistreated them as former soldiers in its land redistribution by exchanging their old plot for several poor, inconvenient strips. Like other petitioners, the brothers emphasized their poverty and that they could not survive on the new land. Moscow informed the brothers that

---

[62] TsGA UR, f. R-204, op. 6, d. 3, ll. 52–71, 85–103. There were thirty-seven signed notes of this kind.
[63] GAKO, f. R-1062, op. 1, d. 74, ll. 94–5. See also GAKO, f. R-1287, op. 1, d. 5, ll. 17–18ob, where a village redistributed land in May 1918 by eater but did not include soldiers who had not yet returned home from the war; GAKO, f. R-1287, op. 1, d. 7, l. 32, in which former soldiers complained that a 1915 agreement of land use was unacceptable because they were away at war at the time and did not approve it.

the soviet had acted within its rights and according to the Basic Law on Land.[64]

Even after soldiers re-established themselves at home, their fellow villagers interfered with their quest for land. Having redistributed land in their favour, peasants were reluctant to give up any gains so quickly, even for those that they valued for their sacrifice and political experience. A typical case was that of Grigorii Konozhev, a soldier returning home in Orlov district. Konozhev had served in the tsarist army for five years and in the Red Army for nine months. In a statement to the *volost* land section, he pleaded that his household held the smallest allotment of land (thirteen *sazhen*'s) in his village. In June 1919, he gathered the village to request a new redistribution of the land in equal parts. While some of his fellow villagers agreed, including a member of the local land section, Konozhev cited two more prosperous peasants who stymied his efforts. The *volost* land section ordered the village to uphold the interests of Konozhev.[65] Konozhev used his status as a soldier and general class arguments to help win his case. He showed himself as a poor peasant who was being exploited by local kulaks. Soldiers like Konozhev turned to the Soviet state because they knew that it would defend their rights and entitlements as natural allies of the new order.

From the Council of People's Commissars (Sovnarkom) to *volost* soviets, the Soviet state promoted soldiers' social rights to land by summoning investigations and ordering the village government to ensure that soldiers and their families received land. This happened in Nizevo village, Orlov district. A Red Army soldier returned home wounded in the Civil War to find his father evicted from his homestead that he had built in 1918. The soldier turned to the Military Revolutionary Soviet to solve the problem and it passed the matter to the provincial land section with the order to review the matter immediately. Likewise, the Slobodskoi district Military Revolutionary Committee ordered all *volost ispolkom*s to guarantee that land of Red Army soldiers remain sown for the benefit of their families (and presumably military and urban needs).[66]

Urbanites across Russia who retained ties to their village fled epidemic unemployment and the daily struggle for basic provisions in the cities with the hope of a more stable life working the rural land.[67] In the Lower

[64] RGAE, f. 478, op. 6, d. 654, ll. 12–13. A bureaucrat in Moscow paid close attention to the petition and noted 'legal' next to the account of the soviet's actions.
[65] GAKO, f. R-1062, op. 1, d. 213, ll. 19–20, 23. For other cases, see ll. 9, 39, 40, 47, 75.
[66] RGAE, f. 478, op. 7, d. 138, ll. 15–17ob, 63; GA RF, f. 1240, op. 1, d. 122, l. 73.
[67] Narskii, *Zhizn' v katastrofe*, 89; Diane P. Koenker, 'Urbanization and Deurbanization in the Russian Revolution and Civil War', in Diane P. Koenker, et al., eds, *Party, State,*

Volga region, the average village had to accommodate nineteen families who returned to their roots. Almost all the villages included the returnees in the land reallotments. The smaller villages of the Urals through the northern regions greeted only three returning families on average. The differences are unclear but peasants in Viatka were more likely to keep land plots while engaging in seasonal work. They also worked in cities like Viatka and Izhevsk that did not witness the remarkable depopulation of Moscow and Petrograd. Viatka's peasants were also more reluctant than those in the Lower Volga to give returnees land, with only sixty-five per cent of villages in the region accommodating this population.[68]

While the majority of workers who returned home from the factory by 1918 received land, those who kept their jobs outside the village did not enjoy such guarantees. Some peasants still working in other provinces attempted to retain their land allotments via mailed requests. For example, a Viatka peasant living in Perm urged the *volost ispolkom* to allow him to keep his land allotment, rented out for the past twelve years while he was away.[69] Peasants working in the high-paying armaments factories in eastern Viatka, however, actually laboured to exclude themselves from the land redistributions. For example, peasants in Bogorodskaia *volost*, Nolinsk district, engaged in out-migration (*otkhodnichestvo*) to factories in Votkinsk and Izhevsk. In winter and spring 1918, several peasants sent letters to the *volost* land section requesting certification that they did not have land in the village. The workers needed to present this certificate to retain their jobs.[70]

Scores of wartime refugees, urban dwellers, and even foreign prisoners and alien citizens also tried to join villages in which they did not have family ties. While exact numbers are impossible to determine, data from the 1922 survey in the Urals region suggests that these outside figures outnumbered returnees three to one. This is in sharp contrast with the Lower Volga, where returnees dominated the non-established population jockeying for land. Communes were even more reluctant to include them in the land reallotments, with only twenty-three per cent of villages in the Urals region giving them land, even though the law demanded that they do so.[71] Tensions from the war carried over in this case and kept outsiders on the margins of the village. Refugees and prisoners either moved on or had to create a space for themselves in the community.

and Society in the Russian Civil War: Explorations in Social History (Bloomington, 1989), 81–104.
[68] 'Sovremennoe', 142–4.   [69] GAKO, f. R-1620, op. 2, d. 2, ll. 51–51ob.
[70] GAKO, f. R-1620, op. 2, d. 2, ll. 5, 7, 9–9ob, 11–14, 17.
[71] 'Sovremennoe', 144–5; Figes, *Peasant Russia*, 138–44.

Peasants also used the 1918 reallocation of land to settle long-standing kinship disputes. In this regard the land sections took the place of the *volost* courts as an official arena to settle family disputes. In a survey after the revolution, peasants commented that 'fights of fathers with sons increased because after the sons returned to the commune from military service, or wherever they were, they knew more about the current situation than their fathers'. Tied to these quarrels and youths' dreams of social independence, household divisions (*razdels*), especially by sons who had been in military service, increased. The land section estimated that the number of peasant households in 1919 increased 12% from 1917 and 17% from 1912.[72] The commune's incorporation and reallocation of land and resources provided an opportunity for younger peasants to break from their family and establish their own household. If there were problems, peasants turned to the commune or land section.[73]

Other disputes were clearly linked to generational strife. For example, in Pudemskaia *volost*, Glazov district, Afanasii Kurpikov petitioned the *volost* land section to use his deceased son's land. The daughter of the deceased brought her own complaint to the land section, arguing that her father had broken away from the household twenty years earlier, so in fact she was entitled to his land. Afanasii appealed to the provincial land section that his son died twenty years ago and his granddaughter had married and moved away. The land section ruled in his favour.

The land section acted as a valve to release pressure in households. *Soldatki* whose husbands were still at war, had perished, or had abandoned the family still struggled to survive. Collective organizations that promoted their need for state subsidies did not help enough. At the First Provincial Congress of *Soldatki* in June 1918, representatives from the villages uniformly complained that they had not received state subsidies since the October Revolution and were starving.[74] Many *soldatki* became lowly members of their in-laws' homes. In 1919, Kseniia Kazakova petitioned the *volost* land section to break from her father-in-law Andrei Kazakov's home because he 'attacks her with slanderous words and even beats her, for which he was jailed for three days by the people's court'. While Kseniia had been the matriarch of a large household, the war had destroyed her family. Kseniia's husband had been mobilized in the army

---

[72] Nauchno-Otraslevoi Arkhiv Udmurtskogo Instituta Istorii, Iazyka i Literatury Ural's-kogo Otdeleniia RAN (hereafter NOA UIIIaL URO RAN), op. 2-N, d. 11, l. 2; GAKO, f. R-1062, op. 1, d. 338, l. 18.

[73] RGAE, f. 478, op. 6, d. 761, ll. 36–7; see also GAKO, f. R-3238, op. 1, d. 22, ll. 1–1ob, 3–3ob, 8, 10–10ob, 12, 14; f. R-2506, op. 1, d. 28, ll. 13–14ob; d. 37, l. 7, 18–18ob, 31–3, 47.

[74] *Obshchegubernskii s''ezd soldatok Viatskoi gubernii 1-go iiunia 1918 goda* (Viatka, 1918).

in 1914 and had not been heard from since; her oldest son was in the military and his wife had moved to a different village to live with her parents. Kseniia's middle son left for work in spring 1917 and had not contacted his family since then. Kseniia and her six-year-old son had to move in with her father-in-law, his wife, and their two children. Although Kseniia lived in Andrei's old house (*izba*) for most of the year, during the winter she had to move in with her father-in-law. At the hearing, Andrei promised that if Kseniia would stay in the home, they would work together, but if she did not want to then he would not grant her a division (*razdel*) of property. The land section ruled against Andrei because he 'has not carried out proper relations with his daughter-in-law and will be brought to trial to bear responsibility for his actions'. It ordered him to carry out a division of property with Kseniia.[75] By 1919, the land section thereby began to go beyond a strict reading of Soviet laws and act as a social arbitrator. It could protect women and victimized family members and help them advance in the rural economy. The Soviet body took root as a mediator and alternative to traditional peasant social institutions.

Soldatki were one of the most likely rural populations to turn to the Soviet administration. They continued their fight for subsidies as they had turned to the tsarist and Provisional governments. The bureau of complaints reported that the greatest percentage of over 2,100 petitions that it received in five weeks in 1919 came from soldiers' wives and families writing that they did not receive their funds.[76] Even though *soldatki* did not receive adequate financial assistance, they still enjoyed a favoured status in the eyes of the Soviet state. *Soldatki* petitioned for free forest materials and allotments guaranteed to them by law, and the provincial authorities pressured the local governments to fulfil these requests. Some villages used the privilege of soldiers' families to get access to forbidden forest material by claiming that they needed to rebuild the families' dilapidated homes.[77] *Soldatki* and soldiers' families were potential allies for the Bolsheviks in a sea of politically unreliable peasants and the government learned by 1919 that they were the key to deterring soldiers from deserting the Red Army. As part of the creation

---

[75] GAKO, f. R-2506, op. 1, d. 37, ll. 34–6. In another case, a *volost* land committee upheld a scheduled division between father and son, but the son went into the Red Army before the inventory of the father's property. The wife, now a *soldatka*, took the matter before the district land committee and it forced the father to carry through with the division with his daughter-in-law. He won on appeal at the provincial level because the matter should have gone through the people's court and not the land committee. GAKO, f. R-3238, op. 1, d. 19, ll. 11, 19.

[76] GARF, f. 1240, op. 1, d. 120, l. 2.

[77] GAKO, f. R-3238, op. 1, d. 19, l. 4; Ivanov, ed., *Pervaia sovetskaia vesna*, 128.

of the modern state, the Bolshevik government also acknowledged its obligations to its citizens and extended social welfare entitlements to family members of model citizen soldiers who risked their lives for the nation.[78] The state also intervened in family affairs and hoped to mobilize soldiers' wives and families for the Soviet project.

While fine when the husband was alive, if the *soldatka* became a widow, Soviet support clashed with village customs. Widows had always held a tenuous position in the village. Their land allotment was tied to their union with their husband. After his death, the village would assign the widow a partial land allotment to survive on. A widow would often instead move in with her children or late-husband's family where she held a subordinate place within the family.[79] Widows used creative ways to improve their lot. In Orlov district, a widowed *soldatka* lived in the household of her son who had recently been killed in war. Incensed that the village gave her the worst land, she petitioned the *volost* land section for land for her son as well. The case made it to the district land section but it discovered that her son had died in June 1917 and the state's confirmation of his death arrived in October 1917, so the widow was not guaranteed his land.[80] The case of Varvara Vagina reveals how the position of the widow in the Soviet legal system hinged on her ties to Red Army soldiers. In 1915, Vagina's husband was entangled in a court battle over a hayfield parcel and building that he sold to Semen Novoselov when he was called away to war, never to return. In 1919, the *volost* land committee took the land and building and Novoselov and Vagina responded with a volley of petitions and complaints to the land committees and, in 1920, to the Kremlin, fighting for ownership of the land and building. Through many twists and turns over questions of property rights in the new order, the central land section finally decided the case based on Vagina's status as a *soldatka*. As one of her children wrote in a statement supporting her case, 'blood from her family was spilled for the sake of the Red Army'. The decision, overturning the district-level land section, underlined that she was after all a mother of three Red Army soldiers and should get the disputed property.[81]

Land section decisions also reveal complex conflicts among peasants in communes and those who separated from the village under the Stolypin reforms. Tensions that had spilled over during the war, and especially in 1917, escalated when the commune redistributed land.

[78] Sanborn, *Drafting the Russian Nation*, 49–53; Kabanov, *Krest'ianskoe khoziaistvo*, 34; GAKO, f. R-3224, op. 1, d. 1, l. 8.
[79] Worobec, *Peasant Russia*, 22–3, 65–70; Moon, *The Russian Peasantry*, 184–98.
[80] RGAE, f. 478, op. 6. d. 761, ll. 70–70ob.
[81] RGAE, f. 478, op. 6, d. 1933, ll. 5–10; d. 1610, ll. 15–25. Quote on l. 10.

Many Stolypin separators returned to the commune to grab part of the newly acquired land. Communes also forced separators back into the village or took their land during redistribution. This trend was repeated in Viatka, especially in the southern part of the province where the number of separators was highest.[82] Some communities simply exacted revenge upon separators. This happened in Kotel'nich district where the Podugoriana village commune and the separator Iakov Vokhmianin sparred in a drawn-out case. The commune implemented a general redistribution of communal land by eater that the *volost* land section approved on 25 April 1918. As the commune explained in a written complaint, seeing that Vokhmianin, who held his land as a private farmstead (*otrub*), still had more land than his fellow villagers and was ploughing up his neighbours' strips as well, the commune punished him by bringing his farmstead into the communal lot and reapportioning his land so he had less than his fellow villagers. The *volost* rejected the new allotment, but the commune implemented a second redistribution, approved by the *volost* land section, that allowed him to retain his private farmstead but replaced his fertile land with poor quality land. Vokhmianin won a grievance against the commune to the district land committee that overturned the resolution and returned his land and the provincial land section upheld his victory following the commune's appeal.[83]

The upper levels of the Soviet state aggressively defended the separator's right to exist. Both the Basic Law and the Provisional Instructions explicitly asserted that separators had an inherent right to their land. Separators could therefore confidently turn to land sections as their protectors. This made the provincial land section, after a peasant in a separate farm (*khutor*) complained that landless peasants had illegally divided his farm, order the district land section to put the guilty peasants before the revolutionary tribunal.[84] In the summer of 1918, the provincial land section even demanded that the Elabuga district government strictly enforce the Provisional Instructions to defend separators against attacks and restore broken up farms (*khutora*).[85] In this way, the state's legal consciousness overrode its aim of class warfare in the countryside.

Separators were not passive victims of the land redistribution. Many turned to the land section and the Soviet legal codes to take advantage of

---

[82] RGAE, f. 478, op. 6, d. 1044, ll. 5–8ob; GAKO, f. R-1062, op. 1, d. 74, l. 54.
[83] RGAE, f. 478, op. 6, d. 761, ll. 41–41ob; l. 94 on peasants from Viatka district who held an *otrub* farmstead and demanded a new division of land.
[84] GAKO, f. R-1062, op. 1, d. 64, l. 457.
[85] GAKO, f. R-1062, op. 1, d. 74, ll. 85, 281.

the situation. In one case, Prokopii Perminov convinced the provincial land section to allow him to keep his private farmstead (*otrub*) that the village of Staraia Piniuga had brought back into the communal pot. Perminov had only begun to work his private plot in the spring of 1918 but *volost* records proved that he had land divided from the commune in 1916 but could not work it as he was called to war that year.[86] In another case, Ivan Koshcheev, a peasant in Nolinsk district, broke from his village in 1914 to establish a private farm (*khutor*). Labour and material shortages from war and revolution prevented him from actually moving. The commune now insisted that he move to the private farm because, according to the petitioner, they wanted his immovable property. Koshcheev understood that the Basic Law promised him the rights to his independent farm, but he asked the land section whether the commune had the right to force him to the private farm.[87]

More often, separators fought to keep their land. For example, in 1914, forty-three households broke from Kypka village, Kliuchevskaia *volost*, Glazov district, a predominantly Udmurt village. They enclosed common land and farmed it privately for the next four years. In June 1918, the remaining villagers demanded that the borders between the village and private farmers be abolished. Presumably, the villagers wanted to incorporate separator land into the commune's redistribution. The separators turned to the *volost* land section for help, appealing all the way to the provincial-level Zemotdel. The land section cited article 32 of the Provisional Instructions, that the commune or village must preserve private farmland (*khutorskie i otrubnye uchastki*) during a redistribution of land.[88] This exchange is even more compelling because the petitioners followed up on their complaints even while their territory was under the rule of anti-Soviet forces in the autumn of 1918.

Village against village

Sparring over land was not limited to individual peasants. Whole villages fought each other over the agrarian revolution's spoils. They claimed rights to long-disputed or coveted meadows and fields that used to be owned by the state or church, or whose ownership had never been determined. Villages acted as cohesive units in their fights with other communities. As with collective peasant action towards forests and other non-village property, the peasantry often seized the disputed land,

---

[86] RGAE, f. 478, op. 6, d. 1044, l. 12.   [87] RGAE, f. 478, op. 6, d. 654, l. 25.
[88] RGAE, f. 478, op. 6, d. 761, ll. 113–14; GAKO, f. R-1062, op. 1, d. 74, l. 100; *Vtoroi Viatskii gubernskii s"ezd*, 100.

leaving the victims to turn to the state for aid. Villagers in Il'inskaia *volost*, Iaransk district, pleaded with the provincial administration to help them because peasants from Vasil'kovskaia *volost*, Kotel'nich district, were illegally mowing their hayfields. The land section came to the petitioners' aid.[89] Similarly, villagers of Voskovishisk grounded their argument on ownership. They acquired a meadow from neighbouring Olnoninska village in 1909 but peasants from Olnoninska apparently had illegally mowed it in 1918 and 1919. The provincial land section decided that both parties had rights to it, as one village had worked it since the revolution, but the other rightfully owned it, and so it divided the meadow in half.[90] However, the provincial land section took ownership and relative wealth into account in mediating a meadow claimed by both Posadska and Permiaki villages in Orlov district. Stepan Savinykh, a peasant of Posadska, had owned the meadow since 1875 and peasants of Posadska had worked it. In 1918, the village appropriated the meadow and put it into communal use. Permiaki village countered that the meadow abutted its land plots and showed legal proof that Savinykh never owned it. The district and provincial land sections could not determine ownership and bestowed the meadow to the citizens of Permiaki because they held less land per eater than Posadska.[91] Similarly, members of Savino village, Urzhum district, were furious when they learned from a surveyor that their *volost* land section laid claim to a 256 *desiatinas* tract of land for the reserve land fund and realloted 169 *desiatinas* of it to a neighbouring village. In a petition that worked its way to Moscow, the villagers demanded all the land 'as toiling peasants' who had worked all 256 *desiatinas* with their own labour for the past fifty years. The central land committee agreed that the land should not have gone to the reserve land fund because there was never a proper redistribution of land, but since the other village was poor and already working the land, they decided to leave the parcel as it was for the time being.[92]

Peasants of Mumzer village, Konganurskaia *volost*, Urzhum district, issued a resolution at a general gathering laying claim to the tract of forest adjacent to their farmland. The peasants posited that the whole *volost* used to own the forest but forty-five years ago four neighbouring villages won ownership. In a plea that fitted both traditional discursive patterns of peasant petitions and the new socialist order, the village

[89] GAKO, f. R-1062, op. 1, d. 74, l. 393; see a similar dispute over a land parcel in Petropavlovskaia *volost*, Sovetsk district, GAKO, f. R-2506, op. 1, d. 37, l. 4.
[90] RGAE, f. 478, op. 7, d. 138, ll. 107–9ob.
[91] RGAE, f. 478, op. 6, d. 1610, ll. 8–8ob; op. 7, d. 138, ll. 128–9ob.
[92] RGAE, f. 478, op. 6, d. 1610, ll. 12–13.

complained that the other villages enjoyed 'a huge amount of land that they are able to sell freely'. It demanded the forest and part of the other villages' arable land, for good measure, and promised that the village would never rent it out. A parallel case happened nearby, when Timofeevo village asked the Urzhum land section for 'surplus land' from three neighbouring villages that had increased their land by ploughing up the neighbouring forest. Timofeevo villagers suffered an acute shortage of land and could only allot half a *desiatina* (1.35 acres) of land per eater, but the land section responded that it was prohibited to transfer land between villages.[93]

Although villages fought over resources, surprisingly, the land redistribution process did not bring out intra-village ethnic hostility. The Urzhum district land congress guaranteed the inviolability of non-Russians' sacred spaces. In the lone violation, Mari villagers posted guards around a local sacred grove after unknown people illegally cut down some of its trees.[94] In multi-ethnic villages, kinship and economic status overrode any ethnic divisions. Moreover, Russian and non-Russian peasants behaved similarly in turning to the state to solve intra-village disputes. While the conflicts revolved around disputed land, in some instances they had ethnic dimensions. In May 1918, Udmurt villagers of Votskii Taimbosh, Elabuga district, used armed force to seize land from a neighbouring village. They reasoned that they were small landowners and the other village did not need the disputed arable land.[95] In a long-standing dispute, Russians and Bashkirs fought over land on the Kama River separating Viatka and Ufa provinces. The Viatka Russian peasants had 'since olden times' used the 1,500 *desiatina*s of land on the other side of the Kama River, the border between Viatka province and Menzelinsk district, Ufa province. The two sides had fought six times in the courts since 1904 over who owned the land, without a resolution. In March 1918, the Menzelinsk land section resolved to let the Viatka peasants keep the land until it was redistributed, but in July, the Menzelinsk Peasant Congress resolved to seize the land from the Russian peasants. In December, the Russian peasants turned for help to the Central Commissariat of Land, emphasizing that the socialization of land had not taken place and that without the meadow they 'did not have one pud of hay to feed our livestock'. Even though the Elabuga land section recognized that the meadow belonged to the Viatka peasants, the issue was never officially resolved.[96]

[93] Ivanov, ed., *Pervaia sovetskaia vesna*, 99–100, 183–4. For other inter-village disputes, see GAKO, f. R-1062, op. 1, d. 74, l. 205, ll. 375–6; GAKO, f. R-1287, op. 1, d. 5, l. 108; RGAE, f. 478, op. 6, d. 761, l. 39; d. 1610, ll. 72–4ob.
[94] Ivanov, ed., *Pervaia sovetskaia vesna*, 235–6.   [95] GAKO, f. R-1062, op. 1, d. 74, l. 88.
[96] RGAE, f. 478, op. 6, d. 1043, ll. 14–14ob, 18; d. 654, ll. 27–8.

The socialization of land affected all agricultural land, regardless of its location. Urbanites found themselves fighting with villages over meadows and land allotments that they had traditionally farmed. Some city dwellers farmed land either in the city or in nearby villages. As the food crisis grew during the tumultuous times, these borderlands became essential for survival. In Viatka, towns owned meadows and hayfields for their own exploitation. In 1918, villages near urban areas looked to incorporate and distribute city-owned meadows and hayfields located beyond city limits. For example, the city of Sarapul and two surrounding villages fought over the city's use of meadows. The city soviet refused to give the meadows to the peasants. The peasants took their case to the provincial-level land section that demanded a new review of the matter by the Sarapul section.[97] The peasants had Soviet law on their side in these disputes. The head of the land section of the Viatka city soviet reported in 1920 that the Second Congress of Soviets' agreement, to give all land outside city borders for peasants' use, went against the spirit of Soviet politics because it hurt the city's relations with the village and strengthened 'kulak' elements. He concluded that the land distribution process in Viatka hurt political organization and was the greatest factor in the destruction of the city economy.[98]

Conclusion

Control of the land, the climax of the revolution for so many of Russia's peasants, had contradictory and unexpected results. The traditional commune had continued its revitalization since the beginning of the war and played the central role in an initial redistribution of land and resources. Orlando Figes casts the conflict over land as one between insiders and outsiders – stable peasants who fought returning soldiers, urban migrants, landless peoples, and other folk who did not benefit from communal governance. This closely resembles Soviet historians' conceptions of class conflict in the countryside while still stressing traditional peasant politics in rural revolution.[99] It only shows part of the picture, however. If the commune reasserted its hegemony at first, the interventionist revolutionary land codes and Soviet administration quickly counteracted its authority. Lenin and Soviet policy makers began their rule promising peasant autonomy in resolving the land question, but quickly changed their minds and established administrative guidelines

---

[97] RGAE, f. 478, op. 6, d. 761, ll. 42–3. The city of Urzhum also fought over a meadow, ll. 60–60ob.
[98] RGAE, f. 478, op. 6, d. 1933, ll. 61–9ob.   [99] Figes, *Peasant Russia*, 101–53.

for the redistribution. Part of this new urge for state intervention was to spur class warfare among the peasantry by empowering the poor against the rich and traditional village leadership. The Soviet regime had fertile ground to work with as war and revolution had shaken an already fractured village. Soviet land law successfully widened existing intra-village cleavages by favouring poorer land-hungry peasants over wealthier ones and giving certain population groups within the village an official outlet to oppose their community.

Soviet administrators put legal order above their aim for class warfare. When rich peasants, priests, separators, or other suspicious elements turned to the state, the Soviet administration looked to the written law for guidance, often undermining the larger class struggle. By acting as largely impartial organs that relied on the Soviet law codes, the land sections proved a valuable resource for peasants to counteract the commune's power and work within the Soviet apparatus to better their position. Land relations offered a relatively stable counterbalance to the tumultuous political breakdown and the Soviet state's coercive tactics that otherwise marked Soviet–peasant relations in the Civil War years.

In order to help resolve problems with their communes, neighbours, and families, and to better their situation, peasants invited the Bolshevik state into their homes. So, while the peasantry's initial decision to divide their land was often autonomous from state intervention, this step was a far cry from peasant rule. As in the tsarist era, peasants did not hesitate to turn to state authorities. Like courtrooms and petitions to outside authorities, the new Soviet land sections offered peasants an alternative to the commune's hegemony and another avenue to get what they wished. Peasant applicants may have had to adopt Soviet rhetoric or work within the polity, but the end result was worth it. The new administration and legal code guided the land redistribution process and allowed the Soviet state to creep into village life. In effect, the so-called Black Repartition, approved by the Bolsheviks in October 1917, brought the peasants closer to the state.

5 Civil War and the village

In the spring and summer of 1918, massive uprisings against the Bolshevik regime erupted throughout Russia. The October order had inherited a crumbling economy, a desperate food supply situation, and a polarized social and political world. The Bolsheviks' willingness to employ aggressive and coercive politics to achieve their goals further promoted Russia's civil conflict. The period between the spring of 1918 and 1919 marked the crucial, defining era of the Communist regime in the Viatka region. It had to defeat organized anti-Bolshevik forces in the south and east and stem the tide of peasant and worker uprisings, while building state infrastructure and popular support. The state's immediate needs of food and military recruits undermined its effort to build a solid administration and legal order, while its thrust to monopolize political power drove away key support. Peasants in Viatka lived in the heart of Russia's social turmoil during this period and cautiously navigated through its bloody civil breakdown.

Four years after mobilization for world war, direct military conflict entered Viatka's villages. First, the People's Commissariat of Food Supply (Narkomprod) turned its attention to the fertile lands of southern Viatka, sending food brigades into the village. To get grain from peasants in an area where they were losing control, central Soviet officials quickly forged what would become the *razverstka* (levy) system for all of Bolshevik Russia. The development of grain policy in the summer of 1918 illuminates the tensions in the peasant–state relationship and the inherent weakness of Soviet authority in the countryside at the time. The Soviet state lacked both political and military might and its attempts to requisition grain undermined its popularity with local peasants and claim to popular-based political power. Rural people therefore did not just experience grain requisitioning; their actions shaped Bolshevik practices.

Viatka was the front line of the Civil War in 1918 and 1919 and conflicts within its borders both shaped Russia's Civil War and challenge our understanding of civil conflict in the countryside. As the Soviets tried to find a way to make peasants fulfil obligations to them, the largest anti-Soviet insurrection to date erupted from the factory city of Izhevsk in eastern Viatka. These two equally significant events, followed quickly by the advance of the White Army, not only highlight the importance of the Viatka countryside in understanding Russia's Civil War, but strikingly illustrate how several political viewpoints and population groups clashed in such a concentrated area. The chaos from the requisitions and other Bolshevik excesses led to a fascinating triangular civil conflict in the countryside among Bolsheviks, the anti-Bolshevik Prikomuch regime, and peasants. While the rebellions arose from concrete disputes over grain requisitions, there were also competing, violent conversations on the best political system for Russia. At the same time, several revolutionary movements offered alternatives to Bolshevik control.

Over the next four chapters, following a roughly chronological order, I examine the Civil War and its aftermath in the village. In this chapter I explore how Bolshevik attempts to force peasants to give up grain in the region created a tumultuous environment in the countryside that fed anti-Soviet forces. When alternative political figures emerged, they had natural, albeit fleeting, support from the peasants. The Soviet's early attempts at grain requisitioning were therefore intertwined with the equally traumatic military campaigns in Viatka. The next two chapters examine how the Soviet regime attempted to reconstruct its relationship with the peasantry from 1919. The final chapter studies the devastating social and economic breakdown and the Soviet state's efforts to rebuild the countryside.

Forging Bolshevik grain policy

The spectre of hunger haunted the Soviet regime. The new rulers, like the wartime tsarist and Provisional governments, struggled to find a workable scheme to extract enough grain from the countryside to provision the army and urban areas. Peasants had already sacrificed grain to the national cause for over three years, in what seemed to them to be a repetitive cycle of the state's empty promises of competitive prices or manufactured goods, followed by armed forces appearing in their village to take their grain at gunpoint. For rural grain producers, the Communist regime intensified the cycle begun during the war. The Bolsheviks maintained the Provisional Government's grain monopoly scheme, but peasants did not produce as much grain as the Bolsheviks wished and the state quickly returned to a policy of armed force to extract and control grain supply.[1] Soviet requisitioning of grain was a central point of contention between peasants and state but it also became a sign of power. The Soviet state, peasants, and anti-Soviet insurgents all used the need for food as a tool to establish power relationships in the countryside. The significance of grain procurement politics in Viatka also went well beyond its borders. In fact, in the late summer of 1918, the sole district of Sarapul became a laboratory for Commissariat of Food Supply officials to test methods to extract grain from peasants that they then applied to the rest of Soviet Russia.

In the first half of 1918, Viatka's provincial and local officials relied on a socialist version of the Provisional Government's grain monopoly scheme. In March, the Viatka Provincial Commissariat of Food Supply (Gubprodkom) called on the districts to establish their own fixed prices or exchange material goods for grain, and to confiscate grain if the peasants refused to sell.[2] The following month Gubprodkom added socialist nuance to a province-wide system of fixed prices on agricultural goods based on its imagined class structure in the countryside. Poor peasants who had less than thirty puds of surplus grain would be supplied a minimum grain ration and paid fifteen rubles a pud for rye and barley and twelve rubles a pud for oats. Peasants of the 'ownership class' (middle and rich peasants, kulaks) would be compensated significantly less: five rubles a pud for rye and barley and four for oats, tied to a sliding scale of their grain inventory. The state declared that it would confiscate grain from peasants who would not sell.[3] The Communist class analysis of the village remained vague; the sliding scale shows that it did not rest on the amount of a peasant's surplus grain. Of course, the success of the plan depended on the ability of the state to inventory household grain and back up its scheme with force. In the spring of 1918, it could do neither.

The system may have worked if the state had as much power as the decree imagined. On paper it gave peasants their main demand of 1917 – fixed prices on both agricultural and manufactured goods. The

---

[1] Holquist and Lih show the mirror image of the continuity in policy. *Making War*, esp. 243–60; *Bread and Authority*.

[2] GAKO, f. R-876, op. 2, d. 27, ll. 302, 309–10; op. 1, d. 27, ll. 55–7. There was a clear distinction in state policy between requisitioning (*rekvizatsiia*) and confiscation (*konfiskatsiia*). When the state requisitioned agricultural goods from a peasant, it guaranteed payment in kind. When state agents confiscated goods, they did not offer recompense and at least threatened force. Soviet officials delineated this difference in a response to a peasant petitioner who wanted more compensation for requisitioned ropes and anchors.

[3] Resolution of the Second Viatka Provincial Congress of Soviets, 20 April 1918, Bystrova et al., eds, *Ustanovlenie*, 483–5.

First Viatka District Congress of Soviets of Peasant Deputies in March 1918 supported the exchange and backed government confiscation of grain from peasants unwilling to sell their surplus at the fixed price.[4] The exchange of goods had the potential to work well for both parties. At the Malmyzh city collection point, peasants of the surrounding villages exchanged 2,100 puds of rye, 5,500 puds of oats, and 1,600 puds of rye flour for manufactured goods and oil in just over two months.[5]

Many peasant communities wanted to establish a moral economic relationship with the state; that is, they would give grain for a loss if the state would make material goods available at a reasonable price. Peasant communities based their drive for a moral economy with the state on tsarist-era relations with their landlords and the state in which the peasants gave their grain and labour and accepted the unequal power relationship in exchange for guaranteed subsistence from the political elite.[6] In February 1918, peasants of Medianskaia *volost*, Viatka district, expanded their terms of the moral economy to have the state also guarantee a minimal subsistence. They stated that they would give rye, flour, and oats at the fixed prices but the government should give every eater sixty funts of flour or seventy funts of rye a month until the new harvest, as well as provide a ration of oats for horses and livestock.[7] Such a relationship could not work in 1917 or at the beginning of the Soviet era. Manufactured goods were in too short supply to please the peasants and they did not give enough grain to please the Soviet government. Provisional Government authorities could not complete a reliable census with experienced personnel and a more stable political relationship with the rural administrations. The Soviet government had neither sufficient experienced personnel nor a warm enough relationship with its peasants when it came to food supply. The Soviets did not even have enough surveyors to chart major tracts of land and they certainly could not inventory individual households' grain.

The province's half measures were trumped in May 1918 by Moscow's food supply dictatorship, a system born of wartime statism and the Provisional Government experience. The food supply dictatorship maintained the state's claim from 1917 to a household's surplus grain and to reliance on coercion to procure it. The Soviets added political agitation and armed food brigade detachments (*prodotriady*). The food dictatorship

[4] GAKO, f. R-879, op. 1, d. 1, ll. 1–5.
[5] Report of the Malmyzh district soviet of supply, 1 June 1918, Bystrova et al., eds, *Ustanovlenie*, 504.
[6] The concept of the moral economy is defined at length in James C. Scott, *The Moral Economy of the Peasant: Rebellion and Subsistence in Southeast Asia* (New Haven, 1976).
[7] Bystrova et al., eds, *Ustanovlenie*, 471.

embodied scientific rationality, the desperation of a country descending into civil war, and the violence of wartime. In principle, the system rested upon a mathematical formula. Experts in the *ispolkom* of Viatka's food-stuffs section calculated in March 1918 that peasants could give up thirty per cent of their projected surplus (1,650,000 puds) without threat to future production.[8] This was the same formula that Provisional Government experts had used. In actuality, the centre pushed its agents to extract more grain, while not wielding enough power to control its agents in the countryside. State agents with experience from the war immediately turned to violence and forced requisitions, paying little heed to Soviet regulations. Requisitions violated peasants' sense of justice and they responded with passive and active resistance. Peasant resistance and conflict with the state occurred simultaneously with peasant attempts to reach out to the state to solve land disputes, as discussed in the previous chapter. This created a picture of juxtapositions where peasants one day took up arms against Soviet grain detachments and the next day petitioned the land committee to support their claims.

By the summer of 1918, the Bolshevik government had lost its main grain surplus regions of Ukraine to Germany, and the northern Caucasus and Siberia to civil war. Moscow pressed the historically grain surplus provinces in European Russia, such as Viatka, for more grain. Fertility of the soil thereby shaped peasants' experience of civil war. Food brigades bypassed the northern and central grain deficient zones with their small, dispersed villages and, as in 1917, concentrated their activities in Viatka's southern breadbasket region. Brigades from Petrograd, Kharkov, and Moscow joined several regiments from the province and roamed the countryside searching for goods and food-stuffs.[9] By the end of June, 2,500 workers had also arrived in Viatka to help get grain. The brigades gathered nearly 500,000 puds of grain in their first six weeks but resorted to base economics and violence to do so.[10] Brigades negotiated higher grain prices with individual regions, rich peasants, and even speculators and ignored whether or not a

---

[8] RGAE, f. 1943, op. 3, d. 160, ll. 2–3ob. The total projected surplus was 5,500,000 puds of grain. Thirty per cent of the calculated 1918 grain surplus was 1,650,000 puds. The foodstuffs section argued that the province needed seventy per cent of the surplus to complete new sowing of fields in districts with grain shortfalls.

[9] RGAE, f. 1943, op. 3, d. 160, ll. 62, 83, 98. Participation of brigades from other provinces was typical. See Delano DeGarm, 'Local Politics and the Struggle for Grain in Tambov, 1918–21', in Raleigh, ed., *Provincial Landscapes*, 60.

[10] Specifically, 63,000 puds of grain in Sarapul district, 200,000 in Malmyzh, 10,000 in Urzhum, 15,000 in Elabuga, and 207,716 puds in the remaining districts. RGAE, f. 1943, op. 3, d. 160, ll. 62, 83, 98; N. Orlov, *Sistema prodovol'stvennykh zagotovok. K otsenke rabot zagotovitel'nykh ekspeditsii A. G. Shlikhtera* (Tambov, 1920), III.

household had surplus grain. They quickly gained notoriety for their violence, hooliganism, alcoholism, and other notorious acts, stealing goods from villagers and arresting peasants who offered no resistance.[11] Peasants in the southern and eastern districts of the province thereby witnessed a more violent, coercive, and interventionist Bolshevik (and anti-Bolshevik) governance in the Civil War than their northerly neighbours who rarely had to fend off forced grain requisitions.

For the peasants, Soviet grain brigades represented an intensification of the much-hated forced requisition policies from the previous autumn under the Provisional Government. Peasants responded through both passive and active resistance, adapting and strengthening their resistance to grain policies begun during the First World War. Peasants resisted Soviet grain procurement in a number of passive manners: they petitioned the administration, hid grain, refused to bring it to collection points, and complained about food brigades. They also used the inefficiency of the new regime and the tension between the central and provincial administrations to their advantage. Such weapons of the weak allowed peasants to disobey Soviet grain policy while not explicitly refusing to follow orders.

Peasants complained to the administration about the brigades' illegal activities. This included a typical complaint by a peasant woman in Pilinskaia *volost*, Urzhum district. Soldiers searched her house and then offered to buy her horse. She refused but they took the horse anyway and later brought her a notice that the horse had been requisitioned. The woman pleaded first to the village soviet and then the district *ispolkom* that this was her only horse and she needed it for fieldwork. Her village soviet supported her claim and demanded that the government return her horse.[12] Representatives of the Soviet sponsored Fourth Iaransk District Congress of Peasant Deputies were so incensed with excesses that they lashed out against the grain monopoly and condemned it as 'state robbery'. The provincial revolutionary tribunal considered trying all the representatives for counter-revolutionary activity, but after a year dropped the case.[13]

Peasants also reduced the amount of land they put under the plough. It is unclear if peasants limited crop land to resist state claims on their grain, or to shore up the village economy that suffered from a shortage of labour, seed, and agricultural instruments. In any case, the state interpreted peasant reduction of crop land as resistance. In July, the Glazov district *ispolkom* published a plea to *volost* and village governments to

[11] GAKO, f. R-885, op. 1, d. 53, ll. 14–14ob, 31.
[12] GAKO, f. R-3454, op. 1, d. 66, ll. 32, 34–5.   [13] GAKO, f. R-1322, op. 1, d. 8, l. 12.

entice its constituency to plant their fields: 'Despite repeated orders about the impermissibility of reducing tilled land, despite many people explaining the disastrous consequences of reduction of crop land, despite the intensification of daily starvation, a significant part of the district's population is decreasing the amount of tilled land.' The district government complained that the *volost* and village administrations did little to curtail such practices: 'The district *ispolkom*, foodstuffs committee, and land section once again clarifies to the population of the district that any reduction of crop land will have disastrous effects on the well being of the country, district, and all citizens.' The district government considered those who refused to use all their land to be enemies of the poor and against Soviet power and threatened to take land away by force from those who were not using it.[14]

When peasants did sell grain they preferred to do it through sackmen (*meshochniki*) who could offer a higher price or more material goods than the state could. These intermediaries then sold the grain on the urban black markets. Bolsheviks lamented that sackmanship was epidemic in Viatka, and for good reason. In Urzhum, sackmen reportedly paid peasants forty to fifty rubles for a pud of flour, thirty-five rubles more than the district's fixed price. The Kukarsk *ispolkom* complained to the provincial leadership that 'thousands of sackmen are arriving by ship to Kukarsk'. Sackmen frequented transportation centres such as rivers and railroad stations, and congregated at the border of Kazan province. One of their favourite spots was the port village of Viatskie Poliany in Malmyzh district where they paid off the village *ispolkom* and transported up to 10,000 puds of grain a day. In April, the district government sent a Red Army detachment to the village but the sackmen paid them off too. The provincial government then got involved and sent another brigade, but they also had little success, only confiscating 5,000 puds of grain over the next month (or half a day's transaction).

In the Tatar village Paran'ga, in Cheremissko-Turekskaia *volost*, Urzhum district, peasants maintained a brisk trade with Kazan province, exchanging grain for manufactured goods, sugar, and other products. Around 5,000 puds of grain a day passed through the village en route to Kazan; on bazaar days the amount would be as high as 30,000 puds. The Red Army was unwilling to confront the better-armed Tatars who had rifles and even machine guns at their disposal. In June, even a brigade of two hundred men could not defeat the villagers. A brigade

---

[14] Announcement of the decree by the Glazov district *ispolkom*, 4 July 1918, Bystrova et al., eds, *Ustanovlenie*, 48–9; Raleigh also finds a major reduction in tilled land in Saratov; see, *Experiencing Russia's Civil War*, 316–17.

accompanied by Red Army soldiers was also unable to requisition grain from the nearby predominantly Tatar village of Ilet. Ilet was on the road to Kazan from Paran'ga and would have been part of the grain network. Cheremissko-Turekskaia *volost* was also in the centre of the autumn 1917 conflagration over grain, a fact that must have appeared to locals as a continuation of state policy.[15]

These villagers and other sackmen from Viatka enjoyed the sanction and protection of the Kazan provincial soviet. When Viatka posted guards on the border with Kazan, the Kazan Province Food Supply Section demanded that the borders reopen to free trade, threatened Viatka's guards, and even sent food brigades into Viatka to help hide goods and aid sackmen.[16] The Kazan soviet promoted a free market in grain and flaunted the centre's complete lack of control over the economy. During the Civil War, bureaucratic conflict was more than a struggle between the centre and periphery. Provinces fought with each other to survive economic shortages. The trade between the mostly Tatar peasants of the region also shows the resilience of traditional economic and social networks. During the late-tsarist era, Tatars of southern Viatka had close economic and cultural ties with Tatars in Kazan. They traded agricultural goods and horses and crossed the border to attend schools.

Peasants throughout southern Viatka went beyond passive resistance to Soviet requisition policy and food brigades. They actively and often violently fought state agents, even more than they had when the Imperial and Provisional Governments relied on coercive pressures. From March to August in Glazov district alone the government reported over eighty incidents of peasants refusing to comply with grain policy.[17] In June, villagers in Malmzyh district killed an agent of the food supply commission and forced the chair of the provincial soviet of food supply to run for his life; Soviet officials described the situation as an armed rebellion. Two peasants were killed in Tsip'ynskaia *volost* while resisting state attempts to inventory grain. A group of peasants attacked the head of the Gyinskaia *volost* land section during an inventory of the local mills' grain. In Iukamenskaia *volost*, a crowd of peasants beat up a member of the

[15] RGAE, f. 1943, op. 3, d. 160, ll. 92ob, 96; Bystrova et al., eds, *Ustanovlenie*, 504–6, 514.
[16] RGAE, f. 1943, op. 3, d. 160, l. 107a.; D. S. Saisanov and B. Sh. Shingareev, 'Krest'ianskie vosstaniia v iuzhnykh uezdakh Viatskoi gubernii v 1918 godu', *Mariiskii arkheologicheskii vestnik* 8 (1998), 120.
[17] T. S. Tomshich, 'O nekotorykh osobennostiakh agrarnoi revoliutsii v Udmurtii v 1918–1919 godakh', *Iz istorii partiinykh organizatsii Urala. Sbornik statei. Uchenye zapiski*, no. 69, vyp. 7 (Sverdlovsk, 1966), 24.

Plate 9   The Iaransk district *ispolkom*, 1919. Courtesy GASPI KO

volost ispolkom for 'incorrectly' distributing grain. In July the whole village of Khodyri, Ukhtymskaia *volost*, appeared at the *volost* soviet and threatened to arrest its personnel after attempts to requisition grain. The district *ispolkom* fined the villagers ten thousand rubles. In Ezhovskaia *volost*, villagers angry about the requisition of grain disrupted a *volost* gathering and attacked the head of the *volost* committee. At the beginning of August, citizens of Afanas'evskaia *volost* murdered the commissar and six Red Army soldiers who were attempting to requisition grain.[18]

As happened the previous autumn, peasants saved their fiercest opposition for state attempts to enter their fields and thresh the grain. In Shakhaiki village, Serdezhskaia *volost*, Iaransk district, a brigade of Red Army soldiers and workers came to thresh the local population's surplus grain. The local soviet billeted the soldiers in peasant houses. That night the villagers spread the word about the brigade's arrival to twenty-one surrounding villages, including villages in neighbouring Urzhum district. The following morning the brigade awoke to a huge crowd of peasants armed with stakes, iron canes, and guns who attacked the regiment in the homes where they were staying. The peasants wanted revenge and

---

[18] RGAE, f. 1943, op. 3, d. 160, l. 99; Emel'ianov et al., eds, *Udmurtiia v period inostrannoi voennoi interventsii i grazhdanskoi voiny* (Izhevsk, 1960), 63, 87, 95; Bystrova et al., eds, *Ustanovlenie*, 511, 513, 520.

attacked the soldiers who escaped the dwellings, beat them senseless, and stole all their possessions, including 20,000 rubles and their clothes. Eight people including the brigade leader died in all, and another fifty-eight were wounded. Other soldiers simply disappeared and were presumed dead. The district soviet immediately sent an armed detachment, which suppressed the uprising and put 'the leaders' in jail. The government later sent three hundred workers to the *volost* and in two weeks they threshed 15,000 puds of rye and brought it to the local collection point. The Iaransk *ispolkom* also imposed a 500,000 ruble tax on all participating villages in retribution for the murders.[19]

The fact that the brigade went to the *volost* to thresh grain shows the degree to which peasants excused themselves from the grain monopoly. The local population had even refused to prepare food to sell at the state collection points. The swift growth and size of the armed resistance also reflects peasant solidarity against outside forces. The brigade became a personal symbol to the villagers of the ill-favoured requisition policy, which helps explain the voracity of peasant violence. Peasants beat and robbed the brigade of its basic materials, as the requisition policies had done to the peasants.

Peasants resisted state horse and livestock requisitions as fiercely as they did grain requisitions. For example, in Bykovskaia *volost*, Glazov district, a large crowd surrounded the *ispolkom* building when the army tried to mobilize the locals' horses. Some peasants burst in, 'inflicted flagrant violence' upon the soldiers and arrested the committee. The crowd brutally attacked the head of supplies and when he was almost dead they broke his neck. The peasants killed two other committee members and threatened to kill the others. The next day a regiment arrived and killed and wounded some of the peasants as an example to the others.[20] Other peasants questioned the state's reason for confiscation. In June the Pasegovskaia *volost ispolkom* in Viatka district informed the peasants that they needed to present six horses for war needs. On the day of the mobilization a group of peasants appeared at the gathering point without the requisite horses. When Soviet officials asked why they did not comply, the peasants stated, 'there is no war so the state does not need our horses'.[21] Peasants of Pasegovskaia *volost* couched their refusal in terms of citizenship duties; the state could ask extraordinary sacrifices

[19] GA RF f. R-393, op. 1, d. 83, ll. 5–6; Hoover Institution Archive, Archives of the Soviet Communist Party and Soviet State (hereafter HIASCPSS), reel 41; Bystrova et al., eds, *Ustanovlenie*, 523–4.

[20] Report of the organization–information subsection of the Glazov district *ispolkom*, 2 July 1918; Emelianov et al., eds, *Udmurtiia v period inostrannoi*, 45–6.

[21] GAKO, f. R-879, op. 1, d. 75, l. 374.

from its citizens only during active wartime. At the Vasil'evskaia *volost* soviet in Glazov district, peasant representatives disagreed on whether they should sell livestock to feed the Red Army and cities. They finally agreed not to sell their livestock because village land needed fertilization.[22]

Regional officials created an ideal peasantry that could not meet reality. Soviet officials constructed the peasantry as a benighted people, as had tsarist and Provisional Government political agents. In tropes that would resound throughout the Civil War, one discursive line held that kulaks, priests, and even the Black Hundreds (which did not have a presence in the Viatka countryside) instigated riots and even forced the other peasants to participate. Officials termed the unrest 'counter-revolutionary' and 'anti-Soviet'. In the midst of a civil war, local soviet leaders saw all resistance to their policies as a threat to the state's existence. Officials attributed the uprisings to a small segment of the peasant population. Economic divisions surely existed within the village and wealthier peasants with more livestock and surplus grain had more to lose than poor peasants during grain requisitions. However, most peasant resistance to the food brigades throughout the Russian countryside was a collective occurrence in which the village united against an outside threat.[23] Other Soviet agents blamed the peasantry as a whole, echoing past representations of the sly peasant who secreted away wealth and fought tooth and nail for autonomy.[24] These views shaped policy. The Narkomprod official A. Glob urged his superiors to go after the peasants in the southern districts because they all, supposedly, had hidden stores of ten to fifteen years of grain.[25]

Bolshevik food supply agents acknowledged that the inefficiency of their state was also to blame. Prices still did not match inflation and market pressures, the state could not supply material items that the peasants demanded, and there was insufficient infrastructure to maintain a centralized foodstuffs monopoly. The Food Supply Military Committee recognized the inherent problems in the system: 'the fixed prices either need to be changed or cancelled altogether, but nothing else can be done without orders from the centre so nothing will be done'.[26] Agents from Moscow blamed Narkomprod. A Moscow official in Viatka

---

[22] GA RF, f. R-393, op. 3, d. 100, l. 23ob; HIASCPSS, reel 42.
[23] The same was true in Tambov. Taisia Osipova, 'Peasant Rebellions: Origin, Scope, Dynamics, and Consequences', and Delano DuGarm, 'Peasant wars in Tambov Province', in Vladimir Brovkin, ed., *The Bolsheviks in Russian Society: The Revolution and the Civil War* (New Haven, 1997), 154–98.
[24] See Shlikhter's comments in Orlov, *Sistema*, I–XI.
[25] RGAE, f. 1943, op. 3, d. 160, l. 107.
[26] *Viatskoe narodnoe khoziaistvo*, August 1918, 17–18.

reported that Narkomprod was filled with incompetent and corrupt personnel who knew nothing of food policy. Their willingness to raise grain prices and allow free trade destroyed the efficacy of the grain monopoly. He concluded that 'the provisions sections [were] the largest hindrance to the stockpiling of grain'.[27] In June and July 1918, Lenin sent daily telegrams to the provinces to alert officials that Moscow's workers and soldiers had only a three-day supply of grain left, demanding that they take decisive action to extract grain from the peasantry.[28] Under such pressure from the centre, the Urzhum district military commissar reported to Moscow that the only way to obtain sufficient grain was 'through the use of armed force'. However, the district *ispolkom* had only fifteen to twenty soldiers in its garrison and so lacked adequate military forces to collect the amount of grain wanted by the centre.[29]

Moscow sent the famous Bolshevik Aleksandr Shlikhter to Viatka in late June to fix what was clearly a grain system in disarray. Internal Party sources commonly referred to the Viatka countryside as anarchic and the state feared a total collapse in food supply from the region. Shlikhter made the port village of Viatskie Poliany his staging area to concentrate on one of the most productive regions of the province and to control the black market grain flowing down the Viatka and Kama rivers. Shlikhter's well-armed brigade confiscated this grain at gunpoint but also tried more creative means to get grain from the peasants.

It was here, among the multi-ethnic villages of Viatka's south-east corner, that the Soviet government forged its defining food supply programme that helped it survive the Civil War. Shlikhter quickly dismissed the policy of inventorying household grain and relying on untrained worker brigades as too cumbersome and adopted a levy-based (*razverstka*) grain programme, supposedly devised by a local soviet representative named Sukhikh, at a 22 July meeting on the grain crisis. The state backed away from its claim that it could inventory individual households and take grain only from well-off peasants. In other regions, the Soviet grain policy called on committees of the poor peasants (*kombedy*) to take grain from fellow villagers, but peasants in southern Viatka resisted Soviet policies so forcefully that hardly any committees were established in the summer of 1918. Instead, Shlikhter compromised and returned to a reliance on scientific rationality. The plan called for more material goods to be given to the peasants and a redistribution of grain to the local population. It allowed bureaucrats in its district Commissariat of Food Supply to calculate the future grain surplus and

---

[27] RGAE, f. 1943, op. 3, d. 160, l. 107.   [28] GASPI KO, f. 45, op. 1, d. 158, l. 2.
[29] Quote from RGAE, f. 1943, op. 3, d. 160, l. 43; GASPI KO, f. 45, op. 1, d. 158, l. 3.

local officials to produce quotas based on these numbers. The Sarapul district government quickly supported a levy of 300,000 puds. The Malmyzh Commissariat of Food Supply followed on 5 August with a levy of 358,000 puds. Behind the compromise rested the threat of armed brigades who would requisition grain from peasants who still did not acquiesce.

Shlikhter and his chroniclers hailed his Viatka *razverstka* experiment as an unparalleled success. They assert that in a two-week period he collected enough grain to send 189,000 puds to Moscow and Petrograd and another 119,700 puds for local urban and state needs. The vision could not have come at a better time of year, for peasants in the area were finishing their harvests and were probably in the best mood to exchange grain for money and goods after wrestling all summer with armed brigades. Shlikhter told Lenin of the accomplishment of the *razverstka* method and Narkomprod adapted the less intrusive decentralized method throughout Soviet Russia for the remainder of the Civil War.[30] Shlikhter's Viatka *razverstka* experiment was never fully implemented, cut short by the tumultuous environment that his armed forces had helped create. Shlikhter appears to have embellished the efficacy of the *razverstka*. He could not have relied on the flimsy local Soviet administration to help gather the grain in such a short and unruly period. An anti-Soviet revolt overthrew the Malmyzh government two days after it agreed to the *razverstka* method in its district. Another rebellion the following week in Sarapul district forced Shlikhter and his men to flee the province.[31] Shlikhter's forces were able to requisition a stunning amount of grain and essentially stop sackmanship in the area, but this was done by the old methods of barter and force for the village as a whole. As we shall see, one version of Soviet power tried to create a working relationship with the peasants; another more violent one ripped the relationship apart.

The Stepanov revolt and political mayhem

While Shlikhter tested the grain policy that would drive the Soviet economy through the Civil War, the other major brigade sent by the centre to the neighbouring districts battled local peasants and turned

[30] Orlov, *Sistema*, 17–25; Lih, *Bread and Authority*, 168–71; GAKO, f. R-885, op. 1, d. 53, l. 30. For more on Shlikhter, see Iu. K. Strizhkov, 'Iz istorii vvedeniia prodovol'stvennoi razverstki', *Istoricheskie zapiski* 71 (1962): 25–42. Sukhikh was not the only exceptional local food provisions representative. Officials raved about a peasant named Zhilin in Tsyp'inskaia *volost* whose energy supposedly convinced the peasants to give up their surplus grain. RGAE, f. 1943, op. 3, d. 160, ll. 343–4.

[31] RGAE, f. 1943, op. 3, d. 160, l. 317.

against the regime. The political officer A. S. Khomak and military commander A. A. Stepanov led the First Moscow Food Brigade Regiment.[32] Stepanov and Khomak's forces were the most equipped state agents in the province but it would turn out that neither leader supported the Soviet regime. When they faced heavily-armed peasant resistance and inefficient district administrations, the Moscow food brigades turned to acting strictly for personal gain.

For a month, Khomak and Stepanov successfully extracted grain from local peasants and delivered it to the Soviet government. Violence often accompanied their visits to villages and the Narkomprod official Levenson criticized 'the most motley of brigades that is completely devoid of proletarian beliefs, doing very little and caring only about money', in a report to the provincial leadership. Peasants complained that the brigades brewed moonshine, marauded, and simply abused their authority.[33] Peasant resistance pushed Khomak and Stepanov to move from hooliganism to robber barons and anti-Soviet rebels. On 13 July a division of Khomak's food brigade entered the Mari village of Toktai-Beliak, Urzhum district, to requisition grain. Peasants there had openly opposed the Soviet's grain policy since May, yelling at Soviet officials that they did not need fixed prices or the Red Army and had suffered when military forces replied by firing upon the crowd killing some villagers. Khomak's brigade nevertheless managed to collect the grain this time and set off to the collection point at Cheremisskii-Turek but the Toktai-Beliak villagers, armed with rifles, revolvers, and machine guns, caught up to the brigade, attacked them, and killed their commissar. Another brigade sent later confiscated the villagers' grain and property. At a meeting of the Urzhum *ispolkom* following the incident, Khomak criticized the regional government's inaction, cited growing peasant armed resistance, declared a military dictatorship of the city and district, and disarmed the local Red Army.[34]

Simultaneously, Stepanov also began making public statements against Soviet power. Stepanov and his forces moved to the city of Malmyzh, overwhelming a small Red Army detachment on the way. On 7 August news about the Whites' capture of Kazan and rumours of anti-Soviet uprisings throughout the region spread across southern Viatka. In the energized atmosphere of popular sentiment against the Bolsheviks and rumours of the unpopular government's imminent fall to the

---

[32] Saisanov and Shingareev, 'Krest'ianskie vosstaniia', 124–5.
[33] RGAE, f. 1943, op. 3, d. 160, l. 486.
[34] GAKO, f. R-3454, op. 1, d., 74, l. 1; GASPI KO, f. 45, op. 1, d. 147, ll. 13–14; d. 142, ll. 19–25; Saisanov and Shingareev, 'Krest'ianskie vosstaniia', 125–6.

Whites, Stepanov's forces revolted against the Soviets. Supported by a leading local SR, P. N. Chirkov, and army officers, Stepanov seized Malmyzh and robbed the city *ispolkom* and state treasury of at least 200,000 rubles.[35] The following day Stepanov's brigade of approximately 700 well-armed men took a steamboat to Turek village, robbed the state coffers and left some forces there, and continued on to Urzhum, which bordered the White-controlled Kazan province. Stepanov's forces tracked down the city *ispolkom* that had fled to a nearby forest, confiscated over 1.4 million rubles, and presumably killed its members.[36]

The Soviets' tenuous hold on political power quickly withered throughout southern Viatka. On 11 August, the city *ispolkom* of the district centre of Iaransk took the city's treasury and fled in fear of an anti-Soviet invasion. Members of the Popular Socialist Party and former officers emerged to lead a coup but two days later a small division of thirty Red Army soldiers overthrew them, restored Soviet power, and shot the leaders. The town of Tsarevosangursk experienced an anti-Soviet uprising two days later.[37] In an atmosphere of diffuse power, groups of citizens (be they prosperous, Tatars, food brigade soldiers, or the Red Army) came together to gain economic and military control over a region, but failed to build a broad-based political order.

Stepanov organized the Provisional Government of the Southern District of Viatka Province.[38] While his long-term political ambitions are unclear, Stepanov banked on images, ideals, and symbols of the Provisional Government to build political legitimacy. He made appeals to the population, calling for the convocation of the Constituent Assembly and the end of fixed grain prices. His men and allied villagers (it is unclear exactly which villagers) also disbanded soviets across Urzhum and reinstated the zemstvo administration. Stepanov gained some success with new recruits from villages and the defection of the thirty-man division of the Petrograd food brigade to his side.

---

[35] GA RF, f. R-393, op. 3, d. 112, ll. 306–7/HIASCPSS, reel 42. One report stated that Stepanov stole 700,000 rubles, another 500,00 rubles. GAKO, f. R-885, op. 1, d. 53, ll. 56–7; GA RF f. R-393, op. 3, d. 119/HIASCPSS, reel 46.

[36] GAKO, f. R-876, op. 1, d. 9, ll. 470–1; Saisanov and Shingareev, 'Krest'ianskie vosstaniia', 129.

[37] GAKO, f. R-1322, op. 1a, d. 1243; *Golos trudovogo naroda*, Iaransk, 7 November 1918, 1; I. Solonitsin, 'Iz istorii grazhdanskoi voiny v gubernii', in I. Danchik, et al., eds, *Oktiabr' i grazhdanskaia voina v Viatskoi gubernii: Sbornik statei i materialov* (Viatka, 1927), 51; Iu. N. Timkin, 'Iaranskoe vosstanie v Viatskoi gubernii 11–13 avgusta 1918 g.', in G. Iu. Krysova, ed., *Istoriia i kul'tura Volgo-Viatskogo kraia (k 90-letiiu Viatskoi uchenoi arkhivnoi komissii)*, 226–9.

[38] RGAE, f. 1943, op. 3, d. 160, ll. 488ob–9; GAKO, f. R-876, op. 1, d. 9, ll. 469–72. P. N. Dmitriev and K. I. Kulikov, *Miatezh v Izhevsko-Votkinskom raione* (Izhevsk, 1992), 82.

Having established control of Urzhum, Stepanov marched north to the city of Nolinsk where he quickly surrounded a minute band of Communists in a school and set the building on fire. Both the Viatka and Central governments feared that Stepanov would seize Kotel'nich and its railroad and either encircle the city of Viatka or move towards Moscow, and so sent decisive force against him. The newly formed Second Battalion of the Ninth Ural Regiment marched to Kotel'nich while the Red Army moved the Volga flotilla, the Poltava shooter brigade, and troops and armoured cars from Perm and Moscow against Stepanov. On 16 August the Reds launched a surprise attack and scattered many of Stepanov's forces. Nolinsk was liberated two days later.[39] As the Soviet forces marched to Stepanov's headquarters in Urzhum, he divided his forces and fled towards Kazan. The Reds captured most of Stepanov's remaining men, but Stepanov and his officers turned towards the city of Cheboksary, south-west of Viatka province, and disappeared.[40]

In the matter of a week, a lone food brigade officer led forces that seized three districts of Viatka, two of which had most of the province's strategically important surplus grain. However, Stepanov had only a tenuous hold on political power, as seen by his precipitous decline. As the leader of an armed food brigade, Stepanov began as a personification of the Soviet system's wrongs and never gained popular support from the peasantry. His forces were notorious for using violence and peasants linked Stepanov with the unpopular grain requisitioning policies. Upon seizing power he sought alliances with people whom the peasantry saw as exploiters – merchants, prosperous urbanites, and better-off peasants.

Peasant resistance to grain requisition helped to destabilize the Soviet regime and create the conditions for Stepanov's meteoric rise, exposing the fundamental weakness of Soviet power in the summer of 1918. The central government did not yet have enough political power to rule from Moscow. It could not rely on the provinces or regions to exert enough military might to make the peasants give up grain, so it had to use tsarist officials to help. The Stepanov revolt shows that the Bolshevik government could not control its own agents in the countryside and, thereby, its relationship with the peasantry. However, politics in the countryside

[39] Rossiiskii Gosudarstvennyi Voennyi Arkhiv (hereafter RGVA), f. 169, op. 1, d. 114, l. 81; GASPI KO, f. 45, op. 1, d. 158, l. 5; Solonitsin in Danchik, et al., eds, *Oktiabr'*, 45–52; N. N. Azovtsev, et al., eds, *2 armiia v boiakh za osvobozhdenie Prikam'ia i Priural'ia. 1918–1919. Dokumenty* (Ustinov, 1987), 41–3.
[40] GAKO, f. R-885, op. 1, d. 53, ll. 92–3, 97; GASPI KO, f. 45, op. 1, d. 147, ll. 53, 69; RGVA, f. 169, op. 1, d. 165, l. 25; f. 169, op. 1, d. 115, ll. 5, 94; f. 169, op. 1, d. 114, l. 306; Saisanov and Shingareev, 'Krest'ianskie vosstaniia', 130–3. The fate of Khomak is also unknown.

also aided in Stepanov's quick demise. Peasants had no reason to support him and were renegotiating their relationship with the Soviet administration. Soviet military might therefore successfully eclipsed Stepanov's unpopular forces. Since peasants did not support the aggressiveness of Soviet grain and conscription policies and the Soviet state still did not have a strong foothold in the villages, political power was still up for grabs in the Viatka countryside.

The Prikomuch alternative

In the summer of 1918, Soviet officials in Viatka felt so threatened by peasant resistance to grain requisitions and the threat of the Whites' advance that they imposed martial law first in Malmyzh and Iaransk in June, and throughout all of Viatka on 2 August.[41] *Volost* military commissariats announced that peasants had to register all hunting firearms or have them confiscated.[42] Indeed, August 1918 was the most critical period for Soviet rule in Viatka. As Stepanov's forces were overrunning Soviet positions with ease, a colossal anti-Soviet revolt erupted in the factory town of Izhevsk. By mid-August, only the northern half of the province remained under Soviet control.[43]

Both the Stepanov and the Izhevsk revolts should be seen as the climax of social, political, and economic conditions in the first year of Bolshevik rule. In the cities the scarcity of agricultural and manufactured goods, and the Bolsheviks' consolidation of their political rule through censorship and exclusion of other parties from their government, exacerbated negative popular sentiment towards the new regime. Resulting urban uprisings dictated the future political landscape and political discourse in the countryside by pushing the Bolshevik government to accelerate its efforts to win peasant support and integrate villagers into the Soviet polity.

The Izhevsk workers' rebellion was the largest and most significant uprising of its kind to date against the Soviet regime. Labourers in Iaroslavl and Ashkhabad resisted the Communist regime in 1918, but their numbers and the duration of unrest did not nearly match Izhevsk. The epicentre of the unrest lay in the Izhevsk armaments factories but the movement became a massive insurgency and reverberated throughout the neighbouring cities and factories and at its height enveloped almost all eastern Viatka and south-western Perm. The revolt also interrupted key armaments production that the besieged Bolshevik

---

[41] Bystrova et al., eds, *Ustanovlenie*, 17.   [42] TsGA UR, f. R-204, op. 59, d. 5, ll. 106–7.
[43] GASPI KO, f. 11, op. 1, d. 2, l. 9.

government desperately needed. The factories of Izhevsk and Votkinsk had manufactured essential military supplies during the war. Izhevsk issued almost a quarter of Russia's infantry rifles and was the sole producer of rifle and revolver barrels. Votkinsk produced the armour for naval ships. Izhevsk's military significance grew during the Civil War. The major armaments factories in Sestroretsk and Tula had closed, while Izhevsk continued to produce significant amounts of barrels and rifles.[44] The uprising also came at the end of the harvest in the region, when it would have been easier to collect grain from peasants. Finally, the revolt radically altered the life and experience of not only the surrounding peasant communities, but also the rest of the Viatka peasantry. The Soviet army called on peasant recruits to help stop the uprising, while the provincial government shaped policies to avoid another massive uprising and gain support among peasant populations (such as the poor and veterans) whom it saw as inherently supportive of the new government.

Izhevsk and Votkinsk's workers were mostly skilled, Russian, and highly paid.[45] According to Bolshevik ideology, Izhevsk's thirty thousand workers should still have been firm supporters of the Soviet government. There was a strong contingent of skilled proletarians whom Lenin believed would guide the rest of the workers in revolution. The Bolsheviks in fact saw Izhevsk as a citadel of socialism at the end of 1917. During 1917, the Bolshevik Party experienced a significant growth in membership in Izhevsk. Simultaneously, however, the Socialist Revolutionary Maximalists also gained popular support.[46]

Although the SR Maximalists and Bolsheviks ruled in coalition in the Izhevsk soviet and *ispolkom* from the autumn of 1917, tensions grew during the winter as the city became politically polarized between the two main forces. In February the Bolsheviks tried to incorporate Izhevsk's Maximalist-dominated Red Guard into the Red Army but the Red Guard responded by attacking its political enemies and confiscating goods.[47] The Treaty of Brest–Litovsk, Bolshevik policies

---

[44] Dmitriev and Kulikov, *Miatezh*, 7–8.
[45] S. L. Bekhterev, *Esero-Maksimalistskoe dvizhenie v Udmurtii* (Izhevsk, 1997), 23–4; Stephen M. Berk, 'The "Class-Tragedy" of Izhevsk: Working-Class Opposition to Bolshevism in 1918', *Russian History* 2 (1975): 176; L. M. Spirin, *Klassy i partii v grazhdanskoi voine v Rossii* (Moscow, 1968), 262.
[46] The Union of Socialist Revolutionary Maximalists (*Soiuz sotsialistov-revoliutsionerov maksimalistov*) were founded during the 1905 Revolution and fought for the immediate transition to a 'maximum' level of socialism; that is, the nationalization of land and factories along with the dictatorship of the working class. As such, they were most akin to the left bloc of the SRs.
[47] Bekhterev, *Esero-Maksimalistskoe dvizhenie*, 6, 60–1; Berk, 'The "Class-tragedy"', 180.

towards the declining material life, and rising unemployment in the city angered the Maximalists and they went into open opposition against the Bolsheviks. In April the Bolsheviks formed their own military brigade to counter the Red Guard and asked for help from the Kazan soviet to deal with the Maximalists. On 20 April the Bolsheviks disbanded the Izhevsk soviet and arrested up to two hundred Maximalist Red Guards. The Maximalists quit the soviet and in May new elections were held. Although not more than twenty per cent of the workers voted, they elected a majority non-Party soviet that favoured the SRs and Mensheviks.[48] The new soviet passed a resolution condemning Bolshevik rule and called for the convocation of the Constituent Assembly. Further elections in June shunned the Bolsheviks by again voting in an SR and Menshevik majority. The Bolsheviks once more turned to Kazan for military aid and together they disbanded the Izhevsk soviet and began to rule alone. Outside political forces altered the polarized world in Izhevsk. In the summer of 1918, Soviet Russia felt itself encircled by enemy forces. Anti-Bolshevik troops concentrated in southern Russia; the Czech regiment easily defeated disorganized Soviet divisions in Siberia; and the remnants of the Constituent Assembly and Socialist Revolutionary Party overthrew Soviet power in Samara province and formed Komuch (Committee of Members of the Constituent Assembly).

In August, Viatka province was a microcosm of the country. Czech forces threatened from the east and on 7 August took Kazan in the south. In the north, British forces landed in Murmansk and Arkhangel'sk, and on 2 August supported the overthrow of its soviet and the establishment of the anti-Bolshevik Supreme Administration of the Northern Region, with Nikolai Chaikovskii as its leader.[49] The encirclement created panic among Viatka's Soviet officials. On 8 August, upon hearing that the Whites had seized Kazan, the Bolsheviks attempted to mobilize First World War veterans in Izhevsk. The *frontoviki*, a large union of front-line veterans and officers that resisted heavy-handed Bolshevik policies elsewhere in Russia, led rallies and organized workers against the mobilization, standard of living, and Bolshevik power as a whole. A popular uprising had begun. For the next three days, Maximalists, *frontoviki*, and workers destroyed the vestiges of Bolshevik rule. The rebel workers hunted down and arrested Bolshevik leaders, paraded around the city

[48] RGAE, f. 1943, op. 3, d. 160, l. 50. Left SRs and Maximalists continued to sit on the *gubispolkom* until 7 July when they resigned as part of the national breakdown of the socialist coalition government.
[49] Chaikovskii and the other socialist leaders of the Supreme Administration of the Northern Region ruled until late September. Chaikovskii then left Russia for exile in France.

and gave anti-Bolshevik speeches. On 10 August they formed a new government.[50]

The leaders of the Izhevsk revolt established a government parallel to the Komuch regime of the Lower Volga region, and adopted the moniker 'Prikomuch' (The Kama Region Committee of Members of the Constituent Assembly). Prikomuch leaders stated that they recognized only the Constituent Assembly as represented within the Komuch government as Russia's true ruling body. The two centres of Komuch engaged in correspondence and shared political ideals but there is no evidence that they linked military forces or political administrations. Prikomuch aided the failing Komuch regime with monetary donations but otherwise maintained autonomy.[51]

Helped by the current political and military weakness of the Soviet government, Prikomuch initially enjoyed great military success. The Red Army was already engaged in Kazan and fighting Stepanov's forces and did not have the reserves, organization, or resources to offer significant resistance to Prikomuch's forces. The workers of Votkinsk joined in the rebellion on 17 August and emboldened the movement to expand westward into Malmyzh district, where the Stepanov revolt was raging, and southward where on 31 August it took Sarapul.[52] Although the Soviet regime had begun to establish an administrative and legal presence in the Viatka countryside, it did not have a large rank of diehard cadres. There were few sympathetic Red Guards and Communist Party members, those who would fight for the Bolsheviks. It was therefore easy for Prikomuch forces to roll through eastern Viatka. At the beginning of September, Prikomuch was at its height of power and ruled thirteen to fourteen thousand square kilometres and close to a million people.[53]

Prikomuch enjoyed much greater popular support than other anti-Bolshevik rebellions in European Russia. It immediately established a People's Army (*narodnaia armiia*) to be filled solely by volunteers. The volunteer army created an army 12,000 strong, composed of *frontoviki*, former military officers, and workers.[54] As the Red Army organized

[50] GASPI KO, f. 45, op. 1, d. 158, l. 56; RGVA, f. 169, op. 1, d. 830, l. 26; A. G. Efimov, *Izhevtsy i Votkintsy: Bor'ba s bol'shevikami 1918–20 gg.* (San Francisco, 1975), 7–11; D. I. Fedchikov's recollection in M. S. Bernshtam, ed., *Ural i Prikam'e noiabr' 1917–ianvar' 1919: Dokumenty i materialy* (Paris, 1982), 337–8; A. Kuchkin, 'K istorii Izhevskogo vosstaniia', *Proletarskaia revoliutsiia* 6 (1929): 153–4; Zubarev, *Prikam'e v ogne* (Izhevsk, 1967), 64–5; Spirin, *Klassy i partii* 264; Raleigh describes an uprising led by the *frontoviki* in May 1918 in Saratov province, *Experiencing Russia's Civil War*, 48–9.
[51] RGVA, f. 39562, op. 1, d. 3, l. 39.
[52] See GA RF, f. R-393, op. 3, d. 112, l. 307; HIASCPSS, reel 41.
[53] Dmitriev and Kulikov, *Miatezh*, 90; Berk, 'The "Class-Tragedy"', 187.
[54] RGVA, f. 176, op. 3, d. 89, l. 102.

against the rebels, Prikomuch mobilized its urban and rural population and swelled its ranks to 35,000 troops.

Peasants also initially supported Prikomuch because it overthrew Soviet power. In the first days of the uprising, peasants captured and killed Red Army soldiers. In one case they slaughtered fleeing soldiers and dragged the bodies back to Izhevsk.[55] Inhabitants of Porez village in Ukhtymskaia *volost*, Glazov district, threw out Soviet personnel and re-elected the old *volost starshina* and scribe.[56] Prikomuch agitators went to the countryside, called *volost* gatherings, rallied the peasants against Soviet food brigades, and began mobilizations.[57] Many local peasants, displeased with Soviet grain policies and tied to Izhevsk and Votkinsk by family members working in their factories or other economic ties, volunteered to join the army. The most ardent peasant support came from the villages of eastern Perm province. Peasants of Agryz and Babkin villages even gave 33,000 rubles to Prikomuch along with military volunteers. Villagers killed the head of the Babkinskaia *volost ispolkom* in Perm province after he tried to conscript them to fight against Prikomuch.[58]

Strong-arm grain procurements by the Soviet military on the frontline also pushed peasants towards Prikomuch. Amazingly, while Stepanov and the Prikomuch regime both threatened to overrun the district on 10 September, Soviet military leaders ordered Narkomprod to take one million puds of grain from the peasants of Urzhum. Narkomprod officials resisted, citing their lack of money, armed strength, and the 'infected' (*zarazheny*) locals with Whitest sentiments. Nevertheless, Narkomprod officials travelled the land over the next two weeks in driving rain, gathering village meetings, and demanding that they grind all of their grain in their storehouses. They levelled grand grain levies to be compensated at a meagre fourteen rubles a pud, threatening villagers with force for non-compliance. The *volost* of Kokshinskaia was given a 33,000 pud levy, with the hope of getting 50,000 puds, because the official saw it as a rich *volost* and unsympathetic to the Soviets. Peasants hesitantly complied. Villagers of Baisinskaia *volost* produced 29,000 puds before Stepanov overran the local Red Army and replaced one evil with another.[59]

Prikomuch leaders also understood that their fate rested on grain. They distributed a leaflet among peasants at the local bazaar, evoking unity among workers and peasants, and played on the peasants' hatred of

---

[55] RGVA, f. 169, op. 1, d. 830, l. 26.   [56] GAKO, f. R-1322, op. 1, d. 9.
[57] RGVA, f. 176, op. 3, d. 159, l. 163; Report on the socio-political life in Malmyzh district, 28 August–8 September, Emelianov, ed., *Udmurtiia v period inostrannoi*, 103.
[58] RGVA, f. 176, op. 3, d. 89, ll. 108–9.   [59] RGAE, f. 1943, op. 3, d. 160, ll. 545, 617a.

Soviet grain policies: 'Citizen peasants, in this trying moment for workers give them grain . . . so that they can make short work out of the oppressors . . . Support your brothers, don't delay with supplies.' The leaflet also announced fixed prices on grain of twenty rubles for a pud of rye and twenty-five rubles for a pud of flour, much higher than the Bolsheviks had set.[60] This price was still lower than peasants could get through sackmen or the black market and peasants did not feel such binding ties with the new regime or its workers to sacrifice precious grain. Market prices of grain rose beyond the reach of workers. For example, on 1 October rye flour cost forty to forty-five rubles a pud while most workers were paid between forty and sixty rubles.[61] Prikomuch's central government became so desperate in mid-October that it reverted to confiscation of all surplus grain, a Bolshevik policy it had rejected.[62]

Like the Bolsheviks, the Prikomuch government tried to win over the peasantry as a group, as well as divide the village for its own political means. Its discursive strategies and varying success among its population reveal the peasantry's complex political ideals at the time. Upon seizing power, the Izhevsk rebels sent detachments and emissaries throughout the Viatka countryside to drum up support, foment unrest, and garner volunteers.

Prikomuch officials, similar to Stepanov and Komuch, used the symbolic image of the Constituent Assembly to ground their legitimacy, even if their policies focussed on general anti-Bolshevik themes and simply staying in power. Each political regime claimed that its political body was the natural heir to Russia's true government, the Constituent Assembly. The Constituent Assembly had symbolic weight among enemies of the Bolsheviks as the binary opposite to Soviet rule and the chaos of civil war. It served as a mode of identification to show that the political actor stood against the current order.[63] The rebels therefore spent most of their propaganda efforts defining themselves as anti-Bolsheviks. They depicted Bolsheviks as robbers who stole grain from the peasantry to line their own pockets and as enemies of the people.[64] As one announcement read:

There is no place among us for the Bolsheviks and provocative elements. You must destroy them immediately. They sold you to the Germans, they bring ruin

---

[60] GASPI KO, f. 1, op. 1, d. 142, ll. 112a–13ob; V. Maksimov, 'Kulatskaia kontrrevoliutsiia i Izhevskoe vosstanie (1918 g.)', *Istorik marksist* 4–5 (1932), 148.
[61] Maksimov, 'Kulatskaia kontrrevoliutsiia', 153.
[62] RGVA f. 176, op. 3, d. 89, l. 16.
[63] Erik Landis, 'Waiting for Makhno: Legitimacy and Context in a Russian Peasant War', *Past and Present* 183 (2004): 218–20.
[64] *Izhevskii zashchitnik*, 23 August 1918, 4; 10 September 1918, 1.

to your villages, and they kill your women and children. Is it possible that you do not have enough sense to deal with the scoundrels comrades Lenin, Trotsky, and their like? Those fronting the 'Worker–Peasant Government' mercilessly annihilate workers and peasants.[65]

In the late summer this message resonated because the Bolsheviks were already unpopular among peasants in southern Viatka, many of whom were victims of the food brigades. Fed up with the heavy-handed nature of Soviet rule a number of villages in Sarapul district threw their support behind Prikomuch. Peasants in Debeeskaia *volost* proclaimed:

we are ruled by former convicts who depend on bayonets . . . Comrades, they promised us peace, bread, and freedom. Did we get this? No! Not freedom, grain, or peace. So let the sackmen perish! Down with Soviet power! Death to them! Long live the Constituent Assembly! All power to the Constituent Assembly! Down with the Bolsheviks![66]

Prikomuch messages, and in turn peasant supporters, emphasized popular themes dominant a year before, such as the Constituent Assembly. At the same time, Prikomuch appropriated and negated Bolshevik linguistic tools from 1917, such as the slogans of peace, bread, and freedom and the contradictions of the worker-peasant government. Messages played on the Brest–Litovsk Treaty with Germany and repeated common rumours of Bolshevik ties to Germany. They also linked Bolsheviks to hooliganism, thievery, and chaos – common themes in the SR press in 1917. Another message from the newly resurrected *volost* zemstvo in Perm welcomed the People's Army as emancipators from 'enshackling work', presumably a play on the Marxist promise of the liberation of workers in a socialist society, and recognized the Constituent Assembly as the only power, denying the legitimacy of Soviet power.[67] In 1918 Russia's political actors used class as their lingua franca. Both the Bolsheviks and anti-Soviet powers imagined the countryside through class divisions of poor, middle, and rich peasantry. Soviet and anti-Soviet officials assumed that there was tension between poor and rich and that the classes would support the appropriate side. Politics and political imagination created reality. As villagers allied and identified themselves with a political force they became either a poor peasant or a kulak.

Prikomuch terrorized supporters of the Bolshevik regime. In Kel'chinskaia *volost*, Sarapul district, an armed detachment from Izhevsk arrived to break up the *volost* soviet but first executed three brothers whom villagers told them sympathized with the Communists.[68] Violent incidents

[65] RGVA, f. 39562, op. 1. d. 2, ll. 37ob–8.   [66] GAKO, f. R-876, op. 1, d. 92, l. 100.
[67] RGVA, f. 39562, op. 1, d. 3, l. 46.   [68] RGVA, f. 176, op. 3, d. 159, ll. 45–9.

within many villages under Prikomuch show the cleavages in peasant society. Intra-village peasant uprisings that took political 'class' structures were often graphically violent. For example, in Sviatogorskoe village (*selo*), Glazov district, 'kulaks' and priests led attacks against Communist supporters and even killed one of the supporter's daughters. In another village, in neighbouring Perm province, peasants and Prikomuch soldiers whipped and dismembered Soviet sympathizers.[69] Prikomuch forces often abetted locals in exacting violence against their fellow villagers. In Grakhovskaia *volost*, Elabuga district, part of the village gathered and decided to root out Red Army soldiers and their families from the village. They began to arm themselves and called on the Prikomuch army to help them. A detachment of sixty soldiers arrived and together with these peasants searched each home, arrested eight people, and killed five others (four soldiers and one father of a soldier). The detachment planned to take one of the captured back to the city, but locals requested that they execute him there and the Prikomuch forces complied.[70]

The Red Army's initial attack on Prikomuch with a small division was quickly repelled. The Red Army gained its first victory on the Eastern Front in recapturing Kazan on 10 September, and the Prikomuch rebellion became the centre of the Eastern Front when the Soviet's Second Army concentrated its forces in an all-out effort to take Izhevsk. By mid-September the Prikomuch forces began to wear down. Their army ran short of weapons when the Red Army cut off the Izhevsk armament factory's supply of metal. Just as important, Prikomuch faced the same problem as their Bolshevik opponents when local peasants did not sell enough grain to feed the army and urban centres. The Prikomuch government had to rely on forced grain requisitions from the peasantry, which destroyed popular support. Its army also suffered from poor morale and mass desertion, a problem that became an epidemic when it turned to forced conscription. The Red Army advanced on Izhevsk. On 5 October, it captured Sarapul and on 20 October began to encircle the region. The Reds battled Prikomuch forces in surrounding villages, hurling artillery against their entrenched opponents. In the first week of November Red Army forces killed up to 1,500 people.[71] On the first anniversary of the Bolshevik Revolution, 7 November, the Red Army captured Izhevsk and on the night of 13 November defeated Prikomuch forces that had fled to Votkinsk. Remaining Prikomuch soldiers either returned to their villages or fled to Siberia to continue their fight against the Bolsheviks.

---

[69] Dmitriev and Kulikov, *Miatezh*, 88–9.   [70] GASPI KO, f. 45, op. 1, d. 158, ll. 14–15.
[71] Report on Second Army advance on Izhevsk, Azovtsev et al., eds, *2 armiia v boiakh*, 99–101.

The Prikomuch government was not able to sustain the active support of the whole peasantry. As Prikomuch's fortunes dimmed, the government expanded those subject to mobilization until 3 November, when all able-bodied males were liable to be called up. To secure and maintain recruits Prikomuch turned to strict discipline, including capital punishment. When the Red Army advanced, peasants quickly switched alliances. The anti-Soviet forces were able to drive a wedge in many villages but did not implement policies to garner widespread peasant support. Prikomuch played on peasants' discontent with Bolshevik requisitioning but was unable to establish a viable alternative polity. Like its parallel Komuch government, Prikomuch did not offer land reform or other pro-peasant policies. Prikomuch remained an urban-based revolt that enjoyed support from workers and members of educated society who had supported the Provisional Government. The government therefore defended private property and demanded that land reform wait to be decided by a future Constituent Assembly.[72] However, unlike the peasantry under Komuch, who supported the Soviet government because it endorsed their seizures of former-landlord property, most of the peasantry under Prikomuch never lived under landlords.

The complex reasons behind the Viatka peasants' rejection of Prikomuch hint that it was more than fear of the return of landlords and a manorial economy that decided the peasants' political support. Prikomuch had symbolically brought back local zemstvos, but it failed to establish an administrative or political connection to its peasants. Where the Soviet regime tried to broker relations within the village, the Prikomuch government never worked towards that end. As with the Provisional Government, the Prikomuch regime envisioned the peasantry as followers; they were regarded as lesser citizens who could not rule themselves. In order to win popular peasant support it would have been necessary to treat the peasants as equal participants in the larger polity and establish administrative links and an accompanying loyal bureaucracy.

Many of the peasants under Prikomuch's rule were non-Russians. Udmurts living around Izhevsk had played a peripheral role in the factory economy. They sold their produce in the city markets and transported wood and other forest materials for the factories. Udmurts and Tatars initially gave their tacit approval to the rebels. However, Udmurt peasants were more apathetic than active in their support for the new Prikomuch rulers. The Prikomuch government never addressed the issue of its non-Russian population in the waning days of

---

[72] Dmitriev and Kulikov, *Miatezh*, 100–1, 120–1.

its rule.[73] When the Reds advanced, non-Russian peasants switched sides and volunteered for the Red Army.[74]

Conclusion

In the spring and summer of 1918, as the Soviet administration mediated land disputes in the village, it grew frustrated with peasants' refusal to part with sufficient grain to feed the urban areas. The popular recognition that food supply for the nation was in a state of crisis established power relationships in the Viatka countryside. Peasants tried to leverage their grain for a just supply of manufactured goods. The Soviet state resorted to coercive practices to extract grain from the countryside. It was willing to negotiate a levy system that mixed coercion and concession with the peasants. The *razverstka* system, born in Viatka's breadbasket, guided Bolshevik grain policy throughout Russia for the remainder of the Civil War. In Viatka, though, the Bolsheviks were too weak to control the population or even their own military forces; the new state fell victim to its violent practices. Food brigades forced peasants to give up their grain and then themselves turned on the Soviet state. Overlapping economic problems, Bolshevik attempts to monopolize power, and social polarization then provoked the workers of Izhevsk to establish the Prikomuch regime. Livid peasants fleetingly supported the alternatives to Soviet power, but they did not provide land or grain. Moreover, the alternatives to Soviet power did not mediate within the village or treat peasants as citizens. To re-establish power, the Soviet administration intervened in the village to bring peasants into the fold.

---

[73] Dmitriev and Kulikov, *Miatezh*, 121, 144–5. A Soviet official noted that Muslims welcomed the Red Army and had 'defied' all White propaganda. GAKO, f. R-876, op. 1, d. 92, ll. 16–16ob.

[74] See Maksimov, 'Kulatskaia kontrrevoliutsiia', 158.

6 The resurrection of Soviet power in the countryside

As the Red Army put down the Stepanov and Prikomuch revolts, the Soviet government reconstructed Soviet power in the region's countryside. The regime liberally resorted to force and terror to re-establish power and then turned to appeasing the unhappy peasants. It offered reconciliation to those who a few weeks earlier had denounced the Communists. To survive over the long-term, though, the Soviet regime needed to bring peasants into the Soviet polity. It was in the landscape of violence and continued mobilization for war that the Soviet regime resurrected the bureaucratic process of institutionalizing Soviet power in the countryside. It countered opponents with the quick establishment of administrative institutions predicated on popular participation. Bolshevik ideology also informed the bureaucratic process as Communist leaders believed that they needed to engage in active state building that incorporated the peasant population into the new order and, by doing so, transform the backward peasantry into lasting allies of the proletariat. This chapter examines Soviet attempts to re-establish power in the Viatka countryside from the fall of the Prikomuch regime in November 1918 through to the end of direct military conflict in the province in June 1919.

Class mattered in the Civil War village. From Lenin's notions of capitalist development in the Russian countryside, Bolsheviks divided the village into three overarching typologies – poor (*bedniaki*), middle (*seredniaki*), and rich (*kulaki*) peasants – and so imposed class identities on peasants that did not exist as such before. The implementation and official discourse surrounding the Soviet government's major rural policies, such as the establishment of local administration, grain extraction, taxation, and the committees of the poor peasantry (*kombedy*) put Bolshevik categories of the rural population into concrete terms. The Bolsheviks' public worries, seen in newspapers and decrees, that they needed to rely on a petty bourgeois peasant population, as well as their courtship of an imagined middle peasantry, only reinforced class delineations.[1] Peasants

---

[1] On the problems of ascribing class during the Civil War, see Sheila Fitzpatrick, 'New Perspectives on the Civil War', in Koenker et al., eds, *Party, State, and Society*, 3–10.

had certainly already based part of their identity on a general sense of relative economic status in the village, but as we saw in negotiations over land disputes, economic status was relative, fluid, and did not match Bolshevik imagination. But Bolshevik reliance on strict categories of class in their policies and discourse, even when it did not apply, in turn shaped and transformed individual peasant identity. To communicate with the state, peasants had to adopt Bolshevik constructions that filtered surprisingly quickly into intra-village communication.

The politics of repression

The Soviet regime set out on a mission of retribution against those suspected of collaborating with Prikomuch and Stepanov. The violent repression joined the Red Terror that followed the assassination attempt on Lenin on 31 August 1918. Sovnarkom declared, 'The Soviet Republic must be safeguarded from its class enemies by isolating them in concentration camps, by shooting all persons associated with White Guard organizations, plots, and conspiracies, and by publishing the names of all those shot and the reasons for the shooting.'[2] The Soviet state initiated a policy of popular fear of denunciation and isolation and extermination of dangerous, infectious social elements.

The Viatka military committees and Cheka suppressed popular anti-Soviet sentiment using all the above methods. The Glazov district military committee ordered all *volost* governments 'to shoot on the spot without trial anyone who is armed and speaking against Soviet power'.[3] In September 1918, the Cheka in Orlov district arrested seventy Prikomuch army officers and Right SRs and shot twenty-three of them.[4] On 3 October, the Kotel'nich Cheka executed sixty-one people.[5] During a two-week period in early 1919, the Iaransk Cheka shot forty people.[6] The Malmyzh Cheka swept the land in October and arrested several people for actions against the revolution, and brought others before the revolutionary tribunal.[7] The

---

[2] James Bunyan and H.H. Fisher. eds., *Intervention, Civil War, and Communism in Russia, April–December 1918: Documents and Materials* (New York, 1976), 239.
[3] GAKO, f. R-3238, op. 1, d. 4, l. 52.   [4] GAKO, f. R-3238, op. 1, d. 4, ll. 242–3.
[5] W. H. Chamberlin, *The Russian Revolution 1918–1921: From the Civil War to the Consolidation of Power*, vol. II (Princeton, 1987), 70–1. Chamberlin describes a letter from the Nolinsk Cheka complaining of 'petty-bourgeois ideology' among the Moscow Cheka and offered its own solution: 'A dangerous scoundrel has been caught. Get out of him what you can and send him to the other world.'
[6] V. I. Bakulin, 'Nasilie kak komponent gosudarstvennoi politiki: Bol'shevizm v Prikam'e (konets 1917–seredina 1919 g.)', in *Revoliutsiia i chelovek: Byt, nravy, povedenie, moral'* (Moscow, 1997), 176.
[7] GAKO, f. R-876, op. 1. d. 92, l. 144.

government sent thousands of people to concentration camps.[8] Reports sympathetic to the White cause regularly recounted Red Army executions of peasant rebels both near the front lines and in the rear, the most bloody of which supposedly transpired in February 1919 when the army shot 2,700 peasants and arrested another 1,500 in Iaransk district. While documentation of this massacre is difficult to find, the Red Army and other coercive arms of the state often relied on violent repression of anti-Soviet protest.[9]

Although the Cheka shot a number of rebels, many more were put in prison or even amnestied. State officials went throughout Khristor-ozhdestvenskaia *volost* and compiled a list of 946 peasants who were soldiers in the Prikomuch army. The documents do not indicate how the state punished them and many of those listed immediately transferred to the Red Army. This did not mean that they switched political allegiances. The head of the Sarapul Bolshevik Party complained in November that transfers from the Prikomuch army were agitating the peasantry against Soviet power.[10] As during the Stepanov revolt, rural populations' loyalties for political centres shifted rapidly in an environment of diffuse power.

The politics of persuasion

While the Soviet government used force to regain power, it more often relied on appeasement and building the peasants' trust in the new political world. The Soviets intensified their efforts to win over and enlighten the peasantry by implementing a propaganda and organizational campaign to plant themselves within the village.[11] The government began by sending agitators through the region to call village *skhod*s and explain that Soviet power was being re-established.[12]

Soviet revolutionary committees provisionally governing the former Prikomuch region let up on the forced grain requisitioning that had been so unpopular. They tried to appease the peasant population and resume coaxing grain out of them with gentle, non-threatening proclamations. Upon freeing the city of Sarapul, the re-established soviet urged local

---

[8] GAKO, f. R-1322, op. 2, d. 12.
[9] 'The Terror' and 'The Bolshevik Rear and Army', *Bulletins of the Russian Liberation Committee* 10, 26 April 1919, 2. The publication also described Viatka as 'a hotbed of insurrection, as the peasants have been completely worn out by requisitions'. On peasant unrest and Bolshevik repression, see Vladimir Brovkin, *Behind the Front Lines of the Civil War: Political Parties and Social Movements in Russia, 1918–1922* (Princeton, 1994).
[10] GAKO, f. R-3271, op. 1, d. 2, ll. 2, 16, 18–32ob; Emel'ianov et al., eds, *Udmurtiia v period inostrannoi*, 185.
[11] GAKO, f. R-876, op. 1, d. 92, ll. 17–18.   [12] GAKO, f. R-876, op. 1, d. 92, l. 19.

peasants to give grain to the starving city but it avoided language of explicit class warfare in favour of pleas for friendship between the village and city. It called on all 'comrade peasants' (regardless of economic position) to 'bring needed food to the city and support the population of Sarapul. Bring it comrades and don't be afraid that someone will take [the food] away. No, this Soviet power does not allow that. For everything will be paid a fair price. Now all of you should feel that we must be committed to supporting each other.'[13]

When the Prikomuch regime declined in late October, peasants repented and proclaimed their support for the Soviet government. As in the Imperial era, villagers who had engaged in unlawful acts admitted their guilt and went out of their way to express their loyalty to the regime. Facing physical punishment, peasants acknowledged that their actions were not acceptable and proclaimed their loyalty to the power relationship. Peasants throughout Uvatuklinskaia *volost*, Malmyzh district, passed formulaic decrees supporting Soviet power. After listening to Bolshevik agitators, peasants now 'wanted' all measures taken to put down enemies of Soviet power. They called for death to all who opposed the people's power and welcomed peasant workers, socialism, and the Red Army as defenders of the working people.[14] *Volost* meetings in Sardykskaia, Elganskaia, Gordinskaia, and other places passed resolutions supporting the Soviet regime during this time of crisis, and welcomed proletarian uprisings in western Europe.[15] The day after the Reds beat back anti-Soviet forces from Vikharevo, village residents proclaimed that they did not support the Whites and agreed to a general mobilization into the army.[16] The Bolshevik state, for its part, put great significance on this discursive process. Bolshevik organizers were certain to get peasants to state their allegiance to the Soviet regime and include formulaic Soviet popular slogans into their village resolutions, going out of their way to get the peasants to 'speak Bolshevik', even if such statements did not reflect popular sentiment.[17]

The *kombedy* and the institutionalization of Soviet power

In June 1918, as part of the grain dictatorship and the attempted co-option of the poor peasantry, the Communist government organized

---

[13] Emel'ianov et al., eds, *Udmurtiia v period inostrannoi*, 120–1.
[14] GASPI KO, f. 1, op. 1, d. 40, ll. 315–16ob, 318–25ob.
[15] Emel'ianov et al., eds, *Udmurtiia v period inostrannoi*, 137.
[16] GA RF, f. R-393, op. 3, d. 112, ll. 309–09ob; HIASCPSS, reel 42.
[17] I take the idea of speaking Bolshevik from Stephen Kotkin, *Magnetic Mountain: Stalinism as a Civilization* (Berkeley, 1995).

Table 6.1 *Number of kombedy in Soviet Russia*

Province	Number of Kombedy	Province	Number of Kombedy
Viatka	15,573	Perm	3,115
Iaroslavl	8,676	Nizhegorod	3,000
Tver	8,612	Tambov	2,831
Kostroma	6,918	Kursk	2,774
Orlov	6,814	Penza	2,710
Severo-Dvinsk	5,335	Riazan	2,658
Vitebsk	5,031	Petrograd	2,471
Vologda	5,000	Saratov	2,267
Vladimir	4,875	Simbirsk	2,000
Kaluga	4,842	Cherepovets	1,893
Novgorod	4,653	Voronezh	1,690
Tula	4,604	Mogilev	1,571
Moscow	4,533	Samara	1,305
Smolensk	4,103	Olonets	1,097
Kazan	3,630	Arkhangel'sk	190
Ivano-Voznesensk	3,428	Astrakhan	138
Pskov	3,300		
		Total	131,637

Data from V. R. Gerasimiuk, 'Nekotorye novye statisticheskie dannye o kombedakh RSFSR,' *Voprosy istorii* 6 (1963): 209–10.

its first mass mobilization project in the countryside – the establishment of committees of the poor peasantry (*kombedy*) in all *volost*s and villages. The Soviet government designed the *kombedy* to empower the poor peasantry with state backing to wage war on village kulaks, confiscate their surplus grain and livestock, and help redistribute them to poor peasants, urban areas, and the army.[18] The *kombedy* project began as a colossal failure. Viatka's provincial *ispolkom* sent out the first order to the districts to establish *kombedy* only on 30 July when many of the villages in the southern districts were in open revolt against the regime.[19] Other peasant communities rejected the committees as another mechanism to take their grain. The little over three hundred *kombedy* that the Soviets had been able to organize functioned poorly in the summer and early autumn of 1918.[20] It seemed that the Soviet vision of the *kombedy* project to encourage poor peasants to turn on their rich neighbours could not penetrate the collective solidarity of the village.

[18] *Izvestiia Glazovskogo soveta krest'ianskikh, rabochikh i krasnoarmeiskikh deputatov*, 16 October 1918, 1–2.
[19] GAKO, f. R-885, op. 1, d. 47, l. 17.   [20] GASPI KO, f. 11, op. 1, d. 2, l. 24.

Table 6.2 *Number of kombedy in Viatka province*

District	Number of Kombedy
Orlov	3092
Kotel'nich	2398
Iaransk	1871
Glazov	1867
Elabuga	1280
Viatka	1300
Nolinsk	1154
Urzhum	920
Malmyzh	638
Slobodskoi	600
Sovetsk	514
Sarapul	354
Total	15888

Data from A. S. Bystrova, *Komitety bednoty v Viatskoi gubernii* (Kirov, 1956), 38.[21]

However, the *kombedy* blossomed in November – after the Sixth Party Congress realized its failure and terminated them as 'kulak infested' institutions. By December 1918, nearly 16,000 *kombedy* had been established in Viatka, almost double that of any other Russian province (Table 6.1 and Table 6.2). As local Party and state officials acknowledged, the *kombedy* project began to function only after the government heightened its attention on the countryside with the end of anti-Soviet revolts, the arrival of agitators, and the end of the harvest.[22] The key to the eventual success of the *kombedy* project in Viatka was that it transcended its original purpose of helping the state extract grain from the village in an alliance with poor peasants. Instead, the *kombedy* movement served as an administrative tool for the Soviet state to establish its presence in the countryside, especially in the southern and eastern districts of the province, the centres of anti-Soviet rebellion. Many peasants in turn joined the *kombedy* to show their loyalty to the Soviet order.

While peasants in 1917 set up local governmental organizations, Soviet agitators in 1918 were instrumental in establishing *kombedy*.

---

[21] Bystrova's totals for Viatka province differ from Gerasimiuk's by 2.6%. The difference can be attributed to the date that the authors calculated the number of *kombedy* and to fragmentary archival records. Both historians still reach the same conclusion, that Viatka had an overwhelmingly greater number of *kombedy* than other provinces.

[22] GASPI KO, f. 11, op. 1, d. 2, l. 23; GAKO, f. R-880, op. 1, d. 171, l. 160.

Agitators spoke at *volost* gatherings and persuaded attendees to organize village *kombedy*.[23] This was especially the case in areas that had been overrun by anti-Soviet forces and *volost*s with close urban ties, such as northern and central *volost*s of Viatka district. In these regions, village *kombedy* were organized in blocks between September and October. In Viatka district all the *kombedy* in Medianskaia *volost* were established during a two-day period between 13 and 15 September; in Bobinskaia *volost* the *kombedy* were all formed on 29 September.[24] In late September, agitators from the political division of the Second Army distributed thousands of copies of the decree on the organization of the kombedy and established *kombedy* in villages on the border between Soviet and Prikomuch Russia.[25] As the Red Army advanced into anti-Soviet territory, so did political agitators intent on spreading *kombedy*. They arrived in a village, hastily sought out peasants who would ally with the Soviets and organized them into a committee of the poor peasantry, often without a vote by the village assembly. They had great success. By January 1919 in the former heart of the Prikomuch revolt, the Izhevsk region of Sarapul district, 266 *kombedy* had been established.[26]

Soviet officials organized in both Russian and non-Russian villages. In October, Red Army agitators in Elabuga district visited seven Tatar villages, called a meeting, gave a speech about the current situation, and established village *kombedy*. The following month instructors travelled throughout the predominantly Udmurt *volost* of Tsyp'inskaia, Malmzyh district, organized *kombedy*, and gave lectures in Udmurt entitled, 'What Soviet Power Gives the Peasantry', 'Who Goes Against Soviet Power', and 'The Rights and Responsibilities of Committees of the Village Poor'.[27] The army also distributed agitation publications in Tatar. Udmurt regions had as many *kombedy* as predominantly Russian areas, showing that Udmurts were willing to participate in Soviet state building and the construction of class identity.

Villagers by this point in the revolution were used to outside agitators showing up to urge them to join a political party or establish an organization, committee, or new governing body. The *kombedy* in this way continued the wave of mass mobilization begun in 1914. By the autumn of 1918, most villagers were familiar with agitators' class rhetoric. Peasants in Viatka did not view the *kombed* as an alien institution that threatened the village. Research on the Black Earth region has

---

[23] GASPI KO, f. 1, op. 2, d. 40, l. 2.   [24] GAKO, f. R-880, op. 1, d. 172, ll. 6–60.
[25] GA RF, f. R-393, op. 3, d. 110, ll. 165–8; HIASCPSS, reel 42; Azovtsev et al., eds, *2 armiia v boiakh*, 238–40.
[26] GAKO, f. R-876, op. 1, d. 110, ll. 146–9; GASPI KO, f. 11, op. 1, d. 2.
[27] GAKO, f. R-876, op. 1, d. 92, l. 3; f. R-885, op. 1, d. 4, ll. 77–77ob.

found most *kombedy* members were peasants who had traditionally been excluded from the community, such as landless labourers, migrant workers, and craftsmen. Many members had not worked the land before the war. Their status as outsiders drew them to the opportunity for power provided by the Soviet state and their disconnect from the community guaranteed the demise of the *kombedy*.[28]

In stark contrast to outsiders or marginal figures in the Black Earth region who manned the *kombedy*, those who joined Viatka's *kombedy* were stable members of the village who had not previously been part of its governance. Viatka and Nolinsk district *kombedy* membership lists reveal that around 90% of those who joined the *kombedy* were local peasants who had worked the land before the revolution.[29] Most enrolees had just returned from the war, like *kombedy* members elsewhere in Russia. In Ekaterininskaia *volost*, Nolinsk district, 62% were veterans and in Il'inskaia *volost*, also in Nolinsk, 46% of members had military experience.[30] As in 1917, the politically–charged veterans had seen the wider world outside old village authority structures and probably had been exposed to Bolshevik propaganda at the front. This was their first time in governance and almost no members had served on a soviet or worked for local government before joining the *kombed*.

The vast majority of members were also not affiliated with the Communist Party; members were listed as non-Party, with a small minority noted as 'sympathetic' to the Party.[31] Membership rolls did not list class or even how much land individuals held. As one village *kombed* simply wrote to the *volost ispolkom*, 'in our organisation and village we do not have kulaks, exploiters, or intelligentsia'.[32] The evidence paints a picture of young veterans who were willing to cooperate with the Soviet regime when they returned to the village, rather than marginal, poor outsiders who wished to use the alien *kombedy* to undermine the cohesiveness of the village. The *kombedy* thereby drew new personnel into the government and the *kombedy*'s membership helped them become established so quickly. Their success in turn aided the foundation of the Soviet state in the countryside.

From late autumn, *kombedy* members were actively engaged in their duties, controlling provisions, leading cultural work, and organizing the poor.[33] Bolshevik leaders had established the committees of the

---

[28] Figes, *Peasant Russia*, 193–5; Raleigh, *Experiencing Russia's Civil War*, 318–19.
[29] GAKO, f. R-880, op. 1, d. 172, ll. 6–60.
[30] A.S. Bystrova, *Komitety bednoty v Viatskoi gubernii* (Kirov: 1956), 36.
[31] GAKO, f. R-876, op. 1, d. 197, ll. 346–88, 425–7, 432–61; f. R-938, op. 1, d. 3, ll. 63–8ob. Every list noted that the members were peasants.
[32] GAKO, f. R-938, op. 1, d. 3, l. 6.   [33] GAKO, f. R-3238, op. 2, d. 1, l. 31.

poor peasantry to help fuel class conflict within the village, and members in Viatka implemented policies that favoured the poor against the rich. They took stock of grain supplies, requisitioned and confiscated 'kulak' grain, and helped food brigades collect goods. In northern, grain deficient districts, the *kombedy* focussed on redistributing grain from individuals they perceived to be rich to the poorer villagers. They redistributed manufactured goods among the poor. The *kombedy* also attempted to redistribute land and heard petitions on local property disputes.[34] Finally, the *kombedy* collected the extraordinary tax, discussed below.

Their policies provoked conflict within the village. For example, in Rodygino village in Kukarskaia *volost*, Sovetsk district, a few peasants who felt singled out by the village *kombed* agitated against it in the *skhod*.[35] While the conflict overtly centred on class (prosperous against poor peasants), it also had generational undertones. More prosperous peasant households were usually large with prominent patriarchal figure heads. *Kombedy* members, many of whom were younger peasants, took goods from these elderly figures and redistributed them to poorer households who themselves were often younger, small families.

Fulfilling their duties to the Soviet state did not stop many committee members from terrorizing their enemies and abusing their powers for self-satisfaction and revenge. The Elabuga district soviet reacted against village *kombedy* improprieties and issued a warning for members to follow the law in confiscations, to take only from those who supported the Whites, and give the items only to the poor and needy.[36] Individual *kombed* members were known to conduct illegal searches, take excess grain for themselves, and not always have the poor peasants' interests in mind.[37] A villager in Nizhne-Ukanskaia *volost*, Glazov district, complained to the district military information section that the head of the village *kombed*, Dem'ian Vladykin, abused his power. Vladykin tried to run the *skhod*, and proclaimed, 'no one has the right to go against me'. When levying taxes, he went to the person's home and swore at them.[38] The new personnel did not only want money and grain from their new positions, but also to gain new social status. Many villages were quite small and families knew each other and had long-held animosities and alliances. The *kombed* gave members a new power to right these personal wrongs.

---

[34] Bystrova, *Komitety bednoty*, 41–59; GASPI KO, f. 1, op. 1, d. 40, ll. 6–7.
[35] GASPI KO, f. 1, op. 1, d. 40, ll. 6–7.
[36] *Izvestiia Elabuzhskogo revoliutsionnogo komiteta*, 26 November 1918, 1.
[37] Rossiiskii Gosudarstvennyi Arkhiv Sotsial'no-Politicheskoi Istorii (hereafter RGASPI), f. 17, op. 5, d. 17, l. 39ob.
[38] TsGA UR, f. R-204, op. 59, d. 2, l. 63. The military information section sent a copy of the complaint to the Glazov district Cheka.

While some *kombedy* members used the organization for personal gain, many of them went out of their way to fulfil their duties, supporting their perceived tasks as poor peasants in the Soviet state. *Kombedy* members felt a social obligation to their community alongside their bond to the Soviet state. For example, in Malmyzh district, Lidiia Efrelovskaia complained to the *volost kombed* that the government expropriated her tea, sugar, tobacco, silver, butter, honey, money, and high quality galoshes to pay for her father's extraordinary tax. The *kombed* agreed and ordered the return and reimbursement of her property.[39] Two representatives sparred at a Smolenskaia *volost kombed* meeting over the legality of their searches of homes. One demanded that members needed formal instructions before carrying out searches, while the other representative argued for autonomy.[40] Many members strove to improve the social and cultural life within their village. In Chekanskaia *volost*, Malmyzh district, *kombedy* members tried to construct a public building and organized a *volost* soviet of education.[41] Showing that they had a vested interest in improving the well-being of their population, peasant representatives at the Malmyzh District Congress of *Kombedy* Members peppered district government officials with demands to improve the local schools, economy, and public health system.[42]

Kombedy members also saw themselves as the true representatives of the people's government, an idea that the Bolshevik leadership continuously broadcast to the countryside. But members refused any official compromise to this idea of class rule. Bolsheviks intended to foment class warfare and show that Soviet power was being built from the bottom up, and so also allowed a broader base of peasants, which included those categorized as 'potentially suspect' middle peasants, to be members of the *kombedy*. Representatives at the First Glazov District Congress of the *Kombedy* in November argued that the *kombedy* should be formed exclusively from the poor and passed a resolution stating, 'at the present time all power must exclusively belong to the poor. Kulaks and *miroedy* (more prosperous peasants) must not have a place in soviets, committees [of the poor] and the district congress of kombedy.'[43]

The *kombedy* movement was only part of the sovietization of the southern Viatka village immediately following Stepanov and Prikomuch's demise. The Bolsheviks also tried to foment class struggle in the village, and bring in much-needed finance, through the extraordinary tax

[39] GAKO, f. R-3271, op. 1, d. 17, l. 12.   [40] GASPI KO, f. 1, op. 1, d. 40, l. 10.
[41] GAKO, f. R-3271, op. 1, d. 38, ll. 2–2ob; f. 3454, op. 1, d. 79, l. 3.
[42] GAKO, f. R-885, op. 1, d. 54, ll. 6–25.
[43] GARF, f. R-393, op. 3, d. 109, l. 18ob; HIASCPSS, reel 41. Bystrova, *Komitety bednoty*, 39.

(*chrezvychainyi nalog*). From the beginning of Soviet rule, the provincial government down to the *volost* soviet had issued class-based and progressive taxes but lacked the strength to force payment.[44] Corresponding to the *kombedy* project that was supposed to root out stores of grain from the kulaks, Moscow also issued a tax on kulaks, speculators, and the well-to-do in the autumn of 1918. It set a 10 billion ruble national target and apportioned 300 million rubles to Viatka; the district governments in turn distributed levies to each of their *volost*s based on population.[45] Moscow encouraged the *kombedy* to impose additional taxes on the propertied class to redistribute local wealth and foment class strife. This time, the *kombedy* served as enforcers – if so-called kulaks did not pay the tax, then the *kombedy* would arrest them or sell their property. The dispossession had its limits. Soviet decrees ordered that kulaks be left a horse, a cow, two sheep, and a home.[46]

When peasants refused to pay, local leaders could not, or would not, force payment, and the Soviet government garnered only a small percentage of what it had hoped for. After trying to wrestle dreamt-up riches from imagined kulaks, most local governments taxed the whole population. This meant that even though the government tried to win over the middle peasantry with favourable policies, it still increased the group's tax burden. In Prosnitskaia *volost*, Viatka district, the *ispolkom* only took 181,955 rubles from peasants it categorized as kulaks out of the *volost*'s 800,000 ruble apportionment and had to collect another 2,000 to 4,000 rubles from middle and poor peasants.[47] *Volost ispolkom*s assigned middle peasants extraordinary taxes from 500 to 10,000 rubles. In Kotel'nich district, NKVD reports noted that middle peasants paid all their taxes, while kulaks paid little; the result was that the district collected less than six million rubles of its twenty-three million ruble tax levy.[48] *Volost ispolkom*s searched for other ways to get the money. Some did not even try to divide their population by class and allocated the tax equally to every person.[49] Other *volost ispolkom*s levied the tax as fines for

---

[44] E. P. Titkov, 'Finansovyi vopros v deiatel'nosti volostnykh sovetov dokombedskogo perioda (na materialakh Nizhegorodskoi i Viatskoi gubernii)', in E. M. Shehagin, ed., *Sovety i drugie obshchestvennye organizatsii; Mezhvuzovskii sbornik nauchnykh trudov* (Moscow, 1989), 106–21.

[45] *Krasnaia mysl'*, 1 January 1919, 3–4.

[46] GAKO, f. R-885, op. 1, d. 44, ll. 48–54, 84, 126.

[47] RGASPI, f. 17, op. 5, d. 17, l. 45. The same situation occurred in Filippovskaia *volost* where the *ispolkom* collected 169,925 rubles out of 600,000 and had the middle peasants pay 4,000 rubles. RGASPI, f. 17, op. 5, d. 17, l. 48.

[48] RGASPI, f. 17, op. 5, d. 20, ll. 3–40; GARF f. R-393, op. 13, d. 94, l. 138; HIASCPSS, reel 53.

[49] *Izvestiia Viatskogo gubernskogo ispolnitel'nogo komiteta*, 17 January 1919, 1.

un-Soviet behaviour. The Berezovskaia *volost ispolkom* taxed 121 individuals for discretions ranging from mild affluence (a 100 ruble tax), speculation (a 500 ruble tax), or great prosperity (4,000 rubles), to hiding grain (5,000 rubles). This led Ivan Ivanovich to petition the provincial finance section for reprieve from his 400 ruble tax. He crafted himself as the model poor Soviet peasant. A wounded veteran, Ivan had little property, an old horse, and seven family members to feed. He had never hired labourers, never engaged in business, and even gave fifteen puds of grain to the Red Army. The Orlov district government investigated the matter, deemed him a 'lower middle peasant', and freed him from the taxes.[50] The central Soviet government did not get as much money as it wished, but once again the peasants who had lived under the Prikomuch regime showed their support for the regime to the tune of nineteen million rubles, even though the collection ran during the small window of uncontested Soviet rule from November 1918 to January 1919.[51]

The *kombedy* did not fulfil any of their requirements to the degree that the central government wanted. Village communes and soviets continued to act independently, and never met the central government's lofty goals for procuring grain. Between August 1918 and April 1919, the province delivered only 7.9 million puds of its 15 million-pud levy.[52] They did build soviet organizations in over 80 per cent of the province's villages. Thus, the *kombedy* became a link between rural and national politics by establishing an active official Soviet administrative presence within the village. This created an opening for the Communist Party. At *volost* and district congresses, Bolshevik officials persuaded representatives in several locales to begin to form Communist Party cells in their village.[53]

The committees of the poor peasantry in Viatka outlived their official termination by three months. Beginning in January 1919, Party language turned against the *kombedy*. In a familiar code for state failure in the countryside – '*kulak* elements' overran the institution. In the mixed Russian–Udmurt *volost* of Vasil'evskaia, Elabuga district, a representative from Elabuga city reported to the *volost kombedy* congress that the kombedy 'are not conducting enough successful work in the villages and *volost*s' and that their membership was corrupted by criminals and demanded the re-election of the membership.[54] Newspapers concurred,

[50] GAKO, f. R-1733, op. 2, d. 1, ll. 7–24ob.   [51] GAKO, f. R-878, op. 1, d. 1, ll. 12–14.
[52] G. G. Zagvozdkin, 'Grazhdanskaia voina', in Tatarenkova et al., eds, *Entsiklopediia zemli Viatskoi*, t. 4, *Istoriia*, 354.
[53] GASPI KO, f. 1, op. 1, d. 40, ll. 3, 30.
[54] GA RF, f. R-393, op. 13, d. 93, l. 20/HIASCPSS, reel 53.

telling their readers that the poor had been passive and let the kulaks control the soviets and *kombedy*.[55] The state leaders ordered the dismantling of the tainted *kombedy* to be replaced by pure proletarian soviets.

The soviet elections of 1919

The Soviet state turned away from the *kombedy* project, but not the idea of co-opting allied peasants into the local administration. Having failed with the *kombedy*, it announced re-elections to the village and *volost* soviets. The elections functioned as more than a means of ridding the local government of unwanted 'kulak' elements. The elections held in January and February 1919 helped lay the foundation of a central myth of active participation in Soviet state building through their orchestration of popular participation in Soviet political culture. The soviet elections were the first time the Russian countryside voted en masse since the Constituent Assembly election in 1917. This revolutionary orthodoxy – an insistence of popular political engagement drawn from the political culture of 1917 – defined Bolshevik activity in the countryside.[56] The difference between 1917 and the Soviet experiment was that the election also marked the beginning of the Soviet government's political disenfranchisement of class enemies. The Soviet constitution of 1918 denied 'exploiters of labour' – those living on unearned income, private traders, monks, the insane, criminals, former police, and gendarmes – the right to vote.[57] In principle, elections to the soviets broadened the quality of participation in the state and active citizenship while contracting those who could henceforth be members in the polity. The election, then, was a key moment in reshaping popular participation in the revolution and of ascribing class identity in the countryside.

In most *volost*s, the local government identified, categorized, and disenfranchised those who it believed had traditionally wielded economic and political power. Officials labelled and disenfranchised kulaks and merchants, as well as speculators, former police, clergy, and 'non-labouring elements'. The labels were decided locally and haphazardly so the number of disenfranchised varied widely, from Iaransk district,

---

[55] *Golos trudovogo naroda*, 25 January 1919, 2; *Krasnaia mysl'*, 5 January 1919, 4.

[56] Holquist, *Making War*, 244–5, 279–81.

[57] Chapter 13, article 65 of the 1918 Constitution. A. I. Lepeshkin, ed., *Sbornik ofitsial'nykh dokumentov (Primenitel'no k kursu sovetskogo gosudarstvennogo prava)* (Moscow, 1964), 48–9; Golfo Alexopoulos, *Stalin's Outcasts: Aliens, Citizens, and the Soviet State, 1926–1936* (Ithaca, 2003). The Soviet regime maintained the Provisional Government's disenfranchisement of monks, the insane, and criminals.

where a remarkable 46% of the potential electorate (72,499 people) was denied the right to vote, to Viatka and Orlov districts where closer to 5% could not vote.[58] Even 5% left a greater percentage of people without the right to vote than in the 1920s or the darkest days of the Stalinist purges.[59] Some communities did not deny the right to vote to any of their members since, as the Toropovskaia *volost* soviet in Kotel'nich district, stated, 'we did not have any of those types of people'.[60] Others did not understand the disenfranchisement rhetoric. One official listed 'Orthodox Christian' (*pravoslavnyi*) as the occupation of the disenfranchised, another simply wrote 'has property'.[61]

Despite Soviet rhetoric that peasants were electing a proletarian organization, the elections created a hybrid of traditional peasant organization and new Soviet administration. In some communities the elections paralleled village selection of peasant officials in the tsarist era, where male elders of the village voted unanimously for the representatives. For example, in a village in Arkhangel'skaia *volost*, Nolinsk district, only eighteen peasants, all middle-aged and older, participated in the election, out of 113 people with the right to vote. The group elected five middle-aged men, three of whom voted and two did not, suggesting that only heads of households actually voted.[62] Elections in most villages had more universal participation. In a neighbouring village in Arkhangel'skaia *volost* equal numbers of men and women of all ages participated in the vote at the village gathering. Six male candidates, averaging thirty-six years old, and all 'middle peasants' stood for election.[63] Both heads of the household and their subordinate members participated and they elected the sons of the heads of households. The election appears to have been highly contested and lasted three hours with only one candidate receiving unanimous support. In other locales, the *kombed* membership spilled into the new soviet.

Voters re-elected younger *kombedy* members along with older peasants to the soviets. Nearly half of the members in the *volost* soviets in Iaransk district had served in the *kombedy*. These young males had the advantage of incumbency and the elections gave their political rule a new legitimacy. Other villages did not hold elections for the soviet and simply

[58] GAKO, f. R-876, op. 1, d. 199, ll. 1–12, 33–8, 55–6; GAKO, f. R-876, op. 1, d. 291, ll. 195–6.
[59] Alexopoulos, *Stalin's Outcasts*, 190, n. 8.   [60] GAKO, f. R-876, op. 1, d. 199, l. 46.
[61] GAKO, f. R-876, op. 1 d. 291, ll. 195ob–6.
[62] GAKO, f. R-876, op. 1, d. 197, ll. 268–70ob. See also ll. 266, 271–71ob, 305–05ob; This pattern can also be seen in Sulaevskaia *volost*, Viatka district, GAKO, f. R-876, op. 1, d. 199, ll. 28–31.
[63] GAKO, f. R-876, op. 1, d. 197, l. 274; f. R-879, op. 1, d. 120, l. 3; f. R-3238, op. 2, d. 8, ll. 35–6.

renamed their *kombed*.[64] The soviet elections, then, were a small retreat for the nascent Soviet state. They entrenched younger people from the *kombedy* in ruling rural governing bodies, but accepted village voting practices and older peasants who did not necessarily embody the characteristics of allies of the proletarian state. New representatives to the soviet were uniformly non-Party. Some were listed as sympathetic to the Communist Party, but a few identified themselves as Left SRs. Most candidates were labelled middle peasants, but this definition was surely loose. For example, in October 1919 the village soviets in Rybno-Vatazhskaia *volost*, Malmyzh district, were comprised of sixteen middle and thirty-four poor peasants. However, seven of the 'poor' peasants also had to pay the extraordinary tax, suggesting that they had property and a degree of wealth.[65]

In contrast to the elections of 1917, when women dominated the electorate, in 1919 they played only a minor role, a point noted by Soviet officials. In many villages, women stayed away from the polls and in communities that had more universal voting, far fewer women participated than they had thirteen months previously. In Slobodskoi district, over half of able males and only a third of able women voted. In Iaransk, only seven per cent of entitled women participated. Female representation on soviets was almost non-existent.[66] The Bolsheviks' acceptance of open voting at communal gatherings, traditionally an elderly male arena, guaranteed male domination in Soviet rural politics. When veterans from the First World War returned in 1918, they pushed women out of village politics and back into the home. Because women viewed themselves in local politics as surrogates of their menfolk, they largely did not resist relinquishing their role in village assemblies. Women by and large did not participate in the official construction of Soviet political culture. By attempting to bring the rural poor to power and quickly build a reliable state apparatus in the countryside, the Bolsheviks reinforced traditional gender divisions, placing class considerations above gender.

The Soviet state burrowed into the locales with the elections, but its triumph was bittersweet. The opportunity to govern the village appealed to specific village populations – those who had been denied access to power in the old regime and those who wanted to hold onto power they had traditionally enjoyed. The Soviet enterprise still did not enjoy popular, active support. The Viatka provincial electoral commission

[64] Bystrova, *Komitety bednoty*, 111–12; TsGA UR, f. R-204, op. 18, d. 8, ll. 40–1.
[65] GAKO. f. R-3288, op. 1, d. 2, ll. 86–104.
[66] GAKO, f. R-876, op. 1, d. 199, ll. 35–41, 57–57ob; f. R-879, op. 1, d. 120, ll. 3–4.

complained that candidates across the province could not get elected on the platform of Soviet power. Provincial officials lamented the endemic absenteeism of the rural voters. In many areas, turnout hovered at a pathetic fifteen per cent. Bolshevik acceptance of traditional village assembly politics, including the exclusion of women who still constituted a majority of the rural population, and de facto re-elections of former *kombedy* drove down numbers. Other peasants, who tried to work with the Soviet state only when it suited them, and had been scarred by the past year's onslaught of state violence and shifting civil war lines, stayed away and still refused to put their name behind the Soviet state. The return of armed conflict to the province made all peasants once again choose sides.

Soviet loyalty tested: the Kolchak offensive

In 1919, Russia's Civil War again transformed the Viatka countryside. In December 1918, the White Siberian Army under General Rudolf Gajda advanced westward with the goal of linking Siberia with the British-controlled north. Viatka lay in between the two anti-Bolshevik powers. The White's brief link between Siberian and southern forces had been broken and Admiral Kolchak, leader of the Siberian Army, knew that in order to receive British material assistance, cut the Bolshevik railroad, and revive the White campaign, he had to take Viatka. The British government acknowledged the military significance of a White seizure of Viatka. British-led Allied forces wanted to pull out of Russia after the anti-Bolshevik forces established a dependable network in northern Russia and Viatka was the key to its success. The British planned to advance to the major northern railroad outpost of Kotlas, directly north of Viatka, and the Siberian Army would capture Viatka, linking the two armies.[67] On 24 December 1918, White forces overran Perm, forcing the evacuation of its soviet administration to Viatka. The Whites crossed the Kama River and the Ural Mountains and entered Viatka province.

The White advance in Viatka in the winter and spring of 1918–19 was a crucial event in the Civil War. The Bolsheviks put state-building

---

[67] United Kingdom National Archives, WO 33/950, 2–3, 7, 43. Viatka was the topic of many top-ranking western powers' strategic conversations. In April 1919, the British told President Woodrow Wilson that they were sending more troops to advance on Kotlas and Viatka. Winston Churchill in private conversation also stated that the British would make 'a good punch towards Viatka to join with Kolchak before we cleared out'. Quoted in Michael Kettle, *Churchill and the Archangel Fiasco: November 1918–July 1919* (New York, 1992), 315.

measures on hold in eastern Viatka and focussed on driving back the Whites. The combination of the White's capture of Perm and movement into Viatka provoked a crisis for the Central Committee over the general disorganization of the Red Army and Trotsky's policy of reliance on military specialists. In spring 1919, White forces advanced through eastern Viatka and easily captured Votkinsk, Sarapul, Elabuga, and Izhevsk, the former heart of the Prikomuch regime. The Whites therefore enjoyed sympathetic support from the urban populations. The Whites continued through Malmyzh district and into Urzhum in the south, and Kaigorod in Slobodskoi district and the northern part of Glazov in the north. In May and June, the Red Army's Second and Third Armies pushed back the Whites in a series of gruesome battles in which over 22,000 people were killed or injured. By 20 June the Red Army forced the Whites out of the province. The White Army's failure to take Viatka in what the British forecast as an easy victory helped to push Britain out of Russia.[68]

The Soviet government was able to rally the necessary support from the peasantry to achieve this decisive military victory only after a troubled evolution in its relationship towards the village. The Bolshevik leaders at first envisioned an all-volunteer force of the proletariat to protect the revolution, but the German advance in the west and Czech- and Cossack-led revolts in the south and east in the spring of 1918 made them quickly rethink their vision of a small force. The conscription-based mass Red Army was born. By 1920, peasants made up seventy-five per cent of a reconstituted army five million strong.[69] The Bolsheviks built this army through a painful mixture of mobilization, institution building, and force. The First World War provided them with the language and expertise for mass conscription, as well as the population's numbness to wartime's accompanying fatalities. Peasants saw civil war as a continuation of the world war; their villages became only further militarized after the Brest–Litovsk Treaty in March 1918.

The Soviet government chose Viatka as one of the first provinces to conscript peasants for the expanded Red Army in the summer of 1918, since it was so close to the eastern front. Results of the initial conscriptions were pathetic. The central government imposed a levy of twenty recruits per *volost*, but local officials had little success enticing more than a handful of conscripts. Bitter villagers already resented

[68] United Kingdom National Archives, WO 33/950, 7–8; WO 95/5487; WO 33/962, 72; WO 106/1189; RGVA, f. 169, op. 1, d. 153, l. 94.
[69] Orlando Figes, 'The Red Army and Mass Mobilization During the Russian Civil War, 1918–1920', *Past and Present* 129 (1990): 168.

Plate 10. Red Army recruits, 1919. Courtesy GASPI KO

official pressure for requisition of grain and horses and they balked at
their local government officials' orders for young men to answer the call
to colours so soon after their return from the First World War. Peasants
overall opposed mobilization into the Red Army but gave up just enough
men to sustain their relationship with the Soviet state.

Ironically, in the autumn of 1918, when the swiftness of Stepanov's
and the Prikomuch regime's advances showed how feeble Soviet power
actually was, peasants began to enter the Red Army and strengthened it.
From August through October, at the height of the military conflict in
the region, the Red Army conscripted 30,000 people across the province. The districts that fielded most of the battles – Glazov, Elabuga,
and Malmyzh – gave up the greatest number of conscripts. The Red
Army impressed many local peasants into its ranks, as was its policy in

areas of battle.[70] But the Civil War also forced peasants to proclaim their political identity publicly and mobilization into the armed forces was a central sign of loyalty to a political side. When Kolchak's forces advanced in December 1918, villagers who had lived under the Prikomuch regime, or had been caught in the fighting with Stepanov, volunteered men and many *volost*s exceeded their levies five- to tenfold. Peasants wanted to protect their villages from hostile forces, but they were also aware that having been part of anti-Soviet opposition, they were politically suspect and so publicly supported the Soviet order by readily giving up their men.

On top of the volunteers, in December and January, the military mobilized over 53,000 peasants and workers born between 1893 and 1898 and another 8,000 petty officers.[71] Both Russian and non-Russian peasants joined the Red Army. For example, in October 1918 as Prikomuch forces advanced towards their villages, peasants in the predominantly Udmurt *volost* of Il'inskaia and the mixed Russian–Udmurt *volost* of Mozhginskaia, Elabuga district, requested that the military revolutionary committee allow them to be mobilized into the army.[72] Tatar peasants in Kitiakskaia *volost*, Malmyzh district, initially resisted Soviet registration for mobilization but by the end of 1918, the *volost* volunteered recruits.[73] Peasants did not want to endure another nightmare of bloody battles and reprisals, but the quick sovietization of the countryside in the region in late 1918 also accounted for the number of volunteers.

The significance of civil conflict upon public political loyalty can also be seen in how peasants outside the danger zone continued to resist the draft in 1919. The spring and summer levies were supposed to net ten to twenty poor and middle peasants from each *volost*. Villagers in the centre, north, and west of the province, untouched by conflict and sovietization, resolutely resisted mobilization. They filed petitions requesting exemption, complained that they were too busy in the fields and did not have able-bodied men to spare, or they simply did not show up to the mobilization point. The May levy in Viatka district produced a scant 78 people and the July levy only 132. While June's levy was more successful, with 335 men successfully called up, over 40%

---

[70] GAKO, f. R-878, op. 1, d. 95, l. 10ob; Sanborn, *Drafting the Russian Nation*, 45–6.
[71] GASPI KO, f. 45, op. 1, d. 178; GAKO, f. R-1585, op. 8, d. 101, l. 5.
[72] Order of the head of the provisional revolutionary military committee of Sarapul, Azovtsev, ed., *2 armiia v boiakh*, 76.
[73] GASPI KO, f. 45, op. 1, d. 178, l. 4; Report on the socio-political life in Malmyzh district from 19–25 September 1918, Emel'ianov, ed., *Udmurtiia v period inostrannoi*, 114.

of conscripted individuals failed to appear, while 15% of men that the village communities sent were elderly, ill, or otherwise unfit to serve. Villagers also sent clergymen and other natural enemies of Communism, whom the Red Army officials did not want to mobilize.

Volost officials reported to their superiors that locals 'absolutely refused' to be mobilized.[74] The provincial *ispolkom* dispatched agitators 'to clarify' the mobilization order, but they had little success enticing peasants to join. An agitator and representative from the district-level government tried to persuade peasants to give up men at a *volost ispolkom* meeting in Bobinskaia *volost*, Viatka district, by speaking on the situation at the front. The representative challenged that there must be men there who would 'stand in defence of the government of workers and peasants', but no one volunteered. The agitator asked those assembled if there 'wasn't just one person who wants to be mobilized'. The representative tired of persuasion and ordered that every village soviet nominate two people from whom twenty nominees would be picked by casting lots, but the peasants still refused and suggested that the government take citizens who worked in the factory instead. A similar situation happened in nearby Iakshinskaia *volost* where men at a general gathering unanimously refused to nominate men to join the army. At a meeting in Nolinsk district, peasants shouted down the local officials who announced the call and then got up and left.[75] Afraid of stirring up anti-Soviet feelings, the provincial *ispolkom* prohibited repressive measures to fight peasant non-compliance. Peasants in the non-combat regions did not have to proclaim their political loyalty like their brethren just to the east. So, when *volost*s did sacrifice a few of their villagers, they were often those who could not help the village economy or were members of the *ispolkom* and obliged to do state service.[76]

To avoid mass rebellion and maintain an army with a core from classes that the Bolsheviks presumed to be friendly to their regime, the state mobilized peasants from populations that had already shown support. Veterans, Party members, and Communist sympathizers were the first to be mobilized into the army, draining the Bolsheviks of natural allies in the countryside. In April 1919, 50 per cent of Communists from district and *volost* cells of Glazov district were mobilized into the army.[77] Often, whole cells were mobilized into the Red Army ranks and the cells were not reconstituted until after the Civil War. The military also

---

[74] GAKO, f. R-879, op. 1, d. 102, ll. 60–60ob, 63, 66, 68–68ob; d. 114, l. 2; f. R-1585, op. 8, d. 265, ll. 72, 79, 94–5, 145; GA RF, f. 1240, op. 1, d. 126, l. 13ob.
[75] GA RF, f. 1240, op. 1, d. 126, l. 1ob.
[76] GAKO, f. R-879, op. 1, d. 102, ll. 5–6, 7–7ob, 9, 31–3.
[77] RGASPI, f. 17, op. 5, d. 21, l. 6. See also GAKO, f. R-3238, op. 2, d. 4, ll. 14, 19.

pushed members of local soviets into the army, despite their pleas to remain at home.[78] These peasants were also often part of the local government, retarding the development of the Soviet administration in the countryside.

As several historians have noted, desertion was the crucial issue for the armies in the Civil War.[79] Many soldiers had been conscripted into a war they did not want to fight. They would have preferred to stay at home to care for their families and help guide changes within the village. Slim rations, ill-fitting clothing, poor arms, administrative disorganization, and unceasing complaints from fellow soldiers spurred soldiers to leave their posts. Desertion was already a social phenomenon from the First World War and by the Civil War, families in the village had come to accept it. Indeed, when deserters returned home, fellow villagers sheltered them in their homes or neighbouring forests from the state's gaze. Former allies of the Soviet state, soldiers when they deserted descended into 'banditry' in Soviet documents. Armed and living on the fringes of society, deserters were clear threats to Soviet power and reminders of the limitations of Soviet control. This would become apparent when deserters attacked Soviet power as the war against the Whites drew to a close in 1920.

Despite the presence of deserters in the countryside, peasants' opposition to conscription diminished. The pressure of the front faded and in the autumn of 1919, mobilization by the Soviet military became more regimented. Peasants understood their duties in the system and saw how the state granted social entitlements to Red Army soldiers and their families. A 1924 study documented that most Red Army soldiers from Viatka who died in colours lost their lives while in service outside the province. If peasants joined the Red Army to defend their villages, they stayed in it beyond the immediate threat to their locale.[80] Those peasants who remained in the Red Army fought for Soviet power and not just in defence of their homes.

Back in the village, the return of the Civil War strained relations between peasants and Soviet officials. Peasants more openly and vindictively attacked the Bolshevik project. A crowd of angry, and reportedly drunk, peasants went after the Bolshevik agitator Zubarev as he tried to rally locals at a popular spring fair in Verkhosunskaia *volost*, Nolinsk district. They yelled him down and chased him into the forest

[78] GA RF, f. 1240, op. 1, d. 126, l. 2.
[79] Figes, 'The Red Army', 198–211; Sanborn, *Drafting the Russian Nation*, 48–55; Evan Mawdsley, *The Russian Civil War* (Boston, 1987), esp. 182–3.
[80] GAKO, f. R-1330, op. 1, d. 7, l. 3.

Plate 11. Red Army brigade. Courtesy GASPI KO

with cries of 'Grab the Bolshevik'.[81] Fed up with constant requisitions, political repression, and false promises, peasants in Viatka, like their brethren throughout Russia, iterated the refrain, 'long live Soviet power, down with the Communists'.[82]

The Soviet state, for its part, obsessed with policing, categorizing, and controlling its population. The government's military and NKVD built on the modes of power used by the tsarist state during the First World War and moulded them as an exigency of the Civil War.[83] Information sections maintained detailed reports (*svodki*) on the population's mood and socio-economic situation as a means of surveillance. *Volost* officials reported to district administrators who then categorized the data and transferred it to provincial leaders. The accounts detailed the unpopularity of Soviet policies (such as taxes and grain requisitions), the extent of Soviet institutions, and the health of the local population. The Bolsheviks in part used this information for self-assessment and to find which areas (both geographically and politically) they needed to improve. They also conducted this surveillance of the population, as Peter Holquist states, 'to transform both society and individual citizens for the better'. Thus, Bolshevik surveillance should be seen as part of government attempts to understand, manage, and shape the peasant population in the same line as the *kombedy* project and establishment of local soviets.[84]

The Soviets expanded the frequency and detail of their reports when anti-Soviet forces threatened the region. In 1919, when the Whites invaded Viatka, officials provided near daily reports, paying special attention to *volost*s that had been within Prikomuch territory.[85] The military even converted the reports into a series of cartograms that categorized monthly aggregate data of whole *volost*s by political allegiance: revolutionary, apathetic indifference, wavering, and counter-revolutionary.[86] Informants showed a highly volatile shift in allegiances in several *volost*s. After the summer of 1919 the Whites no longer seriously threatened Viatka but the now entrenched Soviet state continued detailed reports from the locales. Immediately following the Red Army's capture of Glazov district from the Whites, emissaries of the Viatka

---

[81] GA RF, f. 1240, op. 1, d. 126, l. 2.   [82] GA RF, f. 1240, op. 1, d. 120, l. 14.
[83] Peter Holquist, '"Information Is the Alpha and Omega of our Work": Bolshevik Surveillance in its Pan-European Context', *The Journal of Modern History* 69 (1997): 415–50.
[84] Holquist, 'Information', 421.
[85] GA RF, f. R-393, op. 12, d. 41, ll. 19–30; op. 13, d. 94, ll. 49ob–131/HIASCPSS, reels 10, 53.
[86] GASPI KO, f. 45, op. 1, d. 178.

provincial *ispolkom* provided detailed, pessimistic reports to their superiors. They blamed both the weakness of the state administration and legal arm, and the psychology of the peasant population. Kulak elements controlled local governments and poor peasants suffered from 'a petty-bourgeois mentality'. Bolshevik political conceptions, in which class analysis was paramount, shaped the reports' language and categories. Informants blamed kulaks and unconscious peasants for failures of policy and incidents of unrest.[87]

Conclusion

The Civil War further politicized the peasant community and categorized individual peasant's experiences and identities. Soviet and White political fortunes depended on peasant support. At the same time, each side imagined peasant society through their own ideological worldview. As Red and White power ascended and descended, individual peasants had to take a side and shape their discourse and political identity to be understood by their respective political ally.

Peasants did not simply oppose or welcome Soviet power. They separated state policy and laws into those that helped and those that hurt their society. Peasants resisted state military force and embraced less violent state encroachment into their village. In a period in which power disseminated throughout the province, only the Soviet state was able to harness the political energy of peasant populations into building a new government. The Viatka Soviet government succeeded in drawing support from key segments of the village population, who agreed to be the administrative links between peasants and power. The Soviets thereby gained a foothold in the village. Most peasants still objected to aspects of Soviet power but the administrative process eventually won over the bulk of the peasantry to the Soviet regime. Bolshevik state building to coalesce political power following the massive rebellions brought the peasantry closer to the Soviet state.

---

[87] GAKO, f. R-1287, op. 1, d. 30, ll. 12–12ob, 15, 18–21ob.

7 Big tent Bolshevism: rule by consent and the construction of the Soviet polity

The Bolshevik state attempted to persuade peasants to consent to its rule through diverse cultural and modernizing programmes. Propaganda campaigns, agricultural modernization drives, and programmes aimed at youths, women, and national minorities, among a litany of other initiatives, would popularize the Soviet system while helping to solve desperate resource problems. Moving away from confrontational politics that sought warfare in the village, Bolsheviks, especially in the latter stages of the Civil War, welcomed as many peasants as possible into their big tent. Rule by consent did not mean giving in to peasant life. Soviet state agents imagined the peasantry as a social group that needed cultural and political enlightenment and identified themselves as the mechanism of such change. In this way they continued the ideals of members of educated society from the Imperial and Provisional Government eras who had worried that an autarkic and backward peasantry prevented Russia from progressing. Soviet agents placed even greater hope, though, in the transformative power of the revolutionary state to create a 'new man' that was class conscious and liberated from capitalist ideals. The resulting mass-participatory and consensus-building projects successfully integrated a significant portion of the peasant population into the new regime.

Rule by consent and transformation rarely turned out as Soviet agents intended. Paltry resources and a still weak administrative apparatus limited Bolsheviks' dreams of peasant enlightenment. Many peasant populations, for their part, agreed to work within Soviet rule and joined forces with the state to build the foundations of Soviet society. They also adapted policies to suit their own needs to gain resources and better their social situation. While most of the projects began in the early days of Soviet rule, and overlapped with the institutionalization of Soviet power discussed in the previous chapter, they did not come into their own in Viatka until the end of the threat of direct military conflict in mid-1919. Each of the projects took place in the latter stages of an era defined by violence and destruction, during which the threat of state force and coercion was often implied in official policies.

Promoting socialism: propaganda and enlightenment campaigns

The Soviet state devoted exceptional resources to propaganda and mobilization efforts directed at all peasants but especially those it categorized as natural allies to its rule. It worked to shape peasants' identities, their hearts and minds, and to act within the Bolshevik worldview. As Peter Kenez notes, in its struggle for the peasantry, '(b)uilding administrative institutions, that is, authority, and carrying out propaganda always went hand in hand'.[1] The central Soviet government therefore initiated a number of multifaceted consensus-building programmes. Especially in the latter stages of the Civil War, the state implemented policies to raise the material and cultural level of Viatka's peasantry with the aim of raising peasant political consciousness, winning them over to Soviet power, and helping to solve desperate resource problems.

Soviet authorities made dramatic efforts to show peasant communities ravaged by the physical destruction from the Civil War that the socialist state cared for their material well-being. After the Bolsheviks beat back the White advance in the summer of 1919, local governments in Glazov district tallied and paid for the damage. In the mixed Russian and Udmurt *volost* of Kliuchevskaia the Soviet state asserted responsibility for repayment and aid to those hurt by the Whites burning their villages. The local government detailed property, livestock, and even clothing that was lost in the fire and placed a monetary value on villagers' losses. The state adapted its assertion of class as the best unity builder. Although authorities listed many households as middle and poor, no peasants were listed as kulaks. Indeed, the class categorization appears rather arbitrary; for example, some families owned two horses, two homes, and a cow and were listed as poor, while others had one horse and were listed as middle peasants.[2] This contrasts with the Bolshevik description of peasants in this region just a year earlier. In 1918–19, anti-Soviet forces took over eastern Viatka and peasants did not actively support the Soviet regime; Bolsheviks ascribed a kulak status to all villagers in their policy reports. Once the Red Army drove out and suppressed anti-Soviet organized opposition, the Bolsheviks had to build popular support, justify devoting resources from the proletariat state to this population, and come to terms with those they wanted to win over.

---

[1] Peter Kenez, *The Birth of the Propaganda State: Soviet Methods of Mass Mobilization, 1917–1929* (Cambridge, 1985), 51.

[2] TsGA UR, f. R-204, op. 6, d. 19.

They thus transformed 'kulaks' into 'poor peasants' and natural
recipients of the state's positive attention. In the Enlightenment tradition of a rational, modern state that legitimizes its rule by caring for
the needs of its people, the Soviet government established a number
of such welfare programmes.[3] Alongside state welfare policies, the
Bolsheviks engaged in propaganda to win peasant support and raise
consciousness. Bolshevik agitators visited villages, organized, and gave
lectures. Peasants, especially men, eager to learn about the Civil War
and major political programmes, attended these events in droves.

Travelling agitation brigades were the most famous of the Bolsheviks'
propaganda tools. Agitation trains, led by the famous 'Oktiabr'' (October)
train, stopped at each station. Lecturers spoke to surrounding towns and
villages, while agitators displayed brightly coloured posters and distributed newspapers and literature. In the summer of 1919, the agitation
steamboat, 'Krasnaia zvezda' (Red Star), travelled along the Volga and
Kama rivers. The ship, decorated with flags, pictures, and slogans,
brought famous Bolsheviks, including V. M. Molotov and Nadezhda
Krupskaia, to Viatka's eastern border. Agitators utilized the ship's huge
hall to show films and they distributed books from its stores, printed
newspapers on its press, collected petitions from peasants and processed
them in its complaints section, and instructed the peasants through an
agricultural exhibit.[4] Since there were only seventeen movie theatres in
the whole province, this was many peasants' first exposure to film.[5] The
ship was a symbol for the new regime – modern, mobile, and embracing
the people. Like the *kombedy* project and state restitution for Civil War
destruction, the 'Krasnaia zvezda' came to win popular support immediately after the Reds had pushed their political opponents out of the
area. Robert Argenbright has shown that agitation vehicles both made
villagers familiar with the Soviet government and were physical representations of the possibilities of Soviet rule. They transformed social
space to at least temporarily create an unrestricted, direct dialogue
between central rule and the rural locale.[6]

State agents created and repositioned holidays to celebrate and insti-
tutionalize the new socialist world. From 1918, the provincial-level

---

[3] For more on the Soviet state as the result of the Enlightenment tradition, see Kotkin,
  Magnetic Mountain; Scott, *Seeing Like the State*, 89–93.
[4] Ts. Gofman, 'K istorii pervogo agitparokhoda VTsIK "krasnaia zvezda" (iiul'–oktiabr'
  1919 g.)', *Voprosy istorii* 9 (1948), 65.
[5] S. A. Fediukii et al., eds., *Kul'turnoe stroitel'stvo v Kirovskoi oblasti 1917–1987.
  Dokumenty i materialy* (Kirov, 1987), 33–4.
[6] Robert Argenbright, 'The Soviet Agitational Vehicle: State Power on the Social
  Frontier', *Political Geography* 17 (1998), 253–72.

administration promoted socialist holidays. The anniversary of the October Revolution, celebrations of international socialist victories, and a Bolshevized May Day came to the countryside.[7] However, the Soviet state only had the resources to implement mass celebrations of holidays in the countryside after the termination of military conflict in the region in 1919. The second anniversary of the October Revolution held special importance as the first major holiday that officials could promote in the village.

Like the mobilization processions in the first months of the First World War, and the parades and holidays of 1917, public rituals dictated the language and symbols of the new era. The villagers of Chutyr, Sarapul district, were treated to a grand celebration of the second anniversary of the October Revolution. The holiday closely resembled celebrations of the February Revolution. Peasants began the day in church with a short service. They moved outside where they sang revolutionary songs with red flags flying overhead and church bells marking the occasion. Celebrants continued on to the cemetery to the sound of the 'Funeral March'. In the afternoon, members of the *ispolkom* gave speeches and went door-to-door to share with villagers their feelings about this great day. A theatrical performance concluded the holiday. As Nylgi-Zhik'inskaia *volost* and other nearby *volost*s held celebrations similar to Chutyr, the holidays must have been scripted by higher Soviet officials. In Nylgi-Zhik'inskaia, peasants sang revolutionary songs and marched to the cemetery where a member of the soviet gave a speech lauding those fallen in the fight for Soviet power. Students staged a school performance that allowed more members of the government to speak on the significance of new socialist education and the holiday.[8] Like the Provisional Government political elite, Soviet officials sanctified the day with religion. They stressed popular participation with socialist songs but controlled the language of the celebration with speeches dictating the meaning of the holiday. Finally, like their predecessors, Soviet agents promoted cultural enlightenment and education to become better Soviet citizens.

The Red ploughman: the week of the peasant and socialist agriculture

In August 1920, the Central Committee declared a 'Week of the Peasant' (*nedelia krest'ianina*), a period of mass mobilization to aid the

---

[7] *Viatskaia zhizn'*, 12 May 1920, 4; *Viatskaia pravda*, 6 May 1920, 3; GAKO, f. R-876, op. 2, d. 32, l. 27.

[8] *Izhevskaia pravda*, 14 November 1919, 4; 15 November 1919, 4.

rural economy and gain peasant support.[9] In images that conveyed both the going-to-the-people movement and military operations, Bolsheviks descended on the village to enlighten the population and to promote modern agriculture. Faced with a devastated rural economy, growing famine, and a peasantry unwilling to sacrifice its grain, the Bolsheviks were in a precarious position. They had to feed their urban population but also needed to win over the peasant constituency whom they purported to champion. By 1920, the village economy had suffered from six years of limited investment and the beginnings of a devastating drought. Agricultural tools, from combines down to wheels, were breaking down and peasants were unable to replace or fix them. The Week of the Peasant was held throughout Russia, but the state concentrated its efforts on Viatka.[10] Like the Week of the Red Front, Week of the Mothers and Children, Week of the Infants, and Week of the Famished, the Week of the Peasant focussed state resources and popular attention on a specific population to solve targeted problems and win public sentiment.

The Bolsheviks mobilized Party organizations like the trade unions (*profsoiuzy*) and urban women's section (Zhenotdel), as well as workers and agricultural specialists to rebuild the peasant economy. Instructions evoked military vocabulary and called for 'regiments' (*otriady*) of workers from district towns to divide up a *volost* and descend on it. In essence, the holiday extended Civil War military methods by attacking economic ruin as an enemy of the socialist state.[11] Red Army regiments joined urban workers, blacksmiths, carpenters, and other skilled professionals to shoe horses, rebuild barns, fix bridges and roads, help bring in the harvest, and repair harrows and wagons. Travelling brigades that aided the agricultural economy continued tsarist-era wartime schemes of migrant prisoner of war labourers. Both the tsarist and Soviet initiatives aided families of soldiers first, although the Soviets also favoured landless peasants, those lacking working hands, and communes and state farms.[12] The holiday succeeded in providing a limited, but still crucial number of implements. Workers supplied scores of wheels and horseshoes throughout the countryside, while specialists built mass quantities of the same tools in each *volost*. In Khlebnikovskaia *volost*, Urzhum

---

[9] RGASPI, f. 17, op. 5, d. 48, l. 1a; *Krasnyi pakhar'*, Kotel'nich, 5 August 1920, 2; Kabanov, *Krest'ianskoe khoziaistvo*, 40–6.
[10] RGASPI, f. 17, op. 5; The state held the same sowing campaign in the Tatar Republic. *Posevoi biulleten'*, Elabuga, 19 April 1921, 1.
[11] GASPI KO, f. 1, op. 1, d. 400, l. 2.
[12] GASPI KO, f. 12, op. 2, d. 103, ll. 1–2. *Krasnyi pakhar'*, 5 August 1920, 1; *Zhizn' krest'ianina*, Glazov, 12 August 1920, 1.

district, specialists produced axes; in Petrovskaia, peasants received over 450 ploughshares.[13]

The holiday went beyond practical economic reconstruction and state care for its population. The Bolsheviks used the week to educate the masses, raise peasants' cultural level, inculcate scientific methods of agriculture, show that the socialist state honoured its peasantry, and further infiltrate the village. Drama troupes, musicians, and lecturers accompanied professionals and helped stage shows that taught peasants the 'right', or scientific, way to engage in agriculture. After three years in which the state took grain from the village to help the urban sector, the Week of the Peasant was meant to show that the urban toilers cared for their still-backward comrades in the village. Instructions informed the workers that they were to be 'the technological advisers' to the peasantry.[14] The Week of the Peasant in this way was a cultural precursor to the economic relief of the New Economic Policy (NEP) – the termination of grain requisitions and the implementation of aid to the peasant economy.

Despite the week's many successes, there were significant shortcomings as well. Trade unions were not strong, could only mobilize the required minimum five per cent of members, and few active members willingly volunteered their time. In Urzhum district, the site of one of the largest Week of the Peasant campaigns, forty-two workers and twenty-four agronomists helped and it was only fully implemented when Viatka city sent another twenty-three people.[15] Ironically, peasants supplied the majority of the labour, mocking the union between workers and peasants.[16] The village economy was devastated and one month's effort could not resolve fundamental problems such as an absence of fuel, iron, salt, and other basic necessities, as well as the continued drought. Peasants complained that breakdowns in communication and administrative confusion restricted the efficacy of the movement. In Afanas'-evskaia *volost*, Glazov district, a peasant went to use one of the new reapers, but officials turned him away telling him that it would hurt the ground. Other villagers had their new implements taken away and did not know where to find tool distribution centres.[17]

In the Week of the Peasant and accompanying scientific, agricultural projects the state mobilized the masses for larger state aims to transform

---

[13] GASPI KO, f. 12, op. 2, d. 104, ll. 31–3. The week produced similar results throughout Sarapul district. RGASPI, f. 17, op. 5, d. 103, ll. 16–17.

[14] GASPI KO, f. 12, op. 2, d. 103, ll. 1–2.

[15] GASPI KO, f. 12, op. 2, d. 103, ll. 434–7.

[16] In Sarapul district, peasants worked 54,400 hours, while *profsoiuz* members put in 26,000 hours. RGASPI, f. 17, op. 5, d. 103, l. 16.

[17] *Zhizn' krest'ianina*, 9 September 1920, 2.

the rural economy and population. State officials used all the resources available to them, including employing refugees as reporters and informants, councillors for peasants, and labourers to fix mills.[18] The Bolshevik government continued to divide the peasants and direct more resources to their allies within the village, but it aimed to build greater peasant support. Peasants appreciated the technical aid and entertainment, and officials reported that peasant–state relations warmed after the holiday.

Soviet agricultural specialists believed that peasants' ignorance of modern agricultural methods drove down production and was partially to blame for the looming famine in Russia. To bring the countryside out of the agricultural disaster peasants themselves had to be transformed and modernized through formal education, cultural enlightenment, and scientific agriculture. Although central Bolshevik leaders described modernization of the peasant economy in terms of class structure, state agricultural projects led by Narkomzem (the People's Commissariat of Agriculture) extended tsarist-era zemstvo programmes and included a number of ex-zemstvo specialists.[19] Modern, rationalized agriculture, according to Lenin and agricultural specialists, would advance the rural economy and eventually eliminate the threat of famine. To build the foundations of a socialist economy in the countryside, state and Party officials promoted collective farming. Peasants signed up for agricultural courses and adopted new technology when it did not threaten their economic viability, but most hesitated to give themselves up completely to modern collectivist dreams. The *kombedy* had organized a few collective farms (*kollektivy* and *kolkhozy*) in late 1918 and peasants who realized that they could gain access to more land in the reserve fund joined. Most often whole families of poorer peasants who did not receive enough land in the initial land divisions entered the ventures, but a few villages reorganized themselves into collective farms. Members expressed their hope of building a socialist society and got on surprisingly well. Their charters allowed anyone from the toiling classes to join and declared full equality for all members, including making decisions in open assemblies.[20]

The few collective farms, though, quickly ran into the same problems as other Soviet ventures – the lack of administrative resources for civilian projects and the placing of law and order over the class struggle. The

[18] GAKO, f. R-1062, op. 1, d. 873, ll. 3a, 9.

[19] For more on this, see James Heinzen, *Inventing a Soviet Countryside: State Power and the Transformation of Rural Russia, 1917–1929* (Pittsburgh, 2004).

[20] GAKO, f, R-1062, op. 1, d. 68, l. 3; d. 116, ll. 1–12ob; d. 118; d. 119, ll. 2–7ob. Figes finds parallel problems with collective farms in the Black Earth region. *Peasant Russia*, 295–308.

former teacher Riabov organized the Zaria Svobody collective and a beekeeper, master blacksmith, and twenty-nine other people joined. They grew oats and clover, built new homes, and managed beehives. But two members had to serve in the local soviet, another two went to war, and another fell ill. Attempts to expand the commune failed because separators held abutting land and they did not want to give it up. The Voskhod collective in Glazov district faced even greater problems in 1919. The district land section bestowed upon it church land, and what it claimed was unused, communal land. Local peasants reacted angrily. They filed a complaint claiming that they worked this land and would starve without it. They also attacked the collective in a more aggressive manner through the summer, trampling Voskhod's fields, breaking down its fences, and cursing and threatening its members. The members of the collective were so distraught that they asked the government to allow them to move their organization to the Don. Meanwhile, the NKVD and Ivan Popov, chair of the provincial soviet, took the extra-ordinary step of supporting the villagers' legal claims. Even though Voskhod was productive, the state liquidated it and gave the land back to the locals.[21]

The few collective farms (*sovkhozy*) organized by state authorities were small and inefficient. A representative of the provincial land section reported that the five collective farms that he inspected were simply too small and could barely survive. Formed on former landowners' property, they were not large enough to feed their members or handle modern techniques. The Lenin collective farm lacked fuel and cows and faced the wrath of the local population, like the other collective ventures. Its members could hardly feed themselves and could only provide 30% of the total levied grain.[22] Popov, like Lenin, derided the collective farms for their inability to produce a surplus.[23] State support provided seed to the strongest farms first, so peasant households received 97% of the seeds and all the state agricultural projects had to fight over the remaining 3%.[24] Artels, organizations that farmed a portion of land collectively or pooled resources for other agricultural activities, were the only collective ventures that enjoyed some success and a steady growth during the Civil War years. Peasants were attracted to artels because they required the least sacrifice and had shown themselves to be worthy establishments in the pre-revolutionary period. Still, less than 7,400

[21] GAKO, f. R-1062, op. 1, d. 213, ll. 66–9, 243–7; GA RF, f. 393, op. 11, d. 61, ll. 3–26.
[22] GAKO, f. R-1062, op. 1, d. 523, ll. 58–61.
[23] *Chetvertaia chrezvychainaia Viatskaia gubernskaia konferentsiia*, 12.
[24] Hoover Archives, American Relief Administration, Russia, box 1, 97.

people belonged to 177 artels in 1921. Some peasants initiated cooperative ventures themselves or embraced top-down programmes, but not enough to shift agricultural production. So many collective farms quickly fell apart or were liquidated by the state that in 1922 Narkomzem reported only twenty-three functioning farms (down from thirty-eight the year before). To add to these paltry numbers only twenty per cent of *kolkhozy* actually farmed their land collectively. The rest just shared livestock or equipment.[25]

Although model socialist farms failed to catch on with the peasants, specialists hoped to transform agriculture within the village by instructing peasants on how to increase production. Narkomzem published articles in local newspapers recommending that the population grow the highly productive and quick growing rape, and to line their fields with nitrogen and phosphorus or potassium.[26] Experts continued to promote rational beekeeping for peasants to have a stable resource when crops failed.[27] During the winter months specialists conducted courses, exhibitions, lectures, and readings.[28] Narkomzem also established agricultural schools and gave lectures to extend rational modern agricultural practices, such as transferring from a three-field to a multi-field system, establishing artels, and predicting the weather.

As in the tsarist era, several peasants adopted modern agricultural technology when it would not threaten their subsistence. For example, in 1922, Narkomzem established two-to-three-month agricultural technical courses throughout the regions. Peasants flooded the agency with requests to enrol. For 42 places for peasant volunteers, 214 applied. The composition of students on the Iaransk district course shows that young male peasants dominated the student population. Out of thirty-two students, thirty-one worked the land, and twenty-eight were younger than twenty years old. Twenty-two had some schooling in the village while ten had no education. Only one student was a member of the Communist Party.[29] This continued the practice of peasant societies in late-tsarist Russia of sending young men to technical schooling. In the early Soviet era, many young men who had experienced the outside

---

[25] GAKO, f. R-1062, op. 1, d. 60b, l. 1; for a slightly higher estimate see RGASPI, f. 17, op. 5, d. 3, l. 70; GA RF, f. R-1318, op. 5. d. 27, l. 168. By comparison, Samara province had 59 communes with 4,558 members, and 49 artels with 4,925 members. RGAE, f. 478, op. 3, d. 1284, l. 2. See also, *Viatskoe narodnoe khoziaistvo* 17–18 (15 September 1919), 24.

[26] GAKO, f. R-1062, op. 1, d. 697, l. 24; *K likvidatsii sel'sko-khoziaistvennoi bezgramotnosti na bor'bu s zasukhoi*, Viatka, 22 March 1922, 2–3.

[27] *Golos trudovogo krest'ianstva*, Moscow, 25 August 1918, 6.

[28] RGAE, f. 478, op. 7, d. 344, ll. 143–4ob.

[29] RGAE, f. 478, op. 7, d. 271, ll. 19–19ob, 23.

world from migratory labour and fighting in the wars were more receptive to non-traditional ideas, such as modern agriculture.

Soviet state specialists also built on pre-revolutionary hydrotechnical modernization projects like draining swamps, restoring and building canals, and developing peat production. Modernization plans were not just imposed from above. Village and *volost skhod*s in Malmyzh, Orlov, and Sarapul districts taxed themselves for ambitious water preservation projects originally offered to them by zemstvo agents. The Soviet state took a special interest in these efforts because they promised to modernize agriculture and improve productivity. Narkomzem retained zemstvo experts to help oversee water preservation and peat extraction projects, surveyed villages on their natural resource needs, and then plotted out the projects versus the location of potential exploitation of further natural resources.[30]

Institutions of Soviet culture

The state mobilized its officials, supporters, and the peasantry and attempted to build a socialist cultural and political polity through cultural enlightenment projects and a strong party system in the countryside. Since the late-Imperial era, peasants sought out educational opportunities for their children to gain functional literacy and strengthen the link with the greater society. Peasants continued to place value on education during the 1917 revolutions by petitioning the Provisional Government for teachers and putting educational figures on the ballots. Especially in the First World War, the state used schooling, reading huts (small public buildings housing books, pamphlets, and newspapers), lectures, and public conversations (*besedy*) for mass mobilization and building civic consciousness. Nevertheless, the war began a period of decline in education. State funds and personnel evaporated, schools became dilapidated, and by the Civil War most had closed down.

The Bolshevik vision to create a new man necessitated that the vanguard bring the proletariat and peasantry out of darkness and into enlightenment but Soviet reality lacked the resources to build new schools or maintain existing ones.[31] With the rural economy in ruins, peasants could not fund the schools. Viatka's rural educational system

---

[30] GAKO, f. R-1062, op. 1, d. 99, ll. 1–126; d. 100, ll. 7–26ob, 33–6ob, 39–40ob, 48a–48aob, 51–2ob; RGAE, f. 478, op. 7, d. 369, ll. 3–3ob, 39–39ob; *Viatskoe narodnoe khoziaistvo*, 15 March 1919, 27.

[31] For more on Russian Marxist visions of the need to create a new man, see Igal Halfin, *From Darkness to Light: Class, Consciousness, and Salvation in Revolutionary Russia* (Pittsburgh, 2000).

could barely maintain minimal efforts. Most regions lacked kindergartens and only began schooling at age nine. Teachers had disappeared with the revolution and the state could not pay those who remained. Dreams of providing students with hot breakfasts and clothing were put aside when administrators realized schools lacked such basic supplies as paper. Parents gave up and stopped sending their children to school. In Iaroslavskaia *volost*, Slobodskoi district, less than half of the students came to school. Peasants blamed the local soviet for not allocating enough resources to schools.[32] After the Reds secured Viatka from the Whites in the summer of 1919, they attempted to improve rural schools. Schools in some regions, such as Riazanskaia *volost*, Kotel'nich district, began to use new socialist-inspired methods, such as having students engage in simple hands-on work, and implementing class committees and student courts. During the 'Week of Aid to the Illiterate' in 1920, the Party pleaded with the population for donations to the school and villagers sacrificed huge amounts of paper, pencils, and pens.[33] However, in November 1921, after the cessation of conflict, the state still did not have building materials to refurnish destroyed schools.[34]

The Bolsheviks had greater success organizing smaller cultural centres. By June 1921, the Bolsheviks organized 3,080 reading huts throughout the countryside of Viatka (Table 7.1). Peasants could read about politics in national newspapers like *Izvestiia*, *Moskovskaia pravda*, and *Petrogradskaia pravda*, provincial newspapers such as *Viatskaia pravda*, *Derevenskii kommunist*, as well as regional newspapers. Party members held literature evenings where they read Maksim Gorky and Anton Chekhov to the villagers.[35] The quantity of reading huts belies the pitiful nature of cultural resources in the countryside. Huts were usually sections of the village tearoom or a corner in a public building. District Party officials and even Lenin himself admitted that most huts did not receive newspapers on a regular basis while others existed 'only on paper'.[36] Viatka, however, enjoyed a significantly greater number of reading establishments than other provinces in Soviet Russia. According to Lenin's estimates, there were more than three times as many reading huts or other types of libraries in Viatka than in any other province. Voronezh was a distant second with 525, Petrograd province had 378,

---

[32] RGASPI, f. 17, op. 5, d. 21, ll. 13, 16, 26.
[33] Fediukii et al., eds, *Kul'turnoe stroitel'stvo v Kirovskoi oblasti*, 36–7. On material and personnel shortages, see GAKO, f. R-885, op. 1, d. 54, l. 13.
[34] RGASPI, f. 17, op. 60, d. 106, l. 5; *Izhevskaia pravda*, 2 February 1919, 4.
[35] RGASPI, f. 17, op. 5, d. 48, ll. 6, 10.
[36] RGSAPI, f. 17, op. 5, d. 20, l. 40; d. 18, l. 70ob; d. 48, l. 1a; GA RF, f. R-1240, op. 1, d. 120, l. 101.

Table 7.1 *Establishments of cultural education in Viatka province, June 1921*

District	Libraries	People's Huts	Reading Huts	Clubs	Cultural Education Circles
Nolinsk	39	19	538	20	44
Iaransk	51	17	300	3	37
Slobodskoi	36	16	310	21	NA
Urzhum	53	22	336	27	82
Orlov	105	10	220	4	NA
Glazov	76	40	362	NA	70
Malmyzh	42	42	220	9	92
Sovetsk	18	3	113	NA	6
Kotel'nich	52	19	270	NA	52
Viatka	29	19	300	NA	NA
Sarapul	73	32	141	15	NA
Total	574	239	3110	at least 108	at least 384

RGASPI, f. 17, op. 5, d. 48, l. 5. Elabuga district was reassigned to the Tatar Autonomous Region by 1921.

and Vladimir only 37.[37] Such a difference between Viatka and other provinces probably stems from the province's tradition of education and conditions continued from the Civil War. Popular expectations for literature and Bolshevik attention to state-building projects and propaganda to win popular support fuelled the growth of these small cultural spaces.

Peasants saw the huts as spaces to gain both news and education. In a telling proclamation, villagers in Kurzeneva, Iukshumskaia *volost*, Iaransk district, evoked the significance of revolutionary events 'not only surrounding us, but in all the land' of Russia and the world in their decision to open a reading hut.[38] Other peasants adopted the cultural definitions of both pre-Soviet educated society and the Bolshevik's, and pleaded to the district *ispolkom* for 'enlightenment of the dark masses of the village' through money for a people's hut.[39]

The Party also established clubs and organizations aimed at segments of the population whom the Bolsheviks believed would be their natural

---

[37] Lenin, *Polnoe sobranie sochinenii*, vol. 32, 128. Lenin gave the figure of 1,703 reading huts in February 1921.
[38] Fediukii et al., ed., *Kul'turnoe stroitel'stvo v Kirovskoi oblasti*, 38–9.
[39] GAKO, f. R-879, op. 1, d. 129, l. 20.

allies. Although weak at first, youth groups quickly gained in popularity. Party officials proudly declared that the majority of 17- to 22-year-olds sympathized with Communism and the youths had a 'revolutionary spirit'. Youth unions had a 'lively spirit and members should be sent to the front because the youth appear to have the greatest reliability for reinforcing cadres of party workers'.[40] Party and state activities provided an opportunity for youths to come together away from their parents' gaze, as an official in Mushakovskaia *volost*, Elabuga district, was dismayed to find out. He was pleased to have around one hundred young people turn out for his lecture on 'primitive man'. Thinking the event would have been something else, the youths left the speech and went to 'a second lecture' – a village party.[41] Nevertheless, young peasants who had grown up during war and revolution joined unions of youths and other official participatory organizations. The Soviet system appealed to young veterans, former migrants to cities, and youths in general who searched for a means to upend the peasant community that privileged older adults.[42]

Party agitators organized non-Party meetings and discussions on topics of concern to the peasantry such as current events, the redistribution of land, and prevention of disease. These meetings could become theatres of direct communication between peasant and state. In Pilinskaia *volost*, Urzhum district, peasants expressed their displeasure towards food brigades. In Buiskaia, Petrovskaia, and Terebilovskaia *volost*s, peasants complained about labour conscription to gather wood. While Party members lectured about the need to pay taxes and give grain, and read Marx to the peasants, peasants demanded salt, iron, and basic materials and complained about officials' behaviour.[43] The meetings created public spaces within the village for the Bolshevik state to build its authority. Party and government officials who called the meetings controlled the agenda and topics for discussion. At the same time, the meetings established a means for direct communication between peasants and the outside elite. As long as the peasants stayed in their subaltern position by listening to the orators and submitting to Soviet authority they could resist official policies and protest their dire situation without fear of reprisal.

---

[40] RGASPI, f. 17, op. 5, d. 19, l. 117. GA RF, f. R-393, op. 3, d. 117, l. 3/HIASCPSS, reel 46. See also, RGASPI, f. 17, op. 5, d. 18, l. 7.

[41] *Krasnyi put'*, Elabuga, 9 February 1921, 2.

[42] David L. Hoffmann, 'Land, Freedom, and Discontent: Russian Peasants of the Central Industrial Region prior to Collectivisation', *Europe–Asia Studies* 46 (1994): 637–48.

[43] RGASPI, f. 17, op. 5, d. 48, l. 13; GASPI KO, f. 1, op. 1, d. 410, ll. 9–14, 16–18; GA RF, f. R-1240, op. 1, d. 126, l. 29.

The Party in the village

The central and provincial-level Communist Party made a conscious effort to establish Party cells in the villages and recruit new members from the poor peasantry. They enjoyed little success. *Volost* cells were only organized in late 1918, as part of the post-Prikomuch wave to sovietize the countryside, but even then they had few members.[44] Often *volost* leaders established a Party cell and attempted to draw in sympathizers to expand the organization. The Multanskaia *volost* cell was typical. On 30 November 1918, at a meeting of the *volost* government, the leader organized a *volost* cell. Eight people joined, five of whom were Party members. Those who joined were uniformly male and averaged thirty-two years old. While all but one of the founding members were listed in the membership rolls as poor peasants, middle peasants soon became the majority of the members. The cell grew, albeit slowly. By April 1919, it had at least eleven members with twelve more petitioning to join.[45] In September 1919, Nolinsk district *volost* cells still struggled to gain recruits. Many cells could barely hold a meeting and claimed two participants – including both members and sympathizers. The strongest *volost* cell in the district enjoyed a paltry seventeen participants.[46] Peasants stayed away during military conflict because Party membership almost guaranteed being shipped to the front. Villagers adapted to the Soviet regime, but most balked at subscribing to the Bolshevik ideology.

Russian male peasants in their mid- to late-twenties, who had some schooling before serving in the military or working in the factory, were most likely to be attracted to the Party. They were young, literate peasants with previous contact with Bolshevik agitators. Many of them had recently been appointed to the soviet and knew that joining the Party was crucial to succeed in power.[47] What is unclear, however, is whether these peasants fitted into Communist class categories or simply identified themselves as poor or even middle peasants. Peasants often quit the Party soon after joining. By April 1920, 4,446 of Viatka's villagers had obtained Party cards or became candidates for membership to the Party. In 1921, the number of rural members dropped considerably,

---

[44] GA RF, f. R-1240, op. 1, d. 120, l. 1.
[45] GASPI KO, f. 8, op. 1, d. 43, ll. 2–8, 25–6.
[46] RGASPI, f. 17, op. 5, d. 6, l. 31.
[47] GASPI KO, f. 10, op. 1, d. 22, ll. 8–313; GA RF, f. R-1240, op. 1, d. 120, l. 1. Figes concludes similarly for the Black Earth region, although he posits that these were peasants living on the margins of the village. *Peasant Russia*, 225–32.

to 2,831.[48] Peasant members left the Party in disgust with Soviet politics or had their membership revoked in the massive purge of that year. Other new members, like Mikhail Kassikhin who was establishing his own household after a family division, found Party work too onerous and turned in their membership cards.[49]

In spite of concentrated Bolshevik efforts, Party membership remained male and Russian. Peasant women largely stayed away from active participation in official organs. After 1917 and the gradual return of peasant men from the front, women left the public sphere and most did not fight to enter the Soviet polity. The Zhenotdel, the main Communist agency directed at women, had only limited success organizing working women in the cities and completely failed to establish rural Zhenotdel organizations or even recruit individuals. Established early on, in February 1918, the Zhenotdel remained essentially inactive until Party officials began an agitation campaign directed at rural women on International Women's Day in 1920. They held general and non-Party meetings but limited resources and peasant ambivalence stunted results. Bolshevik public sources admitted that in Sarapul district the Party could only find two women trained at the Party school to agitate in the village and even then they lacked sufficient literature to distribute. The Bolsheviks allowed such honesty in their failings because they deflected blame to their target audience. A newspaper quoted a peasant woman in Nolinsk district as saying, 'It is true that many women among us are against organizing. Women say to those who have joined that the *baba* needs to be in the home, and not wander off to public meetings.'[50] The few peasant women who attended regional Zhenotdel conferences in the cities heard lectures on building class consciousness among peasant women and the equality of men and women, but women's sections remained with traditional female occupations. Zhenotdel organs oversaw 'maternal' roles by establishing children's cafeterias and helping in schools.[51] In this case, Bolsheviks accurately portrayed popular resistance. Most peasant women had no interest in joining the Party because it did not serve their purpose. Men dominated organized politics in the public sphere and women used other official agencies (such as land courts and petitions to government departments) to fight

---

[48] V. V. Legotin, ed., *Kirovskaia oblastnaia organizatsiia KPSS v tsifrakh, 1917–1985* (Kirov, 1986), 19.
[49] GASPI KO, f. 10, op. 1, d. 130, l. 8.
[50] *Viatskaia zhizn'*, 13 May 1920, 3.; RGASPI, f. 17, op. 10, d. 177, ll. 2–3; GASPI KO, f. 1, op. 1, d. 383, l. 18.
[51] RGASPI, f. 17, op. 10, d. 244, l. 18; d. 322, l. 1–2, 10.

for issues. In 1920 women comprised only 5.1 per cent of the total Party membership of Viatka.[52]

Soviet cultural and propaganda efforts thereby extended pre-revolutionary efforts to connect the village to the larger political world. Where zemstvo agents worked to spread culture and mobilize the village during the world war, Soviet agents did the same with a Bolshevik accent during the Civil War.

Officially imagined communities, or making Udmurts revolutionary

In December 1919, a drama troupe from the regional teachers' institute staged a series of performances for the inhabitants of the Udmurt village of Ludoshur. The troupe intermingled traditional Udmurt songs with conversations on Soviet politics and the current political situation, all in the national language. During intermissions performers engaged youths in conversation. Local Udmurts eagerly attended the shows and there was often not enough room to accommodate them. Similar cultural events were held in villages throughout the land inhabited by Udmurts in the latter days of the Civil War.[53] Organized by Narkomnats (People's Commissariat of Nationalities) to popularize the socialist system, mobilize the masses, and bring culture and national awareness to non-Russian peasants, they represented a crescendo in a years-long process by national minority agents to disseminate their own national culture among the populace.

Central figures in the national minority causes, specifically educators and the Bolshevik state, maintained consistent ideas that non-Russians were uneducated, unenlightened, and culturally backwards. As early as 1918, Bolsheviks and national agents voluntarily joined together to impose a modern consciousness upon Viatka's mosaic of nationalities. Soviet officials' ideologically grounded views of national evolution shaped their attempts to make national minorities revolutionary. While state officials and national minority agents dominated the discourse, they engaged in a dialogue with peasants over what constituted acceptable culture. The creation of national minority identity was also a means of official mass mobilization, categorization, and integration of segments of the population into the larger polity. Far-reaching ideological

---

[52] Legotin, ed., *KPSS v tsifrakh*, 109.
[53] TsGA UR, f. R-204, op. 18, d. 9a, l. 216; GAKO, f. R-876, op. 1, d. 302, l. 8; A. I. Bobrova and A. S. Korobeinikova, eds., *Kul'turnoe stroitel'stvo v Udmurtii: Sbornik dokumentov (1917–1940 gg.)* (Izhevsk, 1970), 67–8.

aspirations to transform national minorities were constantly stymied at the local level, however, by local politicians, administrative weakness, and popular ambivalence.

Most non-Russian peasants experienced revolution and civil war much like Russian peasants – they struggled to become part of the larger polity, used the state in land disputes, and were victims of requisitions and conscriptions. Like almost all other non-Russian peasants, Udmurts and Maris clearly saw themselves as distinct ethnicities, but did not have a strong consciousness of themselves as nationalities. The Soviets ascribed and worked to instil a national identity upon them. Udmurt and Mari peasants recognized that they could gain resources and positive attention for cultural growth from the state if they played up their respective 'national' identities.

The Bolshevik state and national agents would form a perfect alliance during the Civil War to extend national minority projects in a radical direction. As Francine Hirsch shows, the Bolsheviks drew on Marxist concepts of national development through historical stages and ethnographic interpretations of cultural evolutionism to come up with their plan of 'state sponsored evolutionism', a project to transform clans, tribes, or nationalities into eventual 'socialist-era nations'.[54] The Soviet government backed national minority causes in part because it needed allies during the Civil War and was willing to concede a degree of political autonomy to nationalities. Bolshevik policy towards nationalities was also based on ideology. Central Communist Party leaders believed that all nations had equal rights and thus attempted to give them opportunity. In a policy that paralleled tsarist ethnographic interpretation, the Soviet regime also saw many of its eastern nations as backward, although the socialist regime based this assessment on such factors as industrialization, urbanization, and literacy.[55] Soviet officials methodically described Udmurts and Maris in internal documents as 'hardly cultured' (*malokul'turnyi*) and 'very backward in the realm of cultural and political development'.[56] This mindset of the uncultured nation included a revolutionary tribunal decision to free two Udmurts charged with counter-revolution and fighting for the Whites because, 'As Udmurts [Votiaki] they lack consciousness and do not understand the aims of Soviet power or what constitutes a crime.'[57] The Bolsheviks therefore adopted a nationalities policy during the Civil War to promote

---

[54] Hirsch, *Empire of Nations*, 7–9, ch. 1–2.
[55] Terry Martin, *The Affirmative Action Empire: Nations and Nationalism in the Soviet Union, 1923–1939* (Ithaca, 2001), 6, 126; Slezkine, *Arctic Mirrors*, ch. 5.
[56] GA RF, f. R-1318, op. 5, d. 3, ll. 26, 96, 299, 424, 528.
[57] GAKO, f. R-1322, op. 1a, d. 894, ll. 1–2.

popular national culture for 'backwards' nations through mass mobilization, education, and culture.

While the Soviet policy of indigenization (*korenizatsiia*) – the advancement of national culture through promoting national language and national elites – officially emerged after the Civil War in 1923, regional sections of Narkomnats were already implementing the essence of this policy in 1918. Moreover, the official Soviet practice of promoting national culture repeated the demands of nationality congresses from 1917 for national education, literature, and the training of indigenous elites.[58] The Bolsheviks and the small group of Udmurt and Mari national agents 'encouraged national consciousness and a sense of inherent primordial ethnicity' among the peasants.[59] The years between 1917 and 1921 thereby saw a massive acceleration and broadening of the national process.

In 1918, national agents and the Soviet state sought each other out. Many of the Udmurt and Mari national agents who had organized congresses in 1917 continued to meet at Soviet-sanctioned congresses to promote popular national consciousness, demand resources for education and culture from the state, and even discuss the possibility of political autonomy. In January 1918, Mari representatives met at Sernur village (*selo*), Urzhum district, formed a district union of Mari, proclaimed the need for Mari language schools, and demanded more resources from the zemstvo. In February 1918, many of the same representatives from Mari congresses in 1917, along with soldiers, met in Kazan. Influenced by discussions on the possible formation of a Tatar–Bashkir state, they discussed for the first time an autonomous ethno-territorial unit for the Mari.[60] Over the next year, national agents and the Soviet state held district congresses attended by village representatives that issued blanket support for Soviet power, formed national unions, and repeated calls from 1917 for national language education.[61]

As early as spring 1918, the Viatka Soviet government gave non-Russians autonomy to establish their own newspapers and schools. Military conflict strengthened the Soviet state's resolve to promote programmes for nationalities. In November, soon after the Red Army crushed the Stepanov and Prikomuch forces in the region, Udmurts held a series of meetings to form cultural circles and publish literature in Udmurt.[62] In December 1918, in part to win an alliance with the Mari in the crucial Elabuga district as Prikomuch forces faded and Kolchak's

---

[58] See Hirsch, *Empire of Nations*.   [59] Suny and Martin, eds, *A State of Nations*, 7.
[60] Lallukka, *From Fugitive Peasants*, 161–2.
[61] *Golos trudovogo naroda*, Iaransk, 28 February 1919, 3; *Viatskaia pravda*, 19 February 1918, 4.
[62] GAKO, f. 3271, op. 1, d. 13, ll. 20–1, 43.

advanced, the Revolutionary Committee of Elabuga city announced the organization of a Mari section to decide all questions relating to its people, a society for the promotion of Mari national consciousness, a district nationality library, a Mari national museum, a press to translate books and print newspapers in Mari, as well as new national schools. *Kombedy* were also ordered to aid the Mari.[63]

Narkomnats synthetically joined the Communist state with local national agents to promote national identity in the village. Following requests from national agents, the Udmurt and Mari sections of Narkomnats were established in mid-1918. Former zemstvo officials, teachers, seminarians, and even Orthodox clergymen dominated the Udmurt and Mari sections. Most were the sons of the Imperial-era Il'minskii system that promoted native language schooling and non-Russians as teachers and clergy. Shrugging off confessional identity, they devoted their lives to promoting national culture within the current state system. The leader of the Mari national movement, Vladimir Mukhin, transformed himself from seminarian, to teacher, to Left SR activist, before becoming the commissar of the Mari section of Narkomnats.[64] Pavel Glezdenev followed a similar trajectory. After completing religious schooling, Glezdenev taught primary school and seminary for non-Russians (*inorodtsy*), and then worked for the Viatka provincial education department and the zemstvo. During the war he edited both the Mari and Udmurt newspapers, then staffed the Provisional Government's education ministry, and joined Narkompros (People's Commissariat of Enlightenment) in December 1918 to continue his promotion of Udmurt and Mari national culture. Kuz'ma Chainikov (K. Gerd), best known as the Udmurt national poet, finished at the Kukarka teachers' institute in 1916 and taught at a local school until the Bolsheviks took power in the district. He spent 1918 peppering the provincial Soviet government with petitions to join the Udmurt section of Narkompros and to get the government to support his efforts to build rural Udmurt schools. Like his fellow national agents, Chainikov later joined Narkomnats and oversaw cultural dissemination programmes, such as drama troupes.[65] Historians have noted that Narkomnats was an instrument to co-opt national elites in order to gain mass support from nationalities and 'the direct representative of the national minorities to the central government'.[66]

---

[63] *Luch kommunizma*, Elabuga, 10 December 1918, 4.
[64] Lallukka, *From Fugitive Peasants*, 161–5.
[65] N. P. Pavlov, *Kuzebai Gerd – syn epokhi* (Izhevsk, 2004), 4–23.
[66] Jeremy Smith, *The Bolsheviks and the National Question, 1917–23*, Studies in Russia and Eastern Europe (New York 1999), 31; Stephen Blank, *The Sorcerer as Apprentice: Stalin as Commissar of Nationalities, 1917–1924* (Westport, CT, 1994), 13.

National agents themselves used the Soviet state and Narkomnats to further nationalist causes and implement their own notions of cultural progress and the Soviet nationalities policy played into and extended the national agents' imagination of their national culture.

Narkomnats, along with the overlapping Narkompros, oversaw national evolutionary programmes among non-Russians. The former students of the Il'minskii pedagogical method continued to preach schooling in the native language.[67] Narkompros ordered the construction of new village national schools. In one instance Udmurt villagers were freed from all other duties while they built a school.[68] Four national pedagogical technical institutes were established to train Udmurts in 1918–19, and courses in medicine, agriculture, and cultural education followed. The Commissariat of Udmurt Affairs advertised in newspapers to attract Udmurt peasants to train as teachers.[69] The state went to great lengths to recruit those able to teach and agitate in the national language. The Viatka provincial *ispolkom* put such significance on the national question that it demanded an immediate survey of all state and Party workers in order to transfer all national minorities to Narkomnats.[70] Officials recalled qualified soldiers and even freed men jailed for desertion and sabotage in order to do cultural work among the nationalities.[71]

Narkomnats agents organized cultural productions throughout the countryside. In Zav'ialovskaia *volost*, Sarapul district, Narkomnats sponsored an Udmurt-language performance. Before the show a representative discussed current affairs and basic subjects like 'what is Soviet power?' and 'why there is civil war'.[72] Narkomnats also organized a wide array of cultural programmes including reading huts, libraries, people's huts (buildings where locals could gather and hold meetings), national drama circles, orchestras, choruses, concerts, lectures in both Russian and the national language, and entertainment programmes every Sunday, and distributed books of poetry, political brochures, and newspapers in the nationality's language.[73] The Mari section of Narkomnats tried to

---

[67] Yuri Slezkine, 'The USSR as a Communal Apartment, or How a Socialist State Promoted Ethnic Particularism', *Slavic Review* 53 (1994): 418; Isabelle Kreindler, 'A Neglected Source of Lenin's Nationality Policy', *Slavic Review* 36 (1977): 86–100.

[68] GA RF, f. R-1318, op. 5, d. 3, l. 91.

[69] *Izvestiia Glazovskogo soveta krest'ianskikh, rabochikh i krasnoarmeiskikh deputatov*, 15 November 1918, 1.

[70] GA RF, f. R-1318, op. 5, d. 3, l. 4.

[71] GA RF, f. R-1318, op. 5, d. 3, ll. 424, 604, 748.

[72] GA RF, f. R-1318, op. 5, d. 27, ll. 11, 15.

[73] GA RF, f. R-1318, op. 5, d. 8, l. 2ob; d. 27, l. 15; d. 8, ll. 22, 25. Bobrova and Korobeinikova, eds, *Kul'turnoe stroitel'stvo v Udmurtii*, 36, 38–9, 42–5, 60–3, 68, 71–3. For more on the Udmurt theatre, see K. Gerd, 'O votiatskom teatre', *Zhizn' natsional'nostei* 2 (1923), 98–102.

identify and enumerate the Mari in Iaransk district in a targeted census in 1919. Based on its data it aimed the Mari-language newspaper *Ioshkar keche* at *volost*s with registered Mari populations.[74] The Udmurt-language newspaper *Voinays ivor*, established in 1915, outlived its zemstvo sponsor by gaining Soviet approval and changing its name to *Udmort*, but retained its editorial staff. *Udmort* and a sister paper, *Vil' sin'* (New Window), continued to publish stories on the need for national education, better hygiene, and national unity but added a Soviet tint to stories.[75]

National agents saw their work under the Soviet gaze as liberating their nation and allowing it to bloom and they were sympathetic to the social message of Soviet power. The state tied national enlightenment activities to political agitation, and incorporation and mobilization into the Soviet system. As a Soviet editorialist wrote in 1921, 'Finally, after many centuries the star of enlightenment begins to shine and burns brighter and brighter every day in the [Udmurt] family. The morality and soul of the forgotten [Udmurt] people under Soviet power is waking from a long nightmare.'[76] Just as the *kombedy* and agitation in the villages taught poor peasants how to be proper Soviet citizens and create new class identities, national minority programmes built a revolutionary national identity. Non-Russians learned about their history through the language of class warfare and the Soviets began to inculcate Communist revolutionary politics. Local soviets made calendars in Udmurt with portraits on them of Marx, Lenin, Trotsky, and Anatolii Lunacharskii.[77] Chainikov translated a biography of Lenin into Udmurt, even though he mistranslated key theoretical phrases and misinterpreted Marxism in his commentary.[78] Communist Party agitators went throughout the countryside to explain Bolshevik politics and ideology among the peasants in the national tongue. The agitator Petr Bagrashov returned to his native *volost* and engaged locals in conversations (*besedy*), including one with students on the lessons from the Paris commune.[79]

Despite their zeal, Bolsheviks and their national agent allies were hampered by practical limitations brought on by the Civil War and institutional weakness. Narkomnats agitators spent much of their conversations in 1920–21 listening to peasant grievances against state requisitions or helping in famine relief, leaving little time to promote national culture. The state lacked infrastructure and resources and had

[74] GAKO, f. R-3319, op. 1, d. 1, ll. 1–5a, 13, 21; d. 13.
[75] Pavlov, *Samoopredelenie, avtonomiia*, 69–104.
[76] *Zhizn' krest'ianina*, 11 January 1921, 1.   [77] GA RF, f. R-1318, op. 5, d. 3, l. 374.
[78] Pavlov, *Kuzebai Gerd*, 15–16.   [79] GA RF, f. R-1318, op. 5, d. 27, l.11.

few ardent supporters among the non-Russians. An effort to distribute the Tatar newspaper *Iarlyrar-taushi* failed because the Party could not find a censor who knew Tatar.[80] Narkomnats agents were always short of paper and begged Moscow to supply them with enough to print even a limited run of newspapers. The state could not even provide the drama troupe in Ludoshur kerosene to hold spectacles at night and one official dismissed support of the effort as 'a joke'.[81] Years of civil war had taken away able personnel and destroyed schools. The regional nationalities division complained to Moscow that it had only 1 agitator for 250,000 Udmurts.[82] Minutes of Narkomnats meetings are filled with the power of rhetoric and ideological conviction unable to meet reality. At one meeting Narkomnats resolved to pursue pedagogical and agriculture courses 'with maximum energy', but resources never appeared to make such efforts a reality. In 1921, after the Bolsheviks had defeated the anti-Soviet forces, local officials reported that almost all the schools were destroyed and they had neither building materials, nor working hands for repairs. The majority of school instructors was inexperienced and there was no money to pay their salary. The few new village libraries in Udmurt had no literature in the national language.[83]

Non-Russian peasants embraced the opportunity of cultural expression and education. They continued their quest from the tsarist era to seek out opportunities for education and embraced schooling and literature in their mother tongue. Many villages readily sent representatives to national meetings and cultural productions remained the one line by which to continue a dialogue with non-Russians hostile to the Soviet government's requisitions and mobilization of their men. In a rowdy village meeting with Narkomnats in Sovetskaia *volost*, Sarapul district, where peasants complained about the war and questioned Soviet power itself, they still asked to learn how to hold performances.[84]

Non-Russian peasants also learned to don the mask of their nationality with a Bolshevik face. They used elite notions of national evolution for their own good. For example, at the First Party Conference of Udmurts in 1920, Udmurt representatives 'confessed' that Udmurts 'have an insufficient understanding of their duties as citizens' and that is why so many of their 'tribesmen' deserted the Red Army. They blamed their poor public spirit on the fact that historically Udmurts had tried to shirk their military duties and they had not yet gained sufficient

[80] GASPI KO, f. 1, op. 1, d. 211, ll. 2–9.   [81] GAKO, f. R-876, op. 1, d. 302, l. 8.
[82] GA RF, f. R-1318, op. 5, d. 27, l. 186; d. 8, l. 2.
[83] RGASPI, f. 17, op. 60, d. 106, ll. 5, 7; GA RF, f. R-1318, op. 5, d. 27, ll. 19ob, 20ob.
[84] GA RF, f. R-1318, op. 5, d. 27, ll. 18–20ob; GAKO, f. R-3319, op. 1, d. 3.

understanding of the difference between the tsarist and Red armies.[85] Representatives at the Ernurskaia *Volost* Congress of Mari in Iaransk district in 1920 also lamented their national 'darkness' from lack of education and pleaded for more books in Mari because, as representative Buketov summarized, 'As every species of bird has its own customary song, its own voice, so does every nationality. We Mari have our own language and customs but we could never learn them from Russians in Russian.'[86] Like the peasants in 1917 who used the popular discourse of enlightenment and citizenship to gain educational opportunities and participation in national politics, these representatives used Soviet tropes of duty, consciousness, and cultural backwardness tied to historical exploitation to support the regime while explaining why they did not want to fight for it.

National minority peasants supported the nationalist cause only to a limited degree. While peasants certainly embraced opportunities for formal education, literature in their villages, and colourful free performances, many resisted having to make additional sacrifices to a nationalist movement developed by outsiders. Peasants already suffered through state requisitions, taxation, and famine. Many Udmurt villagers refused to pay or even send representatives to national conferences.[87] Local officials even threatened a delegate returning home from a congress with arrest after he tried to call a *volost* gathering to discuss nationalist issues.[88] Some Mari peasants in Ernur village disagreed with representatives at the *volost* congress and complained, 'We do not need our own language. Give us the Russian language and a Russian school.'[89] While seeking out education like other peasants before the revolution, national minorities were split on whether education in their own language or the dominant Russian language would serve them best in the larger world.

National minorities embraced state-sponsored cultural programmes, but steered clear of becoming a full part of the Soviet system, even more than ethnically Russian peasants. In 1920, for example, only 7 Tatars out of almost 16,000 belonged to the Party in the Viatka countryside.[90] The regional and central Communist Party leaders were keenly aware of their failure to recruit non-Russians and around 1920 they began to devote considerable resources to rectify the problem. For example, in

---

[85] GASPI KO, f. 1, op. 1, d. 211, l. 29.
[86] GAKO, f. R-3316, op. 1, d. 3 ll. 82ob–83.; see also ll. 4–5, 6, 25–25ob.
[87] GAKO, f. R-876, op. 1, d. 85, l. 47ob.
[88] L. S. Khristoliubova, 'Prosvetitel'naia i etnokonsolidiruiushchaia rol pervykh udmurtskikh gazet i kul'turno-prosvetitel'nykh obshchestv v pervoi chetverti XX v.', 47.
[89] GAKO, f. R-3316, op. 1, d. 1, l. 117.   [90] RGASPI, f. 17, op. 61, d. 131, l. 3.

the Votiak (Udmurt) Autonomous Region, the Soviets recruited a number of Udmurts to study at the urban Party school. When some of the students did not show up, the Party went to the extreme measure of seeking them out in their village. In another instance, the Party devoted resources to teach an illiterate potential political Udmurt agitator to read.[91] Still, at the beginning of 1922, Udmurts accounted for only 14.8 per cent of Party members in the Votiak Autonomous Region.[92]

The establishment of the Mari and Votiak autonomous regions, announced simultaneously on 4 November 1920, created a logistical nightmare for local governments as Moscow divided (and sometimes redivided) districts, assigned regions to different provincial jurisdictions, and moved boundaries among provinces and the newly established regions.[93] In July 1920 the centre employed the provincial-level administration to categorize the population by ethnicity and pass along the material by August. If the centre lacked knowledge about its land, the provincial-level administration also struggled to comprehend and classify data to understand the population. Unable to make the deadline, in November the province pleaded to have more time. It finally used a partial census from 1920 and, it appears, the 1917 census to draw the boundaries for the new autonomous regions.[94] No one was satisfied with the results.

Regional Party and state leaders fought the territorial divisions. In January 1920, M. Agapitov, the chair of the Sarapul district Party, and N. Turanov, the chair of the *ispolkom*, sent the central Narkomnats leadership a letter of protest against the establishment of the Votiak Autonomous Region, writing that they were, 'not only against the annexation of the district to a Votiak republic, but also the very establishment of an independent Votiak unit since the Votiaks are too scattered and most of them are mixed with Russian peasants. Moreover, they are not interested in their nation.'[95] Agapitov and Turanov

---

[91] GA RF, f. R-1318, op. 5, d. 3, ll. 442, 593.

[92] V. I. Katkov et al., eds, *Udmurtskaia oblastnaia organizatsiia KPSS v tsifrakh, 1921–1985* (Ustinov, 1986), 86.

[93] For example, the state changed the jurisdiction of Elabuga district to Kazan province and reassigned most of it to the newly formed Tatar Autonomous Oblast in May 1920, only to reassign Elabuga back to Viatka. The borders of Viatka province and the Mari, Komi, and Votiak Autonomous Oblasts continually shifted during 1921 as jurisdiction of *volosts* and villages transferred among the territories based on ethnicity. *Administrativnoe raionirovanie RSFSR. Sbornik postanovlenii, kasaiushchikhsia administrativno-territorial'nogo deleniia Rossii, za peiod 1917–1922 g. po dannym administrativnoi komissii VTsIK k 10 noiabria 1922 goda* (Moscow, 1923), 30–47.

[94] GAKO, f. R-876, op. 1, d. 234, ll. 5, 8, 76, 90–108. For the Mari, see GAKO, f. R-3319, op. 1, d. 1, ll. 1–5a, 13, 21; d. 13.

[95] Quoted in K. I. Kulikov, *Natsional'no-gosudarstvennoe stroitel'stvo vostochno-finskikh narodov v 1917–1937 gg.* (Izhevsk, 1993), 5.

correctly noted that the centre was attempting to separate an intermixed population. The acknowledgement of popular indifference to national identity by officials shows the extent to which Soviet nationality administrators and national agents tried to construct and impose new identities upon non-Russian peasants. The Viatka provincial government also protested against the establishment of the Udmurt and Mari autonomous regions because it took away the province's breadbasket in a time of famine and central government pressures to requisition grain.

Peasants also showed that economic considerations and geographic identity took precedence over their sense of unity with their ethnicity. Several predominantly Udmurt villages and even whole *volost*s successfully voted and petitioned to remain inside Viatka province. They cited geographic proximity to their current district centre, economic ties, or more elemental problems like 'bad roads' to the new district centre 'that are submerged under a river for the whole season of spring'.[96] The population of Elabuga and Malmyzh districts was infuriated when it learned that the centre of the Votiak Autonomous Oblast would be placed in the northern town of Glazov. To reach their new capital by rail, peasants would have to travel either to Viatka city or Ekaterinburg, since a north–south line had not been built. In the end, Izhevsk became the capital. Having recently been the centre of one of the largest anti-Soviet movements in the Civil War and lacking strong transportation ways, Izhevsk was not Moscow's choice.

National agents and Soviet ideology worked together to create a national awareness among non-Russians. Whereas the tsarist state stood in opposition to these cultural figures (many of them were arrested after forming national circles), the Soviet state and national leaders created a symbiotic relationship. National agents enjoyed state resources, but most importantly their concept that national minority peasants' cultural backwardness had to be overcome through specific cultural education coincided with Bolshevik policy and images of nationalities. Full participation in the polity could only be achieved through national consciousness-building measures. The Soviets thereby maintained the discourse of cultural development and promoted national culture in order to bring the nationalities up to the level of the Russians and build a rational, socialist utopia. This may give high politics and cultural figures too much credit, though. The unruly rural Soviet administration, the Civil War environment, and limited resources undermined the nationalist effort, while national minority peasants bent the projects to favour

---

[96] GAKO, f. R-876, op. 1, d. 234, ll. 5, 90–91, 117, 118–23. Quote on l. 125 repeated by another *volost* on ll. 134–134ob.

programmes that served their own purposes or that they enjoyed, such as national language education and cultural performances. For the first years of Soviet rule, national minorities learned to speak and take advantage of revolutionary Bolshevism.

Conclusion

Overlapping with the violence and devastation of Civil War, the Bolshevik regime built a system of persuasion and consensus through projects to strengthen and enlighten nationalities, to spread the word of socialism, and to disseminate class warfare. Bolsheviks and the peasant populations approached the rationale behind the projects differently. The Bolsheviks believed that various populations, such as Udmurts, Maris, Tatars, poor peasants, women, youths, and the peasantry as a socio-economic category, needed and would accept their tutelage. In this way, Marxist–Leninist ideology, as well as a belief in the transformative abilities of the rational modern state, guided early Bolshevik rule. Peasants accepted and became a part of the Soviet state–building project. At the same time, peasant populations used Bolshevik imagination and state programmes to further their own good. For example, nationality projects and propaganda campaigns gave peasants educational opportunities and additional state resources.

Bolshevik policies shaped peasant identities. Individual peasants learned to live with and accommodate state needs and they retooled their language and presentation of themselves to fit into the new socialist polity. For some peasants, like many national minorities, living under Soviet rule changed how they spoke about and framed their plight. For others, the changes went still further. New peasant identities incorporated state ideas of the socialist peasant, thereby bringing Soviet society even further into the village. Peasants also used state projects for their own good and re-centred state apparatuses to suit their own interests. They found language and arenas to communicate with state officials and resist state policies without fear of reprisal. Peasants accepted and shaped Soviet rule, creating a consensus that was not what Soviet leaders had originally envisioned.

8 The citizens' hunger: famine relief efforts and the Civil War economy

The Civil War was a long season of hunger. The emaciation of the village began during the First World War. Since late 1916, grain detachments and armies pilfered villagers' fields and homes. By 1919, storehouses ran low and desperately needed to be filled. Since 1915, tuberculosis and typhus threatened the countryside and only needed the Civil War environment to become epidemic.[1] The Red Army victory over Kolchak's forces in the summer of 1919 may have eased the constant threat to peasants' goods in Viatka but in the winter of that year the combination of crop failure, disease, famine, and mass population displacement finally crushed the peasant community. These disasters highlight the fragility of the peasant economy and village structure. Famine and Civil War engendered transformative social changes in the rural community by destroying the subsistence of peasant households, moving tens of thousands of peasants out of their villages, and putting society in a state of even more dynamic flux.

As death and disease from the famine and Civil War dragged the countryside down, they also transformed society and politics. Famine and accompanying social disasters shaped government policies and, in turn, the peasant–state relationship. Mass hunger, disease, and upheaval were daily reminders of the nascent Soviet regime's limitations and failures. Rural dwellers reacted outside and against the state, ignoring state codes and rebelling against the Soviet system. At the same time, hunger and war drew peasants and the Soviet state closer together. Peasants turned to the government with an expectation that it would provide for them in times of need, while government officials began to build what would become the Soviet welfare state in which the government embraced its duty to try to care for the population, while simultaneously mobilizing them to build a socialist society.

---

[1] *Belyi tsvetok*, Viatka, 20 June 1915. For a similar picture of the everyday struggle to survive, see Narskii, *Zhizn' v katastrofe*.

The backdrop of famine

Between 1919 and 1922, a series of meteorological disasters befell the Russian countryside, resulting in wholesale crop failure and massive famine. In 1919–20, a drought hit European Russia, destroying most winter and spring crops. In 1920, frost destroyed the harvest and seed. Given the precarious nature of the peasant subsistence farming at the time – without surplus labour, stored grain, and non-agricultural income to fall back on – the rural economy collapsed. Years of war, government requisitions, and other external strains on the rural demography and economy had weakened the peasant economy and the extraordinary weather made the loss of crops catastrophic.[2] The chaos of the times makes calculations of the loss of life from famine and disease nearly impossible, but estimates range from 5 to 15 million souls.[3] Although starvation was worst in the Lower Volga region, the Volga–Kama region (including Viatka province) suffered like the rest of Russia.

Crop failure hit Viatka's southern districts (the province's traditional breadbasket) the hardest because the area was heavily reliant on agriculture. Sarapul district produced 8,627,334 puds of grain in 1916, but only 625,145 puds in 1921.[4] Peasants were forced to eat their seed grain and slaughter livestock and the agricultural economy spiralled downwards. As the number of working hands, livestock, and amount of seed grain declined, peasants limited their sown land further, continuing a decline in cultivated land that began during the First World War. In 1922, peasants of Kotel'nich district sowed slightly more than half of the land that they did in 1916. In neighbouring Nolinsk district, villagers only sowed forty per cent of the land they had six years earlier. As a whole, peasants in the southern and central districts restricted the land that they put under the plough more than those in the northern districts. Weather conditions also hit the southern districts' more intensive agriculture harder than the hardier yet less productive crops of the northern region.[5]

Their emergency supplies eaten or taken by the state, peasants became desperate. The situation was so bad that starving villagers in

---

[2] Hoover Archives, American Relief Administration, Russian operations, box 414, folder 3, general questionnaire. *Otchet o deiatel'nosti Viatskoi*, 3.

[3] Narskii, *Zhizn' v katastrofe*, 93–4.

[4] Hoover Archives, American Relief Administration, New York office, box 30, folder 2, Report of inspection trip in the Kazan region, 12 October 1922.

[5] B. Perfil'ev, 'Posevnaia ploshchad'', in *Viatskaia guberniia na Vsesoiuznoi sel'sko-khoziaistvennoi i kustarno-promyshlennoi vystavke v 1923 godu: Sbornik statei* (Viatka, 1923), 30–4; GA RF, f. 1318, op. 5, d. 14, l. 1.

southern districts travelled over a hundred versts just to collect dirt that they had heard could nourish them. Locals blocked the travellers from the soil, and fights between the two populations broke out.[6] Peasants turned to surrogates for grain such as potato peel, cabbage leaves, acorns, pig weed, flax, blood, sawdust, straw, and tree bark, causing nausea and malnutrition. Not knowing what to do, parents abandoned their children at the district government building. Others committed suicide.[7] Hundreds of thousands of peasants in Viatka were malnourished or starving. In the winter of 1921–22, a census showed that 170,595 people were starving in Malmyzh district and up to 50,000 starved in Nolinsk district.[8] The famine was gendered and generational in nature. Most portrayals of famine in the world centre on the suffering of women and children as innocent victims.[9] During the Soviet famine, young and old of both sexes were quicker to succumb to hunger and disease than adults, but males overall died at greater rates than females. Males in the village were disproportionately elderly, or wounded veterans, and they may not have been able to withstand famine.[10] Around 70% of children were registered as starving in June 1922, even though those younger than seven years old represented only 21% of the total famished population.[11]

As famine grew, so did disease. Unsanitary conditions and general ignorance of disease had long made the Viatka countryside prone to epidemics. In 1892, cholera devastated Viatka, as it did the rest of European Russia. Disease grew during the First World War and the revolution. Soviet officials wearily reported that the Spanish flu, a local manifestation of the influenza pandemic sweeping across the globe, caused 'colossal damage' in October 1918 in Kotel'nich district and killed 170 peasants. A typhoid epidemic ravaged Nolinsk in spring 1919.[12] Villagers, assuming they wanted to, could not turn to modern

---

[6] Hoover Archives, American Relief Administration, Russian operations, box 29, folder 2, Report of the Central Committee of Relief, 16 November 1921; GAKO, f. R-783, op. 1, d. 79, l. 72ob; d. 5, ll. 26, 120ob.

[7] GAKO, f. R-783, op. 1, d. 1, ll. 26, 120.

[8] GAKO, f. R-783, op. 1, d. 74, l. 4ob; d. 5, l. 136.

[9] Margaret Kelleher, *The Feminization of Famine: Expressions of the Inexpressible?* (Durham, NC, 1997), 2.

[10] Serguei Adamets, 'Famine in Nineteenth- and Twentieth-Century Russia: Mortality by Age, Cause, and Gender', in Tim Dyson and Cormac O Grada, eds., *Famine Demography: Perspectives from the Past and Present* (Oxford, 2002), 172–7; David Arnold, *Famine: Social Crisis and Historical Change* (Oxford, 1988), 88–91.

[11] GASPI KO, f. 1, op. 2, d. 229, ll. 5–5ob; GAKO, f. R-783, op. 1, d. 74, l. 401. Based on records of Malmyzh district.

[12] GA RF, f. R-393, op. 3, d. 117, l. 7/HIASCPSS, reel 46. GAKO, f. R-1620, op. 2, d. 13, l. 37.

medicine for help as the government mobilized most doctors and *fel'dshers* for the war and Civil War.[13] In 1919 in Glazov district there remained only four doctors, two for the city hospital and two for the countryside. With unsanitary conditions, malnutrition, and the lack of medical resources, massive epidemics were inevitable. From 1920–22, tuberculosis, scurvy, dysentery, relapsing fever, and especially typhus ravaged the rural population.[14]

Disease, pestilence, famine, and requisitions further decimated peasants' livestock. Cases of glanders jumped and mange went from less than 400 cases in 1913 to almost 7,000 cases in 1920. Anthrax, the deadly parasite that the zemstvo fought against during the war, hit the hardest. In 1913, 262 heads of livestock were struck with the pest, 514 in 1914 and almost 4,000 in 1921.[15] The various state powers had mobilized veterinarian specialists, leaving a void in the countryside. Without medicine and training, peasants could not contain these parasites. The environment also spread pests. Anthrax most often attacked cattle and horses when they grazed in swampy areas. During the drought, peasants were forced to feed their cattle in these dangerous lands even though veterinarians before the war had instructed them as to the associated dangers. In the area that formed the Votiak Autonomous Region, the number of cows dropped by 46%, working horses by 47%, and bulls by an amazing 95% (see Table 8.1). Peasants slaughtered two-thirds of their sheep and pigs, fast growing farm commodities before the First World War but extra mouths to feed in the now non-existent cash economy.[16]

Wartime dragged down the number of horses per household and created more horseless peasants, one of the tsarist ethnographers', and Lenin's, main barometers for peasant wealth. In 1916 in Sarapul district there were 1.37 horses per household, and by 1920 there were 0.80. The ratio declined further in 1921 to 0.70, and in 1922 bottomed out at just 0.55 horses per household.[17] In 1922, around thirty-five per cent of

---

[13] RGASPI, f. 17, op. 5. d. 21, l. 4; GAKO, f. R-3300, op. 1. d., 1, ll. 50–1.
[14] *Otchet o deiatel'nosti Viatskoi*, 13–14. The state recorded thousands of cases for each disease and over 11,000 cases of typhus in the first half of 1922. Hoover Archives, American Relief Administration, Russian Operations, box 29, folder 29–3. Narskii, *Zhizn' v katastrofe*, 128–39.
[15] P. Trapeznikov, 'Veterinarnoe delo', in *Viatskaia guberniia na Vsesoiuznoi sel'skokhoziaistvennoi*, 84–5; RGAE, f. 478, op. 3, d. 1284, l. 1.
[16] GAKO, f. R-890, op. 1, d. 2, l. 64. Narskii finds a similar picture in the other provinces of the Urals, *Zhizn' v katastrofe*, 93–8.
[17] Hoover Archives, American Relief Administration, New York office, box 30, folder 2, Report of inspection trip in the Kazan region, 12 October 1922.

Table 8.1 *Decline of livestock and harvest in Votiak Autonomous Region*

	1916	1921	1922
Cows	164,425	107,527	89,707
Bulls	11,725	1,037	503
Draft horses	160,523	104,322	85,369
Colts	39,907	29,985	22,018
Grain harvested (in puds)	28,000,000	4,000,000	8,213,000

Data from RGAE, f. 478, op. 2, d. 384, ll. 17, 19–21.

peasant households did not own a horse.[18] The decline began in 1914 when military conscription took horses away at the height of their breeding. Not only did the number of horses go down, so did the potential rebirth of the population. Soviet directives targeted requisitions of horses at 'prosperous', multi-horse households and in effect levelled the number of horses per household, although the downward shift resulted in a growth of the impoverished 'poor' peasant segment.

Material shortages continued through 1922. Poor supply lines prevented the state from importing salt, kerosene, and iron to Viatka and even the abundant firewood from the northern part of the province could not reach the central and southern districts.[19] Shortages strangled the peasant economy. Peasants could not fix agricultural equipment, prepare meals, or even properly heat their homes. Shortages in both the countryside and the national economy also destroyed the non-agricultural sector. The *kustar'* market was hit the hardest. A December 1918 report on the *kustar'* industry in Viatka district summarized the problems: '[O]ften the market lacks necessary raw and factory materials, such as paint, lacquers, extracts, hardware, instruments, oils, spirits, and so forth; there are high prices for materials and working hands, transportation has been disrupted, there are insufficient horses in the countryside, and the Civil War has affected the market.' The report went on to mention the outflow from villages of the best workers to the army.[20] Even if the peasants could produce handicrafts, the economy was so ruined that urban dwellers would have been unable to buy them. The disappearance of the *kustar'* economy therefore deprived most peasant households of their main safety net.

---

[18] *Otchet o deiatel'nosti Viatskoi*, 11–12.
[19] GAKO, f. R-885, op. 1, d. 46, l. 7.
[20] GAKO, f. R-879, op. 1, d. 75, l. 539. See also *Viatskoe narodnoe khoziaistvo*, 15 March 1919, 26, 27.

A population upturned

Famine and civil war exacerbated the massive displacement of the population brought on by the First World War. Calls for lost friends and relatives took up pages of newspapers and reflected how the fabric of Russian society had become torn apart. People searched for those lost in evacuations, service to the Red Army, and wartime captivity in foreign lands. A man hunted for his wife lost during a robbery; family members of Red Army soldiers tried to find sons and husbands who never returned home or disappeared from the ranks; others pleaded for news of their loved ones. The state also put out calls in the newspapers for information on the Viatka district provisions committee chair who was wanted for corruption, the head of the Urzhum district Party who had gone missing, and scores of people convicted of crimes.[21] In these pages, the state openly admitted its limitations and asked the public to help each other beyond the purview of the state.

The transient, displaced rural population can only be understood in the context of war and revolution. Prisoners of war, alien citizens, and refugees reminded local peasants that the hardships of the world war continued. In June 1918, there were still 1,419 German and Austrian soldiers in captivity in Viatka district alone. Another 1,597 prisoners arrived that July. Almost 1,000 German, Austrian, Turkish, and Bulgarian enemy aliens remained imprisoned in the district, of whom 271 were women and 261 were children. Some prisoners joined the revolution and issued proclamations supporting the Soviet state and an international socialist revolution, but most restlessly awaited their return home.[22] The Viatka College of Prisoners and Refugees oversaw a mass evacuation project through the summer and autumn of 1918, shepherding most of the prisoners and former enemy aliens back to their country of origin.[23]

While foreign citizens and prisoners left Russia, urban refugees and peasant soldiers returned to the countryside. Urbanites went to the country to look for food and escape social turmoil, and the state evacuated people from the cities. Villagers and local governments at first

---

[21] GAKO, f. R-876, op. 2, d. 43; *Krasnyi nabat*, Glazov, 19 July 1919, 4.

[22] Article from *Izvestiia Viatskogo gubispolkoma sovetov RS i KD*, 8 June 1918, Bystrova et al., eds, *Ustanovlenie*, 368.

[23] See, for example, GAKO, f. R-876, op. 1. d. 9, ll. 89–89ob, 113. The college administered an enormous number of travellers passing through Viatka. By 20 August the medical staff at the Viatka evacuation point saw over 3,000 Russians, 300 Germans, and 28,500 Austrians. GA RF, f. R-393, op. 3, d. 107, l. 151/HIASCPSS, reel 41. In May and June the Glazov district *ispolkom* sent 758 German and Austrian citizens back to their native countries. GA RF, f. R-393, op. 3, d. 109, l. 208/HIASCPSS, reel 42.

tried to accommodate them but the refugees soon outgrew the locales' limited capabilities. In Ludoshurskaia *volost*, Glazov district, refugees who had arrived during the war and were living in the zemstvo schools spilled over to local dwellings and in 1918 the *volost* soviet requested that no more refugees be placed in the region.[24] There were 1,640 refugees in Viatka district alone in the beginning of September 1918, and that figure grew to 2,143 by the middle of November. The central People's Commissariat of Supply evacuated thousands of Muscovite children to Elabuga district and in 1918 there were over 12,000 refugees in Viatka. Given the desperate food situation, violent material destruction from the Civil War, and shifting political control, neither villagers nor Soviet governmental administrations could handle the influx of refugees and some transplants died from starvation.[25]

Peasant men also slowly returned to their households. Although soldiers from the war began to return home following the February Revolution, soldiers formerly imprisoned in countries of the Central Powers trickled back only in the late summer of 1918 and flooded the province that winter. In August, the Viatka district government reported that up to 4,800 soldiers had returned home.[26] The Soviet government saw the formerly imprisoned veterans, like other soldiers, as potential allies and actively agitated among them. At the disembarkment station in Viatka city, Party members made speeches and the returnees could listen while enjoying free tea, a hot meal, and reading literature from a library established for their use.[27] District soviets even paid those delivering the mail to transport these men back to their *volosts*.[28] Records indicate that within five months of their return almost half of the formerly imprisoned soldiers left again for the Red Army, creating a revolving door effect in which men returned only to leave a short time later.[29]

While thousands travelled back to Viatka or made the province their temporary home, thousands more wandered around the region or tried to resettle in other parts of the country. Peasant migration or flight from unliveable circumstances was a compensatory survival technique in Russia, the origins of which can be found well before enserfment. As in the tsarist era, poor land, epidemics, failed harvests, and rumours of

[24] GA RF, f. R-393, op. 3, d. 107, l. 115ob/HIASCPSS, reel 41.
[25] GASPI KO, f. 45, op. 1, d. 158, ll. 36, 54. A note from Moscow indicates that 100,000 children were evacuated to Elabuga, but no other document supports this number.
[26] GAKO, f. R-876, op. 1, d. 79, l. 95. Several soldiers also returned home in December to Malmyzh district. GAKO, f. R-3300, op. 1, d. 1, ll. 1–17.
[27] GA RF, f. R-393, op. 3, d. 107, ll. 149–50, 299/HIASCPSS, reel 41.
[28] GA RF, f. R-393, op. 3, d. 117, l. 1/HIASCPSS, reel 46.
[29] In Bogorodskaia *volost*, forty-seven of the ninety-seven soldiers went into the Red Army by May 1919. GAKO, f. R-1620, op. 2, d. 13, ll. 1ob–9.

prospects in distant lands spurred peasants to migrate.[30] The political turmoil, government requisitions, and, most of all, unfavourable weather conditions pushed even more peasants to seek opportunities elsewhere.[31] From 1914 to 1922, the vast majority of peasant migrants in Viatka attempted to travel eastward following similar paths that their relatives, neighbours, and acquaintances took in previous years. However, the cataclysmic changes during the Civil War also disrupted local migration.

In the second half of the nineteenth century, Viatka's peasants maintained stable, balanced settlement patterns, moving both within and out of the province. Before the Great Siberian migration, equal numbers of people migrated to other districts within the province as to other provinces. Peasants from the northern and central districts, who suffered from poor land, tended to resettle to the neighbouring warmer, more fertile southern districts, especially Sarapul. Those in the south preferred to leave the province. Seventy-one per cent of migrants from Viatka district moved to other districts within the province, while ninety-two per cent from Sarapul district migrated to another province.[32] The proximity to the settler's home made intra-provincial migration safer and less dramatic but villagers hoping for new opportunities and greater lifestyle change resettled to the Siberian and Far Eastern provinces of Perm, Tomsk, Tobolsk, Eniseisk, and Irkutsk. In a manner resembling labour migration to urban factories, peasants in the same district or village tended to resettle in the same area, using local people from their native land (*zemliaki*) to ease the transition. In 1881, the tsarist government state lifted restrictions on peasants who wished to leave their commune, marking the beginning of the turn towards encouraging peasant migration.[33] The tsarist government promoted resettlement to Siberia in the 1880s and offered state land to settlers. On the eve of world war the state even published brochures providing information on the conditions in Asiatic Russia and ordered local officials to distribute

---

[30] Jerome Blum, *Lord and Peasant in Russia: From the Ninth to the Nineteenth Century* (Princeton, 1961), 106–13, 247–9; Barbara A. Anderson, *Internal Migration During Modernization in Late Nineteenth-Century Russia* (Princeton, 1980); Willard Sunderland, 'Peasants on the Move: State Peasant Resettlement in Imperial Russia, 1805–1830s', *The Russian Review* 52 (1993): 477–8; Willard Sunderland, 'Peasant Pioneering: Russian Peasant Settlers Describe Colonization and the Eastern Frontier, 1880s–1910s', *Journal of Social History* 34 (2001): 898–901.

[31] GAKO, f. R-1062, op. 1, d. 282, l. 151; d. 513, l. 5.

[32] N. Romanov, *Pereseleniia krest'ian Viatskoi gubernii. Issledovanie Viatskago gubernskago zemskago statistika* (Viatka, 1880), 119–20. Data is from 1859 to 1879.

[33] David Moon, 'Peasant Migration, the Abolition of Serfdom, and the Internal Passport System in the Russian empire c. 1800–1914', in David Eltis, ed., *Coerced and Free Migration: Global Perspectives* (Stanford, 2002), 333–6.

them free of charge.[34] Like peasants throughout European Russia, Viatka's peasants flocked eastward from the 1880s. If during the whole twenty-year period from 1859 to 1879, around 19,800 people left Viatka, between 1895 and 1908 over 100,000 people migrated to Siberia and the Far East.[35] While the numbers of pioneers increased, the paths they took remained stable.

Wartime mobilization began a decade-long period of constant movement and migration in the countryside on an unprecedented scale.[36] The number of migrants vacillated greatly during the revolutionary era. The war economy shut down traditional peasant market networks and the outflow of able-bodied men to the army made migration a riskier venture than during peacetime. Peasant migration from Viatka dropped significantly with the outbreak of war, falling from 17,817 in 1913, to 6,079 in 1915.[37] The economic upheaval from the revolution and the Civil War dried up out-migration to the urban areas, depopulating the cities with the closure of factories and scarcity of food and basic necessities, but many peasants did not sit idle in their villages.[38] If some peasants returned to or remained in the village, others fled the tumult. The weak local governmental apparatus in 1918, as well as the temporary overthrow of Soviet power in the eastern half of the province by the Prikomuch forces, makes quantifying peasant resettlement difficult. However, even the partial numbers compiled by the provincial land section show that migration to other provinces grew sharply soon after the October Revolution. By January 1919, the land section counted almost 9,000 applicants for resettlement and only received information on settlers from six of the eleven districts. Of those applicants, 28% had relatives and acquaintances in Siberia and 9% had been there before. Men and women left in almost equal numbers – 53%

---

[34] GAKO, f. 976, op. 4, d. 213, l. 17.

[35] GAKO, f. 976, op. 4, d. 213, l. 17; *Obzor Viatskoi gubernii za 1913 g.*, 43; Donald W. Treadgold, *The Great Siberian Migration: Government and Peasant in Resettlement from Emancipation to the First World War* (Princeton, 1957), 147–8; *Pereselenie i zemleustroistvo za Uralom v 1913 g. (Otchet o rabotakh pereselencheskago upravleniia za 1913 g.). Prilozhenie k smete dokhodov, raskhodov i spetsial'nykh sredstv Pereselencheskago Upravleniia G. U. Z. i Z. na 1915 g.* (Petrograd, 1914).

[36] Joshua A. Sanborn, 'Unsettling the Empire: Violent Migrations and Social Disaster in Russia during World War I', *Journal of Modern History* 77 (2005): 290–324.

[37] *Obzor Viatskoi gubernii za 1915 g.*, 61–2; *Pereselenie i zemleustroistvo*, 4. For comparison, in 1913, 10,835 families migrated from Viatka: 10,492 came from Tambov province, 12,790 from Poltava, and 8,047 from Saratov.

[38] Inhabitants of Izhevsk applied to leave the city and migrate to Siberia to engage in fieldwork, even though two-thirds of the applicants did not have agricultural skills. GAKO, f. R-1062, op. 1, d. 282, ll. 81–2ob.

of settlers were men and 47% women.[39] Already in the spring of 1918, the provincial land section had telegrammed all of its district affiliates that the central points of resettlement suffered from 'massive congestion'. The governments of the Siberian regions of Omsk and Tomsk pleaded with the Viatka government to stop peasant migration to their lands. The Tomsk government complained that most settlers had the appropriate certification to migrate and were taking all the unused land, driving local landless peasants to the brink of ruin.[40]

Peasant migration in fact violated the law since state officials wanted to be able to document and control the movement of its population and resources. Extending tsarist practices to control migration, Soviet officials sought to limit social disruption while promoting the rearrangement of the land to favour social restructuring.[41] The February 1918 Basic Law on Land prohibited free migration to Siberia and Asiatic Russia until the completion of the socialization of land, a restriction that lasted throughout the Civil War. The People's Commissariat of Agriculture (Narkomzem) as late as 1921 prohibited migration to Siberia on the grounds that it needed the return of 'normal conditions' to maintain data on land ownership and to improve the transportation system before resettlement could continue.[42] Until that time, settlers needed either a written resolution from the commune permitting them to leave or certification from the resettlement organization that the migrant would resettle only on state (*kazennaia*) land.[43]

Peasants tried to slip through the front to Siberia while the Red and White Armies battled in eastern Viatka in early 1919. *Volost* land sections from Glazov district in the autumn of 1919 reported that whole families were still leaving without authorization. Some peasants clearly were trying to flee Soviet power. The Iusovskaia *volost* land section found twelve peasant families, including 'saboteurs', attempting to leave and 'deliver themselves' from Soviet power.[44]

---

[39] GAKO, f. R-1062, op. 1, d. 282, ll. 146ob-7, 150-1ob. This number excludes Slobodskoi, Iaransk, Urzhum, Elabuga, and Malmyzh districts.
[40] GAKO, f. R-1062, op. 1, d. 42, ll. 29-30, 32, 34, 36, 39.
[41] Nick Baron and Peter Gatrell, 'Population Displacement, State-Building, and Social Identity in the Lands of the Former Russian Empire, 1917-23', *Kritika* 4 (2003): 51-100.
[42] GAKO, f. R-1062, op. 1, d. 38, ll. 137, 140. Temporary prohibition on migration due to inadequate data was not new. In 1812, the tsarist government banned resettlement (except to New Russia) for the same reasons. Sunderland, 'Peasants on the Move', 481.
[43] GAKO, f. R-1062, op. 1, d. 42, l. 16; *Golos trudovogo naroda*, 1 November 1918, 1.
[44] GAKO, f. R-1062, op. 1, d. 282, ll. 1-14, quote on l.14. On the continuation of avoidance protest during collectivization, see Sheila Fitzpatrick, *Stalin's Peasants: Resistance and Survival in the Russian Village after Collectivization* (New York, 1994), 5-6.

The Soviets banned free passage, but embraced state sponsored migration, including peasant resettlement programmes. In August 1918, the Viatka land section compiled lists of over 1,740 potential settlers from each district to resettle to Irkutsk, but had to close resettlement with the growing strength of the Whites.[45] Showing surprising flexibility, the Soviet government still issued complimentary passage to Siberia in 1918 for 120 families, amounting to 1,800 people.[46] Official sanction of some migration left the door open for peasants to try to work with the state in their efforts to flee Viatka.

Peasants also relied heavily on their traditional networks and the strategy of 'working the system' to overcome the new barriers and migrate eastward. According to official records, nine per cent of potential pioneers had already been in Siberia. These scouts now led new pioneers back. Peasants also followed 'wonderful rumours of Siberia's freedom'.[47] Official descriptions of the roads to Siberia suggest peasant mass movements – migrants joining together at each stop and forming large migrant brigades. Several peasants petitioned the state to allow them to resettle and 'misunderstood' anti-migration laws. For example, a series of petitioners in Malmyzh district stated that since the law forbade them to travel to Siberia by rail, they asked for permission to travel by foot. The district land section passed the applications to the provincial land section, which clarified that all migration, by foot or by rail, was forbidden.[48]

Once crop failures and famine hit Viatka, the number of those wishing to migrate jumped dramatically and reached epidemic proportions by 1921. In 1920, up to 50,000 people asked to resettle in the east.[49] Reacting to the catastrophic situation in the countryside, the central government in July 1921 eased its restrictions and allowed 20,000 people from Viatka to resettle in Siberia.[50] Incomplete records show that between September and December 1921 alone over 22,000 people applied to migrate beyond Viatka's borders and around 10,200 actually resettled to Siberia, both legally and illegally. The largest number of applicants in 1921 came from the southern districts, where the famine hit hardest; 5,569 people in Iaransk district alone applied to resettle eastward and 12,002 actually migrated.[51] This reversed the migratory trend of pre-revolutionary Russia when peasants across Viatka moved

---

[45] GAKO, f. R-1062, op. 1, d. 65. Numbers from ll. 40–40ob.
[46] GAKO, f. R-1062, op. 1, d. 282, ll. 150–1ob.
[47] GAKO, f. R-1062, op. 1, d. 282, ll. 8, 81–2ob, 150–1ob.
[48] GAKO, f. R-1062, op. 1, d. 514, l. 5.
[49] GAKO, f. R-1062, op. 1, d. 38, l. 164.   [50] GAKO, f. R-1062, op. 1, d. 514, l. 181.
[51] GAKO, f. R-1062, op. 1, d. 888, ll. 8–35; RGAE, f. 478, op. 7, d. 188, l. 14.

into Iaransk.[52] Officials recounted enormous numbers of peasants fleeing their homes without a concrete destination. In Slobodskoi district, a
region not considered famished, up to 1,637 households fled their
homes in the spring of 1922.

Refugees overran railroad and steamship stations even though most
did not have permits or tickets. Between March and June 1922, almost
22,000 people arrived at the Viatka city train station. Over a hundred
peasants died en route to the station while other peasants, having arrived
there, were too weak from hunger, fell on the street, and lay there to
die.[53]

Official discourse surrounding peasant migration during the famine
reflects the traditional dominator–dominated power dichotomy. State
records described peasant flight as 'aimless', 'disorganized', and cited a
primal survival instinct, denying the rationale behind leaving one's
house. In fact, migrating to potential sources of food was a rational
survival strategy in which peasants used personal and legal contacts to
aid their cause.[54]

The social turmoil of war and civil war changed the composition of
migrants. Before the First World War, migrants were either families or
single men looking for new opportunities.[55] From the beginning of
the war until the crop failure in 1919, the typical applicant wishing
to migrate was a female head of a household who wanted to resettle to
Siberia or Asiatic Russia with her family. As men died in combat or were
stuck at the front, women began to play a leading role in migratory
patterns. Rather than viewing resettlement as an adventure, as men had
before the war, women saw it as a last resort in the struggle to maintain
their household. *Soldatki* struck out on their own or led their families as
the surrogate head of the household to join kin and fellow villagers in
Asiatic Russia.[56]

Highlighting the destruction of traditional society and the prevalence
of long-range networks, many applicants to resettle to Siberia were
peasant refugees from the world war on the western front, involuntarily
living in the province. Having fled the war for Siberia, they were stopped
in Viatka by the approaching Civil War. Trapped in Viatka's towns and

---

[52] Romanov, *Pereseleniia*, 70–7.   [53] *Otchet o deiatel'nosti Viatskoi*, 11, 13.
[54] British officials in nineteenth-century India provided the same descriptions for peasants
fleeing famine. Mass migration, however, is a regular companion to famine and is one of
the transformative qualities of this phenomenon. Famine in Brazil in 1878 spurred on
the settlement movement and subsequent famines in the twentieth century pushed
peasants into urban factories. Arnold, *Famine*, 91–5.
[55] See, for example, GAKO, f. 940, op. 1, d. 677, ll. 1–2.
[56] GAKO, f. R-1620, op. 2, d. 2, ll. 19–39.

villages, these refugees had no means of survival and pleaded with the Soviet government to allow them to continue on to Siberia. In their petitions, refugees defined themselves as the true allies of Soviet power and logical recipients of their aid – poor peasants with young children who fled their village because they could not sustain their family. One group of refugees even formed an agricultural artel during their stay 'to work the land and help Soviet power'.[57] Nevertheless, the Soviet government did not let these people continue on to Siberia. Only in the face of famine in the countryside and mass peasant flight, did the Provincial Committee to Aid the Hungry (Gubkompomgol) evacuate the starving to Siberia in August 1921. Between August 1921 and June 1922, the government evacuated over ten thousand people.[58]

The scope of the social breakdown forced the Soviet state to allow more migrants to move eastward but it still tried to control population movement. State resettlement programmes tried to direct migrants to move to the north and south. Representing a major shift in migratory patterns (from west to east) several peasants resettled in the north-western province of Severo-Dvinsk. Upon the outbreak of war, the tsarist government actively pursued internal colonization of peasants to under-populated areas to increase the country's agricultural output. The Provisional and Soviet governments continued this policy. As early as 1918, the central, Viatka, Vologda, and Severo-Dvinsk land sections communicated about resettling peasants from Viatka to the north.[59] In a unique situation shaped by Russia's turmoil, Estonian private farmsteaders in Severo-Dvinsk invited peasants from Orlov and Kotel'nich districts to take over their estates since they were returning to their motherland. Many Estonian peasants wrote letters to the Viatka land section asking them to allow specific families to resettle on their farm.[60] Seeing the desperate plight of the Viatka peasantry in 1920–21, both the Viatka and Severo-Dvinsk land sections facilitated the resettlement to around 450 farms (khutora) with up to 1,000 desiatinas of arable land.[61]

In April 1919, the Soviet government, as part of its decossackization policy, issued a plan to colonize the Southern Don region with true believers and sympathizers of Soviet power.[62] It extended invitations directly to families of Red Army soldiers, hoping to bring 2,000 citizens from Viatka in the first group of settlers. If that number would be

---

[57] GAKO, f. R-1062, op. 1, d. 514, ll. 9–10, 31–2ob. Quote from l. 31.
[58] The Hoover Archive, Russia. Tsentral'naia komissiia pomoshchi golodaiushchim, box 1, 'Totals of the Struggle against Famine in 1921–22', 218.
[59] RGAE, f. 478, op. 6, d. 1342, ll. 1, 9–9ob, 132–132ob.
[60] GAKO, f. R-1062, op. 1, d. 513, ll. 5–7, 10, 28, 32–3, 36, 39, 43, 47, 49–56.
[61] GAKO, f. R-1062, op. 1, d. 38, l. 119.   [62] Holquist, Making War, 166–205.

insufficient, it requested the local governments to 'form groups from the village poor, members of agricultural communes, associations . . . and other collective organizations as well as others who would want to engage in collective agriculture' in the Don.[63] In May, the Bolsheviks advertised their plan and the Viatka land section even ordered forty train cars to transport settlers to the gathering point in Moscow. By mid-June, the Viatka land section began to receive a steady stream of petitions of those wishing to resettle. Significantly, more refugees than peasants wanted to begin a soviet life in the Don. For example, a refugee family from Vilnius living in Viatka city argued that they had land at home and wanted to resettle to Siberia but the Whites controlled both territories. They desired to work on a commune and supported Soviet power. Although Moscow forbade refugees and other unorganized groups from settling in the Don programme, several families from as far away as Perm and Kostroma came to the Viatka city train station to be a part of the programme. In 1919, refugees did not have opportunities for survival that local peasants enjoyed and therefore jumped at the chance to move to the Don. Social circumstances reshaped this Soviet population policy from resettling a peasant vanguard to transporting desperate refugees. Changing military fortunes in the Don forced the Soviet government to cancel the resettlement project in mid-June and prohibit all migration to the Don region. Nevertheless, petitions still came to the land section and those wishing to resettle continued to appear at the Viatka train station.[64]

To add to the picture of the upturned population, many migrants gave up on their journey and tried to return home. In June 1921, about a thousand refugees returning from Siberia were unable to make the journey all the way home and resorted to living at the Viatka city railroad station. They petitioned the famine relief organization to finance their transportation home so they could help in the harvest.[65]

Peasant migrants relied on established routes, connections with settlers, and rumours of a better land. Without these national networks, peasants could not have made the trips successfully. It is also important not to diminish the everyday role of the state in peasant networks. The state at times facilitated peasant migration and occasionally worked against it. Peasants, for their part, used the state infrastructure, laws, and

---

[63] GAKO, f. R-1062, op. 1, d. 278, l. 3; d. 64, ll. 38–38ob.
[64] GAKO, f. R-1062, op. 1, d. 278, l. 3; d. 64, ll. 1–88.
[65] Hoover Archives, Russia. Tsentral'naia komissiia pomoshchi golodaiushchim, box 1, 'Totals of the Struggle against Famine in 1921–22', 218.

progressive policies to further their cause and moulded their networks to take advantage of official benefits.

Resistance, relief, and responsibility

An upturned population and social and economic collapse joined together with Bolshevik repression of its people to lead to a crisis of authority. Across rural Russia, politically complex armed insurrections against Communist authority drove out Soviet power. In the spring of 1920, rural uprisings led by former Red Army officers erupted in the Lower Volga, while an alliance of Bashkir, Tatar, and Russian peasants briefly captured the Ural region in what was named the War of the Black Eagle. Most famously, Nestor Makhno in Ukraine, and Aleksandr Antonov in Tambov, led huge partisan armies against Red power. Both the Bolshevik leadership and insurrectionary armies imagined that the movements had greater connections than they actually did. The Bolsheviks suspected an international SR–Menshevik conspiracy and partisan leaders believed that they were part of a national political movement against Bolshevism and for a resurrection of the Constituent Assembly.[66] Whatever the possibility that these various partisan groups could coalesce to overthrow Soviet power, both sides agreed that they threatened the very existence of the Soviet regime.

A partisan movement on the scale of Antonov or the Black Eagle never appeared in Viatka, although the latter petered out as it reached the province's southern tip. Nevertheless, armed bands appeared throughout the Viatka countryside that reminded villagers and state officials of how weak the Soviet military arm was, and how it was incapable of preventing the collapse of the rural society. In Iaransk district, well-armed bands under the leadership of (former Colonel) Ivanov formed in the summer of 1920 and regularly attacked trucks, mills, and collection points and stole their grain. Local peasants aided Ivanov's men and district authorities could do nothing to stop them for over a year. In the village of Dymkovo, just across the river from the provincial capital, a band outgunned a crack unit of the provincial Cheka and wounded its commander.[67]

Displaced persons from social breakdown and deserters joined together and attacked Communists and kept the state from fully

---

[66] Landis, 'Waiting for Makhno'; Figes, *Peasant Russia*, 321–53; V. P. Danilov and T. Shanin, *Krest'ianskoe dvizhenie v Povolzh'e. 1919–1922 gg.: Dokumenty i materialy* (Moscow, 2002); Raleigh, *Experiencing Russia's Civil War*, 382–7.
[67] GASPI KO, f. 1, op. 2, d. 215, ll. 21, 24.

imposing its will upon the village. Deserters from the First World War met the growing scores of deserters from the Civil War and formed groups in the forests and margins of the village. Bands of deserters roamed the banks of the Pizhma River in Iaransk. Soviet reports counted over 1,000 deserters in Bataevskaia *volost*, Kotel'nich district, and a Soviet spy found trenches and bunkers elsewhere in the district.[68] Soldiers took their weapons with them when they deserted their posts and were well armed with machine guns and rifles. Deserters were a potential threat to Soviet power when they remained in the forests. When the bands left the wilderness and attacked Communists, Soviet authorities labelled them insurgents. They linked deserters in official records to partisan, or Green, movements elsewhere in Russia, but there is no evidence to support these claims. The groups were instead a manifestation of the deep social upheaval from civil war. Members lived on the fringes of the village. Some were friends of local soviet members, and district officials often reprimanded soviets for providing food and materials to the bands.[69]

Peasants who were able to keep their home in the villages also bitterly attacked the Soviet order for failing to provide for them. In Elabuga district, crowds of forty peasants gathered everyday to demand grain from the administration. In Kuknurskaia *volost*, Urzhum district, nearly 700 peasants met secretly to agree on collective refusal to bring their grain to collection points and to hide the key to the storehouse. The authorities learned of the meeting and broke it up. Three hundred starving peasants from nearby Multanskaia and Starotrykskaia *volost*s marched en masse to the local grain collection point to demand a distribution of its collection. The militia stopped the marchers with gunfire. A similar incident occurred in Sovetsk district.[70] Peasant resistance, then, was intrinsically tied to peasants' beliefs that the state had to provide for them in a time of famine.

The introduction of the New Economic Policy (NEP) in the spring of 1921 soothed tensions between state and peasant by exchanging forced requisitions for a fixed tax in kind and limited private trade. Newspapers portrayed the transition as part of state famine and agricultural relief efforts after years of hardship.[71] Secret reports, though, recorded a rumour that peasants believed the Kronstadt sailors had demanded free

---

[68] GA RF, f. 1240, op. 1, d. 126, ll. 1, 4, 13ob, 19, 25; d.122, ll. 70, 73; d. 120, l. 34.
[69] GA RF, f. 1240, op. 1, d. 126, ll. 13ob, 19.
[70] GASPI KO, f. 1, op. 2, d. 215, ll. 34, 44.
[71] *Krasnyi put'*, 2 April 1921, 2; 16 April 1921, 1; GAKO, f. R-3271, op. 1, d. 43, l. 12.

trade and the Soviet state had given in. In any case, peasants welcomed the decree on free trade and the end of the *razverstka*.[72]

Even though the NEP was supposed to ease the burden on the countryside and win over the peasantry, the transition was still tumultuous. Crop failure meant that most peasants could not pay even the much-reduced natural tax of one pud, twenty funts of grain per *desiatina* of land. The provincial government complained that regional food inspectors in charge of collecting the tax were illiterate and dim-witted.[73] The NEP gave the peasants what they had demanded in 1917 and 1918, the exchange of manufactured goods for agricultural products, but with famine, the peasants had nothing to offer.[74] Instead, peasants attacked barter points. In Elabuga district, peasants staged multiple raids to destroy the stations and take the grain.[75] Official labels of the peasants as thieves (*pokhishchenie*) with the aim to abduct (*uvoz*) grain and create chaos (*razgrom*) shows the continued disconnect between state images of the peasantry and peasants' social identity. The NEP and the distribution points were to benefit the masses and give them what the Bolsheviks supposed they wanted as primitive, semi-capitalists. However, peasant actions show they believed that the state should have provided them with grain since they were starving.

It was only in the autumn of 1921 that the Soviet central government organized a coherent famine relief operation. The Provincial Committee to Aid the Hungry (Gubkompomgol), the regional sector of the famine relief organization established by Maksim Gorky and other leading cultural figures, began to implement relief efforts, but it was international aid, especially from the American Relief Administration (ARA) that saved the Viatka countryside from ruin. Herbert Hoover and the Central Committee agreed to the ARA operations on 31 July 1921 and the ARA famine relief began distributing relief that autumn.[76] Because Viatka occupied a liminal space in Russia, neither part of the ARA's Volga, nor its Kazan region, the organizations initially ignored the province. The ARA began to feed southern Viatka in the waning days of

---

[72] GASPI KO, f. 1, op. 2, d. 215, l. 14; GAKO, f. R-938, op. 1, d. 113, l. 5.
[73] GAKO, f. R-890, op. 1, d. 21, l. 1.
[74] GAKO, f. R-890, op. 1, d. 26, ll. 581–581ob, 584.
[75] GAKO, f. R-3271, op. 1, d. 43, l. 20.
[76] The most complete account of the ARA's efforts is that in Bertrand M. Patenaude, *The Big Show in Bololand: The American Relief Expedition to Soviet Russia in the Famine of 1921* (Stanford, 2002). See also, Hoover Archives, American Relief Administration, New York office, box 30, folder 2, Report of an inspection of Ossa, Sarapool (Perm Government) (sic.) and of Votskaia oblast (19–28 July 1922); H. H. Fisher, *The Famine in Soviet Russia 1919–1923: The Operations of the American Relief Administration* (New York, 1927), 49–111.

1921. The ARA and the Committee to Aid the Hungry organized food and grain distribution points and turned many schools into feeding stations. By July 1922, more than 8,500 stations fed over 113,000 people in Viatka. Besides meals and grain, the ARA distributed winter clothing.[77] Peasants did not fully understand the nature of the ARA's aid or that it came from the United States, but they accepted the relief without question.[78]

Women had a significant role in famine relief as care-givers for the children. Since peasant women were responsible for the private sphere and family matters, such as preparing food, it was often the senior female of the household who gathered aid. A relief worker described a typical recipient:

The committee is busy at the scales, and the yellow corn, an unfamiliar sight to most of those assembled, is heaped into a bin before the fascinated eyes of this hungry crowd . . . A name is called and an old woman slowly pushes her way through the crowd. Her costume and her swarthy wrinkled face plainly show she is a Tartar. Around her neck still hang twenty or more silver fifty-kopeck pieces, evidence of a former prosperity. The two silver roubles hanging from the two braids down her back indicate that she has been married. The American field man through his interpreter learns that her name is Fatme Habeullin; that her husband died from hunger last December; that she has had six children, the oldest of whom, a son in the Red Army, has not been heard from for two years; that the second, a daughter, died of typhus in 1920; that of the four small children remaining, two are being fed in the A. R. A. kitchens of the village; and that she is not old, only forty-six.[79]

The Soviet state had called on its people to provide additional resources to combat the nation's enemy, as the Imperial and Provisional Governments had done in wartime. Although the state lacked the resources and know-how to distribute relief like the ARA, it mobilized several population groups, including young and female peasants, workers, specialists, and Party members and drew them into the collective effort to defeat the country's latest enemy. Throughout the province already, by autumn 1921, district- and *volost*-level famine relief organizations (kompomgol) were established to mobilize the population and gather local resources to fight famine. The provincial kompomgol immediately organized a province-wide 'Week of Aid to the Hungry

---

[77] Hoover Archives, Russia. Tsentral'naia komissiia pomoshchi golodaiushim, box 1, 'Totals of the Struggle against Famine in 1921–22', 215–17.

[78] Hoover Archives, American Relief Administration, New York office, box 30, folder 2, Report of an inspection of Ossa, Sarapool (Perm Government) (sic.) and of Votskaia oblast (19–28 July 1922).

[79] Quoted in Hertha Kraus, *International Relief in Action, 1914–1943: Selected Records, with Notes* (Scottdale, PA, 1944), 54–5.

Child' during which factory workers contributed their labour, workers went door-to-door to collect donations, and volunteers staged shows and concerts to raise money. The state targeted taxes for the struggle to fight the famine. It used part of the New Economic Policy's natural tax to fund grain and clothing shipments.[80] The People's Commissariat of Finance (Narkomfin) also imposed a tax on all citizens (*obshchegrazhdanskii nalog*) and deducted 1 to 10% of monthly salaries for famine relief.

Famine relief accented the continuing prominence of duty in the relationship between peasant citizen and the socialist state. In both kompomgol activities and Narkomfin's taxation, the state proclaimed that it was the duty of all citizens to help in the struggle against famine. The brochure, 'All to the Struggle Against Famine', stated that 'each citizen must do everything to assist in the collection of the tax and not oppose it in any way'.[81] Regional declarations on land use also demanded that all citizens support the needy. The Sarapul district congress proclaimed that it was '"the patriotic duty" of every citizen to aid needy comrade peasants who will not have the ability to work and sow their land'.[82] The Provincial land section and Narkomzen ordered that all surplus grain from the northern half of the province, that did not suffer as badly as the south from the famine, must go to those starving populations in the southern districts.[83] Peasants did not dispute their responsibility to pay a just, minimal amount to the state, but they assumed that the state must in turn provide for them in time of famine and harvest failure – the central component of a moral economy. However, the Soviet state altered the moral economic relationship to include popular responsibility. It was now not only the state, but all citizens that had a moral responsibility for public sustainability. Soviet officials expanded the language and images of citizenship and its accompanying civic duties from the wartime tsarist regime and the Provisional Government to mobilize peasants to help defeat a national threat.

The moral economic relationship between peasants and the Soviet state stemmed from the tsarist era when peasants had turned to their landlords and the state during times of need with the expectation that their social superiors would take care of them as good paternalists. During the first Soviet famine, the peasants once again petitioned the local state for aid. In Elabuga district the government and Cheka reported that since peasants 'do not have any emergency stores' the 'starving masses by the hundreds are going to the *volost* soviets' and

[80] GAKO, f. R-783, op. 1, d. 1, ll. 10–11, 21–21ob.
[81] GASPI KO, f. 1, op. 2, d. 179, l. 5.   [82] RGAE, f. 478, op. 6, d. 760, l. 27ob.
[83] RGAE, f. 478, op. 11, d. 372, l. 3.

requesting grain.[84] Peasants of Nolinsk district even sent numerous petitions to the province centre threatening to withhold their famine tax payments, not because they saw them as unjustly taxing an already impoverished population, but because they felt that the province was not giving them enough attention.[85] The residents of Mel'nikov village, Nylgi-Zhik'inskaia *volost*, complained about the exorbitant grain levy that did not come close to matching the actual harvest of the village, while claiming their right to withhold grain: 'We never let up from our work and our aid to our Soviet power, but the present apportionment is beyond our capability and it leaves us starving. We believe that we have the right (*pravo*) to defend our interests. The administration doing this deed must review our petition.'[86] Seven villages in Urzhum district protested to the land section that they were already starving the previous year when the army had seized grain on top of the levy. Now over half of the inhabitants were starving and, lacking seed, villagers reduced their sown area from 245 *desiatinas* to a mere 96 *desiatinas*. They were forced to exchange with speculators their milk and eggs for salt, and demanded that the state reduce the levy on butter and eggs by seventy-five per cent and free them from additional natural taxes.[87]

Workers and peasants accepted their public duty and actively contributed to the cause. While peasants fought against extraordinary taxes and requisitions, they sacrificed almost three million rubles to the all-citizen tax and donated money to medical relief efforts. In contrast, in peasants' attempts to get the state to provide them with famine relief, they resorted to traditional peasant–elite moral language and responsibilities.

Peasants expected the state to provide relief as long as they fulfilled duties, so Bolshevik manoeuvres to confiscate church valuables to help pay for famine relief seemed that much more duplicitous to the spiritual rural population. Bolsheviks had engaged in relentless diatribes against religion and the Orthodox Church through newspapers and brochures, but rarely went out of their way to harm local clergy.[88] The Bolsheviks even allowed thousands of religious peasants to make their annual June pilgrimage and processional around the villages surrounding the city of Viatka.[89] Peasants opposed the anti-religious nature of Bolshevism. In a

[84] GAKO, f. R-3271, op. 1, d. 43, l. 19; GASPI KO, f. 1, op. 2, d. 215, l. 10.
[85] See GAKO, f. R-1620, op. 2, d. 20, ll. 27–48; f. R-890, op. 1, d. 2, l. 27.
[86] GA RF, f. R-1318, op. 5, d. 14, ll. 3–4.
[87] RGAE, f. 478, op. 3, d. 1296, l. 222.
[88] See for example, *Krasnaia mysl'*, Votkinsk, 29 January 1919, 4; *Proletarskaia gazeta*, Glazov, 19 February 1919, 2; *Sovetskaia vlast' i krest'ianstvo*, Viatka, 7 April 1921.
[89] GAKO, f. R-878, op. 1, d. 2, l. 126.

village outside Votkinsk, peasants regularly approached a local Communist and asked him if it was true that the Bolsheviks were servitors of the anti-Christ and Lenin was the anti-Christ incarnate.[90] When Soviet officials and representatives of the soviet in Urzhum district went to Petrovskaia *volost* to seize church goods, peasants passionately defended their religious space. Word of the aim to take church possessions got out across the *volost* and nearly six hundred peasants came to surround the church. When the officials entered the holy church, the peasants let out a cry, 'beat and hang the Communists and *ispolkom*', and attacked them. Only a representative of the district *ispolkom* was rescued from the crowd. The militia soon arrived at the scene, dispersed the crowd, and searched homes for missing church valuables. Although they confiscated church belongings, the official report called on the Soviet government to liquidate the Cheka for the time being in order to win over the locals. The official report blamed peasant action both on local kulaks who agitated at congresses and *skhods* against the government and the whole *volost* peasant population, 'ninety per cent of which is prosperous' and had supported the Stepanov anti-Soviet bands.[91] Several other village communities also reacted violently to Bolshevik attempts to seize church valuables.[92] Orthodox Christian villagers would not let the Soviet state invade their religious world. The church, as a sanctified space, was a physical representation of this struggle and a rural place the Soviets could still not penetrate.

Civil War remakes the village

Seven years of war, revolution, and civil war devastated the Viatka countryside, as it did the whole of Russia. On the eve of world war, in 1913, 3.65 million people inhabited the Viatka countryside. By 1920, less than 2 million remained, a loss of almost fifty percent of the population.[93] Mobilization, famine, disease, flight, and state terror ruptured family relations and destroyed whole households. By the time the decommissioned men staggered home in 1921, the village had suffered seven years of military conscription of their working-age men. Added to the loss of working hands, the disappearance of livestock and agricultural instruments made the peasant economy a hollow shell of

---

[90] *Krasnaia mysl'*, 26 January 1919, 4.   [91] GASPI KO, f. 1, op. 2, d. 229, ll. 67–8.

[92] GASPI KO, f. 1, op. 2, d. 229, ll. 112, 126; *Otchet Viatskogo gubernskogo ispolnitel'nogo komiteta. Oktiabr' 1921–oktiabr'1922 gg.*, tom II (Viatka, 1922), 21–2. For more on the push and pull between peasant and Bolshevik state over anti-religious campaigns, see Young, *Power and the Sacred*, esp. ch. 2–3.

[93] Frenkel, 'Klimat', in *Entsiklopediia zemli Viatskoi*, t. 7, *Priroda*, 55.

what it once was. The political troubles destroyed personal lives. There was a surge in divorce, family abandonment, and suicides.[94] Almost every household lost at least one of its members, while many soldiers who did return from war came back traumatized, wounded, or incapacitated and no longer able to add to the household economy.[95]

Conscription of men for war and the sheer loss of life put severe pressure on the peasant household economy in which the number of working members was a foundation of the family's wealth.[96] Large families usually survived diminished to one or two working members, but many other smaller households often had no workers by the latter years of the Civil War and struggled to remain economically viable.[97] There were several ways in which a household could break down during Russia's turmoil. The parents could be killed from disease or starvation, military struggle, or as a victim of the crime epidemic; they could be imprisoned, abandon the village, or simply disappear en route to the field or market. Communes had extended their safety nets during the world war and continued to do so in civil war, but had limited resources. The number of homeless children and orphans, while always a greater problem in the cities, grew in the rural areas as well. The Soviet government and citizen groups coped as best they could and established children's colonies and children's homes for orphans and homeless children. Children were schooled, fed, and clothed in the colonies but they also worked the land, learned skills for *kustar'*, kept bees, felled trees and performed tasks on the railroad, helping the economy function and providing hard-to-find manufactured goods for the villages.[98]

Peasants in depleted households toiled longer and harder in the fields, in a process of self-exploitation, without necessarily reaping more goods. Since larger families were often wealthier than smaller ones, the more prosperous households suffered less from the demographic disasters than poorer peasants. Although Soviet taxes and politics, as well as the land redistribution, often mitigated richer peasants' advantages,

---

[94] Viktor Berdinskikh, *Rossiia i russkie (krest'ianskaia tsivilizatsiia v vospominaniiakh ochevidtsev)* (Kirov, 1994).

[95] GAKO, f. R-1330, op. 1, d. 7, l. 3; GAKO, f. R-1053, op. 1, d. 188; GAKO, f. R-2506, op. 1, d. 46, ll. 2–5.

[96] Here I am thinking of A. V. Chayanov's theory of a natural peasant economy in which there is a greater degree of consumer satisfaction, less self-exploitation, and a thriving household when it enjoys a higher ratio of working members to non-working members. See Chayanov, *The Theory of Peasant Economy*.

[97] GA RF, f. R-1240, op. 1, d. 122, l. 73.

[98] *Kratkii ocherk o vozniknovenii, zadachakh i deiatel'nosti v techenie 1918 g. Soiuza pomoshchi besprizornym detiam v Viatskoi gubernii* (Viatka, 1919?); Alan Ball, *And Now My Soul is Hardened: Abandoned Children in Soviet Russia, 1918–1930* (Berkeley, 1994).

Communist government policy could hit the poor households harder than the rich. District Party members were aware that local officials, unable to squeeze enough revenue from peasants categorized as kulaks, often allocated taxes on the whole village population. State grain and livestock requisitions (as seen in Chapter 5) were often haphazard and corrupt and took from the whole village regardless of individual households' class status.[99]

The destruction of the revolutionary era and the political and economic changes allowed young Red Army veterans to assert themselves inside the village upon their mass return at the end of the military campaigns of the Civil War. In the spring of 1921, a final wave of redistributions and levelling of land accompanied a significant rise in household divisions (*razdely*). Every *volost* had already recorded a rise in the number of households between 1916 and 1920 that was disproportionate to the change in population – Viatka district had a 10% net increase in households, Nolinsk a 9%, and Kotel'nich an 8% increase.[100] While some were post-mortem divisions after the death of heads of households from war and famine and the return of their sons, the majority of divisions appear to have been pre-mortem fissures. The freedom of revolution and military service made sons bristle when they returned to live under their father's rules. Peasants remarked on the frequency of quarrels between fathers and sons in this period.[101] Wives who had lived alone with their in-laws must have pressured their husbands to establish their own home. The redistribution of land and the liberal land laws provided further impetus to divide the home. The young males' rise to political prominence contrasted sharply with their everyday subaltern status within the household and division was a logical step to solve their dilemma.

Communities elected returning soldiers to the local government and pushed elderly peasants out of office. Villagers saw soldiers as a link to the larger polity and understood that they were the favourite rural sons of the Soviet regime. Villagers recruited and elected soldiers to governing bodies because soldiers were knowledgeable about the outside world, knew how to speak the Soviet language, and had a vested interest in the new regime. These men often turned down the opportunity to govern because they had to rebuild their homes.[102] One soldier stated that his family had divided three times since he went to war and he had to put his household in order. Another elected soldier wrote that there

---

[99] GA RF, f. R-1240, op. 1, d. 122, l. 95.
[100] *Statisticheskii Spravochnik po Viatskoi gubernii, 1917*; *Predvaritel'nye itogi perepisi naseleniia 1920 goda* (Viatka, 1921).
[101] NOA UIIIaL URO RAN, op. 2-N, d. 11, l. 2.
[102] Figes finds a similar phenomenon in the Black Earth region, *Peasant Russia*, 225.

was enough farm work for five souls and there were no workers left in his household, only women and children. The state freed these petitioners from service.[103] Even though veterans often declined executive positions, several of them did join village politics and concluded the generational shift in rural governance that began with Soviet power.

Conclusion

The fatigue and loss of home from war and revolution is almost palpable in reading people's accounts from the time. Peasants witnessed their village wasting away. Beautiful homes fell into disrepair, with broken glass panes, shuttered windows, and dilapidated roofs. Once vibrant homesteads had sick, starving elderly and children struggling to survive. Fields returned to the wild and neighbours abandoned their homes to seek food elsewhere. Peasants sought answers in the political and civil order. Some rebelled against the regime, but most turned to those above them for aid. This time, though, peasants could demand aid as a right of citizenship in the socialist nation. They could go beyond the traditional moral economic relationship with the state and seek out official channels within the emerging welfare state to get aid. Peasant efforts were buoyed by the institutionalization of Soviet bureaucracy and guided by state and Party efforts to integrate the rural population into the new system. The Soviet order tried to control a society (that in part it had helped to break down) by mobilizing the populations, intervening in their movements, and promoting social citizenship within the welfare state. Economic destruction and famine therefore brought peasant and state closer together by building a personal relationship as the populace reached out to the official elite for aid.

[103] TsGA UR, f. R-204, op. 59, d. 22, ll. 78–84.

Conclusion: Peasant citizens
in a modern state

In 1923, as the countryside steadied itself following the chaos of the revolutionary era, the noted ethnographer Pavel Luppov and his students knocked at the doors of Viatka's peasants to survey how the revolution had affected their lives. The peasants assured their questioners that the internal fabric of the village remained intact. They complained that land reforms did not significantly alter the size of personal allotments. Men still ruled the house and controlled village governance. Older peasants were still religious, went to church, and pestered children to follow Orthodox traditions. If the peasants stopped there, it would have been easy to conclude that traditional peasant parochialism had bested some of the most cataclysmic events in Russian history – world war, revolution, and all out civil war. However, after reading their answers in full it is clear that while certain cultural and social structures remained intact, a fundamental transformation both within the village and towards the national polity had occurred during the revolutionary era of 1914 to 1922.

Soviet projects to co-opt the peasants and build an enlightened, rational society were evident in Viatka's villages. Peasants described using reading huts, reading literature on modern agriculture, and joining village Party cells and artels. They commented upon how much the revolution empowered youths. If the size of land allotments did not change, more, and younger, peasants tilled their land as the heads of new households. Young women slowly asserted themselves in the new village: 'Udmurt women, like in times gone by, are controlled by men', one respondent started, 'but in all the Udmurt lands more young women are joining the Zhenotdel and are more independent.'[1] The youth quickly distanced themselves from the church, stopped attending weekly services, and favoured non-religious Red weddings over, or alongside, Orthodox services. The New Economic Policy milieu presumably

[1] NOA UIIIaL URO RAN, op. 2-N, d. 11, l. 3.

263

shaped the respondents' answers, but it was still clear that national politics had reshaped the village.[2]

Non-ethnographic sources concur that the Soviet state had made strong inroads in both Russian and national minority villages. Party membership of young male and female peasants rose steadily in the 1920s; in most districts, the number of members tripled between 1922 and 1927.[3] Reading campaigns and increased access to schooling quickly drove up literacy, especially for youths. By the end of 1923, the Udmurt-language newspaper *Gudyri* (Thunder) enjoyed distribution to every Udmurt village and acted as the main conduit between Udmurts and the nation, controlling the discourse on nationality issues and cultural education in the village.[4] The NEP produced favourable markets for agricultural goods and peasants expanded upon pre-revolutionary ties with the national market. The changes within the village went beyond the material manifestations brought in by the state and Party, such as libraries, newspapers, medical facilities, and even electricity. Peasant identity itself had changed remarkably and peasants now saw themselves as citizens of the Soviet state. The key to understanding how villagers changed so dramatically, and how the Soviet state was established, is to understand the tight relationship between peasants and the state in the revolutionary era beginning in 1914.

In this book I have argued that war and revolution brought Viatka's peasants closer to the local state and into the national polity. The First World War provided fertile soil for the transformation of rural subjects into modern citizens. Wartime mobilization inaugurated a period that witnessed an interventionist state whose success rested on the active participation of the populace. Indeed, throughout the revolutionary era, the village served as a laboratory for the revolutionary state efforts to mobilize, intervene, and transform society. This could not be accomplished through will and imposition alone, though. Mobilization for war allowed peasants to see themselves as deserving members of the Russian nation, a point that they pushed forward as newly empowered free citizens in 1917. Peasant patriots became active citizens, with a sense of inclusion in a national civic and political enterprise.

---

[2] NOA UIIIaL URO RAN, op. 2-N, d. 11; P. Luppov, 'O vliianii revoliutsii na byt natsmen', *Trudy Viatskogo pedagogicheskogo instituta imeni. V. I. Lenina*, t. II, vyp. II (Viatka, 1927), 59–64.
[3] Legotin, ed., *KPSS v tsifrakh*, 18–19, 109–10.
[4] L. S. Khristoliubova, 'Prosveshchenie i razvitie nauki', in N. F. Mokshin, ed., *Narody Povolzh'ia i Priural'ia: Komi-zyriane. Komi-permiaki. Mariitsy. Mordva. Udmurty* (Moscow, 2000), 49–50.

During the 1917 democratic experiment, peasants and rural educated society engaged in an intense discussion of what citizenship should mean in the reinvented Russian nation. Acrimonious public debates over citizens' rights and duties, and how peasants should engage the nation, underscored the growing social polarization and helped to push social groups further apart. Discussions of citizenship expanded under early Soviet rule, although they were articulated in the language of class. State agents and peasants still debated who should be members of society, but the Soviet government simultaneously moved the parameters of citizenship from one focussed on political citizenship to one focussed on social citizenship, including rights to economic and social services and security within the welfare state. Citizenship wove peasants and polity together, creating ties that bound the population.

I have also argued that Viatka's peasants did not shy away from the changes around them. They sought out the state and actively worked to be part of the nation and revolution. They were guided in their relations with the state by a sense of rightful inclusion and a political morality. Part of this was their sense of rights and obligations as citizens within the tsarist, Provisional Government, and finally the Soviet state. So, when the Bolsheviks gave peasants the freedom to take the land in 1917, peasants turned to the Soviet administration to solve the village disputes that emerged as they apportioned their newfound resources, asking the Bolsheviks into their homes. And when the famine and economic devastation of the Civil War killed thousands of villagers and threatened their future, peasants once again asked that the state respond.

Most of Viatka's peasants ultimately decided to accept the Bolshevik state because it promoted their interests. Their political decision went beyond simply choosing the Reds over the Whites or Prikomuch alternative as the lesser of evils, or siding with the Soviet state because it granted them land rights, as many historians have argued. For many ones, especially younger ones who had lived in the village but had not previously governed, the Soviet state gave them the opportunity to participate in state building. Peasants also responded favourably to Soviet publicized attempts to extend social welfare for peasants injured by war and civil war, and mobilization of state resources to repair the agricultural sector as a whole. The Soviet state also successfully created practices that established hegemonic control of politics while promoting peasant populations' own interests. For example, non-Russian peasants found an ally in the Soviet administration when they wanted to continue to promote their national identity. As long as the national groups embraced the Bolshevik language of national evolution, then the state tried to provide resources. Similarly, the Soviets held public meetings to promote policies and targeted populations that they saw as naturally sympathetic to the Soviet experiment. Local state agents played a key role in all of these programmes as mediators between peasant communities and the national polity. The Bolsheviks had the advantage of inheriting both a political system already engaged in mass mobilization and a population who longed to have a greater role in Russia's governance. Nevertheless, the new Bolshevik rulers created even more opportunities for peasants to become part of the Soviet system.

This created a strange situation for peasants, who allied with a state whose policies they often opposed. Marxist and statist ideologies, modern warfare, and civil war pushed forward the Bolsheviks' reliance on coercion and mass mobilization and their almost immediate repression of democratic voices. The Bolsheviks derided what they perceived as peasants' backwardness and petty bourgeois instincts and devised schemes based on wrong-headed ideological precepts of class conflict in the village. They violently repressed political enemies and declared war on peasants who did not, or could not, give them grain. At the same time, peasants needed a state to provide stability and alleviate the unbearable pressure of everyday life. The Bolshevik state's response was based in part on the immediate historical precedence of Provisional Government practice of the state as a social mediator, a larger pan-European shift towards a more modern welfare state that sought to improve the well-being of its members, and its own modernist ideological focus on raising the consciousness of a 'backward' peasantry.[5] By sublimating its aim for class warfare in favour of building order and stability, and creating spaces of dialogue between state and the diverse peasant populations, the Soviet state opened up several spaces for its population to interact with and even shape national politics.

I have also argued that a study of the Viatka countryside allows us to re-examine assumptions of peasant activity and recognize the diversity of peasants' experiences of war and revolution. Peasants in the Viatka countryside experienced revolution and civil war differently from their brethren in the Black Earth region, Central Russia, and Ukraine – the most studied regions of rural Russia. Viatka's peasants had neither the memory of a private serf economy nor the land hunger of the more central lands. Most of Viatka's peasants, as well as the millions of peasants of the northern and western Siberian regions, did not seek to redress the failings of the 1861 emancipation from serfdom or exploitation of a squire. The dramatically different experiences of peasants in

---

[5] David Hoffmann, 'European Modernity and Soviet Socialism', in Kotsonis and Hoffmann, eds, *Russian Modernity*, 245–60.

Viatka and several similar provinces and the Black Earth region accents the need to account for Russia's rich diversity in its revolutionary era. Economic structure, geography, environmental conditions, and local political flavour must be accounted for in the narrative of the revolutionary era. We need to shed ourselves of the assumption of peasant parochialism and single-minded obsession with land. Divesting such assumptions, drawn in part by privileging the Black Earth experience, allows us to draw new conclusions about peasants' relationship to the state. Peasants of Viatka viewed the revolution beyond the borders of the village and from this vantage point saw themselves as active citizens in the polity.

A regional view of the revolutionary era also decentres the revolutionary narrative in general. The revolution was ultimately decided not in the cities of Moscow and Petrograd, but in the towns and fields of the provinces. It was there that the peasants gave up the grain and men needed to defend the Soviet state. While Viatka was a key battleground in the Civil War in its own right, it was also, contradictorily, the site of the largest anti-Soviet worker uprising, the place where the Red Army stopped the furthest advance of Kolchak's White Army, and the testing ground for the Soviet Civil War grain requisitioning policy. Rather than the clear narrative of Soviet progress, these stories underscore the messiness and contradiction of revolution on the ground when imposed from above.

If the experiences of Viatka's peasants tell us more about the Russian Revolution, they also add to a larger, global story. Russia's peasants were not alone in their struggle for emancipatory politics. Peasant demands to be active citizens with legal rights in the modern state could be heard concurrently in countries undergoing revolutionary transformations of their own, from the anti-colonial movements in French Syria and the British Indian subcontinent, to nation-building projects in Mexico and Peru, and popular post-war political and cultural realignments in Germany and France.[6] While political circumstances and popular experiences varied widely among these lands, rural denizens demanded a greater voice in the reconstruction of their nation. Peasants did not long for the simple, untainted, autonomous life, nor could they have achieved it if they had wanted to do so. Peasants helped dictate political change throughout the world at this global conjuncture, but we should not see their participation as a triumph of emancipatory politics. Peasants won land reforms, social benefits, and a muffled voice in politics, but the system that they

---

[6] See Elizabeth Thompson, *Colonial Citizens: Republican Rights, Paternal Privilege, and Gender in French Syria and Lebanon* (New York, 2000); Mallon, *Peasant and Nation.*

joined often resulted in a repressive, undemocratic regime.[7] By the beginning of the twentieth century, most peasants could not easily escape the eyes of the state. Nevertheless, these global voices should make us rethink definitions of peasants as transitional figures in a modernizing world who are reactionary and insular by nature. Peasants shaped the modern state just as much as it shaped them.

---

[7] Discussed in detail by Richard Lee Turits, *Foundations of Despotism: Peasants, the Trujillo Regime, and Modernity in Dominican History* (Stanford, 2003).

Works cited

ARCHIVAL MATERIALS

Gosudarstvennyi Arkhiv Kirovskoi Oblasti (GAKO),
Kirov: State Archive of Kirov Region

    f. 115 Zagarskii volostnoi sud
    f. 574 Viatskii gubernskii statisticheskii komitet
    f. 582 Kantseliariia Viatskogo gubernatora
    f. 584 Viatskoe gubernskoe prisutstvie
    f. 589 Bobinskoe volostnoe pravlenie
    f. 593 Zagarskoe volostnoe pravlenie
    f. 714 Viatskoe gubernskoe zhandarmskoe upravlenie
    f. R-783 Viatskaia gubernskaia komissiia po bor'be
        s posledstviiami goloda
    f. R-876 Otdel upravleniia Viatskogo gubernskogo ispolkoma
    f. R-878 Viatskii gubernskii voenno-revoliutsionnyi komitet
    f. R-879 Viatskii uezdnyi ispolkom
    f. R-880 Otdel upravleniia Viatskogo uezdnogo ispolkoma
    f. R-885 Malmyzhskii uezdnyi ispolkom
    f. R-890 Ekonomicheskoe soveshchanie pri Viatskom
        gubernskom ispolkome (Gubekoso)
    f. 927 Bogorodskoe volostnoe pravlenie
    f. R-935 Ankushinskii volostnoi ispolkom
    f. R-938 Stulovskii volostnoi ispolkom
    f. 940 Arkhangel'skoe volostnoe pravlenie
    f. 941 Il'inskoe volostnoe pravlenie
    f. 976 Vodozerskoe volostnoe pravlenie
    f. R-1053 Statisticheskii otdel Viatskogo gubernskogo ispolkoma
    f. R-1062 Zemel'noe upravlenie Viatskogo gubernskogo ispolkoma
    f. 1254 Viatskaia gubernskaia zemleustroitel'naia komissiia
    f. 1276 Viatskii voenno-tsenzurnyi punkt
    f. R-1287 Vodozerskii volostnoi ispolkom
    f. 1292 Shalegovskoe volostnoe pravlenie
    f. R-1322 Viatskii gubernskii revoliutsionnyi tribunal
    f. R-1330 Komissiia po vyiavleniiu ubytkov ot interventsii pri
        Viatskom gubernskom ispolkome
    f. 1345 Viatskii gubernskii komissar Vremennogo pravitel'stva

f. 1349 Viatskaia okruzhnaia izbiratel'naia komissiia po
      vyboram v Uchreditel'noe sobranie
f. 1351 Iaranskii uezdnyi komissar Vremennogo pravitel'stva
f. 1353 Malmyzhskii uezdnyi ispolnitel'nyi komitet
f. 1362 Urzhumskii uezdnyi zemel'nyi komitet
f. 1368 Pishtanskii volostnoi zemel'nyi komitet
f. R-1585 Upravlenie territorial'nogo okruga Viatskoi gubernii
      Narodnogo komissariata po voennym delam SSSR
f. R-1620 Bogorodskii volostnoi ispolkom
f. R-1733 Berezovskii volostnoi ispolkom
f. R-2506 Petropavlovskii volostnoi ispolkom
f. R-3224 Arkhangel'skii volostnoi ispolkom
f. R-3238 Balakhninskii volostnoi ispolkom
f. R-3271 Otdel upravleniia Malmyzhskogo uezdnogo ispolkoma
f. R-3288 Rybo-Vatazhskii volostnoi ispolkom
f. R-3300 Starotrykskii volostnoi ispolkom
f. R-3316 Iaranskii uezdnyi voennyi komissariat
f. R-3319 Otdel po delam natsional'nostei Iaranskogo
      uezdnogo ispolkoma
f. R-3454 Urzhumskii uezdnyi ispolkom

**Gosudarstvennyi Arkhiv Sotsial'no-Politicheskoi Istorii
Kirovskoi Oblasti** (GASPI KO),
Kirov: Centre for the Documentation of Contemporary History of Kirov Region

f. 1 Viatskii gubernskii komitet VKP(b)
f. 8 Malmyzhskii uezdnyi komitet VKP(b)
f. 10 Nolinskii uezdnyi komitet VKP(b)
f. 11 Slobodskoi uezdnyi komitet VKP(b)
f. 12 Urzhumskii uezdnyi komitet VKP(b)
f. 45 Istpart Viatskogo gubkoma

**Tsentral'nyi Gosudarstvennyi Arkhiv Udmurtskoi
Respubliki** (TsGA UR),
Izhevsk: Central State Archive of the Udmurt Republic

f. 94 Zemskii nachal'nik 11 uchastok, Glazovskii uezd
f. 96 Glazovskii uezdnyi s"ezd zemskikh nachal'nikov
f. R-204 Volispolkomy

**Nauchno-Otraslevoi Arkhiv Udmurtskogo Instituta Istorii, Iazyka i
Literatury Ural'skogo Otdeleniia RAN** (NOA UIIIaL URO RAN),
Izhevsk: Scientific Subject Archive of the Udmurt Institute of History,
Language and Literature of the Russian Academy of Sciences, Urals Branch

op. 2-N Otvety na anketu 'Vliianie revoliutsii na byt natsmen'

Rossiiskii Gosudarstvennyi Istoricheskii Arkhiv (RGIA),
St Petersburg: Russian State Historical Archive

f. 391 Pereselencheskoe upravlenie MVD

f. 395 Otdel sel'skoi ekonomiki i sel'skokhoziaistvennoi statistiki Ministerstva Zemledeliia
f. 397 Otdel sel'skogo stroitel'stva
f. 426 Otdel zemel'nykh uluchshenii MZ
f. 1284 Departament obshchikh del (MVD)
f. 1291 Zemskii otdel
f. 1292 Upravlenie po delam o voinskoi povinnosti
f. 1405 Departament ministerstva iustitsii vtorogo ugolovnogo otdeleniia

Rossiiskii Gosudarstvennyi Arkhiv Ekonomiki (RGAE),
Moscow: Russian State Archive of the Economy

f. 478 Narodnyi komissariat zemledeliia
f. 1943 Narodnyi komissariat prodovol'stviia

Gosudarstvennyi Arkhiv Rossiiskoi Federatsii (GA RF),
Moscow: State Archive of the Russian Federation

f. 102 Departament politsii Ministerstva vnutrennikh del
f. R-393 Narodnyi komissariat vnutrennikh del (NKVD)
f. R-1240 VTsIK
f. R-1318 Narkomnats
f. 1788 M. V. D. vremennogo pravitel'stva
f. 1791 Glavnoe upravlenie po delam militsii
f. 1810 Uchreditel'noe sobranie

Rossiiskii Gosudarstvennyi Arkhiv Sotsial'no-Politicheskoi Istorii (RGASPI),
Moscow: Russian State Archive of Socio-Political History

f. 17 Otdel po rabote v derevne

Rossiiskii Gosudarstvennyi Voennyi Arkhiv (RGVA),
Moscow: Russian State Military Archive

f. 169 Upravlenie 2 armii
f. 176 Upravlenie 3 armii vostochnogo fronta
f. 39562 Arkhiv beloi armii Izhevskogo raiona

United Kingdom National Archives, London

War Office 33 Siberia 1918–19
War Office 95 War Diaries (1914–18)
War Office 106 Directorate of Military Operations and Intelligence 837–1960

Hoover Institute Archive on War, Revolution, and Peace,
Stanford University, Stanford, California

Archives of the Soviet Communist Party and the Soviet State
American Relief Administration
Russia. Tsentral'naia komissiia pomoshchi golodaiushchim

United States National Archives, Washington, DC

State Department Records

NEWSPAPERS AND PERIODICALS

Belyi tsvetok
Bulletins of the Russian Liberation Committee
Elabuzhskaia malen'kaia narodnaia gazeta
Gody bor'by
Golos trudovogo krest'ianstva
Golos trudovogo naroda
Izhevskaia pravda
Izhevskii zashchitnik
Izvestiia Elabuzhskogo revoliutsionnogo komiteta
*Izvestiia Glazovskogo soveta krest'ianskikh, rabochikh i
    krasnoarmeiskikh deputatov*
Izvestiia Kotel'nicheskago vremennago ispolnitel'nago komiteta
*Izvestiia soveta krest'ianskikh, soldatskikh i rabochikh
    deputatov Orlovskago uezda*
Izvestiia Viatskogo gubernskogo ispolnitel'nogo komiteta
K likvidatsii sel'sko-khoziaistvennoi bezgramotnosti na bor'bu s zasukhoi
Kama
Krasnaia mysl'
Krasnyi nabat
Krasnyi pakhar'
Krasnyi put'
Krest'ianskaia gazeta Viatskago gubernskago zemstva
Krest'ianskaia sel'sko-khoziaistvenno-tekhnicheskaia gazeta
Kukarskaia zhizn'
Luch kommunizma
Malmyzhskaia zhizn'
Narodnoe delo
Posevoi biulleten'
Proletarskaia gazeta
Severnoe slovo
Slovo i zhizn'
Sovetskaia vlast' i krest'ianstvo
Viatskaia pravda
Viatskaia rech'
Viatskaia zhizn'
Viatskoe narodnoe khoziaistvo
Viatskoe pchelovodstvo
Vlast' naroda
Vo imia svobody Rossii
Zhizn' krest'ianina
Zhizn' natsional'nostei

OTHER PUBLICATIONS

Administrativnoe raionirovanie RSFSR. Sbornik postanovlenii, kasaiushchikhsia administrativno-territorial'nogo deleniia Rossii, za peiod 1917–1922 g. po dannym administrativnoi komissii VTsIK k 10 noiabria 1922 goda. Moscow: Izdanie VTsIK, 1923.

Alexopoulos, Golfo. *Stalin's Outcasts: Aliens, Citizens, and the Soviet State, 1926–1936.* Ithaca: Cornell University Press, 2003.

Anderson, Barbara A. *Internal Migration During Modernization in Late Nineteenth-Century Russia.* Princeton: Princeton University Press, 1980.

Anderson, Benedict. *Imagined Communities: Reflections on the Origins and Spread of Nationalism.* New York: Verso, 1991.

Anfimov, A. M. ed. *Krest'ianskoe dvizhenie v Rossii v gody pervoi mirovoi voiny iiul' 1914 g.– fevral' 1917 g.: Sbornik dokumentov.* Moscow and Leningrad: Izdatel'stvo nauka, 1965.

Rossiiskaia derevnia v gody pervoi mirovoi voiny (1914–fevral' 1917 g.). Moscow: Izdatel'stvo sotsial' no-ekonomicheskoi literatury, 1962.

Antsiferov, Alexis N., Alexander O. Bilimovich et al. *Russian Agriculture during the War.* New York: Greenwood Press, 1968.

Argenbright, Robert. 'The Soviet Agitational Vehicle: State Power on the Social Frontier'. *Political Geography* 17 (1998): 253–72.

Arnold, David. *Famine: Social Crisis and Historical Change.* New Perspectives on the Past. R. I. Moore, editor. Oxford: Basil Blackwell, 1988.

Atkinson, Dorothy. *The End of the Russian Land Commune, 1905–1930.* Stanford: Stanford University Press, 1983.

Azovtsev, N. N. et al., eds. *2 armiia v boiakh za osvobozhdenie Prikam'ia i Priural'ia. 1918–1919. Dokumenty.* Ustinov: Udmurtiia, 1987.

Badcock, Sarah. *Politics and the People in Revolutionary Russia: A Provincial History.* Cambridge: Cambridge University Press, 2007.

'Talking to the People and Shaping Revolution: The Drive for Enlightenment in Revolutionary Russia'. *The Russian Review* 65 (2006): 617–36.

'Women, Protest, and Revolution: Soldiers' Wives in Russia During 1917'. *International Review of Social History* 49 (2004): 47–70.

'"We're for the Muzhiks' Party!" Peasant Support for the Socialist Revolutionary Party During 1917'. *Europe–Asia Studies* 53 (2001): 133–49.

Badov, N. A. *Sostoianie pchelovodstva v Viatskoi gubernii (po dannym ankety 1910 goda).* Viatka: Tipografiia i khromolitografiia Shkliaevoi, 1912.

Baker, Mark. 'Rampaging Soldatki, Cowering Police, Bazaar Riots and Moral Economy: The Social Impact of the Great War in Kharkiv Province'. *Canadian–American Slavic Studies* 35 (2001): 137–55.

Bakulin, V. I., ed. *Iz istorii Viatskogo kraia kontsa XIXpervoi poloviny XX veka: Sbornik nauchnykh statel.* Kirov: Viatskii gosudarstvennyi pedagogicheskii universitet, 1998.

Ball, Alan. *And Now My Soul is Hardened: Abandoned Children in Soviet Russia, 1918–1930.* Berkeley: California University Press, 1994.

Balyberdin, A. G. et al., eds. *Viatskaia zemlia v proshlom i nastoiashchem (K 500-letiiu vkhozhdeniia v sostav Rossiiskogo gosudarstva). Tezisy dokladov i soobshchenii k nauchnoi konferentsii Kirov, 23–25 maia 1989 goda.* Kirov: Kirovskii gosudarstvennyi pedagogicheskii institut imeni V. I. Lenina, 1989.

Baron, Nick and Peter Gatrell. 'Population Displacement, State-Building, and Social Identity in the Lands of the Former Russian Empire, 1917–23'. *Kritika* 4 (2003): 51–100.

Bassin, Mark. *Imperial Visions: Nationalist Imagination and Geographical Expansion in the Russian Far East, 1840–1865.* Cambridge: Cambridge University Press, 1999.

Batalden, Stephen K., ed. *Seeking God: The Recovering of Religious Identity in Orthodox Russia, Ukraine and Georgia.* DeKalb: Northern Illinois University Press, 1993.

Bekhterev, S. L. *Esero-Maksimalistskoe dvizhenie v Udmurtii.* Izhevsk: Udmurtskii institut istorii, iazyka i literatury URO RAN, 1997.

Berdinskikh, Viktor. *Rossiia i russkie (krest'ianskaia tsivilizatsiia v vospominaniiakh ochevidtsev).* Kirov: Izdatel'stvo GIPP Viatka, 1994.

Berk, Stephen M. 'The "Class-Tragedy" of Izhevsk: Working-Class Opposition to Bolshevism in 1918'. *Russian History* 2 (1975): 176–90.

Berkevich, A. B. 'Krest'ianstvo i vseobshchaia mobilizatsiia v iiule 1914 g.'. *Istoricheskie zapiski* 23 (1947): 3–43.

Bernshtam, M. S. ed. *Ural i Prikam'e noiabr' 1917–ianvar' 1919: Dokumenty i materialy.* Issledovaniia noveishei Russkoi istorii. Paris: YMCA Press, 1982.

Blank, Stephen. *The Sorcerer as Apprentice: Stalin as Commissar of Nationalities, 1917–1924.* Westport, CT: Greenwood Press, 1994.

Blum, Jerome. *Lord and Peasant in Russia: From the Ninth to the Nineteenth Century.* Princeton: Princeton University Press, 1961.

Bobrova, A. I. and A. S. Korobeinikova, eds. *Kul'turnoe stroitel'stvo v Udmurtii: Sbornik dokumentov (1917–1940 gg.).* Izhevsk: Udmurtiia, 1970.

Bohac, Rodney. 'Peasant Inheritance Strategies in Russia'. *Journal of Interdisciplinary History* 26 (1985): 23–42.

Bonhomme, Brian. *Forests, Peasants, and Revolutionaries: Forest Conservation and Organization in Soviet Russia, 1917–1929.* Boulder: East European Monographs, 2005.

Bourdieu, Pierre. *Outline of a Theory of Practice.* Translated by Richard Nice. Cambridge Studies in Social and Cultural Anthropology. Cambridge: Cambridge University Press, 1995.

Bradley, Joseph. 'Subjects into Citizens: Societies, Civil Society, and Autocracy in Tsarist Russia'. *American Historical Review* 107 (2002): 1094–1123.

Brooks, Jeffrey. *When Russia Learned to Read: Literacy and Popular Literature, 1861–1917.* Princeton: Princeton University Press, 1985.

Brovkin, Vladimir. *Behind the Front Lines of the Civil War: Political Parties and Social Movements in Russia, 1918–1922.* Princeton: Princeton University Press, 1994.

Brovkin, Vladimir. ed. *The Bolsheviks in Russian Society: The Revolution and the Civil War.* New Haven: Yale University Press, 1997.

Browder, Robert and Alexander F. Kerensky, eds. *The Russian Provisional Government, 1917: Documents.* Vol. I. Stanford: Stanford University Press, 1961.

Brower, Daniel R. and Edward J. Lazzerini, eds. *Russia's Orient: Imperial Borderlands and Peoples, 1700–1917*. Bloomington: Indiana University Press, 1997.

Brubaker, Rogers. 'In the Nation of the Nation: Reflections on Nationalism and Patriotism'. *Citizenship Studies* 8 (2004): 115–27.

Nationalism Reframed: Nationhood and the National Question in the New Europe. Cambridge: Cambridge University Press, 1996.

Bunyan, James and H. H. Fisher, eds. *Intervention, Civil War, and Communism in Russia, April–December 1918: Documents and Materials*. The Walter Hines Page School of International Relations, Johns Hopkins University. New York: Octagon Books, 1976.

Burbank, Jane. 'An Imperial Rights Regime: Law and Citizenship in the Russian Empire'. *Kritika* 7 (2006): 397–431.

Russian Peasants Go to Court: Legal Culture in the Countryside, 1905–1917. Bloomington: Indiana University Press, 2004.

Burds, Jeffrey. *Peasant Dreams and Market Politics: Labor Migration and the Russian Village, 1861–1905*. Pittsburgh: University of Pittsburgh Press, 1998.

Bystrova, A. S. *Komitety bednoty v Viatskoi gubernii*. Kirov: Kirovskoe knizhnoe izdatel'stvo, 1956.

Bystrova, A. S. et al., eds. *Ustanovlenie i uprochenie sovetskoi vlasti v Viatskoi gubernii: Sbornik dokumentov*. Kirov: Kirovskoe knizhnoe izdatel'stvo, 1957.

Chamberlin, W. H. *The Russian Revolution, 1917–21*. 2 vols. Princeton: Princeton University Press, 1987.

Channon, John. 'The Bolsheviks and the Peasantry: the Land Question During the First Eight Months of Soviet Rule'. *The Slavonic and East European Review* 66 (1988): 593–624.

Chayanov, A. V. *The Theory of Peasant Economy*. Edited by Daniel Throner et al. Madison: The University of Wisconsin Press, 1986.

Chelintsev, A. N. *Russkoe sel'skoe khoziaistvo pered revoliutsiei*. 2nd edn Moscow: Novyi agronom, 1928.

Chetvertaia chrezvychainaia Viatskaia gubernskaia konferentsiia RKP(b) 1919. Viatka: Gubernskaia sovetskaia tipolitografiia, 1919.

Christian, David. 'Prohibition in Russia, 1914–1925'. *Australian Slavonic and East European Studies* 9 (1995): 89–118.

Chulos, Chris J. *Converging Worlds: Religion and Community in Peasant Russia, 1861–1917*. DeKalb: Northern Illinois University Press, 2003.

Clark, Katerina. *Petersburg: Crucible of Cultural Revolution*. Cambridge, MA: Harvard University Press, 1995.

Crews, Robert D. *For Prophet and Tsar: Islam and Empire in Russia and Central Asia*. Cambridge, MA: Harvard University Press, 2006.

Danchik, I. et al., eds. *Oktiabr' i grazhdanskaia voina v Viatskoi gubernii: Sbornik statei i materialov*. Viatka: Istpart Viatskogo gubkoma VKP, 1927.

Danilov, Iu. N. *Rossiia v mirovoi voine, 1914–1915 gg*. Berlin: Slovo, 1924.

Danilov, V. P. *Rural Russia under the New Regime*. Translated by Orlando Figes. Bloomington: Indiana University Press, 1988.

Sovetskaia dokolkhoznaia derevnia: sotsial'naia struktura, sotsial'nye otnosheniia. Moscow: Nauka, 1979.

Danilov, V. P. and T. Shanin, eds. *Krest'ianskoe dvizhenie v Povolzh'e. 1919– 1922 gg.: Dokumenty i materialy.* Moscow: Rosspen, 2002.

Desan, Suzanne. 'What's After Political Culture? Recent French Revolutionary Historiography'. *French Historical Studies* 23 (2000): 163–96.

Dewey, P. E. *British Agriculture in the First World War.* New York: Routledge, 1989.

Dmitriev, P. N. and K. I. Kulikov. *Miatezh v Izhevsko-Votkinskom rainoe.* Izhevsk: Udmurtiia, 1992.

Dowler, Wayne. *Classroom and Empire: The Politics of Schooling Russia's Eastern Nationalities, 1860–1917.* Montreal: McGill-Queen's University Press, 2001.

Dubrovskii, S. M. *Stolypinskaia zemel'naia reforma: Iz istorii sel'skogo khoziaistva i krest'ianstva Rossii v nachale XX veka.* Moscow: Akademiia nauk, SSSR, 1963.

Duprat, Catherine. 'Lieux et temps de l'acculturation politique'. *Annales historiques de la Révolution française* 66 (1994): 387–400.

Dyson, Tim and Cormac O Grada, eds. *Famine Demography: Perspectives from the Past and Present.* Oxford: Oxford University Press, 2002.

Efimov, A. G. *Izhevtsy i Votkintsy: Bor'ba s bol'shevikami, 1918–20 gg.* San Francisco: Self-published, 1975.

Eklof, Ben. *Russian Peasant Schools: Officialdom, Village Culture, and Popular Pedagogy, 1861–1914.* Berkeley: California University Press, 1986.

Eklof, Ben and Stephen Frank, eds. *The World of the Russian Peasant: Post-Emancipation Culture and Society.* Boston: Unwin Hyman, 1990.

Eklof, Ben, John Bushnell and Larissa Zakharova, eds. *Russia's Great Reforms, 1855–1881.* Bloomington: Indiana University Press, 1994.

Eley, Geoff and Ronald Grigor Suny, eds. *Becoming National: A Reader.* New York: Oxford University Press, 1996.

Eltis, David, ed. *Coerced and Free Migration: Global Perspectives.* Stanford: Stanford University Press, 2002.

Emel'ianov, I. P. ed. *Oktiabr'skaia sotsialisticheskaia revoliutsiia v Udmurtii: Sbornik dokumentov i materialov (1917–1918 gg.).* Izhevsk: Udmurtskoe knizhnoe izdatel'stvo, 1957.

Emel'ianov, I. P. et al., eds. *Udmurtiia v period inostrannoi voennoi interventsii i grazhdanskoi voiny: Sbornik dokumentov.* Vol. I. Izhevsk: Udmurtskoe knizhnoe izdatel'stvo, 1960.

Emmausskii, A. V. *Istoriia Viatskogo kraia v XII-seredine XIX veka.* Kirov: Kirovskaia oblastnaia tipografiia, 1996.

Emmausskii, A. V., ed. *Voprosy istorii Kirovskol oblasti.* Kirov: Kirovskii gosu-darstvennyl pedagogicheskii institut imeni V. I. Lenina, 1974.

Emmons, Terence and Wayne S. Vucinich, eds. *The Zemstvo in Russia: An Experiment in Local Self-Government.* Cambridge: Cambridge University Press, 1982.

Engel, Barbara Alpern. *Between the Fields and the City: Women, Work, and Family in Russia, 1861–1914.* Cambridge: Cambridge University Press, 1994.

'Not by Bread Alone: Subsistence Riots in Russia during World War I'. *Journal of Modern History* 69 (1997): 696–717.

Women in Russia, 1700–2000. Cambridge: Cambridge University Press, 2004.

Eriksen, Thomas Hylland. *Ethnicity and Nationalism: Anthropological Perspectives.* Boulder: Pluto Press, 1993.

Evans, Peter B., Dietrich Rueschemeyer and Theda Skocpol, eds. *Bringing the State Back In.* New York: Cambridge University Press, 1985.

Farnsworth, Beatrice. 'The Soldatka: Folklore and Court Record'. *Slavic Review* 49 (1990): 58–73.

Farnsworth, Beatrice and Lynne Viola, eds. *Russian Peasant Women.* New York: Oxford University Press, 1992.

Fediukii, S. A. et al., eds. *Kul'turnoe stroitel'stvo v Kirovskoi oblasti 1917–1987. Dokumenty i materially.* Kirov: Volgo-Viatskoe knizhnoe izdatel'stvo Kirovskoe otdelenie, 1987.

Figes, Orlando. *A People's Tragedy: A History of the Russian Revolution.* New York: Viking, 1996.

  Peasant Russia, Civil War: The Volga Countryside in Revolution (1917–1921). Oxford: Clarendon Press, 1989.

Figes, Orlando and Boris Kolonitskii. *Interpreting the Russian Revolution: The Language and Symbols of 1917.* New Haven and London: Yale University Press, 1999.

Fisher, H. H. *The Famine in Soviet Russia 1919–1923: The Operations of the American Relief Administration.* New York: The Macmillan Company, 1927.

Fitzpatrick, Sheila. *Stalin's Peasants: Resistance and Survival in the Russian Village after Collectivization.* New York: Oxford University Press, 1994.

  Tear off the Masks! Identity and Imposture in Twentieth-Century Russia. Princeton: Princeton University Press, 2005.

Frank, Stephen. *Crime, Cultural Conflict, and Justice in Rural Russia, 1856–1914.* Berkeley: University of California Press, 1999.

Frank, Stephen P. and Mark D. Steinberg, eds. *Cultures in Flux: Lower-Class Values, Practices, and Resistance in Late Imperial Russia.* Princeton: Princeton University Press, 1994.

Fraunholtz, Peter. 'State Intervention and Local Control in Russia, 1917–1921: Grain Procurement Politics in Penza Province'. PhD diss., Boston College, 1998.

Frierson, Cathy A. *All Russia is Burning! A Cultural History of Fire and Arson in Late Imperial Russia.* Seattle: University of Washington Press, 2002.

Gatrell, Peter. *A Whole Empire Walking: Refugees in Russia During World War I.* Indiana–Michigan Series in Russian and East European Studies. General editors Alexander Rabinowitch and William G. Rosenberg. Bloomington: Indiana University Press, 1999.

  Russia's First World War: A Social and Economic History. London: Pearson, 2005.

Gaudin, Corinne. *Ruling Peasants: Village and State in Imperial Russia.* DeKalb: Northern Illinois University Press, 2007.

von Geldern, James. *Bolshevik Festivals, 1917–1920.* Berkeley: University of California Press, 1993.

Geraci, Robert P. *Window on the East: National and Imperial Identities in Late Tsarist Russia.* Ithaca: Cornell University Press, 2001.

Gerasimiuk, V. R. 'Nekotorye novye statisticheskie dannye o kombedakh RSFSR'. *Voprosy istorii* 6 (1963): 208–11.

Gerasimova, N. V. 'Zemskaia reforma na territorii Chuvashii: vybory v volostnye i uezdnye zemstva (iiun'–dekabr' 1917g.)', *Vestnik Moskovskogo universiteta* series 8 (January–February 2003): 70–87.

Gerd, K. P. and V. P. Malimova. *Votiaki. Sbornik po voprosam byta, ekonomiki, i kul'tury votiakov.* Moscow: Tsentral'noe izdatel'stvo narodov soiuza SSR, 1926.

Gertsen, Aleksandr. *Byloe i dumy.* Moscow: Gosudarstvennoe izdatel'stvo khudozhestvennoi literatury, 1962.

    Sobranie sochinenii v tridtsati tomakh. Tom 1. Moscow: Izdatel'stvo akademii nauk SSSR, 1954.

Gill, Graeme J. *Peasants and Government in the Russian Revolution.* New York: The Macmillan Press, 1979.

Gillis, John R., ed. *The Militarization of the Western World.* New Brunswick: Rutgers University Press, 1989.

Gleason, Abbott, Peter Kenez, and Richard Stites, eds. *Bolshevik Culture: Experiment and Order in the Russian Revolution.* Bloomington: Indiana University Press, 1985.

Gnedovskii, B. V. and E. D. Dobrovol'skaia. *Dorogami zemli Viatskoi.* Moscow: Izdatel'stvo iskusstvo, 1971.

Gofman, Ts. 'K istorii pervogo agitparokhoda VTsIK "krasnaia zvezda" (iiul'–oktiabr' 1919 g.)'. *Voprosy istorii* 9 (1948): 63–70.

Golovine, N. N. *The Russian Army in the World War.* New Haven: Yale University Press, 1931.

Gramsci, Antonio. *Selections from the Prison Notebooks.* Edited and translated by Quintin Hoare and Geoffrey Nowell Smith. New York: International Publishers, 1992.

Guha, Ranajit. *Dominance without Hegemony: History and Power in Colonial India.* Cambridge, MA: Harvard University Press, 1997.

    Elementary Aspects of Peasant Insurgency in Colonial India. Delhi: Oxford University Press, 1983.

Gur'ianova, N. P. and V. E. Musikhin, eds. *Viatskomu Zemstvu – 130 let: Materialy nauchnoi konferentsii 8–9 oktiabria 1997 goda.* Kirov: Kirovskaia ordena pocheta oblastnaia nauchnaia biblioteka imeni A. I. Gertsena, 1997.

Halfin, Igal. *From Darkness to Light: Class, Consciousness, and Salvation in Revolutionary Russia.* Pittsburgh: The University of Pittsburgh Press, 2000.

Heinzen, James. *Inventing a Soviet Countryside: State Power and the Transformation of Rural Russia, 1917–1929.* Pittsburgh: University of Pittsburgh Press, 2004.

Herlihy, Patricia. *Alcoholic Empire: Vodka and Politics in Late Imperial Russia.* New York: Oxford University Press, 2002.

Hickey, Michael C. 'Discourses of Public Identity and Liberalism in the February Revolution: Smolensk, Spring 1917'. *The Russian Review* 55 (1996): 615–37.

    'Local Government and State Authority in the Provinces: Smolensk, February–June, 1917'. *Slavic Review* 55 (1996): 863–81.

    'Urban Zemliachestva and Rural Revolution: Petrograd and the Smolensk Countryside in 1917'. *The Soviet and Post-Soviet Review* 23 (1996): 143–59.

Hirsch, Francine. *Empire of Nations: Ethnographic Knowledge and the Making of the Soviet Union*. Ithaca: Cornell University Press, 2005.

Hobsbawm, E. J. *Nations and Nationalism since 1780: Programme, Myth, Reality*. Cambridge: Cambridge University Press, 1993.

Hoch, Steven L. *Serfdom and Social Control in Russia: Petrovskoe, a Village in Tambov*. Chicago: The University of Chicago Press, 1986.

Hoffmann, David L. 'Land, Freedom, and Discontent: Russian Peasants of the Central Industrial Region prior to Collectivisation'. *Europe–Asia Studies* 46 (1994): 637–48.

Peasant Metropolis: Social Identities in Moscow, 1929–1941. Ithaca: Cornell University Press, 1994.

Stalinist Values: The Cultural Norms of Soviet Modernity, 1917–1941. Ithaca: Cornell University Press, 2003.

Holquist, Peter. '"Information is the Alpha and Omega of our Work": Bolshevik Surveillance in its Pan-European Context'. *The Journal of Modern History* 69 (1997): 415–50.

Making War, Forging Revolution: Russia's Continuum of Crisis, 1914–1921. Cambridge, MA: Harvard University Press, 2002.

Hunt, Lynn. *Politics, Culture, and Class in the French Revolution*. Studies on the History of Society and Culture. Edited by Victoria E. Bonnell and Lynn Hunt. Berkeley: University of California Press, 1984.

Ivanov, A. A. ed. *Pervaia sovetskaia vesna v derevne: Krest'ianstvo Mariiskogo kraia i zemel'nyi vopros v 1918 godu: Dokumenty i materialy*. Ioshkar–Ola: Mariiskii gosudarstvennyi universitet, 2002.

Jahn, Hubertus F. *Patriotic Culture in Russia during World War I*. Ithaca: Cornell University Press, 1995.

Kabanov, V. V. *Krest'ianskoe khoziaistvo v usloviiakh 'voennogo kommunizma'*. Moscow: Nauka, 1988.

Kabytova, N. N. *Vlast' i obshchestvo v Rossiiskoi provintsii: 1917 god v Povolzh'e*. Samara: Samarskii universitet, 1999.

Kak ustroit' krest'ianskii soiuz. Viatka: Izdatel'stvo Viatskoi gubernskoi organizatsii komitet krest'ianskago soiuza, 1917.

Katkov, V. I. et al., eds. *Udmurtskaia oblastnaia organizatsiia KPSS v tsifrakh, 1921–1985*. Ustinov: Udmurtiia, 1986.

Kelleher, Margaret. *The Feminization of Famine: Expressions of the Inexpressible?* Durham, NC: Duke University Press, 1997.

Kenez, Peter. *The Birth of the Propaganda State: Soviet Methods of Mass Mobilization, 1917–1929*. Cambridge: Cambridge University Press, 1985.

Kettle, Michael. *Churchill and the Archangel Fiasco: November 1918–July 1919*. Russia and the Allies 1917–1920, vol. 3. New York: Routledge, 1992.

Khalid, Abeed. *The Politics of Muslim Cultural Reform: Jadidism in Central Asia*. Berkeley: University of California Press, 1998.

Khranilov, Iu. P. '"Chto im delo do chuzhikh pisem, kogda briukho syto": voennaia tsenzura Viatskoi gubernii v bor'be za pobedu nad germantsami'. *Voenno-istoricheskii zhurnal* 2 (1997): 22–9.

Kingston-Mann, Esther and Timothy Mixter, eds. *Peasant Economy, Culture, and Politics of European Russia, 1800–1921*. Princeton: Princeton University Press, 1991.

Kiriukhina, E. I. ed. *Ocherki istorii Kirovskoi organizatsii KPSS*. Kirov: Volgo-Viatskoe knizhnoe izdatel'stvo, 1965.

Kiselev, A. F., ed. *Vlast'i obshchestvennye organizatsii v Rossii v pervoi treti XX stoletiia*. Moscow: MIP NV Magister, 1993.

Klimov, K. M., ed. *Slavianskii i finno-ugorskii mir vchera, segodnia. Sbornik statei*. Izhevsk: Izdatel'stvo udmurtskogo universiteta, 1996.

Koenker, Diane P. et al., eds. *Party, State, and Society in the Russian Civil War: Explorations in Social History*. Bloomington: Indiana University Press, 1989.

Kolonitskii, B. I. *Simvoly vlasti i bor'ba za vlast': K izucheniiu politicheskoi kul'tury rossiiskoi revoliutsii 1917 goda*. St Petersburg: Dmitrii Bulanin, 2001.

Kondrat'ev, N. D. *Rynok khlebov i ego regulirovanie vo vremia voiny i revoliutsii*. Moscow: Nauka, 1991.

Korolenko, G. V. ed. *Delo multanskikh votiakov, obviniavshikhsia v prinesenii chelovecheskoi zhertvy iazycheskim bogam*. Moscow: Russkie vedomosti, 1896.

Kosarev, S. N. *Zemel'noe ustroistvo v Viatskoi gubernii*. Viatka: Gubernskaia Tipolitografiia, 1917.

Kotkin, *Magnetic Mountain: Stalinism as a Civilization*. Berkeley: University of California Press, 1995.

Kotsonis, Yanni. '"Face-to-Face": The State, the Individual, and the Citizen in Russian Taxation, 1863–1917'. *Slavic Review* 63 (2004): 221–46.

Making Peasants Backward: Agricultural Cooperatives and the Agrarian Question in Russia, 1861–1914. New York: St Martin's Press, 1999.

Kotsonis, Yanni and David L. Hoffmann, eds. *Russian Modernity: Politics, Knowledge, Practices*. New York: Macmillan Press 2000.

Kratkii ocherk o vozniknovenii, zadachakh i deiatel'nosti v techenie 1918 g. Soiuza pomoshchi besprizornym detiam v Viatskoi gubernii. Viatka: Gubernskii sovetskii tipolitograf, 1919.

Kraus, Hertha. *International Relief in Action, 1914–1943: Selected Records, with Notes*. Scottdale, PA: Herald Press, 1944.

Kreindler, Isabelle. 'A Neglected Source of Lenin's Nationality Policy'. *Slavic Review* 36 (1977): 86–100.

Krysova, G. Iu. et al., eds. *Istoriia i kul'tura Volgo-Viatskogo kraia (K 90-letiiu Viatskoi uchenoi arkhivnoi komissii). Tezisy dokladov i soobshchenii k mezhregional'noi nauchnoi konferentsii*. Kirov: Volgo-Viatskoe knizhnoe izdatel'stvo, Kirovskoe otdelenie, 1994.

Kuchkin, A. 'K istorii Izhevskogo vosstaniia'. *Proletarskaia revoliutsiia* 6 (1929): 153–62.

Kukoviakin, S. A. *Zemskaia meditsina Viatskoi i drugikh severnykh gubernii evropeiskoi Rossii*. Kirov: Viatka, 1998.

Kulikov, K. I. *Natsional'no-gosudarstvennoe stroitel'stvo vostochno-finskikh narodov v 1917–1937 gg*. Izhevsk: UIIIaL URO RAN, 1993.

Kumyshkaez an no iue, en no pos'te. Viatka: Gubernskaia tipolitografiia, 1916.

Kurenyshev, A. A. *Vserossiiskii krest'ianskii soiuz, 1905–1930 gg.: Mify i real'nost'*. Moscow: AIRO XX, 2004.

Lallukka, Seppo. *From Fugitive Peasants to Diaspora: The Eastern Mari in Tsarist and Federal Russia*. Helsinki: Academia Scientiarum Fennica, 2003.

Lallukka, S. and T. Molotovaia, eds. *Etnicheskaia mobilizatsiia vo vnutrennei periferii: Volgo-Kamskii region nachala XX v*. Izhevsk: UIIIaL URO RAN, 2000.

Landes, Joan. *Women and the Public Sphere in the Age of the French Revolution*. Ithaca: Cornell University Press, 1988.

Landis, Erik. 'Waiting for Makhno: Legitimacy and Context in a Russian Peasant War'. *Past and Present* 183 (2004):182–236.

Lavrov, V. M. *'Krest'ianskii parlament' Rossii (Vserossiiskie s"ezdy sovetov krest'ianskikh deputatov v 1917–1918 godakh)*. Moscow: Arkheograficheskii tsentr, 1996.

Legotin, V. V. ed. *Kirovskaia oblastnaia organizatsiia KPSS v tsifrakh, 1917–1985*. Kirov: Volgo-Viatskoe knizhnoe izdatel'stvo, 1986.

Lehning, James. *Peasant and French: Cultural Contact in Rural France during the Nineteenth Century*. New York: Cambridge University Press, 1995.

Lenin, V. I. *Polnoe sobranie sochinenii*. 5th edn Moscow: Gosudarstvennoe izdatel'stvo politicheskoi literatury, 1959–1965.

Lepeshkin, A. I. ed. *Sbornik ofitsial'nykh dokumentov (Primenitel'no k kursu sovetskogo gosudarstvennogo prava)*. Moscow: Izdatel'stvo iuridicheskaia literatura, 1964.

Letiagin, V. D. et al, eds. *Za vlast' sovetov: Sbornik vospominanii starykh bol'shevikov–uchastnikov Velikoi Oktiabr'skoi sotsialisticheskoi revoliutsii i grazhdanskoi voiny v Viatskoi gubernii*. Kirov: Kirovskoe knizhnoe izdatel'stvo, 1957.

Lih, Lars. *Bread and Authority in Russia, 1914–1921*. Berkeley: University of California Press, 1990.

Lohr, Eric. 'Enemy Alien Politics Within the Russian Empire During World War I'. PhD diss., Harvard University, 1999.

  Nationalizing the Russian Empire: The Campaign Against Enemy Aliens During World War I. Cambridge, MA: Harvard University Press, 2003.

  'The Ideal Citizen and Real Subject in Late Imperial Russia'. *Kritika* 7 (2006): 173–94.

Luppov, P. 'O vliianii revoliutsii na byt natsmen'. *Trudy Viatskogo pedagogicheskogo instituta imeni V. I. Lenina*. Tom II, vyp. II (Viatka, 1927): 59–64.

Maksimov, V. 'Kulatskaia kontrrevoliutsiia i Izhevskoe vosstanie (1918 g.)'. *Istorik marksist* 4–5 (1932): 109–62.

Maliavskii, A. D. *Krest'ianskoe dvizhenie v Rossii v 1917 g. mart-oktiabr'*. Moscow: Nauka, 1981.

Mallon, Florencia E. *Peasant and Nation: The Making of Postcolonial Mexico and Peru*. Berkeley: University of California Press, 1995.

Marshall, T. H. *Citizenship and Social Class, and Other Essays*. Cambridge: Cambridge University Press, 1950.

Martin, Terry. *The Affirmative Action Empire: Nations and Nationalism in the Soviet Union, 1923–1939*. Ithaca: Cornell University Press, 2001.

Martynova, M. M., M. I. Gnedin and N. P. Ligenko, eds. *Agrarnye otnosheniia v Udmurtii vo vtoroi polovine XIX-nachale XX vv.: Sbornik statei*. Izhevsk:

Nauchno-issledovatel'skii institut pri Sovete Ministrov Udmurtskoi ASSR, 1981.

Materialy po issledovaniiu promyslov Viatskoi gubernii, Viatskii uezd osnovnyia tablitsy (podvornoe izsledovanie 1909 goda). Statisticheskoe otdelenie Viatskoi gubernskoi zemskoi upravy. Viatka: Tipografiia i khromolitografiia Shkliaevoi, 1912.

Materialy po zemel'noi reforme 1918 goda. Raspredelenie zemli v 1918 godu. Moscow: Izdatel'stvo narodnogo komissariata zemledeliia, 1919.

Matsuzato, Kimitaka. 'The Role of Zemstva in the Creation and Collapse of Tsarism's War Efforts During World War One'. *Jarbücher für Geschichte Osteuropas* 46 (1998): 321–37.

Mawdsley, Evan. *The Russian Civil War*. Boston: Allen and Unwin, 1987.

Mesiatsev, P. ed. *O zemle: Sbornik statei o proshlom i budushchem zemel'no-khoziaistvennogo stroitel'stva*, vyp. 1. Moscow: Gosudarstvennoe izda-tel'stvo, 1921.

Mints, I. I. ed. *Leninskii dekret o zemle v deistvii: sbornik statei*. Moscow: Nauka, 1979.

Moon, David. *Russian Peasants and Tsarist Legislation on the Eve of Reform: Interaction between Peasants and Officialdom*. Basingstoke and London: Palgrave Macmillan, 1992.

The Russian Peasantry, 1600–1930: The World the Peasants Made. London: Longman, 1999.

Mokshin, N. F., ed. *Narody Povolzh'ia i Priural'ia: Komi-zyriane. Komi-permiaki. Mariitsy. Mordva. Udmurty*. Moscow: Nauka, 2000.

Morozov, V. I. et al., eds. *Entsiklopediia zemli Viatskoi*. Tom 8, *Etnografiia, fol'klor*. Kirov: Oblastnaia pisatel'skaia organizatsiia, 1998.

Narskii, Igor'. *Zhizn' v katastrofe. Budni naseleniia Urala v 1917–1922 gg.* Moscow: Rosspen, 2001.

Naselenie Rossii za 100 let (1897–1997). Population of Russia: 1897–1997. Statisticheskii sbornik. Statistical Handbook. Moscow: Gosudarstvennyi komitet Rossiiskoi Federatsii po statistike, 1998.

Neuberger, Joan. *Hooliganism: Crime, Culture, and Power in St Petersburg, 1900–1914*. Berkeley: University of California Press, 1993.

Nikitina, G. A. *Sel'skaia obshchina buskel' v poreformennyi period (1861–1900 gg.)*. Izhevsk: Udmurtskii institut istorii, iazyka i literatury Ural'skoe otdelenie Rossiiskaia akademiia nauk, 1993.

Novikov, A. *Ekonomicheskiia nuzhdy Viatskago kraia (po dannym zemskoi statistiki)*. Viatka: Tipografiia Maisheeva, 1896.

O p'ianstve. Viatka: Gubernskaia tipografiia, 1915.

Obshchegubernskii s"ezd soldatok Viatskoi gubernii 1-go iiunia 1918 goda. Viatka: Tipografiia pechatnik, 1918.

Obzor Viatskoi gubernii za 1913 g. Prilozhenie k vsepoddanneishemu otchetu Viatskago gubernatora. Viatka: Gubernskaia tipografiia, 1914.

Obzor Viatskoi gubernii za 1915 g. Viatka: Gubernskaia tipografiia, 1916.

Orlov, N. *Sistema prodovol'stvennykh zagotovok. K otsenke rabot zagotovitel'nykh ekspeditsii A. G. Shlikhtera*. Tambov: Otdelenie gosizdatel'stva, 1920.

Orlovsky, Daniel. 'Corporatism or Democracy: The Russian Provisional Government of 1917'. *The Soviet and Post-Soviet Review* 24 (1997): 15–25.

Ostrovskaia, M. *Iz istorii Viatskikh inorodtsev.* Kazan: Tipolitografiia imperatorskago universiteta, 1912.

Otchet o deiatel'nosti Slobodskogo otdela obshchestva pomoshchi sem'iam zapasnykh i ratnikov opolcheniia, prizvannykh v mobilizatsii 1914–1915 gg. Slobodskoi: Tipografiia M. A. Miasnikovoi, 1916.

Otchet o deiatel'nosti Viatskoi gubernskoi komissii pomoshchi golodaiushchim za period s 5-go avgusta 1921 goda po 15-e oktiabria 1922 goda. Viatka: 1-ia tipolitografiia bumazhno-poligraficheskogo tresta, 1922.

Otchet Viatskogo gubernskogo ispolnitel'nogo komiteta. Oktiabr' 1921–oktiabr' 1922 gg. Tom II. Viatka: Viatskii gubispolkom sovetov, 1922.

Pallot, Judith. *Land Reform in Russia 1906–1917: Peasant Responses to Stolypin's Project of Rural Transformation.* Oxford: Clarendon Press, 1999.

Pallot, Judith, ed. *Transforming Peasants: Society, State and the Peasantry, 1861–1920.* Houndmills: Macmillan, 1998.

Pamiatnaia knizhka Viatskoi gubernii i kalendar' na 1915 g. Viatka: Gubernskaia tipografiia, 1915.

Pape, Carsten. 'The "Peasant Zemstva": Popular Education in Vjatka Gubernija, 1867–1905'. *Jahrbücher für Geschichte Osteuropas* 27 (1979): 498–519.

Papyrina, A. A. *Revoliutsionnoe dvizhenie v Viatskoi gubernii v 1905–1907 gg.* Kirov: Volgo-Viatskoe knizhnoe izdatel'stvo Kirovskoe otdelenie, 1975.

Patenaude, Bertrand M. *The Big Show in Bololand: The American Relief Expedition to Soviet Russia in the Famine of 1921.* Stanford: Stanford University Press, 2002.

Pavlov, N. P. *Kuzebai Gerd – syn epokhi.* Izhevsk: Udmurtiia, 2004.

Samoopredelenie, avtonomiia: Idei, realii. Izhevsk: Udmurtiia, 2000.

Pereselenie i zemleustroistvo za Uralom v 1913 g. (Otchet o rabotakh pereselencheskago upravleniia za 1913 g.). Prilozhenie k smete dokhodov, raskhodov i spetsial'nykh sredstv Pereselencheskago Upravleniia G. U. Z. i Z. na 1915 g. Petrograd: Tipografiia A. E. Kollins, 1914.

Perminova, N. I. et al., eds. *Entsiklopediia zemli Viatskoi.* Tom 7, *Priroda.* Kirov: Oblastnaia pisatel'skaia organizatsiia, 1997.

Pershin, P. N. *Agrarnaia revoliutsiia v Rossii: Agrarnye preobrazovaniia Velikoi Oktiabr'skoi sotsialisticheskoi revoliutsii (1917–1918 gg.).* Vol. II Moscow: Nauka, 1966.

Pesni revoliutsii. Slobodskoi, 1917.

Piontkovskii, S. A. ed. *Sovety v oktiabre: Sbornik dokumentov.* Moscow: Izdatel'stvo kommunisticheskoi akademii, 1928.

Pipes, Richard. *Formation of the Soviet Union: Communism and Nationalism, 1917–1923.* Cambridge, MA: Harvard University Press, 1964.

The Russian Revolution. New York: Alfred A. Knopf, 1990.

Polner, Tikhon J. *Russian Local Government During the War and the Union of Zemstvos.* New Haven: Yale University Press, 1930.

Ponomarev, V. F. et al., eds. *Entsiklopediia zemli Viatskoi.* Tom 10, *Remesla.* Kirov: Oblastnaia pisatel'skaia organizatsiia, 2000.

Popova, E. D. *Krest'ianskie komitety Viatskoi gubernii v 1917 godu.* Kirov: Kirovskoe otdelenie Volgo-Viatskogo knizhnogo izdatel'stva, 1966.

Porshneva, O. S. *Krest'iane, rabochie i soldaty Rossii nakanune i v gody pervoi mirovoi voiny.* Moscow: Rosspen, 2004.

Postanovleniia gubernskago krest'ianskago s"ezda v Viatke 6–10 iiunia 1917 goda. Viatka: Tipografiia A. A. Sil'vinskago, 1917.

Postanovleniia i resheniia s"ezda mari (cheremis') Viatskoi gubernii. Viatka: Gubernskaia tipolitografiia, 1917.

Pravila obiazel'nogo vzaimnogo zemskogo strakhovaniia ot ognia stroenii v Viatskoi gubernii. Viatka: Viatskaia gubernskaia zemskaia uprava, 1915.

Predvaritel'nye itogi perepisi naseleniia 1920 goda (Viatka: Gosudarstvennoe izdatel'stvo, 1921).

Protasov, L. G. *Vserossiiskoe uchreditel'noe sobranie: Istoriia rozhdeniia i gibeli*. Moscow: Rosspen, 1997.

Pyle, Emily E. 'Peasant Strategies for Obtaining State Aid: A Study of Petitions during World War I'. *Russian History/Histoire Russe* 24 (1997): 41–64.

'Village Social Relations and the Reception of Soldiers' Family and Policies in Russia, 1912–1921'. PhD diss., University of Chicago, 1997.

Rachamimov, Alon. *POWs and the Great War: Captivity on the Eastern Front*. Oxford: Berg, 2002.

Radkey, Oliver. *Russia Goes to the Polls: The Election to the All-Russian Constituent Assembly, 1917*. Studies in Soviet History and Society. Ithaca: Cornell University Press, 1989.

The Agrarian Foes of Bolshevism: Promise and Default of the Russian Socialist Revolutionaries, February to October 1917. Studies of the Russian Institute. New York: Columbia University Press, 1958.

Raleigh, Donald J. *Experiencing Russia's Civil War: Politics, Society, and Revolutionary Culture in Saratov, 1917–1922*. Princeton: Princeton University Press, 2002.

Raleigh, Donald J. ed. *Provincial Landscapes: Local Dimensions of Soviet Power, 1917–1953*. Pittsburgh: Pittsburgh University Press, 2001.

Revolution on the Volga: 1917 in Saratov. Ithaca: Cornell University Press, 1986.

Read, Christopher. *From Tsar to Soviets: The Russian People and their Revolution, 1917–21*. Oxford: Oxford University Press, 1996.

Reports of Delegates of the Embassy of the United States of America in St Petersburg on the Situation of the German Prisoners of War and Civil Persons in Russia. Zurich: Art. Institut Orell Fussli, 1917.

Riabukhin, E. I. *V bor'be s kontrrevoliutsiei (Pomoshch' trudiashchikhsia Viatskoi gubernii vostochnomu frontu v 1918–1919 gg.)*. Kirov: Kirovskoe knizhnoe izdatel'stvo, 1959.

Romanov, N. *Pereseleniia krest'ian Viatskoi gubernii. Issledovanie Viatskago gubernskago zemskago statistika*. Viatka: Tipografiia Kuklina, 1880.

Rosenberg, William. 'Social Mediation and State Construction(s) in Revolutionary Russia'. *Social History* 19 (1994): 168–88.

Rossiia 1913 god: Statistiko-dokumental'nyi spravochnik. St Petersburg: BLITs, 1995.

Rossiia v mirovoi voine. 1914–1918 goda (v tsifrakh). Tsentral'noe statisticheskoe upravlenie. Moscow: tipografiia M. K. Kh imeni F. Ia. Lavrova, 1924.

Rozenblium, D. S. *Zemel'noe pravo RSFSR*. Moscow: Gosudarstvennoe izdatel'stvo, 1925.

Rubin, Barnett R. and Jack Snyder, eds. *Post-Soviet Political Order: Conflict and State Building.* New York: Routledge, 1998.

Rybnikov, A. A. *Kustarnaia promyshlennost' i sbyt kustarnykh izdelii.* Moscow: Tipografiia P. P. Riabushinskago, 1913.

Sadakov, M. 'Udmurtiia v gody pervoi mirovoi imperialisticheskoi voiny'. *Zapiski Udmurtskogo NII.* vyp. 16 (1954): 54–82.

Sadyrina, E. S. *Oktiabr' v Viatskoi gubernii.* Kirov: Kirovskoe knizhnoe izdatel'stvo, 1957.

Said, Edward. *Orientalism.* New York: Vintage Books, 1979.

Saisanov, D. S. and B. Sh. Shingareev. 'Krest'ianskie vosstaniia v iuzhnykh uezdakh Viatskoi gubernii v 1918 godu'. *Mariiskii arkheologicheskii vestnik* 8 (1998): 119–36.

Sanborn, Joshua A. *Drafting the Russian Nation: Military Conscription, Total War, and Mass Politics, 1905–1925.* DeKalb: Northern Illinois University Press, 2003.

'The Mobilization of 1914 and the Question of the Russian Nation: A Re-examination'. *Slavic Review* 59 (2000): 267–89.

'Unsettling the Empire: Violent Migrations and Social Disaster in Russia during World War I'. *Journal of Modern History* 77 (2005): 290–324.

Sbornik dokumentov po zemel'nomu zakonodatel'stvu SSSR i RSFSR, 1917–1954. Moscow: Gosudarstvennoe izdatel'stvo iuridicheskoi literatury, 1954.

Scott, James C. *Domination and the Arts of Resistance: Hidden Transcripts.* New Haven: Yale University Press, 1990.

Seeing Like the State: How Certain Schemes to Improve the Human Condition Have Failed. New Haven: Yale University Press, 1998.

The Moral Economy of the Peasant: Rebellion and Subsistence in Southeast Asia. New Haven: Yale University Press, 1976.

Weapons of the Weak: Everyday forms of Peasant Resistance. New Haven: Yale University Press, 1985.

Seregny, Scott. 'A Different Type of Peasant Movement: The Peasant Unions in the Russian Revolution of 1905'. *Slavic Review* 47 (1988): 51–67.

Russian Teachers and Peasant Revolution: The Politics of Education in 1905. Bloomington: Indiana University Press, 1989.

'Zemstvos, Peasants, and Citizenship: The Russian Adult Education Movement and World War I'. *Slavic Review* 59 (2000): 290–315.

Shanin, Teodor. *Russia as a 'Developing Society'.* The Roots of Otherness: Russia's Turn of Century. Vol. 1. New Haven: Yale University Press, 1985.

Shatenshtein, L. S. *Multanskoe delo 1892–1896 gg.* Izhevsk: Udmurtskoe knizhnoe izdatel'stvo, 1960.

Shchagin, E. M., eds. *Sovety i drugie obshchestvennye organizatsii; Mezhvuzovskii sbornik nauchnykh trudov.* Moscow: Izdatel'stvo prometei, 1989.

Shestakov, A. V. *Sovety krest'ianskikh deputatov i drugie krest'ianskie organizatsii.* Tom 1, ch. 1 [Mart–Oktiabr' 1917 g.]. Moscow: Izdatel'stvo kommunisticheskoi akademii, 1929.

Sigov, I. *Arakcheevskii sotsializm: Doklad o khlebnoi monopolii, zaslushannyi Vol'no-Ekonomicheskim Obshchestvom 25 maia 1917 goda.* Petrograd: Tipografiia P. P. Gershunina, 1917.

Slezkine, Yuri. *Arctic Mirrors: Russia and the Small Peoples of the North*. Ithaca: Cornell University Press, 1994.

'The USSR as a Communal Apartment, or How a Socialist State Promoted Ethnic Particularism'. *Slavic Review* 53 (1994): 414–52.

Slovar'-spravochnik. Pri chtenii knig i gazet. 2nd edn. Viatka: Tipografiia A. A. Sil'vinskago, 1917.

Smirnov, A. S. 'Zemliacheskie organizatsii rabochikh i soldat v 1917 g.'. *Istoricheskie zapiski* 60 (1957): 86–123.

Smith, Jeremy. *The Bolsheviks and the National Question, 1917–23*. Studies in Russia and Eastern Europe. New York: St Martin's Press, 1999.

Smith, S. A. 'Citizenship and the Russian Nation during World War I: A Comment'. *Slavic Review* 59 (2000): 316–29.

'Sovremennoe zemlepol'zovanie po dannym spetsial'noi ankety TsSU 1922 g'. *Vestnik statistiki* no. 1–3 (1923): 131–53.

Spirin, L. M. *Klassy i partii v grazhdanskoi voine v Rossii*. Moscow: Mysl', 1968.

Stanziani, Alessandro. 'Spécialistes, Bureucrates et Paysans les Approvisionnements Agricoles Pendant la Première Guerre Mondiale 1914–1917'. *Cahiers du Monde Russe* XXXVI (1995): 71–94.

Statisticheskii spravochnik po Viatskoi gubernii, 1917. Viatka: Gubernskaia tipolitografiia, 1917.

Statistika zemlevladeniia 1905 g. Svod dannykh po 50-ti guberniiam Evropeiskoi Rossii. St Petersburg: Tsentral'nyi statisticheskii komitet M. V. D., 1907.

Stauter-Halsted, Keely. *The Nation in the Village: The Genesis of Peasant National Identity in Austrian Poland, 1848–1914*. Ithaca: Cornell University Press, 2001.

Steinberg, Mark D. *Voices of Revolution, 1917*. New Haven: Yale University Press, 2001.

Steinmetz, George, ed. *State/Culture: State-Formation After the Cultural Turn*. Ithaca: Cornell University Press, 1999.

Stites, Richard. *Revolutionary Dreams: Utopian Visions and Experimental Life in the Russian Revolution*. New York: Oxford University Press, 1989.

Stockdale, Melissa. 'United in Gratitude: Honoring Soldiers and Defining the Nation in Russia's Great War'. *Kritika* 7 (2006): 459–85.

Strizhkov, Iu. K. 'Iz istorii vvedeniia prodovol'stvennoi razverstki'. *Istoricheskie zapiski* 71 (1962): 25–42.

Sunderland, Willard. 'Peasant Pioneering: Russian Peasant Settlers Describe Colonization and the Eastern Frontier, 1880s–1910s'. *Journal of Social History* 34 (2001): 895–922.

'Peasants on the Move: State Peasant Resettlement in Imperial Russia, 1805–1830s'. *The Russian Review* 52 (1993): 472–85.

Suny, Ronald Grigor 'Toward a Social History of the October Revolution'. *The American Historical Review* 88 (1983): 31–52.

Suny, Ronald Grigor and Terry Martin, eds. *A State of Nations: Empire and Nation-Making in the Age of Lenin and Stalin*. Oxford: Oxford University Press, 2001.

Tatarenkova, L. S. et al., eds. *Entsiklopediia zemli Viatskoi*. Tom 4. *Istoriia*. Kirov: Oblastnaia pisatel'skaia organizatsiia administratsiia, 1995.

Thatcher, Ian D., ed. *Late Imperial Russia: Problems and Prospects. Essays in Honour of R. B. McKean.* Manchester: Manchester University Press, 2005.

Thompson, Elizabeth. *Colonial Citizens: Republican Rights, Paternal Privilege, and Gender in French Syria and Lebanon.* New York: Columbia University Press, 2000.

Timkin, Iu. N. *Smutnoe vremia na Viatke. Obshchestvenno-politicheskoe razvitie Viatskoi gubernii vesnoi 1917–osen'iu 1918 gg.* Kirov: Viatskii gosudarstvennyi pedagogicheskii universitet, 1998.

Titov, A. A. ed. *Nikolai Vasil'evich Chaikovskii: Religioznyia i obshchestvennyia iskaniia.* Paris: Rodnik, 1929.

Tomshich, T. S. 'O nekotorykh osobennostiakh agrarnoi revoliutsii v Udmurtii v 1918–1919 godakh'. *Iz istorii partiinykh organizatsii Urala. Sbornik statei. Uchenye zapiski* no. 69, vyp. 7. Sverdlovsk, 1966: 22–9.

Treadgold, Donald W. *The Great Siberian Migration: Government and Peasant in Resettlement from Emancipation to the First World War.* Princeton: Princeton University Press, 1957.

Trudy komissii po issledovaniiu kustarnoi promyshlennosti v Rossii. vyp. XI. St Petersburg: Tipografiia V. Karshbauma, 1884.

Trudy mestnykh komitetov o nuzhdakh sel'sko-khoziaistvennoi promyshlennosti. St Petersburg, 1903.

Turits, Richard Lee. *Foundations of Despotism: Peasants, the Trujillo Regime, and Modernity in Dominican History.* Stanford: Stanford University Press, 2003.

Urban, Greg and Joel Sherzer, eds. *Nation–States and Indians in Latin America.* Austin: University of Texas Press, 1991.

Vasil'eva, O. I. *Udmurtskaia intelligentsiia. Formirovanie i deiatel'nost'. 1917–1941 gg.* Izhevsk: Udmurtskii institut istorii, iazyka i literatury UrO RAN, 1999.

Verdery, Katherine. *Transylvanian Villagers: Three Centuries of Political, Economic, and Ethnic Change.* Berkeley: University of California Press, 1983.

Vereshchagin, G. E. *Votiaki Sosnovskogo kraia.* St Petersburg: Tipografiia ministerstva vnutrennikh del, 1886.

Verner, Andrew. 'Discursive Strategies in the 1905 Revolution: Peasant Petitions from Vladimir Province'. *Russian Review* 54 (1995): 65–90.

Viatskaia guberniia na Vsesoiuznoi sel'sko-khoziaistvennoi i kustarno-promyshlennoi vystavke v 1923 godu: Sbornik statei. Viatka: Pervaia tipolitografiia GSNKh, 1923.

Viatskoe gubernskoe zemskoe sobranie 56-i chrezvychainoi sessii, 15 sentiabria 1915 g. Viatka, 1915.

Volobuev, P. V., ed. *Revoliutsiia i chelovek: Byt, nravy, povedenie, moral'.* Moscow: Institut Rossiiskoi istorii RAN, 1997.

Vtoroi Viatskii gubernskii s"ezd sovetov krest'ianskikh, rabochikh i soldatskikh deputatov. Viatka: Tipografiia Pechatnik, 1918.

Wade, Rex A. *The Russian Revolution, 1917.* 2nd edn. Cambridge: Cambridge University Press, 2005.

Weber, Eugen. *Peasants into Frenchmen: The Modernization of Rural France, 1870–1914.* Stanford: Stanford University Press, 1976.

Werth, Paul. *At the Margins of Orthodoxy: Mission, Governance, and Confessional Politics in Russia's Volga–Kama Region, 1827–1905.* Ithaca: Cornell University Press, 2002.

Wildman, Allan. 'The Defining Moment: Land Charters as the Foundation of the Post-Emancipation Settlement in Russia, 1861–63'. *The Carl Beck Papers in Russian and East European Studies.* 1205. 1996.

Worobec, Christine. *Peasant Russia: Family and Community in the Post-Emancipation Period.* DeKalb: Northern Illinois University Press, 1995.

Young, Glennys. *Power and the Sacred in Revolutionary Russia: Religious Activists in the Village.* University Park, PA: The Pennsylvania State University Press, 1997.

Zaitsev, K. I., N. V. Dolinsky and S. S. Demosthenov. *Food Supply in Russia During the World War.* New Haven: Yale University Press, 1930.

Zelenin, D. K. *Kama i Viatka: Putevoditel' i etnograficheskoe opisanie Prikamskago kraia.* Viatka: Tipografiia Ed. Bergmana, 1904.

Zubarev, S. P. *Prikam'e v ogne.* Izhevsk: Udmurtiia, 1967.

Za respubliku sovetov. Kommunisty Prikam'ia v bor'be protiv burzhuaznoi parlamentskoi respubliki (mart 1917–noiabr' 1918 g.). Izhevsk: Udmurtiia, 1970.

Index

Lightning Source UK Ltd.
Milton Keynes UK
UKOW04f1814210415

250064UK00001B/121/P